05/07

UNIVERSITY OF WOLVERHAMPTON

ONE WEEK LOAN

24. 2- 10		
- 3 MAR 2011		
- 4 APR 2011		
16 JUN 2016		

Telephone Renewals: 01902 321333 or 0845 408 1631
Please RETURN this item on or before the last date shown above.
Fines will be charged if items are returned late.
See tariff of fines displayed at the Counter. (L2)

Research Themes for Tourism

Research Themes for Tourism

Edited by

Peter Robinson

University of Wolverhampton, UK

Sine Heitmann

University of Wolverhampton, UK

and

Dr Peter Dieke

George Mason University, USA

www.cabi.org

CABI is a trading name of CAB International

CABI Head Office	CABI North American Office
Nosworthy Way	875 Massachusetts Avenue
Wallingford	7th Floor
Oxfordshire OX10 8DE	Cambridge, MA 02139
UK	USA
Tel: +44 (0)1491 832111	Tel: +1 617 395 4056
Fax: +44 (0)1491 833508	Fax: +1 617 354 6875
E-mail: cabi@cabi.org	E-mail: cabi-nao@cabi.org
Website: www.cabi.org	

A catalogue record for this book is available from the British Library, London, UK.

Library of Congress Cataloging-in-Publication Data

Research themes for tourism / [edited by] Peter Robinson, Sine Heitmann, Dr. Peter Dieke.
    p. cm.
 Includes bibliographical references and index.
 ISBN 978-1-84593-684-6 (alk. paper)
 1. Tourism--Research. 2. Heritage tourism--Research. I. Robinson, Peter, 1979-
II. Heitmann, Sine. III. Dieke, Peter U.C. IV. Title.

 G155.A1R474 2010
 338.4'791072--dc22

                    2010020954

ISBN-13: 978 1 84593 684 6

Commissioning editor: Sarah Hulbert
Production editor: Kate Hill

Typeset by Columns Design, Reading, UK
Printed and bound in the UK by MPG Books Group

Contents

Contributors

The Editors

Peter Robinson is a senior lecturer at the University of Wolverhampton and a member of the Tourism Society, the Tourism Management Institute, the Institute of Travel and Tourism and the British Academy of Management. His previous experience includes senior management positions in the public, private and voluntary sectors, as well as working as a consultant. Peter is involved in the UK-based 14–19 Travel and Tourism Diploma and has previously published books including *Operations Management in the Travel Industry* and *Events Management*. His research interests include community-based tourism, sociology within events and tourism and the application of new technologies to these industry sectors.

Sine Heitmann, following her postgraduate studies, has been teaching tourism and leisure students at both undergraduate and postgraduate level. Her previous experience includes working with organizations within the public and private tourism and hospitality industries, from which her interest in human resource management derives. Current research areas include the sustainability of tourism and events, the relationship between tourism and media, and festival tourism. Sine has published chapters and journal articles on human resource management in tourism, sustainable tourism and film tourism and has presented papers on authenticity in festivals.

Dr Peter U.C. Dieke is Associate Professor of Tourism and Events Management at George Mason University, USA. A leading scholar in international tourism development, he has written extensively on the developmental aspects of tourism in less developed countries, focusing on policy, planning and implementation issues, including regional interests in sub-Saharan Africa. Dr Dieke is the Africa regional editor for *Tourism Review International* and also serves on the editorial boards of many other scholarly tourism journals.

The Contributors

Dr Glen Croy is a senior lecturer and a member of the Tourism Research Unit at Monash University, Australia. Glen's teaching and research interests are in tourism. His special areas of research interest are in the role of media in tourism and in tourism education. He also has an active research interest in tourism in natural and protected areas. Glen completed his PhD on the role of film in destination decision making and has been a co-convener of the International Tourism and Media conference since 2004.

Crispin Dale is a senior lecturer at the University of Wolverhampton and has taught tourism at the undergraduate and postgraduate levels for a number of years. Crispin has published widely on tourism in peer-reviewed journals. His research has focused upon strategic management and business development in the tourism, hospitality, sport and events industries. Crispin is also involved in dark tourism research and more specifically the mobility of the dark tourism experience.

Mike Evans is a lecturer in hospitality and tourism management at Salford Business School, University of Salford. He has worked in the hotel and catering industry for a considerable number of years, during which he has acquired a valuable wealth of experience in hospitality management. Michael's interests are in service systems management, business enterprise development and tourism industry operations. Currently, he is undertaking a research project on internal quality service delivery in small- to medium-size enterprises within the hospitality and tourism industry.

Dr Paul Fallon is a senior lecturer in the School of Sport, Performing Arts and Leisure at the University of Wolverhampton. Having worked for a variety of service organizations since the 1980s, he returned to academia in 1996 where he progressed from a BA(Hons) in Hospitality Management to completing his PhD in 2006. He is especially interested in customer satisfaction-related issues. His work has been presented at a variety of national and international conferences and published in a number of books and journals. His research has also been used by a variety of organizations, including the British Educational Travel Association and the organizing committee of the One Earth Festival.

Dr Helen Farrell is a lecturer at the University of Lincoln. She teaches at the undergraduate and postgraduate levels, specializing in the fields of rural tourism, sustainability and geographical aspects of tourism. Before moving to the University of Lincoln, she worked as a part-time lecturer in GIS and environmental management while also studying at the Dublin Institute of Technology, Republic of Ireland. Her research interests lie in the fields of GIS, community participation in planning, rural and outdoor tourism and recreation.

Gemma Gelder is a visiting lecturer in event and venue management at the University of Wolverhampton and a visiting teacher at the City of Wolverhampton College. She is involved in the organization of numerous charity events and facilitates student-led event projects. Her most recent and pioneering research activity focuses on new perspectives in event and festival motivation, research that has been published in the *Event Management Journal* and presented at major industry conferences.

Duncan Marson is a lecturer in adventure tourism at the University of Derby. His ongoing doctoral research focuses on the ideological uses of destination advertising. His research interests include issues surrounding the cultures of adventure and recreation incorporating conflict and attitudes of recreational user groups.

Patsy Morgan worked for many years in the hospitality industry, including managing hotels and restaurants, private enterprise, the licensed trade and hospitals. For over 11 years she was a chef lecturer in further education, and also taught food service and restaurant training. Patsy now works full time in higher education and her main focus is on the development of cruise education. She is currently studying for her PhD, which is based on experiences in the cruise industry. Patsy is working closely with cruise organizations as well as with senior lecturers within the tourism team at Southampton Solent University who are currently developing the BA(Hons) Cruise Industry Management degree, commencing 2010.

Ade Oriade is a senior lecturer in tourism and a postgraduate programmes course leader at the University of Wolverhampton. Having worked in the industry in different capacities, Ade brought these experiences to bear in delivering customer service, quality management and operations modules. Ade specializes in quality management in tourism, and also has a special interest in tourism/hospitality education and career analysis and transportation for tourism. Ade's interest in the travel industry was fuelled by his research findings when he was studying for his postgraduate diploma in transport studies. His current research works focus on quality perception and career development in travel and tourism.

Ghislaine Povey has worked in and researched tourism and hospitality for a number of years, following a career in industry that included managing restaurants and working as a consultant worldwide. She has been based at University of Wolverhampton since 1992 and has been involved in a range of food-related projects, from supervising a knowledge transfer project at an award-winning sandwich factory to delivering taste workshops for Slow Food. She has written a number of articles and book chapters in the areas of culture, heritage and gastronomy. She is particularly interested in the links between food, tourism and heritage, and is currently pursuing a PhD in this area.

Lisa Power is a senior lecturer in tourism at Southampton Solent University. Her research concentrates on cross-cultural interaction in tourism, with a particular focus on tour guides and tour managers as cultural brokers. A current research interest explores the role of enrichment programmes on cruise ships.

Christine Roberts is a teacher within the University of Aberdeen's Sport and Exercise Team. Having dedicated her scholastic and work-based career to the domain of sport, health and recreation, Christine has studied and lectured in a broad range of sport and adventure tourism-related areas within varied educational institutions, alongside implementing the programme design, management and delivery of 'sport tourism' as an academic subject, forming a component of wider leisure-based higher education degree programmes. Her professional experience within sport and leisure establishments and industrial familiarity informs her current and ongoing research agenda.

Neil Robinson lectures at Salford University Business School (Faculty of Business, Law and Built Environment), teaching at both the undergraduate and postgraduate levels. Neil has research interests in dark tourism, and in particular the commodification and promotion of sites associated with assassination/disaster and the use of dark tourism as a methodological tool in the investigation of unsolved cold case files.

Sheila Russell is a lecturer in events management at the University of Derby. Previously project leader on the Food from the Peak District initiative from 2003 to 2008, Sheila has several years of working in the field of rural tourism and was instrumental in the promotion of the local food economy through publications, festivals and events.

Geoff Shirt grew up on a dairy farm in Derbyshire on the edge of the Peak District National Park. Spending the first 25 years of his working life in agriculture, he took his understanding of and love for the countryside into an academic setting by undertaking a masters in tourism management at the University of Derby in 1997. Since that time, he has worked closely with several national park authorities; particularly that of the Yorkshire Dales, where he has assessed the success of several initiatives that have encouraged black and ethnic minority people to visit the rural environment. Indeed, his PhD investigates the attractiveness or otherwise of the Peak District to Asian communities that live in large urban conurbations around the edge of the second most visited national park in the world.

Carol Southall is a visiting lecturer at the University of Wolverhampton and an associate lecturer at Sheffield Hallam University and Staffordshire University. Her previous experience includes 12 years of teaching tourism in further education, course team leadership for a Higher National Diploma in tourism management and over 20 years of working in the tourism industry as a resort representative, contracts manager and tour manager. Maintaining industry contacts and experience is a vital aspect of Carol's role and to this effect she still continues to work as a tour manager and, more recently, having gained a PCV licence, as a coach tour driver, escorting tours throughout the UK and Europe. Carol's research interests include quality management and its correlation with cultural awareness and gay tourism.

Dr Richard Tresidder is a senior lecturer in marketing at Sheffield Business School, Sheffield Hallam University. He has a keen interest in the social and cultural relationship between tourism and the tourist or between the host and guest. He has published in the area of the time and space of tourism and more recently in the semiotics of tourism and food. He has also undertaken research into ethnicity and belonging in national parks and the impact of European-funded projects on communities. Richard currently teaches critical marketing in tourism and hospitality.

Peter Wiltshier is a senior lecturer and programme leader at the University of Derby, where he is researching community regeneration, an interest born out of an abiding concern for the role of the resident and host in local communities and the ways in which visitors and tourists are treated and welcomed. His research is underpinned by responsible, dedicated and creative tourism development through partnerships in the public and private sectors. He enjoys creatively supporting communities to provide resources for their welfare and is dedicated to the pursuit of a responsible future.

Research Themes in Tourism: an Introduction

Peter Robinson, Sine Heitmann and Peter U.C. Dieke

The Theme of Tourism

Tourism is a central feature of modern society and affects every part of the world and every person in the world. Within Western societies, it is hard to imagine a world without holidays and opportunities for travelling to new places for new experiences. There are still a number of people for whom this remains a distant possibility, and others who may never holiday, but perform a part of the tourist experience through their cultural heritage. Within destinations, whether in the developed or developing world, new attractions are built or existing ones adapted. Accommodation, entertainment, transport and other ancillary services are central to the experiences.

Tourism's essence is the physical movement of people. Ever since beginning of humanity, people have travelled for various reasons. During ancient times, the main reason for travelling was war and the territorial expansion of countries through conquest. This continued throughout the Middle Ages with the discovery and exploration of America and later Australasia, although during these times religion was a major motivator as worshippers set out on pilgrimages. Until the 1840s tourism remained a pursuit of the rich who were able to travel for months at a time, exploring Europe and the edges of Africa and Asia to learn about cultures and bring back new ideas for architecture and society. Many treasures were traded and researched through these travels, expeditions that became known as 'the Grand Tour', resulting in collections in national museums of treasures brought back from abroad for cultural enlightenment at home. Within Europe, the Grand Tour had a major influence on travelling. After the rich and aristocratic had led the way, the rest of society was able to follow – the advance of steam railways, advent of paid holidays and emergence of seaside resorts resulted in the working classes travelling in masses.

Tourism as we know it today has developed from further transport developments, particularly in cars and the airline industry, which have allowed more people to travel further and more frequently. The 1950s can be bemoaned for the impact of tourism on coastlines around the world. As air travel was suddenly accessible but few destinations were yet developed, hotels were unsympathetically built along seafronts, replacing countryside and providing accommodation for thousands of holidaymakers each year and leading to sudden urban growth. On the other hand, tourism has been a catalyst for development in many countries and the economic impacts have often justified the development of tourism and its associated industries. While mass tourism dominated the latter half of the 20th century and it was assumed that people travelled as part of a large group to inclusive resorts (as exemplified by the popularity of destinations such as Spain, Mexico and the Caribbean), the late 1980s and 1990s resulted in a shift away from this model. First, many tourists became more experienced and rejected the idea of mass travel in favour of more individualized holidays. Secondly, the negative impacts that tourism brought with uncontrolled development provoked negative reactions from local communities and governments.

The idea that there are two types of tourism – mass tourism and niche tourism (catering for more specialized interests) – is still a popular juxtaposition but, as Chapter 1 demonstrates, it is not really so simple.

Regardless of who travelled where, people travelled; they moved, migrated, explored and discovered, while satisfying their need for education, collection and art. This book investigates the primal notions of travel as exploration. Grand Tourists were often considered explorers and much travel literature from the 18th and 19th centuries, and indeed from the early 20th century, posits travel as a story of exploration and discovery. This is not something that has been lost among the modern tourist; rather, it is an activity that can generally only be emulated. Discovery for the sake of society is, with the exception of a few unvisited corners of the world, broadly complete. Tourism today then is about exploration and discovery for the self; hence the focus of this book on motivations, behaviours and the issues that exist around authenticity and imagery in tourism. The main purpose of travel may have shifted in focus, but the tourist of today has not changed, although tourism is no longer about collecting new territories or original artwork, but about collecting experiences and sights (and sometimes photos and souvenirs as visual reminders).

What has happened in the last 20–30 years is an increased sophistication in the travel consumer, and the growing body of tourism research is evidencing that the act of travel and the role of a tourist is complex and laden with sociological discourses around the reasons why people travel, what they seek and how they remember a tourist space. It is a consequence of increased awareness, better education and increased competition in the marketplace and a better understanding of customer requirements, combined with improved media and technology that have led to more specialized tourism activities.

The Evolution of Research Themes

To some critics tourism is considered to be an indiscipline. It is a relatively young field and therefore still seems to lack intellectual credibility (Tribe, 1997). In terms of tourism research, two seminal works have justified tourism to be studied from an academic perspective: MacCannell's *The Tourist* (1976) and Urry's *The Tourist Gaze* (1990). Both of these books use a sociological approach to the study of tourism. Since then there have been many attempts to describe and define tourism studies, but given that tourism makes use of many different approaches (such as psychology, sociology, geography and management studies), it is considered a multidisciplinary field. Interestingly, in contrast to the two key works by Urry and MacCannell, most tourism study is epistemologically grounded in business and management (both in academic publications and education courses). Nevertheless, despite fierce criticisms against the integrity of tourism as an academic field, this book shows that any approach provides extensive opportunities for research. Furthermore, we attempt to show that different approaches can by combined to add to the study, thereby arguing that tourism is an entity that is worth considering with more insight, both from students and academics.

This book does not seek to follow the juxtaposition of mass versus niche tourism by identifying 'niche' markets, but to demonstrate the themes that exist within tourism, based upon contemporary research, and to provide an insight into a number of new and emerging fields of tourism research. Take gay tourism as an example (see Chapter 16). Being gay is not a new niche, nor is being gay and travelling or visiting a gay bar. What has changed is the acceptability of personal choice across a range of tourist activities. This does not mean that there is now a new niche market for tourism called 'gay tourism', because this would suggest that, rather like sex tourism, people travel for this purpose. What gay tourism really refers to is an assessment and evaluation of the value and importance of gay tourists as a distinct market, and this applies to any type of tourist activity.

Take environmental issues and the growth in interest in ecotourism, a valid issue for any travellers concerned about the environment. In this book it is the growth in ecotourism destinations and the debates around their operational practices and wider benefits that are considered. Likewise, when people visit places associated with a dark and sad past, such as concentration camps and sites of bombings, this is made acceptable by the argument that these sites are not designed for entertainment but for education, and a new product, 'educational tourism', is created – although this is not new, but something that many traditional attractions have delivered for many years. A final example of this type of pigeonholing, which is product focused rather than research focused, is the idea of cruise tourism. This comprises many elements of tourism, with 'cruise' only really denoting a type of travel and accommodation, and it is again important to look not just at the cruise element, but at the relationship that exists between the cruise as an industry and the tourism industry that benefits from cruising.

It is essential then, in reading this book, that the various chapters are read and indeed explored as an evaluation of the broader concepts of tourism in the context of specific tourism products. It is the aim of the book to provide an introduction and explanatory overview to the varied range of classic and contemporary themes that exist in tourism. The book does not attempt to acknowledge product-led tourism, but to look at the broader issues in tourism research, inspire and guide research projects among students and provide practitioners with an introduction to a host of topics that can be adopted in tourism practice.

Other Themes

While this book attempts to cover a wide range of topics for tourism teaching, research or general interest, the list of chapters is by no means a complete list of all the themes that exist within tourism and, therefore, reflects some selectivity. The current state of tourism research opens up new possibilities and opportunities on a continuous basis and attempting to cover every single area would go beyond the scope of this book. Additionally many 'themes' of tourism belong to other categories. For example, disaster tourism is a form of dark tourism (Chapter 15), while educational tourism can be linked to rural tourism, heritage tourism, film tourism and dark tourism (Chapters 8, 13, 14 and 15, respectively) among others.

Likewise, extreme tourism is a form of adventure tourism (Chapter 11) and other products that have been identified as niches may be little more than tourism products, and consequently more closely related to tourist motivation (Chapter 3) and parts of mass tourism (Chapter 1) than a specific and economically valuable theme. Types of tourism that may fit into this category include wedding tourism, sex tourism, archaeological tourism and water tourism. Of course this entire discussion is open to debate, which is the purpose of this book.

The chapters have been selected for their flexibility, as they introduce ideas and concepts that are easily translated and adapted to topics not covered. For example, wine tourism can borrow ideas from the chapters on mass and niche markets, tourist behaviour and gastronomy, and is indeed discussed within the gastronomy chapter. The chapter on authenticity (Chapter 4) may provide ideas for exploring areas such as volunteer tourism, whereas wildlife tourism and ecotourism are discussed in the chapter on sustainable and alternative tourism (Chapter 6).

The ethical discussions surrounding dark tourism can be applied to other types of tourism of ethical concern, such as sex tourism, while the moral debates around newly emerging themes such as medical tourism are explored within the context of the more established niche of health tourism (Chapter 19). The chapters cover a range of interesting topics, although these are just a small overview of the vast possibilities in tourism research.

Using this Book

This publication is designed to introduce a broad range of themes within tourism research. As such, it seeks to provide some explanation and contextualization of each topic, supported by applied case studies (where appropriate), international examples and detailed discourse around some of the current contemporary debates in tourism management. These discussions commence in Chapter 1, which provides an overview of the concepts of mass tourism and niche tourism, explaining the way that tourism has historically evolved and the ways in which the shape, scope and nature of tourist activities have sculpted the definitions and practices that define contemporary tourism. The chapter discusses the ways that tourists themselves have contributed to the changing nature of tourism through activities such as backpacking, and finally explains how this can be used for the purposes of forecasting tourism market demand. Chapter 1 introduces the context for the subsequent chapters in the book as it explores generic theories such as the tourism system, the tourism lifecycle and the multiplier effect to demonstrate how the development of different tourism markets into specialist products creates economic growth and the way in which different regional and national destinations can cater for diverse consumer expectations, thus revealing the value of the specialist niches discussed in the subsequent chapters.

Chapter 2 introduces concepts and issues around tourism development, notably with a focus on developing countries, where tourism can be an important tool for economic growth and sociocultural development. In doing this, the chapter draws important comparisons with westernized destinations and travellers, and explores the notion of niche market tourism within the context of a global industry. The chapter finally explores concepts around tourism planning and sustainability, both of which provide the bedrock for strategic tourism development.

Chapter 3 focuses primarily on 'the tourist' by exploring theories on tourism motivation and introducing a range of different tourist typologies to familiarize the reader with sociological and psychological aspects of travelling and tourism. Understanding the reasons for travelling is essential to understanding tourism management and the ways in which tourists behave.

Chapter 4 then provides a historical overview of the key debates that surround authenticity in tourism, starting with an understanding of the term 'authenticity' and its origins. Concepts such as 'staged authenticity', perceptions of authenticity and 'emergent authenticity' are introduced and exemplified with case studies. The chapter also takes into account the postmodern view on authenticity and how the understanding of this concept is consistently evolving, giving consideration to the implications for tourism destinations, tourism management and tourism marketing.

Chapter 5 moves on from the discussion around authenticity to provide an overview of the ways in which the semiotics of tourism have evolved over the past 25 years. It analyses why, unlike other areas of tourism studies, this has not developed as a subject area at the same pace. The chapter then goes on to suggest that the semiotics of tourism is still of great significance in contemporary tourism and can provide an in-depth understanding of the relationship between the image, the individual and the cultural and political representations of peoples and places within tourism texts, exploring how these reinforce both past and current discourses in tourism.

Sustainable and alternative tourism is discussed in Chapter 6, examining and analysing varying views, issues and prospects for sustainable tourism. No doubt the term is one of the most controversial in the study and management of tourism. Despite non-consensus among academics and practitioners on definition, the majority agree that effective planning and management decisions are the underlining principle, and ideas revolving around alternatives to mass tourism are usually advocated. The focus throughout this chapter is on the development of tourism in the context of the unique sociocultural, economic and physical environment of a given community. The chapter also goes further to examine the key theories and ideas related to environmental tourism, exploring a range of management and planning principles associated with sustainable tourism development.

Chapter 7 discusses community tourism and investigates the relationship within various stakeholders and between community interest groups. The chapter assesses ways that local communities can work with the public and private sectors to develop resources within urban areas to create focal points for visitors and 'visiting friends and relatives' markets. The chapter considers the concept of social capital and uses case studies to place specific attractions in areas of sustainable and responsible development to demonstrate how to adopt community learning to take those attractions into the future as social and cultural resources.

Chapter 8 focuses on rural communities in particular and explores the concept of 'the countryside' and the theme of rural tourism. The chapter provides a definition of the countryside and addresses the relationship between rural tourism and rural life. Included is an exploration of the themes of government and rural policy; the protection of the countryside and the role of national parks; and the impacts of rural and urban development. Finally, it includes the tourist perspective by exploring the nostalgic appeal of the countryside.

Following on from themes of previous chapters on sustainability and authenticity as well tourism motivation, Chapter 9 introduces the growing research around 'slow activities'. It introduces the 'slow' concept, from its inception in the Slow Food movement and the concept of 'Cittaslow' (Slow Cities), and relates these to the tourism industry, before moving on to discuss slow travel and slow tourism. In each case examples are given to explain how tourism is related to and can benefit communities adopting slow principles, but also critiques the notion of 'slow' as a new tool for sustainable tourism.

Chapter 10 discusses the relationship between tourism and events, exploring the typology of events and the relationship between these typologies, the host destinations and communities. The chapter uses international case studies to discuss the rationale and justification for hosting events and the value of the event 'legacy' to the development of tourism destinations. It also assesses the growing size of the festival tourism market and addresses the challenges this brings, together with the increased value of festivals to the tourism economy. Finally, the chapter considers the role of art in tourism and in regeneration for the purposes of growing tourism markets, as well as the importance of architecture and design in the built environment in the context of tourism spaces.

Chapter 11 explores the context and scope of sports and adventure tourism. Rooted in theoretical underpinning, the chapter discusses how industrial growth reflects today's emerging society and the role that sport and adventure activities play. Intrinsic and extrinsic motivations for active participation are investigated alongside an analysis of sport and adventure tourist typologies. Through the use of international case studies, the chapter then explores the wider effects of the industry, paying particular attention to the politics of health, the economy and societal impacts.

In Chapter 12, the notions of culture and access within tourism, and the way in which they can act together to create tourism demand, are explored. Reference is made to the way in which groups have lived or live their lives. Consideration is given to a range of cultures, including popular/high culture, national/regional culture, ancient/modern culture and primitive/advanced culture; each is discussed as a tourism motivator. As cultural and heritage tourism attractions have seen rapid and sustained growth, case study examples are identified and investigated. The chapter then moves on to assess issues surrounding the right of access, which is contested across geographical and indeed national boundaries. The chapter investigates several examples where access has been encouraged, restricted or denied.

Following on from culture and access, heritage tourism as a form of cultural tourism is discussed in more detail in Chapter 13. This chapter explores the development and current trends in heritage tourism, identifying key stakeholders and reflecting on the work of the United Nations World Tourism Organization as a body set up to protect international cultural heritage. The chapter debates the value of World Heritage status, management methods used to manage and protect historic environments and challenges faced by allowing public access, before finally looking at the interpretation and presentation of heritage as a tourism commodity.

Film tourism is discussed in Chapter 14. It initially reviews what is understood by film tourism, before going on to discuss its scope by providing an overview of the development of film tourism, exploring motivations for visiting film locations and outlining impacts of film tourists. Case studies include discussions surrounding authenticity as well as the implications of film tourism planning, stakeholder participation, potential conflicts and sustainability. The chapter concludes by discussing the future of the film tourism industry.

Chapter 15 explores the emergent concept of dark tourism. In reviewing the definitions and understandings of dark tourism, appraising dark tourism motivations and management of dark tourism attractions in environmental, educational and financial terms, and interpreting dark tourism attractions within the context of commodification and authenticity, this chapter picks up previous themes and adapts them to a new concept. The chapter moves on to discuss politicizing the dark and issues concerning propaganda and the use of dark sites for communicating political ideology, as well as the internationalization of the dark with the 'Disneyization' and 'McDonaldization' of dark tourism attractions. The conclusion considers a discussion around the future of the dark tourism industry.

Lesbian, gay, bisexual and transgender (LGBT) tourism is discussed in Chapter 16. This chapter considers the evolution and dimensions of LGBT tourism, giving consideration to the impacts, economic value and opportunities presented by this growing market sector and its increasingly diverse demographic. Further attention is paid to events and destination management as the tourism industry starts to recognize the size, value and importance of this niche market.

Chapter 17 explores the fundamental links between tourism and gastronomy. It considers definitions of gastronomy and investigates the development of the dynamic relationship between food and the different sectors of the tourism industry. In addition, it examines influences on the food tourism relationship, the phenomenon of gastro-tourism and key trends such as the standardization of hotel food offerings, the growth in consumption of fast food and the influence of consumer movements. The chapter goes on to discuss the links between food, culture and consumption; the role of food at destinations; and the value of food to the tourist experience, before discussing the future of this dynamic aspect of tourism.

Chapter 18 takes up the cultural and heritage theme to investigate religious tourism in more detail, highlighting its origins and discussing the increasing variety of typologies of religious tourism (genealogy, cultural learning, education, architectural interest and the renaissance in community interest in religious sites). It also looks at the issues surrounding multiple uses of religious sites, from nature conservation to visitor centre to craft workshop. The chapter uses case studies to identify the ways in which the clergy can attract key players to cooperate and create clusters of heritage products without compromising the purpose of religious sites.

Chapter 19 explores the relationship between health and tourism from a historical perspective to current trends in spa tourism. This aspect of tourism has shifted during recent times to include people travelling to less developed countries and the former communist states for medical purposes, whether for aesthetic purposes or to bypass long waiting lists or expensive private hospitals in the West. This new wave of medical tourism forces us to challenge and re-visit the power relationships that exist within contemporary tourism and the host–guest relationship.

Chapter 20 examines cruise tourism as one of the largest components of tourism. The chapter starts with an historical overview and examines the principles and practices of the cruise industry. The supply and demand perspective is assessed to outline the characteristics of cruise tourists as well as the marketing and management of cruises. The relationship between globalization and cruises is further explored, as is the impact of cruise tourism on host destinations and tourism development. The chapter concludes with a view on future developments in this sector.

The concluding comments provide a review of the themes discussed in this book, while exploring the ways in which tourism may continue to develop and propagate new concepts and ideas that will broaden the base for research in this constantly evolving and diversified sector.

References

MacCannell, D. (1976) *The Tourist – a New Theory of the Leisure Class*. Schocken Books, New York.
Tribe, J. (1997) The indiscipline of tourism. *Annals of Tourism Research* 24, 638–657.
Urry, J. (1990) *The Tourist Gaze*. Sage, London.

1 From Mass Tourism to Niche Tourism

Duncan Marson

Unless a traveller makes himself at home and comfortable in the bush, he will never be quite contented with his lot; but will fall into the bad habit of looking forward to the end of his journey, and to his return to civilization.

(Galton, 1872)

Introduction

A discussion surrounding how a Victorian text from 1872 emphasizes the importance of comfort when travelling may be a strange way of beginning an exploration into mass and niche tourism (and, indeed, the subsequent chapters of this book). On closer inspection, however, this quote on 'comfort in the bush' emphasizes the interrelationship between forms of tourism that have global popularity for a large tourist market and those that could be considered appealing to a smaller specialist clique of tourist types.

On one side of this debate there is the obvious distinction between mass tourism and niche tourism in terms of the specific nature of the attraction. Western comforts and amenities (the inclusion or exclusion of) act as a strong pull factor for tourists towards tourism. This attractive presence or absence of a variable used to sell tourism helps identify differences in size of market demand. Niche markets such as independent travel, while having grown exponentially, are still defined as a niche product (although there is an argument proposed in this chapter and others in this volume that these could be considered the new form of modern mass tourism). Even supplementary products that complement tourism within a destination

could be argued as growing to a point where they will have to be redefined. A modern adventure product such as 'zorbing' (the thrill of rolling down a hill in an oversized inflatable ball) will still only appeal to a certain type of person, even though there is growing evidence to suggest that this bracket of extreme sports (as well as adventure tourism in general) is growing. Dark tourism, too (with its penchant for the attraction of death and destruction), is a product that has grown in demand for a variety of motivational reasons.

Further analysing current research themes, it is evident that all forms of tourism rely on similar variables that allow them to grow (regardless of whether they are globally popular or only interesting to a smaller, more specialized group). This chapter and book, therefore, aim to explore the understanding of niche tourism and mass tourism by initially evaluating some of the variety of available previous definitions. This book also provides the opportunity to identify similarities and differences in these terms, the components that make up the terminology and the subsequent interrelationship between the two concepts. The suggestion posed here is that there is a tangible link between the development of mass tourism and the development of niche tourism, and potentially back again towards mass tourism.

This chapter defines the concepts of mass and niche tourism, explaining and defining their characteristics and evaluating the interrelationship between the two terms. This raises an interesting line of questioning: what variables comprise what we can classify as a form of mass tourism and a form of niche tourism? Can a form of niche tourism turn into a form of mass tourism if demand increases and, if so, when? This then provides the opportunity to look at how one form of niche tourism can evolve into what is defined here as a 'contemporary mass tourism' product. The chapter concludes with a discussion surrounding the impacts of such a transition from niche to 'massified' and how this process of evolution can help in forecasting tourism development from mass to niche and what is further defined here as 'micro-niche'.

The Historical Context of Mass and Niche Tourism

Francis Galton (1822–1911) can be best described as a man of many talents. In 1872, his textbook *Art of Travel* provided an opportunity for a growing market of travellers to use his years of experience to benefit their own travel plans (including such novel ideas as using cats to measure the effects of altitude and innovative methods of preventing scurvy). Research on Galton, including that of Walker (2004), and the continued publication of his guide help conclude that travel to Europe, the Middle East and in particular South America helped shape Galton's contribution to the sciences of meteorology, ethnography, medicine and other academic disciplines. Galton (a first cousin of Charles Darwin) began travelling at a time when the Grand Tour had essentially become obsolete (largely due to the increasing danger of travel in the era of the Napoleonic War of 1799–1815) and continued as the first signs materialized of travel and tourism opening up to a wider socioeconomic class (the first excursion of Thomas Cook took place on 5th July, 1841).

Chronologically, this period of history is an important timeframe for a discussion of 'mass' and 'niche' tourism. If, for example, the Grand Tour (1600–1800) is examined, Weaver and Opperman (2000) cited evidence from Towner (1996) that 15,000–20,000 members of the British leisure class were abroad at any one time during the mid-1700s. Hardly a large market by contemporary standards, but at the time a significant movement of people, helping to dictate the pattern of travel that was to come later. The significance of this lies in whether the Grand Tour was an early example of niche tourism, but one that also (relative to the numbers travelling at the time) fits the banner of 'mass' tourism. What makes this more interesting, and almost suggests a paradigm of the scale and scope of mass tourism, is that the Grand Tour was more akin to modern independent travel, which is now commonly defined as niche tourism.

As with the Grand Tourists of the 16th century, groups of individuals with like-minded characteristics (who would today be referred to as tourist markets) are identified and segmented by similar traits such as demographics (age, gender, ethnicity, religion), psychographics (motivation, behavioural characteristics), geographical tourist-generating zone, socio-economic status and education. Galton's example of bush travel (which in modern terms finds its equivalent in wilderness camping) is useful as he was emphasizing the art of being comfortable in areas that are potentially inaccessible, environmentally harsh and with few or no modern amenities. It is appropriate to argue here that this was a type of product at the time that was only attractive to would-be travellers or explorers who had the inclination and resources to undertake this type of activity.

Fast-forward to the modern era of tourism and travel and it is possible to see this type of wilderness experience becoming more and more popular (see Table 1.1).

This phenomenon is not just restricted to domestic USA markets. We can also see a form of modern Grand Tour appearing in the development of independent travel markets and in what is popularly termed in Europe and Australasia as 'backpacking' (which is different to the USA concept of backpacking). Are these forms of leisure and tourism sufficiently large to now be considered 'mass' or are they smaller 'niche' tourism products that will always appeal to smaller groups of consumers? At this point, it is worth distinguishing the terminology.

Robinson and Novelli (2005), in one of the most significant contributions on the subject of niche tourism, begin with a discussion surrounding mass tourism because, as a term,

Table 1.1. Growth in selected nature-based outdoor activities, all USA.

Outdoor activity	Participants		1-year % change
	2007	2008	
Downhill telemarking	1,173,000	1,435,000	22
Snowshoeing	2,400,000	2,922,000	22
Backpacking	6,637,000	7,867,000	19
Cross-country skiing	3,530,000	3,848,000	9
Hiking	29,965,000	32,511,000	9
Backyard and car camping	31,375,000	33,686,000	7
Recreational kayaking	4,702,000	5,025,000	7
Bouldering, sport and indoor climbing	4,514,000	4,769,000	6
Bird watching	11,783,000	2,417,000	5
Wildlife viewing	22,974,000	24,113,000	5

Source: Outdoor Foundation (2009).

'niche tourism' is relatively recent. When taken from a historical perspective, however, it can initially be concluded that the basic foundations of niche tourism existed before the modern conventions of mass tourism (examples are given above). While considering this, it is appropriate to begin with a discussion about the image of mass tourism, leading into a definition and then to the concept of niche tourism.

Mass Tourism

From a historical perspective, the components of leisure time, affluence and mobility have shaped the way in which modern tourism is defined and how it has influenced demand. History suggests that the significance of having time to indulge in leisure and recreation is a key component in making decisions of where and when to travel. The development of regulations in working hours and paid leave has contributed towards this ability to indulge in 'successful leisure time'. This in turn has allowed the accumulation of disposable income, which contributes to the effective use of leisure time. Affluence further influences the ways in which we detach ourselves through tourism activities; increased working hours in Europe and the importance of employment enact a feeling of needing rest and relaxation on holiday. This can be described as one of the reasons why mass

tourism began to grow in significance from the 1950s onwards, as this period corresponds to changes in work patterns, coupled with increased leisure time (Weaver and Opperman, 2000).

References to 'mobility' relate not only to the infrastructure that allows us to move as tourists from generating to destination region, but also to the increased level of pleasure we experience through tourism. This pleasure can come in the form of the quality of transport (and cost to the tourist) as well as speed and efficiency of travel so the product can be indulged in as quickly as possible ('are we there yet?' is a question posed by tourists as well as by children).

Mass tourism, with its perception of ease and comfort for the tourist and the potentially large market base for countries wishing to obtain the maximum revenue, may inevitably seem like a positive result for all. History, however, tells us that the situation is infinitely more challenging than this: while mass tourism does indeed indicate a large market from which to develop a tourism infrastructure, in its traditional form it has impacts that, in some cases, have created more problems than mass tourism has solved.

Authors, too, have wrestled with the dilemma of mass tourism when constructing a definition. History has acted as a conduit for helping develop a definition that allows for both the positive and negative impacts of such mass development, while allowing for the varying degrees of what constitutes mass tourism. Table 1.2 provides a chronological synopsis of the current discussions surrounding how modern mass tourism is defined. In part, the objective here is to identify the variety of factors that have helped not only to define the traditional concept of mass tourism, but also how the current discussions on mass tourism help us understand the modern term.

This (by no means exhaustive) list identifies a variety of issues in relation to mass tourism and the focus on different issues in tourism studies. In terms of defining mass tourism, there are a number of similarities. Mass tourism's relationship with the word 'large' features in two main components: large tourist numbers and consequently large development. Digance (2006) used the concept of mass tourism to define its origins within pilgrimages from 500 to 1500 CE and large-scale participation relates to the mass movement of religious pilgrims to areas with symbolic images. This symbolism transformed from religious importance into a tourism business opportunity. For example, the pilgrimage 'business' at Durham Cathedral (UK) – where there were nine altars designed for pilgrims to exchange money for prayers and relics (demonstrating an early form of mass souvenir consumption) – changed the monastery into a contemporary tourist attraction.

As consumerism replaces for many the significance of religious observation, so new forms of pilgrimage enter everyday life. Mass leisure and tourism enter as significant components in everyday life and from this perspective it is possible to see the relationship that religious forms of pilgrimage have with more traditional forms of the mass tourism industry. For mass tourism from the 1960s onwards, one cannot exist without the other, and mass demand requires a likeminded approach to supply. Vanhove (1997) related this further towards the rigidity of the mass tourism product, and Richards (2001) and Vanhove drew on similar examples to help understand this discussion. 'Fordism', or early forms of mass production, have paved the way for the development of a variety of industrial bases, including tourism. Like the manufacturing of mass products, early mass tourism has been

characterized by Fordist principles of rigid, standardized development throughout the world. If we relate this to the discussion surrounding tourist motivation (see Chapter 3), it is possible to deduce tourist typologies such as Poon's (1993) shift from 'old tourist' to 'new tourist' and conclude that these early rigid forms of mass tourism development complemented perfectly the rigid novelty and climatic motivational properties of the early 'old tourist'. The popularity of mass tourism in areas of the Mediterranean in the 1950s, for example, was reinforced by a standardized perception of service delivery and expectations of participation and even climate, which is a dominant force in Poon's early discussion.

The increased significance of supply and demand issues, coupled with the consolidation of mass tourism products and the growth in niche products, has resulted in tourism research themes paying more attention to identifying the stages of development within particular destination products and subsequent markets. Destinations are particularly vulnerable to fluctuations in demand, and various attempts have been made within tourism research to further quantify these stages. Most notable is the model proposed by Richard Butler (1980). The destination lifecycle model (adapted from the product lifecycle) attempts to show the specific life stages occurring in single destinations (Fig. 1.1). Similar work has been undertaken in relation to pinpointing the life-stage-specific products within a destination. Benefits of this vary, but it can provide information as to which tourism products are in a state of growth and which are in a state of flux (stagnation). Understanding the positioning of such products (including mass and niche products) will help develop effective strategic tourism planning and rejuvenate products that have witnessed a levelling out or decrease in demand. Questions are also raised here as to the future feasibility of some niche products (and whether public marketing budgets at destinations should be spent on perceived 'ailing' products).

The examples provided in the model (Fig. 1.1) identify the stages of tourism products in Italy in 2006. As shown, emerging niche products within tourism saw further growth in

Table 1.2. Examples of discussions and definitions related to mass tourism.

Reference	Examples of discussion surrounding mass tourism
Cohen (1972)	Mass tourists have a higher likelihood of experiencing culture shock because of the mass tourism method of confining the tourist to a bubble
Murphy (1985)	Mass tourism not only means a larger number of tourists; it also means the concept of mass merchandising
Poon (1993)	The trend for demand to move away from mass tourism to more alternative niche forms
Shaw and Williams (1994)	The negative effects of mass tourism: spatial and temporal polarization, dependency and external control, intense environment pressure
Wheeler (1994)	The future trend for mass tourism to continue to grow in popularity and increase in scale, raising the term 'mega-mass tourism'
Vanhove (1997)	Mass tourism contains two characteristics: participation of large numbers of tourists; and a standardized, rigidly packaged and inflexible product
Wang (2000)	The lure of consumption: a synopsis of the discussions surrounding mass packaged tourism degenerating the significance of places and events
Richards (2001)	The distinction and popularization of high culture and mass culture in cultural attractions
Shaw and Williams (2002)	The association between high sustainability costs and mass tourism. The total sustainability costs of mass tourism may be less when compared to the same amount of tourists spread over a larger geographical area, as with forms of niche tourism
Clarke (2004)	Gives a chronological example of the movement from the traditional perception of mass tourism to the development of sustainable tourism, using a continuum approach. Again highlights how forms of sustainable tourism have utilized parts of the infrastructure embedded within mass tourism
Bramwell (2004)	Mass tourism as a quantitative notion since its increase in the 1960s. Focuses on an evaluation of the impact of mass coastal tourism and that of alternative coastal tourism. Mass tourism as a product that can adapt to the growing demands of modern tourists by offering a wider variety of supplementary products
Urry (2005)	The development of mass travel by train in the second half of the 19th century. This revolution caused further class distinction in forms of tourism, where destinations became ridiculed and mocked through the term 'mass'
Pender (2005)	Mass tourism as a relatively young phenomenon that is reaching the end of immaturity and entering early maturity
Beaver (2005)	Mass tourism as defined by the words 'large scale'. Also noted is the incorrect assumption of tourism as 'not being sustainable', helping to develop a definition for the term
Page and Connell (2005)	Emphasizes the work of Clarke (1997) as mass tourism and sustainable tourism as polar opposites, but containing similar components. Sustainable tourism as the future core component of mass tourism
Holloway and Taylor (2006)	Use of the word 'masses' and development in relation to the Ford Model T car and mass production to mass consumption
Beech and Chadwick (2006)	Identification of traditional seaside resorts as a clear indication of the development of mass tourism. Interesting here is their identification of the misunderstanding of the benefits of mass tourism towards the host population (the realistic impacts of more tourists)
Digance (2006)	While defining the concept of pilgrimage, the first example of mass tourism is suggested as being the initial medieval pilgrimages between 500 and 1500 CE.
Van Egmond (2007)	Sustainable tourism should not be solely attributed to small-scale tourism. Mass tourism should not be considered 'unsustainable' because of the size and components of development

Continued

Table 1.2. Continued.

Reference	Examples of discussion surrounding mass tourism
Holden (2008)	The movement from mass tourism to alternative tourism as characterized by the tourist's over-familiarity with the concept of 'mass destination'
Obrador Pons et al. (2009)	The movement away from the image of mass tourism as an evil of capitalism and globalization. Mass tourism as having the ability for greater depth and the ability to develop the self (meaning and significance in leisure and lifestyle from this type of tourism activity)

2006, whereas more sustained products such as spa tourism were perceived to be in stagnation or decline. Products can be positioned within specific stages for a number of reasons, including: competition within the regional or global marketplace; economic turbulence influencing tourist consumption based on price; shifts in consumption patterns; uniqueness of the niche product; service quality reputation or image; investment in tourism infrastructure; environmental quality; marketing and branding strategies; or one-off or continued significant political events.

The concept of the lifecycle also helps us to understand the shifting fragmentation of tourism products into further specific niche markets. This is useful, as one general term such as 'sport tourism' cannot be identified as broadly exhibiting symptoms of exploration and growth. Mass tourism, too, as a general term,

should not be pigeonholed into one general area of stagnation or decline. The popularity of mass tourism within destinations may be based on the factors above.

Positive and negative impacts: implications

One key feature inherent in the use of the traditional term of mass tourism, as seen in Table 1.2, is the impacts it has. These are both positive and negative, but due to the nature of development the negative impacts of mass tourism are far more prominent in tourism literature. This imbalance has had an influence on the traditional definition. As identified above, the initial growth in demand for mass tourism and the subsequent rush to supply focused more attention on the perceived positive economic

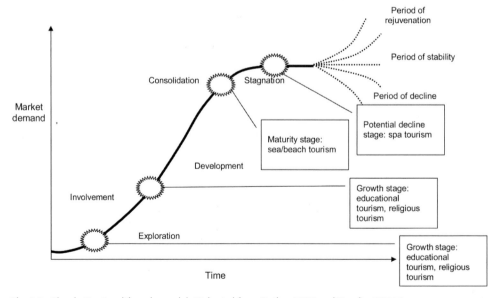

Fig. 1.1. The destination lifecycle model. (Adapted from Butler, 1980 and Trunfio, 2006.)

impacts and less on the negative environmental and sociocultural impacts, which are now well documented through research examples in the tourism literature. Socioculturally, these include issues such as displacement, polarization and dependence theory:

- 'Displacement' describes an impact on local populations and decision-making power when mass tourism is used as a catalyst for economic development. One central argument here is that external investment is required to develop the traditional mass tourism infrastructure. This then causes issues in relation to leakages from the economy and restricted employment opportunities due to lack of access to specialist training and education. Historically, a favourable development location also prioritizes the construction of supplementary tourism products over the local population.
- 'Polarization' describes the increasing separation between host and guest due to phenomena such as the 'tourist bubble'. This is exemplified by the spatial appropriation of areas for traditional tourists, such as private beaches. While this cannot be considered as redefining the dichotomy between 'master and servant', it has raised discussions surrounding tourism being a form of neo-colonialism and further issues in relation to traditional mass tourism and power relations between stakeholders
- 'Dependency theory' describes the process of developing regions becoming dependent on the constant supply of income from tourism, and subsequently on Western nations. This consequently has environmental and cultural implications. The amenities used for tourism can become distorted in the form of 'staged authenticity' (discussed further in Chapter 4), which essentially refers to the staging of host cultures and heritage, through traditional events and performances, for the purposes of tourism, potentially resulting in a loss of significance for the host population. 'Reconstructed ethnicity' describes the impact of the commodification of culture for the purpose of tourism on host belief systems.

Impacts such as these have helped shape the definition of modern mass tourism and have fostered a true need for a global emphasis on developing more sustainable forms of tourism. Traditional mass tourism is known from this perspective as offering economic prosperity, and yet the traditional examples of modern mass tourism have provided so much less. This helps strengthen the resolve for developing more sustainable forms of tourism product.

The word 'sustainable' is interesting in terms of definition. One application of 'sustainability' is in relation to accessing and maintaining sustainable market segments. Access to substantial existing markets (such as mass tourism) allows for increased access to the lucrative economic benefits of tourism. The development of modern mass tourism in the 1960s allowed access to a large (initially perceived as sustainable, some would argue) lucrative market. Research in travel and tourism has shown that the environmental and sociocultural impacts of modern mass tourism have outweighed the economic benefits. Tourism destination regions (both developed or developing) now search for the new 'holy grail' of modern mass tourism: sustainable forms of tourism that appeal to larger markets.

Figure 1.1 shows additional reasons for the movement away from mass tourism and its initial economic benefits. Holden (2008) suggested that over-familiarity with the term 'mass tourism' has decreased demand for mass products. This clichéd nature of how consumers define mass tourism has caused further problems for countries that have adopted development processes that are akin to mass development. It could also be argued that this movement from dominant image to clichéd nature is a constant cycle that is repeated throughout different periods of history. Urry (2005) discussed how the advent of mass transportation in the 19th century led to earlier forms of tourism being ridiculed and mocked due to their popular nature. In this sense, modern mass tourism could also be included in this cycle of movement from popular to unpopular. While modern mass tourism has declined in demand, other forms of tourism are increasing in popularity and becoming more dominant forces in tourism consumption – and, as a result, more dominant forces in tourism literature.

Mass tourism as a result is a tricky concept in both definition and in the understanding of its significance. Table 1.3 attempts to show that throughout history, the image of mass tourism has morphed from heroic saviour, in its capability to act as a method of eroding traditional class boundaries, to the villain of the piece, consuming without care or understanding. This change in significance explains how the concept of mass tourism now denotes a number of factors that have contributed to the overall growth and development of the global tourism product as it is known today. In essence,

mass tourism is the catalyst for many research themes that have developed because destinations have sought new products and research has pigeonholed some tourism activities into classifications and niches – and the two together have evolved into the variety of niches that now exist.

Of particular interest in Table 1.3 are the positive and negative implications that mass tourism can have. While mass tourism is directly responsible for positive and negative impacts

Table 1.3. The historical change in image of mass tourism.

Example	Date	Significance of activity
The advent of the first tour for profit by Thomas Cook between Liverpool, Leicester, Nottingham and Derby (Thomas Cook, n.d.)	1845	The creation of profitable tour management in the UK and a precursor for opening travel to a mass market, while also eroding the perception of tourism and travel as a preserve of specific socioeconomic groups
The advent of jet engine development after World War II utilized for commercial civil aviation	1950 onwards	Technologically, this is a significant period in history as it may be described as the catalyst for the modern civil aviation industry (lowering prices with constant innovation and opening up mass travel to new markets)
Development of tourism on the Spanish coastlines of Costa Brava and the Costa Del Sol	1950 onwards	As Holden (2008) summarized, the development of the jet engine for civil aviation allowed areas such as Spain (which at an early period would still have been considered exotic) to cater for a growing European market. This push to supply demand created issues of over-development, with both environmental and social impacts
Development of tourism in The Gambia	1965 onwards	The Gambia's reliance on tourism has had positive and negative implications on development and the economy (Sharpley, 2007; Sharpley and Tefler, 2008). The Gambia demonstrates the classic example of the perceived attraction of mass tourism development, with subsequent leakages out of the local economy
The introduction of low-cost airlines	1971 (Southwest Airlines) (Bjelicic, 2007)	Low-cost airlines have had a major impact on regional development. Increased transit routes have provided some destinations with access to new markets. This access can change if the route does not remain profitable. This has a major impact on the viability of tourism in a destination that relies on low-cost networks
The development of sustainable mass tourism?	A point of contention, but as Weaver (2007) proposes, it is linked to the increase in green consumers in the early to mid 1990s	This envisages more conventional mass tourism operating an increased policy of sustainable and responsible development processes. The inclusion of sustainable principles by tourism organizations can be a positive force for development, but can also be perceived as 'window-dressing' and, as a result, be counter-productive

associated with environmental, sociocultural and economic areas, it can be argued that the larger framework of modern globalization and capitalism have spurred these impacts on. The mass tourist, for example, could be accused of 'knowing better' in terms of the fair and equal treatment of a local population when they are on holiday. Mass tourists are, however, following a well-trodden path, as Poon (1993) hinted when discussing tourism consumption as a form of escape and novelty, rather than a method of contributing towards to the development of the local community or environment (this may be a more contemporary motivation for the modern green consumer). It may therefore be more appropriate to understand mass tourism as a result of a move towards modern free market economics, the use of capitalism and tourism as a political tool for development and as a feature of global production and consumption.

This is a cautionary nod to understanding the significance of such a term when discussing differing tourism markets and products and the growth and significance of tourism in general. Authors on this subject have also expressed the need to approach the discussion surrounding tourism with a balanced approach. Impact models proposed by authors such as Sharma (2004) raise the important point that all tourism contains negative impacts, and examples provided from the historical development of tourism in Spain show us that mass tourism contains impacts that can be considered to a lesser or greater extent. Weaver (2006) also raised the important discussion that while the history of mass tourism is chequered in negative connotations, its future lies in the relationship between mass and niche forms of tourism – for example, with different forms of 'sustainable tourism' perhaps being grouped together as 'sustainable mass tourism'.

Niche Tourism

As many authors have proposed, including Yeoman (2008), niche tourism can be considered to be an alternative, almost antithesis to modern mass tourism. While mass tourism is homogenous in nature (a standardized, uniformed product for a large market segment),

niche tourism is defined by its heterogeneous nature (higher demand for a more distinctive and unique product). It can be argued that niche tourism is growing in significance because of the shift in motivational factors for travellers. Tourism motivation has, in recent years, demonstrated a move away from the old-style standardized rigid motivations of tourists to a more unique approach where wants and needs are focused upon (and consumers are willing to pay for) experiences that may be more adventurous and meaningful. If this is matched to the differences between mass and niche tourism, it is clear that niche tourism is seen as more specific, conforming to the new motivational factors.

Niche tourism can, therefore, be defined as catering to the needs of specific markets by focusing on more diverse tourism products. The reasons for this change in motivation and the subsequent growth in niche forms of tourism vary in accordance with the type of tourist market. Gibson and Connell (2005), when discussing the growth of music tourism, related this to a general change in the attraction of culture as a leisure pursuit, moving towards forms of mass culture (music as a form of mass culture, but music tourism as a form of niche tourism). Here there is the identification of one key component in the discussion surrounding niche tourism: the continuing growth in niche tourism products to what eventually would be described as a mass product. Other significant components in the definition include the following:

- The distinct qualities of niche tourism products. For example, Swarbrooke *et al.* (2003) described this in relation to adventure tourism: distinct qualities of eco-tourism, distinct qualities of adventure and shared qualities.
- The importance of niche products 'specialization' of tourism, providing a conduit to access new and varied markets. This, as Deuschl (2006) has suggested, is the key area of future growth for destinations. The word 'specializing' also helps identify the competitive advantage in focusing on these types of products and markets.
- Market size being smaller and more specific. The product contains attractions that only appeal to a smaller group.

- Niche tourism as being a more sustainable approach to tourism development than mass tourism.

Niche tourism markets and products: a discussion surrounding size

According to Gibson and Connell (2005) in their discussion surrounding music tourism as a niche tourism product, history can be considered to be one of the first niche markets to be explored in depth in terms of its use to a mass market. As mass tourism has risen to a point of consolidation and stagnation, tourists themselves have realized that other forms of product have more to offer. Indeed, history is one example of a key component of a variety of forms of tourism, including mass, that can also be considered on its own to be niche. The development of Egyptian resorts, such as Sharm El Sheikh, shows us that modern mass tourism is complemented by (one could argue reliant on) the use of history as a supplementary (niche) attraction that influences the consumer decision-making process.

All destinations contain unique elements of heritage and culture that are used for the purposes of tourism. Still, it can be argued that some types of heritage culture (past or present) are more attractive to a variety of tourist markets than others. The significance of the pyramids is known throughout literature and is a prominent feature of any modern mass tourism itinerary to Egypt. The word 'niche' in this context refers to the principle motivation, which is also the actual product and, therefore, a significant pull factor within destination regions. History also shows the significance of heritage products in other ways. The pyramids at Giza and the ancient historical sites of Karnak and Luxor were visited by early tourists on Grand Tours.

With the change in demand and image for mass tourism, niche tourism products and markets have become more significant, both for the development of global tourism and for specific destinations. Current key forms of niche tourism are shown in Example 1.1.

The examples shown in Example 1.1 are current growth markets where the pull of niche products and markets continues to facilitate an

---

Example 1.1. Current examples of niche tourism in literature, together with the relevant chapters in this book.
- Adventure tourism (Chapter 11)
- Agri-tourism
- Cruise tourism (Chapter 20)
- Culture/heritage tourism (Chapters 7, 12, 13)
- Dark tourism (Chapter 15)
- Ecotourism (Chapter 9)
- Educational tourism
- Indigenous tourism (Chapter 7)
- Lesbian, gay, bisexual and transgendered (LGBT) tourism (Chapter 16)
- Medical tourism (Chapter 19)
- Music tourism (Chapter 10)
- Religious tourism (Chapter 18)
- Sports tourism (Chapter 11)
- Volunteer tourism

---

increase in demand. The interesting question here is whether these components will increase in demand to such an extent that they will become as significant as mass tourism within some destinations (in relation to size). This chapter has already identified that the global movement of tourism is seemingly showing an increased focus on the niche product (based on a core product in its own right and also as a supplementary feature to modern mass tourism). In this case, the question seems to be whether the further growth in demand for niche tourism products will continue until they become a form of mass tourism (massified). Arguments against this simply suggest that it is a case of modern motivational factors. Tourism was conceived as a mass market product because it satisfied the wants and needs of a larger group. Those needs simply reflect the type of product it is (a standardized product for standardized motivations). Niche tourism, on the other hand, is a product that can only appeal to a select smaller group. Take the example of adventure tourism. The concept of adventure as a leisure, recreational and tourism product has the potential to appeal to a large market (and does so, with products such as winter tourism). As Swarbrooke *et al.* (2003) suggested, a variety of motivations make up the lure of adventure as a tourism product. Some of these motivational factors are ingrained within human history.

Adventure tourism provides the opportunity to satisfy the urge for exploration, for discovery. This will, however, only appeal to a select few. Adventure tourism will therefore only appeal to a select type of tourist, and yet there is currently a global increase in the demand for adventure tourism products. In this sense, niche tourism products such as adventure may become a modern form of mass tourism (where 'mass' is defined by a significant market size).

Further arguments surrounding niche markets suggest that an increase in demand allows organizations or destinations to specialize and focus on different types of tourism product. This allows the industry to 'fragment' into smaller components that appeal to specific niche markets under the bracket of, for example, adventure. In this sense, we could call adventure (as with culture, sport, music, educational and religious tourism) a new form of mass tourism. As niche tourism grows, it begins to fragment into smaller products and markets. This means that the size of a niche grows, but the fact tourists are participating in it in different ways (with no initial standardized, rigid approach) defines different sectors of the niche. It is then how they fragment that allows a newer definition of niche to be formulated. Figure 1.2 shows how adventure morphs into sub-sectors, which then fragment into specific activities, which subsequently fragment further into more unique products. These unique products are termed here as 'micro-niches'.

While it could be argued that these are merely forms of supplementary activities, it is argued here that tourism has exhibited growth through differentiation, fragmentation and reinvention of modern tourism products.

Figure 1.2 shows how a form of niche tourism (adventure tourism) has morphed into various sub-sections (e.g. mountain tourism) and how this has in turn morphed into further forms, culminating in micro-niches within an activity such as snowboarding. Initially, this could merely be described as fragmentation into supplementary activities that do not have the potential to be focused on by destinations as specific niches. Yet, as can be seen in modern resorts, these forms of snowboarding have become a significant component to resort segmentation and differentiation, culminating in a service offering that is distinct between destinations. In North America, for example, the resort of Stratton is embedded within modern snowboard folklore as not only being the destination where snowboard pioneers crafted their trade, but also the first destination to fully deregulate the use of snowboards. Snowboarding has now become a more significant niche product, such that resorts now differentiate themselves by focusing on specific forms of micro-niches (e.g. snow parks and off-piste 'backcountry' for snowboarding). Some resorts have now started to develop an image as heli-board destinations (flying by helicopter to clear, untouched powder snow to indulge in pure forms of snowboarding, creating brand new lines on pristine snow).

The term 'micro-niches' can be related to more recent discussions surrounding micro-markets (specific selling to individuals), but it is important to remember that these micro-niches are not specific individuals or small groups, but constantly growing groups within groups, evolving to become further important features within niche tourism. It is, therefore, quite feasible that the types of niche markets detailed in Example 1.1 contain a far more specific breakdown of markets and products and will continue to become larger niche markets in the future. What is more interesting is that it may be feasible for certain niche products to become so popular that they are designated as 'mass' tourism products. Independent travel, such as modern backpacking, may be considered as containing features that potentially show this growth from micro-niche to niche and then to mass tourism.

It is this potential of these niche markets and products in tourism that have resulted in destinations focusing more time, energy and money on effectively selling towards a tourist who is being offered more fragmented choices. This focus can have its limitations and risks for a destination. Niche products such as adventure tourism, for example, need a prior appropriate skill set and regulatory framework in place for them to be safe and also a comparable quality with other more established destination products. Failure to solve these initial challenges

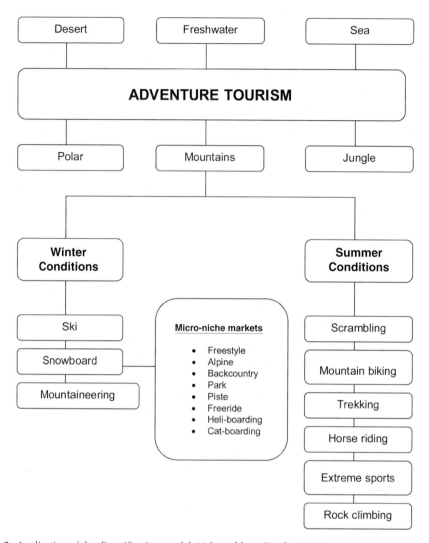

Fig. 1.2. Application of the diversification model. (Adapted from Beedie, 2003.)

can cause major issues later on in the product lifecycle. Examples of this can be seen in the unregulated introduction of adventure sports in areas such as the Caribbean and South-east Asia. Even countries such as New Zealand, with its image of high-quality, safe adventure experiences, are not immune to the impact that issues of regulation and management can have on a destination's image and resulting arrival figures and tourist expenditure.

It is not surprising that destinations choose this approach from which to become com-

petitive within the global tourism marketplace. The use of niche products and markets can give an increased product offering, resulting in differentiation and diversification of markets. When related to the tourist area lifecycle, it is again obvious that destinations that are at a tenuous stage of consolidation and stagnation can use the concept of 'niche' to refresh their tourist offering and enhance the destination image as a 'playground for all'. Economically, niche tourist markets can form a lifecycle in themselves: if a destination is able to gain a foothold by creating a destination brand surrounding specific niche products, the economic value of this will not only become stronger as the market becomes more dominant, but a variety of markets will enhance the economic multiplier effect of tourism by contributing to tourist expenditure. This will further have an impact on tourist movement and subsequent tourist expenditure flowing into localized economies (based on the type of niche and the location of the resources required to successfully participate).

Conclusion: a Movement Towards Mass Tourism?

Tourism exhibits an unusual set of principles that govern demand and supply, largely because it is a service industry and is, therefore, characterized by intangibility and heterogeneity. This chapter has attempted to show how the initial definitions of mass tourism have been formulated and how they are influenced by the inclusion of modern tourism activities, which become forms of niche tourism products and markets in themselves. Tourism in this sense (from a demand perspective, initially) may be described as evolving, where leisure and recreation develop into something more substantial. As demand grows in areas of popularity that can be initially described as niche tourism, so does supply. Mass tourism has manifested from the early development of travel and been facilitated in its growth through technological, social, cultural and political developments. Mass tourism continues to raise complex and challenging debates; both in term of its definition and development, and its impact and significance. The future of tourism in this sense can be argued as being firmly rooted in the development of niche products and markets, as well as in the growing development of forms of mass tourism.

The following chapters of this book provide a synopsis of some of the current discussions taking place surrounding forms of niche tourism. Sustainable and alternative tourism, as described by Ade Oriade and Mike Evans in Chapter 6, addresses the controversial relationship between sustainable development as a tool for environmental and economic development. The word 'environment' is useful here to pinpoint the focus of a tourism type that is becoming increasingly fragmented (into sustainable tourism, eco-tourism, green tourism and responsible tourism, to name just a few similar terms). The chapter on community tourism by Peter Robinson and Peter Wiltshier (Chapter 7) further emphasizes the various methods by which forms of niche tourism can be sustainable in outlook, and helps inform the later chapters on events tourism (Chapter 10; Gemma Gelder and Peter Robinson), adventure tourism (Chapter 11; Christine Roberts) and heritage tourism (Chapter 13; Carol Southall and Peter Robinson). The last of these topics is further explored when looking at how tourism and popular culture exist in a symbiosis of tourism products and attractions. Film tourism, as analysed by Glen Croy and Sine Heitmann (Chapter 14), is an increasingly popular area of debate, from the direct and indirect approaches to how tourists apply significance to destinations based on popular films (and how destinations, in turn, use this to increase arrival numbers and expenditure). Lesbian, gay, bisexual and transgendered (Chapter 16), gastronomy (Chapter 17) and medical (Chapter 19) tourism are also examples that demand further investigation into size, motivations, patterns of demand and growth. Chapters included in this text also take a traditional approach by focusing on what could be described as historical and contemporary 'stalwarts' of tourism, most notably religious tourism (Chapter 18; Peter Wiltshier), cultural tourism (Chapter 12, Geoffrey Shirt) and cruise tourism (Chapter 20; Patsy Morgan and Lisa Power). Other significant areas of discussion surrounding niche tourism not in this series are music tourism (Gibson and Cornell, 2005), the controversial topic of sex tourism (Clift and Carter, 2000; Ryan and Hall, 2001; Bauer and McKercher, 2003), health and wellness tourism (Smith and Puczkó, 2009) and nature-based tourism (Newsome, Moore and Dowling, 2002; Hall and Boyd, 2005).

Review Questions

1. Look again at Table 1.2 and identify the other arguments proposed in relation to mass tourism:
(a) Identify examples of 'positive' and 'negative' themes in the discussion surrounding mass tourism.
(b) How does this influence how we define mass tourism?

2. This chapter has identified the importance of symbolic attractions in further complementing a variety of tourist markets. What kind of products could the Egypt tourism authorities focus on as an alternative to Ancient Egyptian culture?
3. Will niche forms of tourism ever become as popular as mass tourism? Why or why not?

References

Bauer, T.G. and McKercher, B. (ed.) (2003) *Sex and Tourism: Journeys of Romance, Love and Lust.* Haworth Hospitality Press, Binghamton, New York.

Beaver, A. (2005) *The Dictionary of Travel and Tourism Terminology.* CAB International, Wallingford, UK.

Beech, J. and Chadwick, S. (2006) *The Business of Tourism Management.* Pearson Education, Harlow, UK.

Bjelicic, B. (2007) The business model of low-cost airlines: past present and future. In: Gross, S. and Schröder, A. (eds) *Handbook of Low Cost Airlines: Strategies, Business Processes and Market Environment.* Erich Schmidt Verlag GMBH and Co, Berlin, Germany, pp. 11–29.

Bramwell, B. (ed.) (2004) *Coastal Tourism: Diversification and Sustainable Development in Southern Europe.* Channel View, Clevedon, UK.

Butler, R. (1980) The concept of a tourist area cycle of evolution: implications for management of resources. *The Canadian Geographer* 24(1), 5–12.

Clarke, J. (2004) A framework of approaches to sustainable tourism. In: Williams, S. (ed.) *Tourism: Critical Concepts in the Social Sciences, Vol. 3: Tourism Development and Sustainability.* Routledge, London, UK.

Cohen, E. (1972) Toward a sociology of international tourism. *Social Research* 39(1) 164–189.

Clift, S. and Carter, S. (eds) (2000) *Tourism and Sex: Culture, Commerce and Coercion.* Continuum, London, UK.

Deuschl, D. (2006) *Travel and Tourism Public Relations: an Introductory Guide for Hospitality Managers.* Butterworth-Heinemann, Oxford, UK.

Digance, J. (2006) Religious and secular pilgrimage: journeys redolent with meaning. In: Timothy, D.J. and Olson, D.H. (eds) *Tourism, Religion and Spiritual Journeys.* Routledge, Abingdon, UK, pp. 36–47.

Galton, F. (1872) *The Art of Travel.* John Murray, London, UK.

Gibson, C. and Connell, J. (2005) *Music and Tourism: On the Road Again.* Channel View, Clevedon, UK.

Hall, C.M. and Boyd, S.W. (2005) *Nature-Based Tourism in Peripheral Areas: Development or Disaster?* Channel View, Clevedon, UK.

Holden, A. (2008) *Environment and Tourism*, 2nd edn. Routledge, Abingdon, UK.

Holloway, C.J. and Taylor, N. (2006) *The Business of Tourism.* Pearson Education, Harlow, UK.

Murphy, P. (1985) *Tourism: A Community Approach.* Routledge, London, UK.

Obrador Pons, P., Crang, M. and Travlou, P. (eds) (2009) *Cultures of Mass Tourism: Doing the Mediterranean in the Age of Banal Mobilities.* Ashgate Publishing Limited, Farnham, UK.

The Outdoor Foundation (2009) *Outdoor Recreation Participation Report, 2009.* The Outdoor Foundation, Washington, DC.

Page, S.J. and Connell, J. (2005) *Tourism: A Modern Synthesis.* Thomson Learning, Andover, UK.

Pender, L. (2005) Introduction: Managing the Tourism System. In: Pender, L. and Sharpley, R. (eds) (2005) *The Management of Tourism.* Sage, London, UK, pp. 1–13.

Poon, A. (1993) *Tourism, Technology and Competitive Strategies.* CAB International, Wallingford, UK.

Richards, G. (ed.) (2001) *Cultural Attractions and European Tourism.* CAB International, Wallingford, UK.

Robinson, M. and Novelli, M. (2005) Niche tourism: an introduction. In: Novelli, M. (2005) *Niche Tourism: Contemporary Issues.* Butterworth-Heinemann, Oxford, UK.

Ryan, C. and Hall, C.M. (2001) *Sex Tourism: Marginal People and Liminalities.* Routledge, London, UK.

Sharma, K.K. (2004) *Tourism and Socio-cultural Development.* Sarup and Sons, New Delhi, India.

Sharpley, R. (2007) Tourism in the Gambia: 10 years on. In: Tribe, J. and Airey, D. (eds) *Developments in Tourism Research.* Elsevier, Oxford, UK, pp. 49–62.

Sharpley, R. and Tefler, D.J. (2008) *Tourism and Development.* Routledge, Abingdon, UK.

Shaw, G. and Williams, A.M. (2002) *Critical Issues in Tourism: A Geographical Perspective,* 2nd edn. Blackwell, Oxford, UK.

Shaw, G. and Williams, A.M. (2004) *Tourism and Tourist Places.* Sage, London.

Smith, M.K. and Puczkó, L. (2009) *Health and Wellness Tourism.* Elsevier, Oxford, UK.

Swarbrooke, J., Beard, C., Lechie, S. and Pomfret, G. (2003) *Adventure Tourism: the new frontier.* Butterworth-Heinemann, Oxford, UK.

Thomas Cook (n.d.) Key dates. Available from: http://www.thomascook.com/about-us/thomas-cook-history/key-dates. Accessed 24 June, 2010.

Towner, J. (1996) The Grand Tour: a key phase in the history of tourism. *Annals of Tourism Reasearch* 12(3), 295–333.

Urry, J. (2005) *The Tourist Gaze.* Sage, London, UK.

Van Egmond, T. (2007) *Understanding Western Tourists in Developing Countries.* CAB International, Wallingford, UK.

Vanhove, N. (1997) Mass tourism: benefits and costs. In: Wahab, S. and Pigram, J.J. (eds) *Tourism, Development and Growth: The Challenge of Sustainability.* Routledge, London, UK, pp. 46–71.

Walker, J.C. (2004) Becoming a Darwinian, the micro-politics of Sir Frances Galton's scientific career 1859–1865. *Annals of Science* 61(2), 141–163.

Wang, M. (2000) *Tourism and Modernity: A Sociological Analysis.* Pergamon Press, Amsterdam, the Netherlands.

Weaver, D. (1994) Ecotourism in the Caribbean basin. In: Cater (1994) *Ecotourism: A Sustainable Option.* John Wiley and Sons, New York.

Weaver, D. (2006) *Sustainable Tourism: Theory and Practice.* Elsevier, Oxford, UK.

Weaver, D. (2007) Towards sustainable mass tourism: paradigm shift or paradigm nudge? *Tourism Recreation Research* 32, 65–69.

Weaver, D. and Opperman, M. (2000) *Tourism Management.* John Wiley and Sons, Brisbane, Australia.

Yeoman, I. (2008) *Tomorrow's Tourist: Scenarios and Trends.* Butterworth-Heinemann, Oxford, UK.

2 Aspects of Tourism Development

Dr Peter U.C. Dieke

Introduction

This chapter examines the developmental aspects of tourism in the context of less developed countries (LDCs). It identifies some of the structural deficiencies inhibiting development in LDCs and discusses the role of tourism in ameliorating the situation. The chapter argues that the structural features of these societies and, in particular, the general patterns of global tourism to LDCs are themselves constraints to the development of the tourism sector. Based on the analysis described, the chapter sets out guidelines that tourism policymakers in LDCs might consider in seeking to embrace tourism as a viable development tool.

As used here, the LDCs are those mainly in Africa, Asia and Latin America. These regional countries have a wide range of levels of development and share, if anything, certain common structural characteristics that pose considerable challenges to their development efforts. 'Development' is an incremental, long-term (and not immediate) process to improve both the economic opportunity and quality of social life and conditions in these regional countries. Development includes human and institutional changes, such as changes in behaviours, aspirations and broader concerns of quality of life (UNDP, 2009). 'Tourism development' refers to the way tourism has developed in LDCs and the nature of tourism activities in those countries. It is expected that through the encouragement of soundly based tourism initiatives, with policy, planning and implementation of the plan being the focal

points (Jenkins, 2007), these countries will be able to decrease their marginalization in the global system and thus become viable members of the international economy. These considerations are discussed below.

Particular Characteristics of LDCs

A number of broad factors are perhaps common to many countries, both developed and less developed. These include an international debt burden, changing geo-political landscapes, acute problems of unemployment, inflationary pressures and so on. While these factors may be common everywhere, they are supplemented by the special situation in LDCs (UNDP, 2009). The particular characteristics in focus can be usefully classified into five main headings: narrow economic resource base; over-reliance on the export of primary products; unfriendly 'terms of trade'; severe population pressures; and the political–economic (independence) nexus (Jenkins, 1997). One might argue that these structural deficiencies have all combined to make the concept of 'development' elusive for many of these countries. These issues need to be put in the wider context of development if we are to understand how they inhibit the development process in LDCs and the role tourism might have in this process.

First, most LDCs are characterized by narrow resource-based economies. This implies that they are limited in their ability to progress development through exports. Namibia and Zambia are classic examples of African countries with large resource bases worthy of development, but for reasons of low technology production, among others, this potential has not been realized (Government of Zambia, 1995; Jenkins, 2000). Second, LDCs depend on the export of primary products mainly related to agriculture. The problem here is that such export products often face quotas or tariff restrictions that further limit LDCs' import possibilities.

A third (and related) problem is over the so-called 'terms of trade', described literally as 'the quantum of exports required to buy a quantum of imports' (Jenkins, 1997). Terms of trade have moved against LDCs, given that export prices that LDCs receive have substantially declined in recent times. A fourth area of concern stems from the increasing population pressures in many of these countries. For instance, Kenya's current population is estimated at 39 million and grows at an annual rate of about 3%, suggesting that the population will double in the next two decades. India also has a similar growth pattern: current estimates put India's population at 1.15 billion and the population is likely to surpass that of China (currently 1.3 billion) by 2030. With more mouths to feed, the governments of these countries face a number of challenges, not least of which is the need to import developmental inputs of capital equipment and expertise to attenuate these pressures. This is a particularly difficult objective to achieve since these imports have to be paid for at global market prices. This situation is further compounded by the declining value and earning potentials of LDCs.

Finally, in the early 1960s many LDCs gained political independence from their colonial masters. With that came the expectation that there would be corresponding economic independence through an expansion in trade freedom. Unfortunately, this was not the case. The result was that the ex-colonies had to rely on the 'mother countries' for their economic survival, thereby deepening LDCs' reliance on the old colonists. It is against such a background that many LDCs have looked at tourism as a potential export sector, to assist them actualize their well-deserved economic freedom. In subsequent sections, this chapter will examine the role tourism plays in this respect: 'Everything seems to suggest that developing countries look upon tourism consumption as manna from heaven that can provide a solution to all their foreign settlement difficulties' (Erbes, 1973).

International Tourism and Development

International tourism refers to movements of tourists between countries involving the crossing of a national frontier. Purpose of travel follows the 1993 UN Statistical Commission's definition of being for leisure and business reasons. Most governments in LDCs encourage international tourism because of its potential contribution to development, which is well documented. Tourism has been viewed as a means of earning foreign currency, a contributor to government revenues, a creator of employment opportunities and therefore an income generator, a stimulus to inward investment and a means of bringing wider economic benefits to regions with otherwise limited economic potential (Oppermann and Chon, 1997; Harrison, 2001; Sharpley and Telfer, 2002; Jenkins, 2007; Brown and Hall, 2008; Telfer and Sharpley, 2008).

It comes as no surprise that in LDCs, tourism is perceived as a panacea for fragile economies that are characterized by a scarcity of development resources such as finance and expertise. These resources are needed to increase the economic surplus, without which these societies would be forced to rely solely on international aid to support their development efforts. This axiomatic view of tourism has, for a long time, gained some support in part because tourism is a highly visible activity. It is unfortunate if this notion of tourism as 'manna from heaven' is accepted without questioning.

Thus, critics might argue that this notion of tourism is rather absurd, if not overly simplistic, given the well-recognized weaknesses of tourism as a viable development option in LDCs (de Kadt, 1979; Dieke, 1995, 2000, 2008, 2009; Lea, 1998; Rogerson, 2007; Sinclair, 1998; Brown and Hall, 2008). In the main, tourism has not delivered its expected benefits; the economic, sociocultural and environmental costs of tourism outweigh the benefits, in terms of high-revenue 'leakages' related to either repatriation of profits and salaries or imports, and therefore low net expenditure retention; the dominance of foreign companies and the instability of the sector; and the lack of low intersectoral or backward linkages. Tourism has also been criticized for exacerbating societal problems, such as the destruction of social patterns, neo-colonialist relationships of exploitation and dependence, and insensitivity of foreign operators to social and cultural norms of host communities; and damage to the environment via unregulated construction, resource over-use, pollution and diversion of water supplies (Brown and Hall, 2008). All of these objections may raise doubts about whether tourism has a 'development' impact on LDC societies. Both positions, admittedly, have merit.

This chapter takes a balanced view. It explores the preceding issues with reference to the characteristics of tourism in LDCs and, finally, provides guidelines for tourism development in LDCs if these countries are to successfully compete in the global tourism marketplace.

General Patterns of Tourism in LDCs

Five characteristics define the general patterns of tourism in LDCs: low volume; nature of tourism development; point-to-point versus regional circuit; trigger market; and seasonality. These features are important in two respects: first, they highlight general 'areas of concern' associated with tourism as a development option for LDCs; and second, they provide a wider platform for remedial actions. Before discussing these features, however, it is helpful to present global tourism trend patterns as the basis for analysis, since such trends help contextualize regional trends, particularly relating to LDCs. In considering this, there are three areas that will be emphasized: global trends; regional trends; and a synthesis.

International and regional tourism trends

Tables 2.1 and 2.2 show the dispersion and growth of international and regional tourism, as measured in terms of volume (or tourist arrivals; Table 2.1) and value (or tourism receipts; Table 2.2) and related to country groupings for the relevant years.

According to the UN World Tourism Organization's (UNWTO's) latest estimate (2008), 903 million tourists travelled worldwide in 2007 (or 56 million more arrivals than in 2006; Table 2.1), a growth rate of 6.6% in comparison with 2006 and 5.5% increases recorded in 2005. It is further estimated (Table 2.2) that US$856 billion was generated in international tourism receipts in 2007 (or US$114 billion more than in 2006; i.e. 5.6% higher than 2006). It is expected that by global arrivals will reach 1 billion by 2010 and 1.6 billion by 2020. Tourism receipts will reach US$2 trillion in 2020.

Regional trends can also be discerned from Tables 2.1 and 2.2. The indication is that the Middle East led the growth ranking in 2007 (Table 2.1), with an estimated 16% rise to nearly 48 million international tourist arrivals. Asia and the Pacific (184 million) followed with >10% over 2006. Africa increased its arrivals by 7% to 44 million. The Americas (an increase of 5%) showed a substantial growth of tourist arrivals, better than in previous years, achieving over 142 million arrivals. Europe maintained its position of leadership in global tourist arrivals, which grew by 5% to reach 484 million, accounting for 54% of all international tourist arrivals.

Relative growth in real receipt terms (Table 2.2) was particularly strong in Asia and the Pacific (+11%; double the world average), Africa (+8%) and the Americas (+6%). The performance of the Americas showed a significant improvement over the previous year's 2% growth. In sub-regions, the strongest increases came from South-east Asia (+13%) and North-east Asia (+12%), followed by Central America, North Africa and Central and Eastern Europe (all at +9%). Only one sub-region, the Caribbean, did not increase its receipts in 2007 (–0.4%), largely as a result of a stagnation in arrivals.

Synthesis

These statistics highlight several interesting features. First is the extent to which many countries, developed and developing, have

Table 2.1. International tourist arrivals (for selected years).

World and regions	International tourist arrivals (million)						Market share (%)	Change (%)		Average annual growth (%)
	1990	1995	2000	2005	2006	2007[a]	2007[a]	2006/05	2007[a]/06	2000/07[a]
World	436	536	683	803	847	903	100	5.5	6.6	4.1
Africa	15.2	20.1	27.9	37.3	41.4	44.4	4.8	11.0	7.4	6.9
North Africa	8.4	7.3	10.2	13.9	15.1	16.3	1.8	8.4	7.9	6.8
Sub-Saharan Africa	6.8	12.8	17.7	23.3	26.3	28.2	3.1	12.6	7.1	6.9
Americas	92.8	109.0	128.2	133.2	135.8	142.5	15.8	1.9	4.9	1.5
North America	71.7	80.7	91.5	89.9	90.6	95.3	10.6	0.8	5.2	0.6
Caribbean	11.4	14.0	17.1	18.8	19.4	19.5	2.2	3.4	0.1	1.9
Central America	1.9	2.6	4.3	6.4	7.1	7.7	0.9	9.9	9.6	8.6
South America	7.7	11.7	15.3	18.2	18.7	19.9	2.2	2.8	6.4	3.9
Asia and the Pacific	55.8	81.8	109.3	154.6	167.0	184.3	20.0	8.0	10.4	7.8
North-east Asia	26.4	41.3	58.3	87.5	94.3	104.2	11.5	7.7	10.6	8.6
South-east Asia	21.1	28.2	35.6	48.5	53.1	59.6	6.6	9.4	12.2	7.6
Oceania	5.2	8.1	9.2	10.5	10.5	10.7	1.2	0.4	1.7	2.2
South Asia	3.2	4.2	6.1	8.1	9.1	9.8	1.1	11.8	8.2	7.1
Europe	262.6	311.3	393.5	440.3	462.2	484.4	53.6	5.0	4.8	3.0
Northern Europe	28.6	35.8	43.0	52.8	56.4	57.6	6.4	6.8	2.2	4.0
Western Europe	108.6	112.2	139.7	142.4	149.5	154.9	17.1	5.0	3.6	1.5
Central/Eastern Europe	31.5	60.6	69.4	87.8	91.5	95.6	10.6	4.2	4.5	4.7
Southern Europe/Mediterranean	93.9	102.7	140.8	157.3	164.8	176.2	19.5	4.7	7.0	3.3
Middle East	9.6	13.7	24.4	37.8	40.9	47.6	5.3	8.2	16.4	10.0

[a]Provisional estimate.
Source: UN World Tourism Organization (2008).

Table 2.2. International tourism receipts.

	International tourism receipts (billion)						Change Current prices (%)			Change Constant prices (%)		
	1990	1995	2000	2005	2006	2007a	2005/04	2006a/05	2007a/06	2005/04	2006a/05	2007a/06
Local currencies							6.3	8.5	9.1	3.1	5.1	5.6
US$	264	405	475	680	742	856	7.3	9.2	15.4	3.8	5.8	12.1
Euro	207	310	513	544	584	625	7.3	8.2	5.7	5.2	5.9	3.5

a Provisional estimate.

	Change local currencies constant prices (%)			Share (%)	US$ receipts			Euro receipts		
					Billion		Per arrival	Billion		Per arrival
	2005/04	2006/05	2007a/06	2007a	2006	2007a	2007a	2006	2007a	2007
World	3.1	5.1	5.6	100	742	856	950	591	625	690
Africa	10.9	10.5	7.5	3.3	24.6	28.3	640	19.6	20.6	460
North Africa	15.3	19.1	8.7	1.2	8.7	10.3	640	6.9	7.5	460
Sub-Saharan Africa	8.8	6.5	6.9	2.1	15.9	18.0	640	12.7	13.1	470
Americas	4.3	1.8	6.4	20.0	154.1	171.1	1200	122.7	124.9	880
North America	4.5	0.8	7.4	14.6	112.5	125.1	1310	89.6	91.3	960
Caribbean	3.3	1.9	−0.4	2.6	21.7	22.6	1160	17.3	16.5	850
Central America	9.3	10.3	8.9	0.7	5.5	6.3	810	4.4	4.6	590
South America	2.0	6.8	8.0	2.0	14.4	17.2	860	11.5	12.5	630
Asia and the Pacific	4.2	11.1	11.4	22.1	156.5	188.9	1020	124.7	137.9	750
North-east Asia	7.9	12.1	12.5	10.4	75.2	89.2	860	59.9	65.1	620
South-east Asia	0.0	16.0	13.0	6.3	43.6	54.0	910	34.7	39.4	660
Oceania	1.0	2.5	8.1	3.8	26.6	32.3	3020	21.2	23.6	2200
South Asia	4.1	10.7	5.4	1.6	11.2	13.4	1370	8.9	9.8	1000
Europe	1.7	3.9	2.7	50.6	376.9	433.4	890	300.2	316.2	650
Northern Europe	8.4	7.7	3.9	8.1	60.3	69.7	1210	48.0	50.8	880
Western Europe	−0.2	3.7	2.1	17.4	131.6	149.1	960	104.8	108.8	700
Central/Eastern Europe	0.1	8.2	8.6	5.6	38.2	48.3	510	30.4	35.3	370
Southern Europe/ Mediterranean	1.4	1.6	1.1	19.4	146.9	166.4	940	117.0	121.4	690
Middle East	2.5	3.6	6.3	4.0	29.9	34.2	720	23.8	25.0	520

aProvisional estimate.
Source: UN World Tourism Organization (2008).

become tourist destinations for foreign travellers; and the competitive nature of tourist activities in which these countries are fiercely engaged to increase their share of the market in volume and value terms. Second, the trend data suggest that tourism is historically a growth industry. It has, with a few exceptions in certain years, exceeded the growth of world trade over the same time period. This trend clearly demonstrates that tourism is a sustainable, long-term growth industry *on a global basis*. The emphasis is important as it does not follow that a global trend is reflected in every country or region. For example, over the last 50 years Europe (and particularly Western European countries) has received over 50% of international tourism arrivals and receipts, although this is now declining. The distribution of both arrivals and receipts is highly skewed, with approximately 80% of international tourist arrivals and 78% of international receipts being received in developed countries.

Third, in relation to forecasting long-term trends in an industry, projections can be considerably dislocated in the short-term by such by events as the attack in the USA on September 11, 2001, the second Iraq war in 2003 and ongoing, and the SARS virus pandemic, all of which present dangers in terms of realizing the forecasts. Brief comments on the above trends might be appropriate, particularly relating to short-haul versus long-haul international travel. Much intra-European travel (that is, travel within and between Western European countries) is relatively short haul (and therefore more comparable with a lot of domestic travel in large countries such as Australia, Canada and the USA). This distinction is important because it helps to explain the dominance of Europe, in volume and value terms, in the global tourism marketplace. Additionally, there has been a global redistribution in the foci of tourism activity associated with the emergence of the 'tiger economies' of the Asia-Pacific Rim (Hong Kong, Singapore, South Korea and Taiwan). Economic growth in these countries has fuelled both growth in demand and awareness of new tourist destinations.

Finally, from these comparative data we can say that not only is tourism an industry of growing importance in the global economy, but it is expected to sustain its vitality. It should also be noted that the financial revenues generated by tourism activity (international tourism receipts) are always understated because, due to national accounting conventions, international fare payments are not included as tourism receipts but are counted in the transportation account of the balance of payments, maintained by the International Monetary Fund. In fact, the separation of international fare receipts (which are a major source of tourism-induced revenue) understates tourism receipts. It is for these reasons that the UNWTO and the UN have endorsed a move towards compiling tourism satellite accounts as a means to improve the collection of tourism financial and economic data and to facilitate comparisons of the impact of tourism activity between countries.

Against the above background, in brief, this chapter now presents the general characteristics of tourism in LDCs, using Tables 2.1 and 2.2 as reference points.

Low volume

Many writers, perhaps starting with Bryden (1973) and others (Cleverdon, 1979; Brohman, 1996) have expressed concern about LDCs' relatively low share of global tourism. The whole emphasis here is on the volume of tourism activity in, and its implications for, LDCs, with volume referring to tourist arrivals and the consequent impact on tourism receipts accruing to LDCs.

Bryden's (1973) 'volume approach' distinguished between a 'tourism country' and a 'non-tourism country' on the basis of gross domestic receipts as a portion of revenue from exports of goods. A tourism country is one where receipts from tourism exceed 5% of national income, or where 10% of visible exports are accounted for by tourism receipts. There are three striking observations that can be made: the significance of tourism to a country's economy; the particular country's level of dependence on tourism; and developing countries' share of volume and value of tourism at destinations.

It is evident (Tables 2.1 and 2.2) that tourism in LDCs is characterized by relatively low volume, although this differs widely from one LDC country and region to another. For example, a record of 1 million tourist arrivals in India in any one year may be considered high, but by developed economies' standards, the number is low. In the same way, tourism receipt of, say, US$1 million for India may be high; from the perspective of the developed world, it is the reverse.

Several writers (Apostolopoloulos *et al.*, 2001; Dunning and McQueen, 1982; Mowforth and Munt, 2003; Telfer and Sharpley, 2008; Sharpley, 2009) have suggested a myriad of factors that influence volume and value of tourism in LDCs, including control of the sector exercised by companies and organizations from developed economies, and how the local residents of LDCs perceive tourism – an activity mainly for the elite, which is either a consequence of the culture of their society or of certain economic realities. It could well be that development resources – physical or material, financial and human – to support tourism are limited, hence government has to intervene. Other considerations include: (i) government development policy objectives for tourism (e.g. the type of market for which it has chosen to cater – low-spending tourists versus high spenders – or scale of development, such as carefully controlled tourism, setting a limit on the number of tourists to be admitted each year, as is the case in Bhutan); (ii) the average length of time spent by vacationers in each country; and (iii) tourist expenditure patterns, themselves the result of factors such as relative prices and spending opportunities.

The nature of tourism development

The nature of tourism development in LDCs must be specific to that particular country. It would be difficult to compare one developing country with another because of diverse tourism attractions available in each country and different types of tourists with different travel motivations. In this sense, the nature of tourism development covers a very wide spectrum: the type of visitors the government

wants to attract; and types of facilities and services available at destinations. It is also directly concerned with organizations that influence the tourism system, especially how the trigger markets encourage demand. In order to understand the significance of these influences, it is necessary to address whether tourism in LDCs is organically or inorganically determined and to review various tourism typologies as applicable to LDCs and pose a question – what are LDCs' options or alternatives?

The field of tourism development remains a controversial area because there is as yet no consensus among scholars on a generally acceptable model of tourism growth. Forster's (1964) 'genetic approach' and later Greenwood's (1972) argument that tourism is a process that 'creates a type of "cumulative causation" and ultimately a new economic base' help shape subsequent thoughts.

Naronha (1977) conceptualized a three-stage model of tourism development: discovery; local response and initiative; and institutionalization. The model assumes that tourism in a relatively novel place derives its initial development impetus from local initiatives, based on spontaneous factors. Stage two is constrained by a lack of a strong local resource base to sustain continued expansion. As might be expected, this situation heralds the way for the external involvement of corporate tourism. Stage three, described as industrial tourism, causes facilities to be increased in terms of both numbers and standards. This model implies that as LDC tourism develops, a host community loses control and its relative share in the total benefits from tourism generally declines (Rodenburg, 1980). Jenkins (1982) conversely argued that the impetus that such tourism provides may not suffice to stimulate sustained local development.

Other studies add to the debate on tourism systems: those in which growth is organic and those in which initial growth is induced from the outside. Stansfield's (1978) 'resort cycle' and Butler's (1980) 'tourist area cycle' are examples of organic development, at least in a geographical sense (see Chapter 1). The model is limited to describing many resorts in the developed world that grew organically. But LDCs' tourism growth has been extraneously triggered, as the example of The Gambia shows (Sharpley, 2008). The Gambia's tourism developed because of Swedish tour operators. Demand was from mass-packaged tourism.

In relation to tourist typologies (see also Chapter 3), three are to be noted: 'sedentary' and 'migrant' (UNDP/ICAO, 1977); 'wanderlust' and 'sun-lust' (Gray, 1970); and 'institutionalized' and 'non-institutionalized' (Cohen, 1972). Basically, these expressions are similar, apparently indicating two distinct categories of visitors at different evolutionary stages. At one end is an individual interested in 'getting away from it all' (migrant, sun-lust, institutionalized), while at the other end is the person who is perhaps motivated most by curiosity (sedentary, wanderlust, non-institutionalized) and describes a vacation as meaning 'to see, do and experience a variety of things, preferably in different locales' (UNDP/ICAO, 1977).

What options do the classifications leave LDCs with? Except for a consideration of revenue maximization, arguably the most crucial policy decision a government of any developing country faces in tourism develop-ment is the intended tourist population. This is important in view of the fact that the population influences the type of tourists attracted to a destination, room capacity to accommodate the visitors, control of the industry and the impact on the host community. The government of a developing country would appear to face two mutually exclusive tourism development options. The first choice is to put a ceiling on tourist population, attracting non-institutionalized vis-itors and thus reducing possible social disruption. This of course is a function of bargaining power, location and scale. Unfortunately, governments cannot exercise these choices because tourism for LDCs countries is, as noted, exogenously determined.

The second alternative open to the government is to go for a large-scale tourist market. Is big necessarily beautiful? But viewed from the notion that tourism development, as noted, is an evolutionary, but not spontaneous, process in which shifts in tourist tastes and whims impact on the system, it is, therefore, only reasonable to assert that the choice between the two categories of visitors is not as cut-and-dry as it would seem. Rather, what is of interest for our present purposes, as Bastin (1984) suggested, is that the choice is used actively 'to inhibit the growth process in order to retain a particular type of tourism'.

At a micro level, in the context of visitor motivation, the desire to experience the host country's culture may be impossible, especially when the number of visitors is increased. On the other hand, attracting institutionalized tourists may result in contrived cultural experiences – a situation Cohen (1972) reckons is made possible by two factors: the pseudo nature of attractions provided, in the main, to woo tourists; and mass tourists' connivance with cultural 'voyeurism' that does not involve any strenuous efforts on the part of the tourists.

Non-institutionalized tourists view the absence of cultural authenticity as a challenge because it deprives them of the opportunity to establish real contact with the host society – an important aspect of the holiday experience. The result – the tourists move on to another competitive location. The question that arises is: why not tailor the facilities to meet the needs of a particular group? In many cases, this is what tourists want.

At a macro-economic level, increased visitor levels set in motion a chain of related reactions. There is a derived demand for increased accommodation for the tourists. From a business-management principles viewpoint, this may cause the indigenous people to lose their control of the accommodation sub-sector, by not only passing the locus of control to external agencies, but indeed actually encourag-ing dependency.

Increased visitor levels may mean decreased economic returns because of lower per capita spending. This may offset any increase in employment opportunities. Again, the multiplier or 'spread' effect of income may not be realized, particularly because of the prepayment patterns of tourists in their countries.

Point-to-point versus regional circuit tourism

The third feature of tourism in LDCs is point-to-point and/or regional circuit possibilities. By 'point-to-point' tourism, we mean either single-centre, single-destination travel, involving tourist point of origin, (e.g. London and destination, Nairobi) or multi-centre, single-destination travel (e.g. London and Nairobi, plus trips outside the Nairobi area but limited to within the Kenyan borders). Often, however, although this is expensive, tourists take 'side trips' on excursions to neighbouring countries, perhaps of the same sub-region. At best, 'point-to-point' can be regarded as 'single destination'. This has two broad dimensions.

From the perspective of tourist motivations discussed, most developing countries or regions offer enough attractions and facilities – historical sites, beaches, folklore, climate, wildlife, mountains and marine life – to satisfy the two extremes of the tourist spectrum (sun-lust and wanderlust). Countries within this category can be regarded as 'single-destination' countries in travel industry jargon, because their product offering is similar. The term also can be used to qualify a destination that appeals to certain nationalities (e.g. French, British) that travel either on scheduled airlines or by charter flights paying low fares.

Regional circuit tourism, on the other hand, can be described as a multi-centre, multi-destination travel arrangement in which two or more contiguous countries participate. The regional circuit may have some good aspects to it. For the cooperating countries, it offers the chance to promote their various attractions, on a regional basis, in order to attract foreign exchange and provide more jobs. They may also take advantage of economies of scale – financial, managerial, marketing, technical and purchasing. For the tourists themselves, such a consortium arrangement enables enrichment of their experience over a wider area.

Problems such as the infrastructure available may hamper efforts at success. However, cooperation at various levels is the key to success – first, between tour operators and travel agents in tourist-generating countries, in soliciting their views as to the feasibility of the programme; and second with civil aviation, as air transport is the travel means mostly used in regional and international tourism. At the end of the day, it is the tour developer who has the most decisions to make: how much to spend and what the return on the investment might be.

Trigger market

The case argued here is that the trigger market presupposes that certain nationalities make tourism happen in chosen destinations. As we have seen, demand for such regional countries is based on mass-packaged tourism, induced from the outside. It is through either charter flights or scheduled airlines that this demand is met.

Weaver's (1983) framework, indicating source markets for LDC tourism, confirms the view that demand in tourism is exogenous and the host country has limited control. Again, since the determinants of demand are outside the influence of receiving countries, strong reliance on a single market will weaken the receiving country by increasing its dependency. Thus, this developmental approach to tourism accentuates the very nature of the tourism trade. This can be seen in two ways.

Analysis of tourism demand and studies by various UN specialist agencies reveals the overall distribution showing the sources of foreign tourists to developing countries. Hoivik and Heiberg (1980), in their 'country-to-country matrix for south-bound European tourism', demonstrated the extent to which certain developing countries depend on specific countries for their tourism business. More recently, Sharpley (2008), writing on The Gambia, indicated how the country depends on a limited number of customers; how Sweden has come to dominate other nationalities as the largest single source of overseas tourists; and the risks that this trend entails.

Although The Gambia may not be typical of other young developing countries, it is nevertheless possible to discern some common problems. The risks of The Gambia became apparent in 1982 when a downturn in the Swedish economy coincided in a spate of bad publicity in the Swedish press concerning shortages of foodstuffs in The Gambia (Wagner, 1981). The numbers of Swedes visiting the country fell by 17% and half of the total decline in the demand for The Gambia's tourist product in that year was accounted for by the fall in demand from one country.

The second aspect of risk relates to the tourism product offered. The risks become apparent if Gray's (1970) scheme is applied to LDC tourism, especially one particular type of resort – the seaside. Tourists are price sensitive; various LDCs offer a similar product – sun, sea and sand – packaged by the tour operators. The idea of substitutability of these tourist products means that destinations compete for customers. One crucial question remains unanswered. The various features so far examined lead to dependency, but can anything be done about this – perhaps by creating an organization or management to handle it. Conscious of this, one may venture to ask: are there bases for the development of tourism that might mitigate dependency evils (Harrison, 2001)?

Seasonality

Seasonality is defined here as a relatively short span of the tourist season, also referred to 'fluctuating patterns of tourist arrivals' Jenkins (2004). Seasonality is of two types: institutional and natural. Institutional seasonality reflects the point of view of the tourist-generating countries, which in part stems from traditional holiday-taking periods – summer, Christmas and Easter – and in part dictated by school holidays. Natural seasonality takes the perspective of the tourist-receiving country, mainly climatic-related, and its impact on the local economy (see also Butler, 1994).

Van Houts (1979) noted that these two seasonality types cause an imbalance between demand and supply. According to him, the tourism season in developing countries is longer than in most developed countries. Most of the countries have a minimum season of 6 months, which can decrease the negative effects of the peak periods. The lack of domestic tourism, on account of their underdevelopment, does not compensate for the absence of foreign visitors.

A UN report clearly considers seasonality features to be a disadvantage (United Nations, 1996). Although tourism can generate revenue and valuable foreign exchange, marked dependence on tourism can also create problems of an economic or sociocultural nature, particularly for a small country. Heavy reliance on revenue from tourism can result in sharp revenue fluctuations since the industry is very

seasonal, as well as being subject to changes in taste or fashion, fears of political instability, allegations of health hazards and so on. A high degree of seasonality not only causes large fluctuations in earnings from tourism, but also implies considerable social costs in terms of under-utilization of productive capacity and, in particular, high levels of seasonal unemployment.

It is further suggested that seasonality has an impact on employment, noting that 25% of tourism employees are temporarily unemployed or seek another job. The people most hit by temporary unemployment are the less qualified. In this category, women are often victims (Bryden, 1973). In terms of planning and management, Hoivik and Heiberg (1980) suggested that under seasonality, tourist facilities may be utilized for purposes other than vacation tourism, such as the conference trade.

For investment purposes, the seasonality factor means that for many LDCs the whole of the investment on tourism must be amortized over a few short months of the year, realizing the central place of payback and the risk element of the industry. Price policies, such as offering substantially reduced rates for hotel accommodations and allied features, can be practised.

Another study (OECD Secretariat, 1980) has suggested many advantages that a country or region can obtain by spreading peak demand for its tourist facilities over a longer period. A number of private capital facilities, in particular hotel accommodation and related facilities, are built for peak capacity. Reduced peak demand, which stretches over longer holiday periods, and in some cases eliminating weekend demand would reduce cost (both public and private) and increase the rate of return on investments. Tisdell (1984) agreed that a country can gain by transferring some of the peak demand to a period of lower demand. At the same time, his belief was that the practice of such a policy can result in a loss to the country concerned. His arguments in support of this hypothesis are, however, beyond the scope of this chapter.

What can we glean from the preceding discussion to guide LDCs in their development of the tourism sector? This is the focus of the next section, to which we now turn.

Fundamental Issues

Fundamental issues considered here pertain to demand and supply forces. These are important because they play a key role in the direction of tourism development in LDCs. In particular, they indicate the issues that LDCs should take into account in developing tourism. Limited space does not permit for a full discussion of these influences, but a summary of them follows.

Demand considerations

Demand factors, for instance, operate in the developed tourist-generating countries (e.g., France, Germany, the UK, the USA), with implications for tourism in LDCs. This is because an international tourism sector is mainly a dependent sector (Dieke, 1993) for two reasons. First, the type, levels of tourism, and extent of tourist flows in LDCs are determined by forces outside of LDCs' control. Second, the nature and scope of LDCs' tourism programmes must reflect these demand determinants. In the context of this chapter the demand variables include the distribution system, investment expertise, competition and image. Thus, LDCs that want to break into the global tourism market, or allocating resources to the sector, are advised to consider these demand forces.

Tourism is characterized by a *distribution channel* that is dominated by tourist-generating countries via their ownership and management of airlines, tour operations and hotels. Given the extensive market connections, established reputations and recognized expertise of developed economies, one difficulty for LDCs is how to minimize these considerable influences. In terms of *investment expertise*, we find that global tourism gives attention to the satisfaction of foreign tourists, implying that the tourist product must reach international rather than domestic standards. Satisfaction of this provision depends on the availability of international tourism management. For these reasons, LDCs have sought foreign investment experience. To entice foreign developers to invest in the sector has meant giving them a generous 'quantum of incentives', without which avail-

able funds and expertise might be competed away by other regions. Global tourism is highly *competitive* in terms of price and customer satisfaction, given that tourists are price-conscious, rather than price-takers, and that many destinations offer similar attractions. This implies that if holiday needs are not met in LDCs, tourists may move on to alternative locations. This means that destinations are substitutable. *Image* is a final external factor that is outside the control of LDCs. From this perspective, we are reminded of how foreign tour wholesalers as image-makers portray the characteristics of tourist attractions in LDCs, based more on their operational requirements that by the real aspirations of tourists themselves or of LDC destinations.

Supply considerations

Supply factors, on the other hand, operate at the LDC level, mainly related to socioeconomic circumstances of a tourist-receiving LDC. They may take various forms, including level of development, resources available, potential for tourism and motivation. They are internal to and can be controlled by LDCs, although at times the forces may be linked with external influences, as noted. Again, LDC tourism authorities are advised to consider these in their development of tourism programmes.

In the first place, in addition to the gross national product per capita and human development index as useful parameters, *level of development* can be measured by the extent to which wealth and skills are distributed among LDCs or the resilience of local cultural tradition. A country's level of development also reflects the nature, extent and scale of tourism programmes required to sustain the industry. Second, tourism development in LDCs depends on the *resources available* within the countries, whether they are physical, human or capital resources; each type, in terms of availability, quality and competitiveness, is needed for a successful tourism development programme. Thus, LDCs need to ask whether and how they can match their own resources with the requirements of different types of tourists. They need to ask what challenges they face in developing them.

Third, *potential for tourism* has to do with determining tourism's future growth and development potential. An analysis of demand and supply will indicate future directions. These development options are needed to determine what priority tourism development in the country is to receive. The assessment may begin by determining how tourism fits into the national development plan. This will be based on the potential that exists for tourism to contribute to earning foreign exchange and for bringing about increases in national income, employment and overall economic development, relative to other sectors. Finally, *motivation* to develop tourism can be economic or non-economic; the economic argument can be macro such as, as seen, earnings of foreign exchange and government revenue. At a macro level, it is related to employment, income and regional development. In social terms, tourism provides LDCs (e.g. The Gambia) with a 'window on an outside world' (Harrell-Bond, 1978), the possibility of foreign travel and the opportunity to learn about foreign cultures and perhaps of 'getting attached' (Wagner and Yamba, 1986).

Future Research

If there is a concept that guides our future research in tourism development, it must be the following:

> As tourism continues to evolve, considerable scope exists to expand and deepen research efforts in this field. Many of the issues that face the development of tourism at present and in coming years, such as the impact of economic uncertainty, climate change and international security, are dynamic, far-reaching and global in nature.
>
> (Pearce and Butler, 2010)

Thus, in the context of this chapter future research will focus on the following: the need for continued investment in the sector; the significance of growing regional competition; local involvement in and control over tourism development; forging private–public sector partnerships for tourism development; developing equity in tourism benefits sharing; building the image of a destination through marketing and promotional campaigns; expanding tourism entrepreneurial initiatives and investment opportunities; and raising gender awareness to enhance women's participation in the tourism sector.

Conclusion

Based on the above analysis, it is possible to draw some general conclusions regarding the tourism development experiences of LDCs. These conclusions take the form of three related lessons: need for planning, need for flexibility and need for caution.

Need for planning

Planning need is largely one of how to ensure that the best use is made of available resources. This is critical because, as discussed, development resources are scarce and there is much competition for what is available. Part of the planning process requires that the benefits of tourism are optimized and the disbenefits minimized. To ensure that that this happens, it is also essential that the institutional and organizational structures with relevant mandates are in place, for a number of reasons: the need to ensure operational standards in the tourism sector and the need to coordinate the various activities that impinge on tourism. As a basis for the exercise of such functions, tourism objectives have to be developed and policies to implement the objectives formulated. In brief, as Jenkins (1987) has succinctly put it, planning 'permits options to be considered and policies to be formulated ... helps avoid the continuous situation of having to take emergency actions ... [and] provides some element of stability to future operations'.

Need for flexibility

In the tourism policy process, planners must respond flexibly to external pressures, especially relating to the market distribution network – tour operators, airlines and hotels. Essentially, these tourism transnationals can make or break tourism in LDCs. For instance, as surrogates for foreign tourists, overseas tour operators decide which destinations to 'sell' or even which holiday and tourist kinds to offer. Part of their business objectives is to ensure that host destinations provide facilities and services of requisite international standards, acceptable to their clients. Such compliance is a *sine qua non* for future sales and possible repeat business, given the discretionary and exogenous nature of tourism demand. Discretionary because taking a holiday is voluntary and exogenous because tourism is induced from outside of LDCs. Cognisant of the constraints facing LDCs, flexible tourism policies are needed in a manner that does not alienate the proverbial goose that lays the golden egg, be it the market (tourist) or the market intermediaries (the travel trade), or still other international organizations.

'enclave tourism' and 'carrying capacity' encapsulate some of the current thoughts on tourism. What may be implied from these catchphrases is the notion that tourism development carries with it considerable economic and non-economic costs and benefits. Since resources are limited, careful resource use and management is critical, not least because of the need to ensure future availability and to enhance the benefits of such an activity. Clearly, without careful, sensitive and planned utilization and management of resources, destinations will, in sustainability terms – economic, sociocultural and environmental – be unattractive, with all the consequences that go with that. Central to sustainable tourism is the concept of community involvement. Hence the need for caution in regard to policies and institutional arrangements for the tourism sector.

Need for caution

In advocating for caution in tourism development, two issues closely related to the earlier discussions of planning and flexibility may be mentioned because of their implications for tourism policy. The first is the question of scale of tourism development (Jenkins, 1982). Expressions such as 'eco' or 'green tourism', 'alternative tourism', 'sustainable tourism',

Review Questions

1. Analyse the impacts of tourism in a developing country of your choice.
2. Critically assess the role of tourism as a catalyst for economic and sociocultural development.
3. Evaluate the factors that must be considered in the management of tourism development.

References

Apostolopoloulos, Y., Sonmez, S. and Timothy, D.J. (eds) (2001) *Women as Producers and Consumers of Tourism in Developing Regions.* Praeger, Westpoint, Conneticut, USA.

Bastin, R. (1984) *Tourism: Transnational Corporations and Cultural Identities.* UNESCO, Paris, France.

Brohman, J. (1996) New directions in tourism for third world development. *Annals of Tourism Research* 23, 48–70.

Brown, F. and Hall, D. (2008) Tourism and development in the global south: the issues. *Third World Quarterly* 29, 839–849.

Bryden, J.M. (1973) *Tourism and Development: A Case Study of the Commonwealth Caribbean.* University of Cambridge Press, London, UK.

Butler, R.W. (1980) The concept of a tourist area cycle of evolution: implications for management of resources. *Canadian Geographer* 24, 5–12.

Butler, R.W. (1994) Seasonality in tourism: issues and problems. In: Seaton, A.V., Jenkins, C.L., Wood, R.C., Dieke, P.U.C., Bennett, M.M., MacLellan, L.R. and Smith, R. (eds) *Tourism: The State of the Art.* Wiley, New York, pp. 332–339.

Cohen, E. (1972) Toward a sociology of international tourism. *Social Research* 39, 164–182.

De Kadt, E. (1979) *Tourism: Passport to Development?* Oxford University Press, Oxford, UK.

Dieke, P.U.C. (1993) Tourism and development policy in The Gambia. *Annals of Tourism Research* 20, 423–449.

Dieke, P.U.C. (1995) Tourism and structural adjustment programmes in the African economy. *Tourism Economics* 1, 71–93.

Dieke, P.U.C. (ed.) (2000) *The Political Economy of Tourism Development in Africa*. Cognizant Communication, Elmsford, New York.

Dieke, P.U.C. (2008) Tourism development in Africa: challenges and opportunities. *Tourism Review International* 12, 167–315.

Dieke, P.U.C. (2009) Africa in the global tourism economy: trend patterns, issues, and future perspectives. *Harvard College Economics Review* 3, 9–15.

Dunning, J.H. and McQueen, G. (1982) Multinational corporations in the international hotel industry. *Annals of Tourism Research* 9, 69–90.

Erbes, R. (1973) *International Tourism and the Economy of Developing Countries*. OECD, Paris, France.

Forster, J. (1964) The sociological consequences of tourism. *International Journal of Comparative Sociology* 5, 217–260.

Government of Zambia (1995) *Medium-Term National Tourism Strategy and Action Plan for Zambia*. Government of Zambia, Lusaka, Zambia.

Gray, H.P. (1970) *International Travel – International Trade*. Heath Lexington Books, Lexington, MA.

Greenwood, D.J. (1972) Culture by the pound: an anthropological perspective on tourism as cultural commoditization. In: Smith, V.L. (ed.) *Host and Guests: The Anthropology of Tourism*. University of Pennsylvania Press, Philadelphia, pp. 265–274.

Harrell-Bond, B. (1978) A window on an outside world: tourism as development in The Gambia. *American Universities Field Staff Reports* 19, 1–23.

Harrison, D. (2001) Tourism and less developed countries, key issues. In: Harrison, D. (ed.) *Tourism and the Less Developed World: Issues and Case Studies*. CAB International, Wallingford, UK, pp. 23–46.

Hoivik, T. and Heiberg, T. (1980) Centre-periphery tourism and self-reliance. *International Social Science Journal* 32, 69–98.

Jenkins, C.L. (1982) The effects of scale in tourism projects in developing countries. *Annals of Tourism Research* 9, 229–249.

Jenkins, C.L. (1987) Manpower planning in tourism. Lecture presented to UNDP/WTO Regional Seminar/Workshop on 'Tourism Training', Colombo, Sri Lanka.

Jenkins, C.L. (1997) Impacts of the development of international tourism in the Asian region. In: Go, F.M. and Jenkins, C.L. (eds) *Tourism and Economic Development in Asia and Australasia*. Cassell, London, UK, pp. 48–64.

Jenkins, C.L. (2000) The development of tourism in Namibia. In: Dieke, P.U.C. (ed.) *The Political Economy of Tourism Development in Africa*. Cognizant Communication, Elmsford, New York, pp. 113–128.

Jenkins, C.L. (2004) Overcoming the problems relating to seasonality: the case of Dubai. Paper presented at the 2nd Tourism: State of the Art Conference. University of Strathclyde, Glasgow, UK.

Jenkins, C.L. (2007) Tourism development: policy, planning and implementation issues in developing countries. In: Judie Cukier (ed.) *Tourism Research: Policy, Planning and Prospects*, Occasional Paper #20. University of Waterloo, Ontario, Canada, pp. 21–30.

Lea, J. (1988) *Tourism and Development in the Third World*. Routledge, London, UK.

Mowforth, M. and Munt, I. (2003) *Tourism and Sustainability: Development and New Tourism in the Third World*, 2nd edn. Routledge, London, UK.

Naronha, R. (1977) Social and cultural dimensions of tourism: a review of the literature in English. *The World Bank Paper*, 326.

OECD Secretariat (1980) *The Impact of Tourism on Environment*. Organisation for Economic Co-operation and Development, Paris, France.

Oppermann, M. and Chon, K.S. (1997) *Tourism in Developing Countries*. International Thomson Business Press, London, UK.

Pearce, D.G. and Butler, R.W. (2010) *Tourism Research: A 20–20 Vision*. Goodfellow Publishers, Oxford, UK.

Rodenburg, E.E. (1980) The effects of scale in economic development: tourism in Bali. *Annals of Tourism Research* 7, 177–196.

Rogerson, C.M. (2007) Reviewing Africa in the global tourism economy. *Development Southern Africa* 24, 361–379.

Sharpley, R. (2008) Tourism in The Gambia: a case of planning failure? *Tourism Review International* 12, 215–230.

Sharpley, R. (2009) *Tourism, Development and the Environment: Beyond Sustainability.* Earthscan, London, UK.

Sharpley, R. and Telfer, D. (eds) (2002) *Tourism and Development: Concepts and Issues.* Channel View Publications, Clevedon, UK.

Sinclair, M.T. (1998) Tourism and economic development. *The Journal of Development Studies* 34, 1–51.

Stansfield, C.A. (1978) Atlantic city and the resort cycle. *Annals of Tourism Research* 5, 238–251.

Telfer, D. and Sharpley, R. (2008) *Tourism and Development in the Developing World.* Routledge, London, UK.

Tisdell, C.A. (1984) Seasonality in tourism demand and the desirability of evening out tourist demand. *Economic Activity* 27, 13–17.

United Nations (1996). *World Investment Report 1995: Transnational Corporations and Competitiveness.* United Nations, New York.

UNDP (2009) *Human Development Report.* United Nations Development Programme, New York.

UNDP/ICAO (1977) *Studies to determine the contribution that civil aviation can make to the development of national economies of African states. (Project RAF/74/021 Final Report).* United Nations Development Programme/International Civil Aviation Organization, Montreal, Canada.

UN World Tourism Organization (2008) *Tourism Highlights,* 2008 edn. Available from: http://www.unwto.org/facts/menu.html. Accessed 24 June, 2010.

Van Houts, D. (1979) The non-economic impact of international tourism in developing countries: a review of recent literature. *Travel Research Journal (WTO)* 1, 81–88.

Wagner, U. (1981) Tourism in The Gambia: development or dependency? *Ethnos* 46, 190–206.

Wagner, U. and Yamba, Y. (1986) Going north and getting attached: the case of the Gambians. *Ethnos* 51, 99–122.

Weaver, D.B. (1983) Tourism as a factor in third world development with special reference to the Caribbean. *Ontario Geography* 22, 47–70.

3 Tourist Behaviour and Tourism Motivation

Sine Heitmann

Introduction

Studies on travel behaviour and tourism motivation concentrate on the tourists and the decision-making process through which they go when booking a holiday. Why do people travel? Why do many British travel to Spain, but not many Spanish to Britain? Why are Germans number one in international travelling, but only a small percentage of Americans own a passport? Why do Afro-Americans travel to African countries and many South Americans to Spain? Why does it seem that American and Japanese tourists travel the whole of Europe in only 2 weeks? Why do only young people travel to Lloret de Mar in Spain? These are just some of many questions that we seek answers for when studying travel activities from a sociological and psychological point of view.

Consumer behaviour is central here as it gives information on the stages that a tourist goes through before booking and how the tourist's background informs the decisions made, while travel behaviour theories explain how tourists behave and in what kind of activities they participate while on holiday. Tourism motivation theories seek to answer why tourists travel and the underlying psychological processes. While these seem simple enough questions, discussions and theories are wide and varied. There is no universally accepted theory, but several frameworks have been offered to understand consumer behaviour, travel behaviour and tourism motivation. At a personal level, no two individuals are alike and there are significant differences in attitudes, perceptions and motivation. An individual's perception of

travelling depends on the individual's perception of the world, but is further determined by a range of external factors such as their childhood, family, work and the media, as well as wider societal and cultural influences.

Despite the difficulty of homogenizing the tourist as a consumer, it is important to the management of tourism to understand the way in which consumers make decisions and consume tourism activities while appreciating the diversity of demand, particularly for the marketing of tourism products and services where an understanding of tourist consumption and consumer behaviour is essential. If we understand what makes the consumer tick, we can cater for their needs and provide the right product and service. It also helps explain why certain types of holiday can be more successful than others and what new products and services might prove popular.

This chapter outlines the decision-making process in tourism consumption before introducing ideas on travel behaviour and tourism motivation from both psychological and sociological perspectives. The chapter also introduces tourist typologies that help us to understand the role of the consumer within the decision-making process and to take personality into account.

Consumer Behaviour and the Decision-making Process

The tourist as a consumer purchases goods and services for personal consumption. The decision process consists of five stages (Kotler *et al.*,

2010). First, there is the recognition of a need; the potential tourist senses a difference between his/her actual state and his/her desired state. This need can be triggered by internal stimuli and from experience – the person has learned what objects, products or services may satisfy this need. The need can also be triggered by external stimuli, through friends, families and other social networks or advertising messages. The theories of tourism motivation that are discussed later provide a valuable insight.

The second stage involves information searching. Some consumers might not search for more information because the consumer's drive is strong and a suitable product/service is near at hand. Information can be obtained from a wide range of sources, such as personal sources (family, friends, neighbours, acquaintances, colleagues), commercial sources (advertising, sales people, displays, other marketing material) or public sources (reviews, newspapers).

Once the customer has gathered sufficient information, the third stage of decision making is the evaluation of alternatives. Given the competitive nature of the tourism industry, there is usually a range of products and services catering for similar needs and the consumer has to decide on one product, service, brand or holiday. The evaluation depends on needs and, as tourism products and services are a combination of different elements or attributes, it depends on what element or attribute caters more towards that need. The consumer attaches different levels of importance to and expects different levels of satisfaction from each of these elements or attributes. Subsequently, the consumer ranks the products or services and forms a purchase intention.

Once the purchase intention is clear, the consumer chooses the most preferred product or services during the purchase decision stage. However, attitudes of others (such as partners, children, friends, family or other social networks) and unexpected situations (increased price, loss of income, illness or other external factors beyond the consumer's control) will have an impact before the purchase is actually made.

The fifth and final stage is post-purchase behaviour. Once a product or service has been purchased and consumed, the consumer will be satisfied or dissatisfied. This in turn depends on the relationship between the expectation the consumer had pre-purchase and the perceived performance of the product or service. If expectations are met or exceeded, the customer is satisfied. If the product or service falls short, customer dissatisfaction is the result. Although this seems straightforward, expectations are not that clear as consumers base their expectations on past experiences, social influences and other information sources. A range of messages about the product or service reach the consumer on a conscious and subconscious level and therefore impact on the expectations. The larger the gap between expectations and product or service performance, the higher the customer dissatisfaction and the less likely it is that the consumer will buy the same product or service again (Kotler *et al.*, 2010).

To complicate this further, the consumer and his/her purchase behaviour are influenced by cultural, social, personal and psychological characteristics. Societies are made up of small groups or large populations – what makes them a society is the interrelationship that connects them; they are united by structured social relationships and share a unique culture. The British society shares the British culture, which distinguishes it from the culture of French society. Cultural factors are the most basic determinants of a person's behaviour as society influences the person from childhood through to old age. While culture can be tangible (in terms of food, art and clothing), it is also manifested in the beliefs and values that a person holds and influences how we think, how we act, how we make decisions, how we travel and how we behave in social situations. This extends to the demand for tourism. Culture (white, black, Asian) or religion (Christian, Muslim, Hindu) can determine the demand for certain types of holidays (e.g. Afro-Americans travelling to Africa to discover their heritage origin; religious festivals attracting members from different parts of the country/world) and we can further identify the influences of subcultures (determined through linguistic, aesthetic, religious, political, sexual or geographical factors or a combination of factors). Further social networks that can have an influence on the tourist are primary groups such as family, friends or colleagues as the consumer interacts with them on a daily basis. However, secondary groups (e.g. religious groups or professional associations) can also impact on the consumer decision-making process.

Demographics such as age, gender and social class influence consumer behaviour as people within a given class or age group tend to exhibit similar behaviours, tastes and preferences for certain products, services or information sources. Personal factors play a central role as life-cycle, occupation, level of income, lifestyle and personality have a significant influence when it comes to choosing a holiday. Consumer classifications are used by marketers to identify and design products and services that cater for certain consumer segments. For example, if we take age as a factor, youth tourism and the student market are characterized by tourism offers such as gap travel, backpacking and activity holidays. The silver market, or consumers aged over 55 years, has entirely different preferences when it comes to choosing a holiday – more attention is paid to comfort and learning about cultures.

Social and cultural influences are not mutually exclusive; they combine. One pressure can be more explicit than the other, and while some are obvious in determining the type of holiday chosen, others are more subconscious and the tourist might not be aware of the influence certain aspects, such as culture, have on them. We can call those economic, technological, social, cultural and political factors within any society *determinants*. Because these drive or set limits on travel demand, they determine the volume of a population's demand to travel.

After outlining the consumer decision-making process, it is now worth looking into more detail at how tourists behave while on holiday and why they choose certain types of holidays. First, tourism behaviour is outlined by introducing roles and typologies of tourists as these are, similarly to the consumer decision-making process, determined by their social environment. This allows us to characterize tourists into different categories and explain and predict consumer behaviour within tourism. Second, in contrast to the more sociological

differentiation of tourists, we then look at tourist motivation from a more psychological perspective, which looks in more detail at why tourists travel.

Tourist Roles and Typologies

Sunlust/wanderlust

A first distinction is provided by Gray (1970), who took the purpose of the trip as the key differentiation and categorizes tourists into *sunlust* and *wanderlust* tourists. While sunlust is essentially about rest and relaxation in the form of the 3 Ss in tourism (sun, sea and sand), wanderlust is characterized by a desire to explore and experience people and culture. As a result, it can be argued that sunlust tourists seek pleasant climates, comfort and familiar aspects from home without too much excitement because the focus is on a relaxing, hassle-free holiday. Wanderlust tourists are seeking more entertainment on holiday in forms of local cultures because experiences and learning are central to the holiday. This first attempt at differentiating different types of tourists is useful and can be used as a basic form of market segmentation. It describes the demand for tourism, but does not give us much explanation of tourism behaviour. Subsequent typologies have expanded this differentiation.

Venturers (allocentric)/dependables (psychocentric)

Plog (2001) divided tourists into simple categories using personality traits to identify tourist types. The key factors that distinguish different tourists are the level of travel and the nature of the travel experience. The original distinction was between allocentric and psychocentric tourists and this is still the model widely used in tourism textbooks. However, Plog updated his classical study and replaced allocentrics with 'venturers' and psychocentrics with 'dependables'.

First, the venturers (or allocentric tourists) are confident and adventurous, seeking challenges and new experiences, and are prepared to take risks. They are confident and energetic people who make decisions quickly, easily and often independently without relying on other people's opinions. As they are intellectually curious, they travel more frequently and go on relatively long trips. When they travel, they use all modes of transport and, compared to other tourists, are more frequent flyers. When on holiday, venturers prefer unconventional or local accommodation and they are more ready to spend their disposable income – any purchases they make are mostly authentic local arts and crafts. These can be found in long-haul destinations or off the beaten track in exotic and unusual destinations that have not been discovered by the tourism trade. Engagement with locals and participation in local customs and cultures as well as active past times are central to their holiday experience. As venturers are rather independent and make individual arrangements, they avoid routines or organized, pre-arranged group tours.

Dependables (or psychocentric tourists) are the opposite. They are less adventurous, home loving and prefer familiar surroundings and safety. They travel less frequently and stay for shorter periods. Dependables are cautious and more conservative, and avoiding risk is a central part of their nature. They tend to rely on relatively known brands as the popularity of these brands indicates a safe choice. They visit popular domestic attractions, international mass tourism resorts or other touristy spots where they feel comfortable being surrounded by family, friends or other tourists. When travelling they prefer a home-from-home environment and preferred transportation is their own car or caravans, with limited use of flights. Accommodation reflects the general personality traits and they prefer mobile homes, hotels or motels. On holiday, dependables spend less money and purchases are dominated by souvenirs as a visual reminder of their holiday. As they are less confident, dependables are rather passive and non-demanding. They engage in little activity while on holiday (or only in familiar recreational activities) and prefer the structure and routine of package holidays, guided tours and all-inclusive resorts. In general, dependables travel with family and friends, and they are most likely to return to destinations they have been to before.

This dichotomy presents two extreme types of personality and tourist behaviour, and it would be too difficult to put most individuals into either one of these categories. The largest number of tourists is situated between the two extremes (see Fig. 3.1) and can be identified as dependable, near-dependable, centric-dependable, centric-venturer, near-venturer and venturer. The numbers for the two extremes are relatively low, with the majority of travellers found to be centric-dependables or centric-venturers.

Plog's original idea placed a lot of emphasis on the geographical location of destinations and used (American) tourists to link the tourist types to different destinations (e.g. dependables travelling to beach resorts, centrics to Europe and Hawaii and venturers to Africa and Antarctica). The concept is also applicable to the destination lifecycle (see Chapter 1). An underdeveloped destination is most attractive to venturers, and during the course of becoming a developed tourism destination it becomes more appealing to centrics first and dependables later. Furthermore, Plog later revised the concept to include types of holidays and thereby removed the geographical focus. While most types of holidays are tried and tested by venturers first, they later have mass tourism appeal. Interestingly, cruise tourism offers a different example as it used to be a holiday mainly aimed at dependables, but recent changes (unusual itineraries, smaller boats and more on- and off-shore activities) has made it a suitable holiday for centrics and near-venturers.

Cohen's typology

Cohen's (1972) typology of tourists identifies four different categories based on the tourist's relationship with the tourism industry and the destination and bases them along a continuum, with familiarity on one end and strangerhood on the other. Cohen suggested that all tourists travel within an environmental bubble and are determined by their home environment, society and culture – the degree to which the home environment determines the tourist results in different reactions to and preferences for new places and cultures. In other words, not all tourists are equally constrained by the

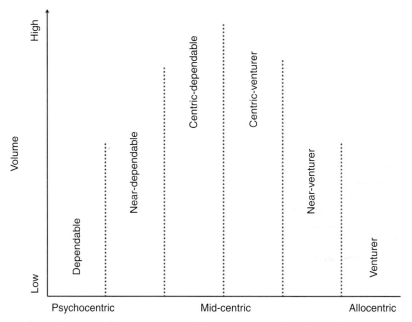

Fig. 3.1. Psychographic personality types – dependable to venturer. (Adapted from Plog, 2001.)

environmental bubble; similarly to Plog's idea, some prefer experiences and places that remind them of their home environment, whereas others are more adventurous and seek out more exciting experiences and places.

The organized mass tourist prefers highly organized package holidays, which are characterized by prearranged itineraries and familiar surroundings. This is the least adventurous type of tourist who prefers to stay within his/her own country or, if travelling abroad, in Westernized hotels and the environment and infrastructure created, supplied and maintained by the tourism industry. This tourist depends on the 'tourist bubble' and prefers all-inclusive, fully packaged holidays that provide the familiar. Any novelty, if sought, is highly controlled.

The individual mass tourist tends to rely heavily on the tourist infrastructure and uses institutionalized facilities (e.g. scheduled flights, tour operator and travel agency services and bookings, transfers) but is more independent than the previous type in that he/she exercises a greater degree of personal choice and does not rely completely on what the industry presents as an option. As much as possible is arranged before leaving home, and when on holiday this

tourist visits the same sights as mass tourists but still retains control of the itinerary.

These first two types are also described as institutionalized tourist types, indicating the heavy influence of the tourism industry in organizing, planning and controlling the travel. Trips are booked with tour operators and while on holiday these types tend to stay on the beaten track without venturing too far from the security of the tourist infrastructure. Domestic tourism and mass tourism within mid- and long-haul destinations are mostly characterized by these types of tourist.

The next two are non-institutionalized tourist types, indicating the individual nature of travelling and its organization. The explorer is an independent traveller who every now and then makes use of the tourist infrastructure, but prefers to travel off the beaten track and engage more with locals. Travel arrangements are made individually and inspiration for activities comes mainly from travel articles, but not so much from brochures. This tourist is keen to stay 'off the beaten track' and only moves back to the 'tourist bubble' if it gets too tough – for the most part of the journey he/she will try to escape the environmental bubble, but every now and then a certain level of comfort and security is required. Finally, the drifter is completely independent and in close contact with locals. There is no fixed itinerary and every attempt is made to immerse in local culture, living and working with locals. Drifters try to avoid any tourism honey pots and the tourism industry as much as possible and instead seek novelty and excitement at all cost, possibly even seeking danger and discomfort

Smith (1989) identified seven tourist types and in what can thus be considered an extension of Cohen's typology, but the establishment is based purely on numbers and the frequency by which these tourist types can be observed. The explorer is the smallest segment, which is not seen very often. This tourist accepts local traditions and cultures fully. Also rarely seen is the elite tourist, who is able to adapt fully to any local traditions and cultures. The off-beat tourist is rather uncommon and adapts well. The unusual tourist occurs occasionally and adapts in part. The incipient mass tourist is more common than the previous types of tourists and 'seeks' (meaning that individual efforts are being made to contribute to the holiday experience), while the mass tourist is arguably the most common tourist nowadays who 'expects' (meaning that minimal effort is coming from the tourist). The last type, the charter, appears in massive numbers and 'demands'.

Having outlined Cohen's, Smith's and Plog's typology, we can also identify overlaps between the different theories, particular if a familiarity–novelty continuum is used (see Fig. 3.2).

Although these typologies are rather useful in understanding the behaviour, characteristics and personal traits of tourists, and can therefore be useful from a marketing perspective in identifying market segments and developing suitable products and services, we have to take a critical stance towards them. These typologies are rather simplistic and based on observable behaviour, but they do not tell us anything about the reasons for this behaviour. Furthermore, they tend to make assumptions about characteristics as well as personality traits. In some cases, they may be very stereotypical.

The differentiation between certain types is not very distinct. For example, in Smith's typology there is little distinction between the mass tourist and the charter tourist. Social

influences such as travel experience, age, gender or income are not taken into account. Furthermore, the models should not be considered as static as the tourist is likely to move between the different classifications, thus the models are more like continuums. Quite often, the more allocentric tourists (or what Cohen and Smith labelled as drifters, explorers and off-beat tourists) pave the way for mass tourism to be developed. For example, Goa in India used to be visited by only a few travellers, but has now become a mass tourism destination.

The more experienced tourists are in travelling, the more likely they will change their preferences and travel behaviour. Taking Plog's dichotomy as an example, the 'old tourist' has more resemblance with the dependable, psychocentric tourist, while the 'new tourist' (or the modern traveller) shares more characteristics with the venturer, allocentric tourist. Advances in technology have resulted in tourists being able to book their own holidays without relying on tour operators and travel agencies. The internet allows easy access to information about potential destinations, products and services, while developments in transportation allow easy access to these destinations. These developments are coupled with the rise of budget airlines and the wider globalization processes that influence tourism development and have resulted in tourism as a whole being more accessible and the world becoming a global village in which even the remotest places are easier to reach.

This also highlights a complication with the typologies in that there is less room for venturers, explorers or independent travellers to find these experiences. While there is an increasingly large number of independent travellers, they still rely on the tourism industry. Backpackers are a good example as they display the characteristics of the explorer or a venturer. They do not have a fixed itinerary, rely on specialist travel guides (e.g. Lonely Planet and Rough Guides) and try to avoid the mass tourism infrastructure as much as possible. However, they often follow popular tourist trails and in many countries (e.g. Southeast Asia and South America), backpacking itself has become a mass tourism industry with a well-established tourism infrastructure. This is a different tourism infrastructure in that it does not have the resorts and Western chain hotels,

Smith (1989)	Cohen (1972)	Plog (2001)	Familiarity
Charter tourist Mass tourist	Organized mass tourist	Dependables/ Psychocentric - - - - - - - - - - - - - - - -	
Incipient Mass tourist	Individual mass tourist	Near – dependables/ psychocentric - - - - - - - - - - - - - - - -	
Unusual tourist		Midcentric	
Off-beat tourist Elite tourist	Explorer	- - - - - - - - - - - - - - - - Near-venturer/ allocentric	
Explorers	Drifter	- - - - - - - - - - - - - - - Venturers/ Allocentric	Novelty

Fig. 3.2. Tourist typologies. (Adapted from Cohen, 1972; Smith, 1989; Plog, 2001.)

but it caters for the needs of the individual traveller in the form of professionally run backpacker hostels and many independent tour operators, thus becoming a more institutionalized form of tourism.

Following on from the changes in tourists, there are further discussions to take into account. There is a long-standing debate around the meaning of tourism and the difference between a traveller and a tourist. Historically, little distinction has been made between the two, but with more places being developed as tourism destinations and the advance of mass tourism and a globally well-established tourism industry and infrastructure, Boorstin (1961) was one of the first critics of mass tourists (see also Chapter 4) and lamented the decline of the traveller as a result of the tourist. While travellers are considered to be active and not shying away from adventure and strenuous travel arrangements as part of their experience, the tourist has become a synonym for a pleasure seeker who is passive and expects everything to be done to and for him/her. This differentiation goes beyond behaviour and extends to philosophical differences and diverse ideologies with opposing ideas on tourism and travelling and reflects wider

discussions on tourism and tourism development. Similarly to mass tourism being blamed for the negative impacts that it brings to local communities and reinforcing social distinction between tourists and locals, the word 'tourist' itself has received negative connotations and is used derogatorily by travellers. Just as the tourism industry is blamed for commodifying local culture and heritage by packaging it into attractive holidays, tourists and their assumed travel behaviour are criticized for not taking an interest in local life and destinations and therefore reflecting characteristics of the psychocentric/old tourist. However, as outlined above, it is questionable whether a differentiation between the two is adequate. Given that tourists can change their preferences over time and might book different holidays during their travel career, any tourist can become a traveller. Furthermore, 'traveller' seems to be a label that those who oppose the institutionalized tourist give themselves, but they cannot consider themselves not to be tourists if they make use of the tourism infrastructure (or use the same infrastructure that is used by the tourism industry – e.g. in the forms of transport used and the sights visited). From a tourist industry perspective, if we compare a 2-week holiday in the sun organized by a large tour operator to a 6-month overland trip by a more specialist tour operator, the whole differentiation between traveller and tourist does not make any difference to the tourism industry, as the process of packaging remains the same – only the style is different. Instead of opposing tourist versus traveller, we should consider these two types along a continuum that opens the possibility for each individual to be a tourist or a traveller, or we should consider the traveller to be another type of tourist (or vice versa).

Similarly, and following on from the criticisms of mass tourists, new niches of tourism and new tourism developments highlight further discussions. While mass tourism is still very popular, new types of tourism are increasing in popularity. Many of these are under the heading of 'sustainability' and new types of tourists are emerging, such as 'the good tourist', the 'responsible tourist' and the 'green tourist'. Special-interest tourists are also on the rise, such as 'cultural tourists', 'nature enthusiasts' and 'adventure tourists'. On the one hand, these could be considered as more the venturer or non-institutionalized tourist type as they are more interested in the local community and culture and therefore benefit locals more directly, instead of relying on the profit-driven tourism industry and its infrastructure. However, considering them to be less institutionalized is wrong, as new types of tourism rely on the existing tourism infrastructure. Although they might engage in different activities, they still enjoy the comfort and security of the tourist bubble. Furthermore, it is wrong to assume that these tourists are 'better' and culturally more sensitive than mass tourists, as closer interaction with the local community might result in more direct benefits, but also more intense interaction and subsequent negative impacts on the local culture and environment. Hence, niche tourists are different, but no better.

The Tourist Gaze

Having discussed some key concepts of tourist typologies, it is worth pointing out one final concept. The tourist gaze, proposed by Urry

(2002), has received substantial attention. The tourist gaze can be argued to form part of tourist motivation as it results in a need to gaze on sights, places and people that are unusual.

Urry's (2002) idea of the tourist gaze originates from the activity any tourist engages in when being on holiday, namely the importance of the visual gaze: we look at places, we look at people, we look at landscapes and buildings and we look at performances. Tourists choose to travel in order to see and experience something different to their usual daily routine, and the visual consumption is inherent to any travel experience. Why do we decide and go to travel to Paris? We want to see the Eiffel Tower, the Mona Lisa in the Louvre and ideally two people kissing as they represent the romantic Paris. Why do we decide to travel to London? We want to see the attractions and museums that London is famous for. Why do we travel to the Amazon? We want to see the natural landscape of the jungle and hopefully catch a glimpse of some Indian tribes living there. Central to the concept of the tourist gaze is the distinction between the ordinary and extraordinary. Attractions are marked as being worth seeing – they have undergone a process of what MacCannell refers to as site sacralization – a sight is named, framed and elevated, enshrined, reproduced mechanically (in forms of souvenirs) as well as socially (in forms of new sights being established and naming themselves after the original sight). Attractions can be unique objects, such as the Eiffel Tower, the Grand Canyon, Buckingham Palace or the Tower of Pisa. But there are also particular signs the tourists is looking for: the typical English village, the typical German beer garden, the typical Italian trattoria, the typical Amsterdam coffee house. Another example listed by Urry is seeing ordinary aspects in an unusual context, such as everyday routines in China as a communist country. Finally, even carrying out everyday activities on holiday (e.g. shopping, eating, drinking) is extraordinary as these are influenced by the visual gaze of an unusual environment.

Urry has differentiated between the romantic and collective gaze. The romantic form of the tourist gaze is characterized by the solitude, privacy and personal relationships with the object of the gaze. In contrast, the collective gaze places emphasis on the people who are present when looking at the object. For example, if you travel up the mountains and see beautiful landscape, you can enjoy it on your own – in fact, if there are too many other people present, it will affect the quality of the experience (this has some overlaps with perceptual carrying capacity, see Chapter 6). Thus, this type of attraction necessitates a solitary, romantic gaze. The collective gaze in turn necessitates the presence of other people – if you attend a festival, all other visitors are essential to the atmosphere and attractiveness of this event. Or travelling to larger cities, where the unique attractiveness is the cosmopolitan character – it would be eerie if you were there on your own and you would not enjoy the experience.

The idea of the tourist gaze has been criticized and developed over the years. Much emphasis is placed on the visual aspects, whereas travelling obviously includes physical and corporeal experiences, touching all senses (think of the importance of eating local food to some tourists, going on wine-tasting trips or the soundscapes when travelling to Latin American countries because of interest in music). Furthermore, limiting the tourist experience to the gaze may also fail to identify the 'second gaze', which goes beyond the superficial experience and realizes that there are things unseen and unsaid that are part of the experience. In contrast, as travelling is inherently about being mobile and on the move with limited time available, tourists have been criticized for not even gazing, but just glancing, having become even more superficial in their holiday experiences (think of the American and Japanese tourists travelling through Europe and visiting 12 countries in 3 weeks because of their tight schedules).

Tourist Motivations

So far, typologies have been introduced that serve to describe and observe tourist behaviour. However, as has been criticized, these typologies do not explain why tourists choose to go on a holiday and why they engage in certain behaviour. At this point, let us turn our attention to motivation theories. Motivation is a state of need or a condition that causes the tourist to take action – in the case of tourism motivation, to take a holiday that is likely to bring satisfaction by addressing the aforementioned state of need or condition. Studying tourist motivation seeks to answer why people want to travel and, if they travel, why they travel to certain destinations and why they engage in certain activities while on holiday. Motivation to travel can be explained as a result of a psychological need (of which the tourist may not even be aware) or through the purpose or choice of the trip. When we refer to the internal factors within individuals, expressed as needs, wants and/or desires, that influence tourism choices, we speak of motivators. No two persons are the same – each individual has a different attitude and different personality, and thus a different motivation to travel. This makes the study of motivation difficult and challenging, but interesting at the same time as we can make some generalizations. However, one has to bear in mind that the motivation to travel is very often subject to societal values, norms and pressures, which are internalized and then become psychological needs. Thus, you can find some overlaps in sociological approaches, mentioned above, and psychological concepts, which are examined next. Travel motivation can be a complex area of research; however, it plays an essential part in the decision-making process. Having determined consumer behaviour and influences on the decision-making process above, we can now turn to investigate different theories on tourism motivation.

Escape-seeking and anomie-enhancement

Iso-Ahola (1982) proposed tourism motivation to be composed of both escape and seeking. While tourists are pushed to escape routine environments, they seek intrinsic rewards. These two motives are not mutually exclusive, but rather act simultaneously. Furthermore, with this idea Iso-Ahola suggested that tourism motivation has both a psychological (personal) and a social (inter-personal) component. Subsequently, he proposed four dimensions – personal seeking, personal escape, interpersonal seeking and interpersonal escape – that act as push factors and the driving force for tourism behaviour. Similarly, Dann (1977) argued that both social and psychological factors influence tourist motivation. The tourist is in a state of anomie within his own society and daily environment, which he seeks to address by going on holiday to achieve a state of ego-enhancement. In both cases, the tourist expects some kind of reward while being away from their usual environment. Travel is motivated by the expectation of being able to enhance or boost ego and status and the possibility of indulging in behaviour that would not be possible within daily life. The key difference is that Dann assumed that escape is socially determined, while Iso-Ahola argued that the need for escape is driven by psychological circumstances.

These two concepts build on the idea of push/pull factors and further highlight the idea that tourism motivation is essentially about addressing needs and the disequilibrium within the tourist's mind. However, these two concepts do not give us any indication regarding possible motivations or what exactly the tourist needs in order to address this equilibrium. Crompton (1979) attempted to address this in his research and suggested seven psychological (push) motives (escape from a perceived mundane environment, exploration and evaluation of self, relaxation, prestige, regression, enhancement of kinship relationships and facilitation of social interaction) and two cultural (pull) motives (novelty and education). At this point, it is worth introducing one of the key theories on motivation, namely Maslow's hierarchy of need, explaining how this can be applied to tourism.

Push/pull factors

Following from Iso-Ahola's and Dann's concepts, push/pull factors have become a central idea to explain tourist motivation. Pull factors can be described as destination-specific attributes or outer motivations – attractions or the destination as a whole is so attractive that it is 'pulling' the tourist towards it. During the information collection stage of the decision-making process, the prospective tourist will have gathered plenty of information about the holiday or destination and attractive products and services will serve as pull factors that influence the final decision. The push factors are internal or inner motivations and the factors that influence an individual when making a decision. These are described as person-specific motivations (e.g. needs, preferences). In this case, aspects such as accommodation, restaurants, entertainment facilities or similar elements of the holiday are not of much relevance to the tourist. Instead, the person just feels the need to 'get away' from his/her current whereabouts.

Although this theory is easily applicable, there are some problems in identifying which factor has more influence on the decision or which comes into play first. Generally, it is the push factors that lead to the decision, but the pull factors can play an equally important role in influencing the final decision. For example, if someone wants to visit one of his two brothers, the push factor is the internal need for love and affection. Assuming that the level of affection and relationship with the brothers is the same, but one of the brother lives near a beautiful beach and the other in noisy and dirty city, the pull factors (beach/city) could be the deciding factor. Similarly, if someone seeks a holiday to relax at the beach, the push factor starts the searching process for various beach holidays, and once enough information on different destinations is available, the pull factors come into play by making one destination more attractive than the alternatives. However, just as the consumer decision-making process is influenced by social, cultural and economic determinants, these determinants can influence push and pull factors.

Maslow's hierarchy of need and its application to tourism

Maslow's hierarchy of need (1943) is considered to be the most influential theory on motivation in general and is easily applicable to tourism motivation. Maslow identified five different needs, namely physiological (thirst, hunger, sleep, sex), safety (security, stability, protection), social (love, affection, belongingness, interpersonal relationships), esteem (self-esteem, self-respect, prestige, status) and self-actualization (growth, advancement, creativity). It is assumed that lower needs have to be satisfied first before the higher needs become relevant – as long as you are hungry, you are not interested in meeting friends; if you are feeling lonely, it is more important to find social belonging before you concentrate on developing yourself as a person or within your career. Of course this is a rather simplified argument, but explains the essential idea of Maslow and the hierarchy of need. When applying Maslow's hierarchy of need to tourism, the central idea of one area of need being more dominant than the other is still valid. For some tourists, relaxation (and addressing physiological needs) is the key driver in choosing a holiday at the beach. Others visit friends and relatives in order to address the need for love and affection or go travelling to make new friends. Some use their travels to boost their self-esteem and develop skills by engaging in activities and learning about new cultures. Certain types of holidays and destinations carry a certain connotation of luxury with themselves and tourists might choose these to enhance their status and show off to their social networks. However, unlike Maslow suggests, it is not necessarily the lower-end needs that drive tourism motivation; rather, any of the needs can become the driving force. Hence, the hierarchical nature is not applicable. Motivations overlap and the application of this theory is limited.

Travel career ladder

Based on Malslow's hierarchy, Pearce (1988) developed the travel motivation theory that is referred to as the travel career ladder (TCL). This suggests that tourist motivation consists of five different levels and the needs of travellers can be organized into a hierarchy or ladder. At the lowest level, we find relaxation needs; stimulation needs are at the second level, relationship needs at the third level and self-esteem/development and fulfilment needs at the fourth and fifth levels, respectively. This is easily applicable to tourism: tourists might be motivated to go travelling to satisfy their need

for rest and relaxation (hence satisfying physiological needs) or they might visit friends and families to satisfy their social needs. Each level of needs can be divided into two further categories: self-directed and directed at others. For example, relaxation needs that are self-directed focus on the need for bodily reconstitution and relaxation, and concentrate on the tourist themselves. Other-directed relaxation needs in turn require other people to cater for the satisfaction of these needs, through external excitement and novelty. Similarly, relationship needs can be self-directed by visiting friends and family to maintain relationships and give love and affection, whereas other-directed needs are more concerned with initiating relationships (meeting new people), receiving affection or being part of a group. Tourists might take part in a special interest or activity holiday to learn and develop new skills, thus they are motivated by self-esteem or self-actualization needs.

Tourists are not considered to have only one level of need, but instead one set of needs in the ladder acts as the most dominant one. The word 'career' suggests that tourists systematically move through the stages or have predictable travel patterns. Some may ascend the ladder, while others may remain at one particular level. A core idea to the TCL is that tourist motivation changes with travel experience; depending on previous travels or life stage, different needs are prevalent and influence tourism motivation. When a tourist travels overseas for the first time, a major concern might be relaxation within a safe environment. The more experienced traveller might start exploring and may become more curious about local culture and history, or even seek a sense of identification with the place.

While the TCL is easily applicable, there are some shortcomings to the theory. First, Pearce argued that stimulation needs are placed along a continuum of risk and safety and the primary focus is safety of self or others. However, there is a real and distinctive difference between these, as either putting one's own safety at risk to help others or the conscious seeking of risk requires a level of personality that does not fit onto the ladder or where another level of need is far more dominant. Second, as tourist motivation is argued to be the desire to leave an environment behind and seek an intrinsic reward, the role of the tourist can change while on holiday. While originally looking to relax, the tourist might become bored after a couple of days and start exploring the environment, hence addressing a different level of need within a short period of time. Coinciding with Maslow's idea, the satisfaction of one need can create awareness of another need that has not been met. Third, tourism demand in general has changed towards several holidays per year and each holiday is assigned a specific function – for example, one holiday is focused on entertaining the children, while a second involves sporting activities and a third might be for visiting extended family. Each holiday caters for a different need. As outlined above, life stage plays another role when deciding to book a holiday (Ryan, 2002).

Motivation by purpose

Travel motivators can also be explained in relation to the purpose of the holiday taken. Referring back to push/pull factors, this approach takes the purpose as the key motivating force. MacIntosh *et al.* (1990) proposed five categories of motivations that reflect the ideas of Maslow's hierarchy (Table 3.1).

As an example, linking these ideas back to the discussion on cultural heritage and its influence on travel behaviour, heritage itself is a suitable example of a motivator by purpose. Tourists might travel to sites because they consider them to be part of their heritage or they might travel to heritage sites that are not necessarily connected to their own heritage. Italian tourists visiting the Colosseum in Rome might have different motivations to travel there than German tourists.

Further Research

As is clear in this chapter, a range of tourism motivation theories has been proposed and many studies have used, borrowed and adapted these theories within different tourism contexts. What is evident within current tourism research is that most concepts are now applied to niche tourism. As motivation and typologies are useful for market segmentation purposes, further differentiation of motivation is attempted within different market segments and tourism types. For example, studies have been carried out among gay tourists (Clift and Forrest, 1999), wellness tourists (Chen *et al.*, 2008) and senior travellers (Jang and Wu, 2006). Furthermore, the recent rise in popular tourism concepts such as film tourism and dark

Table 3.1. Travel motivation.

Travel motivator	Explanation
Physical	Physical motivators indicate the need for physical activities. This can be either the need for rest, relaxation and simple things like getting a suntan or the need for active participation in exercises and health-related activities – any activity motivated by the desire for reducing tension or refreshing the body while on holiday
Emotional	Emotional motivators indicate the influence of emotions on travel behaviour and may include travelling activities related to romance, adventure, spirituality, escapism or nostalgia
Cultural	Cultural motivators indicate the need or desire to explore and learn about the destination, its culture and heritage, or to generally expand one's horizons and knowledge by travelling to new places
Interpersonal	Interpersonal motivators indicate the need for maintaining existing relationships or developing new relationships. This includes visits to family, friends and relatives, or the holiday is taken in order to meet new people
Status and prestige	Travelling is motivated by the desire for enhancing ones status and receiving attention and appreciation from others, but can also include travelling for the purpose of personal development (e.g. increasing knowledge or learning new skills)

tourism (see Chapters 14 and 15, respectively) have sparked more interest in motivation and seeking to adapt theories to more specialist types of tourism. Nevertheless, there are some areas that still beg further clarification and invite more in-depth research. Particular determinants and factors influencing the individual provide endless opportunities for research.

While tourism motivation assumes that all tourists have the potential to travel and engage in activities while in holiday, research on barriers and constraints to tourist motivation and decision making is still rather limited. For example, physical and mental disability can prevent people from travelling or change their motivation. The tourist gaze is a very central idea to travelling, but there have only recently been there more investigations that challenge the visual focus and incorporate the role of other senses into the tourist experience. Furthermore, are tourism motivations completely obsolete if we refer to non-travellers? Reasons for not travelling can give further insight into tourism motivation.

Similarly, as highlighted above, cultural differences also influence tourism motivation; hence, cross-cultural comparison of traveller motivation presents further opportunities for study. Culture not only influences tourism motivation and tourist behaviour, but most motivation theories have a very Western-centric approach as they originate from Western research. While it is generally assumed that these motivation theories are universally applicable, different cultural philosophies and research paradigms can offer alternative explanations. On a different note, tourism in general borrows heavily from other disciplines (e.g. geography, business, law, anthropology), which makes the study of tourism both a vice and a joy. In the case of tourism motivation, theorists look unsurprisingly at social psychology to explain travel behaviour. Further theories are available that can be adapted – both from sociology and psychology, but also from other disciplines – and added to the body of explanations.

In line with technological advances and globalization processes, current studies challenge the traditional definition of tourism as a temporary movement. As the physical movement has become so easy, new generations are establishing connections with many localities and the concept of 'home' or 'origin' becomes less and less valid to these global nomads. While the majority of young people might take a gap year, a growing number of people work and live in different corners of the world for short periods of time without necessarily settling down. If there is no home or mundane, daily environment that can be escaped, then what is sought? Similarly, as the internet presents us with the world on a silver plate and allows us to travel it virtually, how does tourism motivation apply here?

Conclusion

This chapter has provided an overview of the key tourism behaviour and motivation theories. While some theories (such as that of Maslow) have been adopted for tourism purposes, others have proposed concepts that are purely tourism focused. Consumer behaviour in general is important to marketing and promotion of tourism products and services, and understanding the tourist consumer is essential for tourism organizations to survive and succeed. However, identifying tourist motivation is not straightforward and, as the chapter has highlighted, a range of factors and determinants influence tourist behaviour and tourism motivation.

Central to the idea of tourism motivation is the idea that motivation is about satisfying one's needs. Needs can be intrinsic or extrinsic, but essentially result in a state of disequilibrium that tourists seek to balance out by going on a holiday. On the one hand, tourism motivation and tourist behaviour can be socially determined and involve extrinsic motivations that are formed by the tourists' social environment. On the other, motivation can be considered from a psychological perspective to allow for individual differences to be taken into account. Depending on the focus of research, both sociological and psychological considerations can be taken into account – but it is not advisable to differentiate the two as there is a constant interaction between them. The problem is that, in theory, tourism motivation should be a logical process if we follow the consumer decision-making process and identify the stages that each tourist goes through before booking a holiday. However, most people are not aware of their motivations as motivators can be latent and subconscious. Hence, most theories on tourism motivation only offer a partial explanation.

Given the range of theories, it is subject to debate whether the diversity of research approaches is counterproductive to finding suitable explanations for tourist behaviour or reflects the postmodern nature of today's research and a society that welcomes diversification and many perspectives that both compete with and complement each other. The theories in this chapter indeed represent competitive views, but are not necessarily mutually exclusive. While sociology and psychology seem to remain the dominant disciplines, there is still room for alternative tourism motivation and behaviour theories.

Review questions

1. Think about the holidays you have taken so far. To what extent have they been influenced by your society and cultural environment (e.g. your family, friends, work, previous experiences)? Can you determine some of these influences? How similar or different are they to those of your friends?

2. For your last holiday, go through the decision-making process. Why did you want to go on holiday? How did you search for potential holidays? On what criteria did you base your final decision? What expectations did you have and how were they met (or not)?

3. Ask your friends and family about their reason for going on holidays and travel experiences. Can you match their responses and apply the tourist typologies and motivation theories?

References

Boorstin, D. (1961) *The Image: A Guide to Pseudo-Events in America.* Harper and Row, New York.

Chen, J.S., Prebensen, N. and Huan, T.C. (2008) Determining the motivation of wellness travellers. *International Journal of Tourism and Hospitality Research.* 19, 103–115.

Clift, S. and Forrest, S. (1999) Gay men and tourism: destinations and holiday motivations. *Tourism Management* 20, 615–625.

Cohen, E. (1972) Towards a sociology of international tourism. *Social Research* 39, 64–82.

Crompton, J. (1979) Motivations for pleasure vacation. *Annals of Tourism Research* 6, 408–424.

Dann, G. (1977) Anomie, ego-enhancement and tourism. *Annals of Tourism Research* 4, 184–194.

Gray, H. (1970) *International Travel: International Trade.* Heath, Lexington, Kentucky, USA.

Iso-Ahola, S. (1982) Toward a social psychological theory of tourism motivation: a rejoinder. *Annals of Tourism Research* 9, 256–262.

Jang, S., and Wu, C. (2006) Seniors' travel motivation and the influential factors: an examination of Taiwanese seniors. *Tourism Management* 27, 306–316.

Kotler, P., Bowen, J. and Makens, J. (2010) *Marketing for Tourism and Hospitality,* 5th edn. Prentice Hall, Upper Saddle River, New York.

Maslow, A. (1943) A theory of human motivation. *Psychological Review* 50, 370–396.

McIntosh, R.W., Goeldner, C.R. and Ritchie, J.R.B. (1995) *Tourism Principles, Practices, Philosophies.* Wiley, New York.

Pearce, P. (1988) *The Ulysses Factor: Evaluating Visitors in Tourist Settings.* Springer Verlag, New York.

Plog, S.C. (2001) Why destination areas rise and fall in popularity – an update of a Cornell Quarterly Classic. *Cornell Hotel and Restaurant Administration Quarterly* 27, 13–24.

Ryan, C. (2002) *The Tourist Experience.* Continuum, London, UK.

Smith, V.L. (1989) *Host and Guests – The Anthropology of Tourism,* 2nd edn. University of Pennsylvania Press, Philadelphia, USA.

Urry, J. (2002) *The Tourist Gaze,* 2nd edn. Sage, London, UK.

4 Authenticity in Tourism

Sine Heitmann

Introduction

The concept of authenticity has been subject of a range of studies, not just in tourism. Definitions and, more importantly, interpretations of the concept are abundant. Indeed, authenticity can be likened to jelly in your hand – depending on the way you look at it, it changes its shape and nature. This results in a variety of interpretations and applications, making it difficult to pinpoint its essence. However, it also presents an opportunity for discussions surrounding authenticity. Several debates have emerged and this chapter outlines the key discussions, starting with definitions and understandings that have been offered. Later, the chapter looks at contemporary debates on the topic and places the discussion within postmodernity.

Context and Setting

From an etymological point of view, the word 'authenticity' is of classical Greco-Roman origin. It indicates a sense of a true, sincere or original element in a historical context. At its (very) simplest it refers to the genuine, unadulterated 'real thing'. The original usage of authenticity comes from the context of museums, where the authenticity of an object is easy to judge if the cultural element is material (e.g. products, works of art, architecture, dress). A certificate of origin or a certificate of authenticity can prove that the object has been untouched since its creation and has not been subject to any modern influence. When referring to immaterial elements (e.g. language, festivals, rituals, or tourism experiences in general) the determination of authenticity becomes more difficult. Most commonly, something is considered as authentic if it is made, produced or enacted by local people according to customs and traditions or if the presentation or performance has a connotation of traditional culture and origin – a sense of the genuine, real or unique, 'made by local hands'.

Authenticity in tourism is well discussed, as it is argued to be one of the key drivers for most tourist experiences and can be likened to the 'holy grail' for tourists. As briefly highlighted in Chapter 3, a central element of any tourist experience is the juxtaposition of the normal day-to-day environment and the unusual and different experience that tourists can encounter while on holiday. If different destinations are visited, a very simple argument can be made in that tourist wants a true insight into the local culture and heritage in order to experience, learn about and understand the local life. Locals in turn provide performances and entertainment that seek to cater for the tourists' quest and give an insight into their culture. While this sounds straightforward and easy to apply, several problems result from this exchange.

The first question that arises is: who defines authenticity? As the definition implies, if a product or performance is made by local hands, it is the producer or creator (i.e. the local) who determines whether it is authentic. Furthermore, when referring to products or objects, authenticity is easily determined by the material that is used and whether this is still the original material. However, the definition and determination become more fluid if we take the function of an object into an account – if the material or the producer changes, but the function and original purpose are still the same, does that make it less authentic? Similarly, we could argue that as long as the concept (the idea of the creator) is still the same, the product is authentic. Furthermore, authenticity can also be determined by the history of an artefact, the ensemble (i.e. the integrity of the whole) or the context in which we find the object in question (i.e. the location). In the context of museums, for example, the concentration camp in Auschwitz shows an original location of where the Holocaust took place. Hence, this museum can be considered an authentic museum in terms of representation. Does this make the Holocaust Memorial Museum in Washington, USA, less authentic, as the context and location are different? The purpose of educating people about the Holocaust is still the same.

Case Study 4.1. South African souvenirs.

The indigenous communities in South Africa used to produce bowls using natural fibres, but now the same bowls are produced using derelict fibre cables that are available in abundance. The material has changed, but it is still produced by locals using the same techniques and the function and purpose are still the same. Furthermore, the concept, history and context have not changed. We could argue that the purpose has changed slightly, as the bowls were originally intended to be used within the household but are now increasingly produced to be sold as souvenirs. The bowls are taken home by tourists who might use them in their original function or as decoration. Have these bowls lost their authenticity?

The discussion can be further complicated if we take immaterial performances into account, such as festivals, dances, religious rituals or similar culture or heritage performances. There are many examples where these performances have been modified and adapted for the tourist audience in order to make them more attractive and more suitable to the tourists' itinerary. As the original meaning (religious, heritage or similar) can be argued to be lost (for an example, see Case Study 4.2),

many critics have lamented the loss of authenticity and blame tourism's inherently economic nature for the commodification of local culture and heritage (see below).

Identifying the determinants for authenticity results in interesting debates, but there is one key actor that we have to pay more attention to – the tourist. As we are looking at authenticity within tourism, we cannot only look at the supply side of products and performances; the tourist plays a key role when looking at authenticity. Furthermore, as is shown below, the perception of authenticity and the interaction between tourists and locals play a significant role in understanding and grasping the idea of authenticity within tourism. The following sections look into this in more detail. The next section introduces one of the key debates on authenticity, namely Boorstin's (1961) ideas on authenticity versus MacCannell's (1999) understanding of authenticity. Later, Cohen's (1988) concepts of authenticity are introduced to add further variable to the discussion, before we then move tourism and authenticity into contemporary, postmodern discourses on authenticity.

Boorstin versus MacCannell

One of the key debates is between Boorstin's understanding of authenticity and MacCannell's interpretation. Both Boorstin (1961) and MacCannell (1999) took the inauthenticity of modern society as a starting point and argued that (American) people are influenced by the contrived and illusory modern society. As a result of globalization, societal changes and technological advances, modernity and modern society are characterized by features such as contradiction, conflict, violence, risk, alienation and differentiation. Nowadays, the standardization of tourism products and services has resulted in beaches, hotels and destinations that look similar – no matter where in the world they are.

As a consequence, Boorstin (1961) argued that tourists do not experience reality, but thrive on 'pseudo-events'. Consequently, tourists fill their experiences with pseudo-events and are satisfied with these experiences. Boorstin titled his discussion the 'lost art of travel' and distinguished between the traveller and the tourist – while the former is active and exploring, the latter is a passive onlooker who seeks the strange, but from within familiar surroundings. This (generalized) type of tourist travels in guided groups, thrives on contrived attractions and is isolated from the locals and host environment. Furthermore, as tourists pay for the holiday, they expect their money's worth in return and demand the whole world to be made a stage for pseudo-events. Tourism providers and locals have no choice but to cater with more contrived versions to satisfy these consumers, and media (through advertisements) reinforce the contrived images until tourists turn into a closed system of illusions that allows for no authenticity. It has to be noted that Boorstin was a historian and his discussion freely mixed observations with opinions. Nevertheless, his essay on the lost art of travel contributed significantly to the study of tourism from a sociological perspective. For example, Cohen (1972) used Boorstin's general insight for his typology on tourists (see Chapter 3). Boorstin's image of the tourist coincides with the two conventional or institutionalized types of mass tourist who prefer to travel within an environmental bubble with less exposure to strange and unfamiliar sights, products and people. Tourism destinations such as Disney theme parks, Las Vegas and Dubai enjoy high popularity and can confirm Boorstin's idea. Taking the definitions of authenticity above, these destinations do not cater for authentic experiences as they are produced and manufactured purely with the aim of attracting tourists. The nature of the products and services they offer plays on the fake and the illusion. These examples will be explored in more detail later on.

Similarly to Boorstin, MacCannell (1999) took the inauthenticity of modern life as the starting point for his discussion on authenticity. In contrast to Boorstin's idea, MacCannell viewed tourists as a model for the modern man in general, seeking to address their predicament and in a constant search for authenticity. He likened the tourist to a pilgrim who is seeking authenticity in other times and other places. As modern society and normal day-to-day life does not satisfy, people use their holidays to search

for an experience on holiday that closes this gap: tourists want to experience a different way of life, learn how a destination differs from one's own and discover places that remain untouched by modernism and still maintain traditional methods and ways of life.

Here we find an overlap with general tourist motivation and authenticity serves as a motivator. Authenticity is thought to be found in other times or other places. Other times can refer to premodern times (i.e. history). This can be the tourists' own history or another culture's history, hence explaining the popularity of heritage tourism. However, other places can also present opportunities for experiencing authenticity – in societies that are thought to be less developed than one's own (modern) society, hence explaining the popularity of tourist destinations in the developing world. As a result, tourists display a fascination for other people's real lives. The more alienated from modern society and a shallow existence, the greater the desire that drives the search for authenticity. Again, authenticity becomes a motivator for tourists. The search for authenticity reflects the needs of urban tourists from industrial countries – they seek something outside their daily lives, something innovative and different. MacCannell's idea is also mirrored in Iso-Ahola's (1982) concept of escape-seeking as a holiday as the search of authenticity in other times and places also serves as an escape from the day-to-day routine of the tourist's home environment.

This paints a more positive (but still generalized) picture of the tourist, and MacCannell's work has been one of the most influential studies at the beginning of academic research into tourism and its sociology. However, MacCannell also expanded his concept and introduced the concept of staged authenticity to discuss experiences of a tourist searching for authenticity while on holiday. First though, it is important to outline the idea of commodification, which is argued to make the search for authenticity impossible.

Commodification/Commoditization

Tourism is a competitive industry in which the suppliers (tour operators, travel agencies and host communities) seek to exploit every opportunity in order to provide a unique travel experience to the consumers. Within the process of 'commoditization', things and activities are evaluated in terms of their exchange value; thus, they become goods (Cohen, 1988). As a result, any object or subject that might appeal to tourists is commodified, packaged and consumed. Within this process objects, places and settings of touristic interest are identified and marked in order to claim them extraordinary and worthy for tourists to gaze upon (MacCannell, 1999). This applies not only to tangible products such as artefacts, souvenirs and handicrafts, but also to intangible products such as performances, culture and lifestyles. The local community – itself a very central part of the tourist experience and subsequently subject to the tourist gaze – joins the industry to cater for tourists' needs and package their heritage and culture into bite-sized pieces that give tourists the experience they are looking for. To the local community, this has several outcomes. On a negative note, commoditization and the subsequent commercialization have an impact on the original meanings of these objects and subjects (particularly religious, cultural and social). Once an 'authentic' ritual of a culture becomes commoditized and a staged performance for money, it loses its intrinsic meaning and significance to the locals (Greenwood, 1989; see also Case Study 4.2). On the other hand, the staging of performances can protect the local culture and heritage – while an aspect of local heritage and culture is adapted for tourist entertainment, the original version is kept for the locals and away from the tourists.

When discussing commoditization, it also worth pointing out that the tourism industry has jumped on the bandwagon and recognizes the value of authenticity as a unique selling point in marketing activities. Tour operators and destination marketing organizations frequently use authenticity or similar promotional slogans such as 'unique', 'true' or 'the real thing' to sell their products and services by appealing to the tourist's quest for authenticity. Referring back to the definitions above and the question of who defines authenticity, tour operators can be considered to be the vendors of experiences, who consider authenticity to differentiate their products over others. While this can be considered to be a sensible marketing strategy, ethical concerns regarding the locals' position and the potential loss of authenticity apply, adding further interpretations of the concept within a tourism context.

Staged Authenticity

Expanding on his idea that tourists are in a constant search for authenticity, MacCannell (1999) coined the term 'staged authenticity', based on Goffman's (1959) 'structural division of social establishments into what he terms *front* and *back* regions.' Front regions are where performances are given in front of customers, while back regions pertain to where performers retire, recuperate and prepare for future

---

Case Study 4.2. Alarde de Fuenterrabia.

Greenwood's study (1989) investigated the Alarde de Fuenterrabia, a major public ritual of a recreation of Fuenterrabia's victory over a French siege in the 17th century. The festival involves the locals in the celebrations, the reenactment of the siege and the parade, which is one of the highlights. The festival is a central element of the local culture, which provides the locals with a chance to celebrate local history, dissolve everyday conventions and rules and an opportunity for communal enjoyment. The importance of the ritual within cultural life is evidenced in the entire town's participation and in the fact that the performance is for the participants.

As the festival takes place during the tourist season, the festival became more and more popular with tourists. Subsequently, under the pressure of tourism development and the local council resulting from national attention, certain aspects of the festival (such as the parade) were put on not just once, but several times in order to allow as many tourists as possible to attend. As a result, locals became opposed to the festival and did not enjoy it for its original meaning of celebrating local heritage, but came to see it as a presentation and performance that catered purely for tourists.

performances. MacCannell adapted the concepts to tourism, choosing instead, the following: (i) 'frontstage' (i.e. front regions) describes spaces manipulated and managed to accommodate tourists; and (ii) 'backstage' (i.e. back regions) refers to spaces where private, everyday lives of the locals are given priority. Back regions provide the ultimate experience as they present the authenticity of local life that tourists seek to experience; instead, tourists encounter front regions, which are staged by locals for touristic entertainment. This front–back dichotomy can be expanded into a continuum, within which six different stages can be identified (MacCannell, 1999; Sharpley, 2008):

- Stage 1: the front region, a social space that the tourist attempts to overcome or penetrate.
- Stage 2: a front region that has been decorated to appear as a back region in some aspects.
- Stage 3: a front region that is totally organized in order to resemble a back region.
- Stage 4: a back region that is open to outsiders and which tourists are permitted to move into.
- Stage 5: a back region that is somewhat altered or cleaned up as occasionally some tourists are allowed to glimpse in.
- Stage 6: the back region, which is the ultimate goal of the tourist, but rarely – if ever – reached.

The divisions of the stages are blurred and the tourist can break through what is pseudo and the 'tourist's quest for authenticity can progress along the continuum' (Sharpley, 1999), until he/she reaches the back region at the final stage. This is said to be unlikely as the tourist rather encounters 'staged authenticity', which is within stages 2–5 (Sharpley, 1999).

Depending on the tourist setting, the divisions between back and front regions can be clearly visible. If we compare this to a theatrical performance, the tourists are the audience members who are not allowed into the dressing rooms or behind the stage where the actors are preparing for their performance. This idea can easily be applied to cultural and heritage performances of locals, where the tourist is allowed to watch but not permitted behind the

stage to see locals dress up for the performance. Within visitor attractions such as museums, the division between visitors and local employees is visible and clearly marked as employees wear uniforms and tourists are not allowed to enter display areas or storage rooms. In Arabic countries, certain mosques are only open to locals and access is only granted for those in local dress. However, there are less visible and more subtle divisions within other tourist settings. For jungle tours, you need expert knowledge to understand flora and fauna and you need basic survival skills in order to not get lost – the division here is less visible as local expertise and knowledge is needed. Finally, MacCannell also suggested that the tourist's role itself prevents the ultimate authentic experience. Tourists from Western countries travelling to African or Asian tourism destinations stand out among the locals due to their appearance and are therefore immediately considered to be outsiders. Further divisions can include language, behaviour and similar invisible differences between locals and tourists.

Negotiating Authenticity

Staged authenticity implies that authenticity means the same to everyone, like a label that can be attached to an object, subject or experience. However, authenticity is not a given, measurable quality, applicable to a particular event or product, nor is it a fixed, static concept; it is negotiable, depending on the individual tourist and his/her perception of authenticity (Cohen, 1988). Furthermore, authenticity can change over time and 'a cultural product, or a trait thereof, which is at one point generally judged as contrived and inauthentic may, in the course of time, become generally recognized as authentic' (Cohen, 1988). This process is referred to as 'emergent authenticity' (Cohen, 1988). Cohen combined the structural approach adopted by MacCannell with a micro, social action perspective in order to achieve a more realistic model of staged authenticity. Two types of setting (staged and real) and two tourists' impressions of the setting are combined to identify four different relationships (see Table 4.1).

Table 4.1. Model of staged authenticity.

	Setting	
	Authentic	Staged
Perception		
Authentic	The setting is authentic and the tourists recognize the authenticity as such	The setting is staged, but the tourists believe it to be authentic
Staged	The setting is real but the tourists are suspicious of its authenticity and therefore believe it to be staged	The setting is staged and the tourists recognize the inauthenticity

This is still a rather simplistic approach, but opens up possibilities for interpretation of what is authentic and what is not. Two tourists might watch the same performance of a Spanish flamenco dancer, but have different perceptions on whether this is authentic. The flamenco dancer might be professionally trained and dance traditional Spanish flamenco, and one tourist might recognize that this is very authentic, but the other might be suspicious of its authenticity. On another occasion, a flamenco dance is performed by an untrained and unprofessional dancer who might not even be Spanish – again, one tourist might think it is authentic, whereas the other might recognize that it is a fake version of a flamenco dance.

Again, tourist behaviour plays a central role. Depending on how experienced a tourist is,

he/she might be more or less suspicious of authenticity. This coincides with theories on tourism motivation and the concept of the travel career ladder (see Chapter 3). Not only does previous travel experience play a significant role, but also the tourist's background in terms of education, social networks and the media. Perception plays a significant role in judging authenticity and further opens up the debate surrounding authenticity as individual tourists have different perceptions and expectations that influence the experience. This in turn is influenced by the individual's reference system and where the tourist collects information.

We have to highlight a distinction between object-related authenticity – objective and constructive, and activity-related authenticity – a tourist's first-person existential experiences.

Case Study 4.3. The San Angel Inns – Salamone (1997).

There are two San Angel Inns. One is located in Mexico City, the other one in the Mexican Pavilion in the World Showcase, Epcot Center at Disney World, Orlando. The San Angel Inn in the World Showcase is owned and operated by the son of the owner and manager of the San Angel Inn in Mexico City. The two San Angel Inns offer two different images of Mexican culture. Many people argue that the San Angel Inn in Mexico City is authentic, while the one at Disney World is not.

In Mexico City, the San Angel Inn is situated in the colonial quarter and the main consumer base consists of upper-class Mexicans who assert their ties to a European heritage; the setting ties the unique Mexican heritage to that wider context. The menu is characterized by European haute cuisine with Mexican influence, and the décor is expensive and elegant. The waiters' uniforms reflect the European style. Selected elements from Mexico's past are integrated and the main motif is a Mexican variation of the modern good life, solidly based on the virtues of inherited elite status. Overall, the San Angel Inn projects a cosmopolitan message with a connection to the Aztec past. Any foreign tourists are welcome to view the performance and enactment of that vision.

Disney's San Angel Inn caters for mainly Western tourists and both the décor and menu are different to those of the Mexico City Inn. The restaurant design features classic Mexican style with a façade looking like Aztec ruins, the inside being dimmed to create a romantic touch and the waiters being dressed in Ballet Folkloric style. Furthermore, the waiters readily translate the Spanish menu and there is no emphasis on European or American dishes, but the food is characterized by Mexican high cuisine (at higher costs than the Mexican counterpart with the main purpose of reflecting the high-quality reputation). A mariachi band offers entertainment to the patrons.

Which exhibits authentic Mexican culture?

Wang (1999) identified three different types of authenticity. First, objective authenticity refers to the authenticity of originals that are toured objects and certified to be authentic without any reason for questioning the authenticity. It relates to physical objects found in museums or on display to tourists that have an official, accepted or legal certification of authenticity.

Second, constructive authenticity is the result of social construction, as Cohen suggested (see above) and implies that authenticity is negotiable and determined by the context in which the object or subject is situated, hence allowing for perception and negotiation to be taken into account. Construction has two different perspectives here. First, as Pearce and Moscardo (1986) highlighted, it is the relationship between hosts and guests that determines authenticity and not only the setting or the object gazed upon. Second, tourists' backgrounds, experiences and preferences for authenticity influence the perception of authenticity.

These two types are object-related authenticity, focusing either on the tourism object or subject or the relationship between tourists and hosts. Hence, these are the most suitable concepts when discussing cultural and heritage tourism. However, Wang's third type is activity-related and focuses on tourists' first-person authenticity and includes tourists' quests for their authentic selves, namely existential authenticity. This involves personal and intersubjective feelings that are activated by the liminal process of tourist activities. Intra-personal authenticity relates to feelings such as pleasure, relaxation or control that can only be met in short periods of time. In a liminal tourist experience, people are said to feel more authentic and more freely self-expressed than in everyday life. Furthermore, interpersonal authenticity refers to the sense of togetherness (with family, friends or other tourists). In this sense, authenticity is not dependent on the 'Other', but the search is directed in, among and between the tourists themselves (Wang, 1999). It neglects the activities structured around the tourist gaze upon the Other. Wang's examples are primarily concerned with beach holidays, ocean cruises and other forms of travel leisure, thus there is an overlap with tourism activities

that cater for physical or self-focused motivation. Subsequently:

> [The] whole issue [of] whether or not tourists are satisfied with their holiday experience demands a full consideration of the nature of the tourist environment, the tourists' perception of that environments and the tourists' need or preference for authenticity.
> (Pearce and Moscardo, 1986; cited in Sharpley, 1999)

Authenticity in Postmodern Tourism

Most discussions on authenticity have a tendency to follow modernist traditions of analysis, which take societies as totalities and take the tourist as a generalized, homogeneous type. Standpoints so far have not captured the variety of tourism practices, but have instead attempted a total portrayal of the tourist (Uriely, 1997). Instead of homogenizing the tourist experience, the discourse of postmodern tourism consists of compromising statements and stresses the multiplicity of tourist motivations, experiences and environments, thus going a step beyond modernist propositions regarding the variety of tourist experiences and the importance of authenticity (Uriely, 1997). Among postmodern tourism scholars, two theoretical frameworks are of importance: 'simulational' and 'Other' postmodern tourism (Munt, 1994; Uriely, 1997). The former follows Boorstin's idea of pseudo-events and focuses around 'hyperreal' experiences in simulated, themed or contrived attractions as postmodern environments. The 'Other' postmodern concept of tourism follows the arguments of MacCannell in regard to the quest for authenticity and the 'real' and identifies the growing appeal of the 'natural' and the countryside as postmodern expressions. These different concepts do not derive from opposing fields; on the contrary, they may include both dimensions. Furthermore, the concepts are rather complementary than contradictory, thus reflecting the 'both-and' attitude of postmodern theories in contrast to the 'either-or' attitude of modern ones (Uriely, 1997).

While postmodernism is widely acknowledged, it is also subject to criticism and not easy to grasp. As complete discussion goes beyond the scope of this chapter, we are going to focus on the aspects relevant to authenticity in tourism. As a result of commodification, post-modern concepts such as semiotics, media society, hyperreality, pastiche and spectacle are of particular interest and inform the discussion that follows.

Simulational Postmodern Tourism

We have already discussed commodification above. Consumption, rather than production, becomes the dominant driver within postmodern society and tourism (with its sub-elements) becomes a commodity to be consumed. As tourists consumes sights, which are marked and therefore indicate some kind of extra-ordinariness (MacCannell, 1999), tourists becomes semioticians, reading the landscape for signifiers of certain pre-established notions or signs that they have derived from various discourses of travel and tourism (Urry, 2002). Contemporary consumerism involves imagina-tive pleasure seeking, day-dreaming and anticipation of new and different experiences from those in everyday life, constructed in the mind through a media-generated set of signs (Urry, 2002). The media plays a central role and we are living in a media society, which means that we are constantly subjected to images and messages from television, the internet and other media channels.

All this information – be it consciously absorbed through tourism promotional material or subconsciously through books we read about destinations or films we see that depict the lifestyle of certain cultures – influences our experience and behaviour while on holiday. Rojek (1997) explained this through indexing and dragging skills that we have developed as part of our socialization of televisual culture. The process of indexing refers to the set of visual, textual and symbolic representational files to the original object, be it in printed texts (travel flyers and brochures, but also novels and poems), plays, cinematic images or television. These indices of representation confer meaning upon actual sights. Before we actually see a certain sight or experience a culture, we have a certain image in our head about how this sight is going to look or what the culture is like. This follows on from Cohen's idea that authenticity is socially constructed. We cannot avoid information coming from the media and, without knowing or wanting it, we already have a preconceived idea on what a destination looks like. Once we are at the destination, we are then experiencing and perceiving the physical landscape or the attraction in a way that has already been influenced by the images we had in our mind. As a result, the quest for authenticity in tourist motivation is questioned, as 'indexing and dragging problematize the proposition that sights have a single or original meaning' (Rojek, 1997). The images in our mind expect things to be in a certain way; thus, tourists are said to be looking for those particular images. Stereotypes are a good way of explaining this – the 'tourist in Japan looks less for what is Japanese than for what is Japanesey' (Boorstin, 1961). Tourists are more concerned with looking for the image or the sign of cultural practices and attraction, but they do not understand their basic meaning or function. In other words, they do not recognize authenticity when it presents itself.

The influence of media is further discussed by postmodernist scholars who argue that our relationship to reality and our way of thinking about reality has changed due to technological advances, primarily within the field of media (e.g. television, the internet.) 'TV is the world' (Baudrillard, 1988); the medium exposes us to a significant amount of information, messages and images, which are fictional or an edited version of reality. Our referent system and the ways in which we communicate have changed significantly, as it becomes harder to distinguish between the image and the real. 'The very definition of the real is that of which it is possible to provide an equivalent reproduction ... The real is not only what can be reproduced, but also that which is always already reproduced: that is the hyperreal ... which is entirely in simulation' (Baudrillard, 1993). This phenomenon is referred to as 'hyperreality' (Eco, 1987; Baudrillard, 1988). Hyperreality erases 'the distinction between historical reality and fantasy ... it is the confusion between copy and original' (Eco, 1987). It is argued that authenticity is rather visual than historical: if something looks real, it is real. Furthermore, reproductions of an object are perceived as being more real – and therefore better – than the original. Seeing the reproduced object, the tourist no longer has any desire to see the original (Eco, 1987; Pretes, 1995).

Within the 'simulational' framework the most often cited examples are places, such as theme parks, wax museums (e.g. Madame Tussauds), shopping malls, Las Vegas and television and film locations (see also Chapter 14). Theme parks such as Disneyland serve as good examples, as their central attraction is built around fantasy, image and illusion. Walt Disney created fictional stories with fictional characters. Based on these fictions, theme parks have been built that cater for tourists' need to immerse themselves in a world full of illusion and fantasy. Disneyland can be considered as the epitome of postmodernism as different styles and symbols from different places and times (both fictional and real) are mixed into a pastiche and packaged into an attraction that requires the tourist to suspend reality and enjoy the hyperreal – something that is better than reality. Not only can you enjoy the whole of Europe in the EPCOT centre and travel to Germany, England, France and Italy without even having to travel to Europe, but you can also enjoy renaissance castles with flush toilets and haunted mansions with moving walkways. The sight becomes a representation of representation, or signs of signs, hence, simulacra (Pretes, 1995; Davis, 2001). Under the condition of hyperreality the tourist is caught up in an industry and encounters staged authenticity and simulacra of real worlds.

In contrast to such sights, which are built purely to attract tourists, other tourist sights have to be markedly distinct in order to be noticed by tourists. Thus, those sights that are not particularly unique, scenic or cultural attractions attempt to outdo each other in spectacle. Contemporary, postmodern society is dominated by spectacle and hence tourism is increasingly concerned with spectacle (Pretes, 1995; Urry, 2002). 'The spectacle can be formed by attaching signifiers to an otherwise ordinary sight' (Pretes, 1995), proclaiming the region or sight to be unique. The attachment of a myth or a fictional character is widely used in current tourism strategies. One of the most prominent examples is New Zealand, which has benefited immensely from the *Lord of the Rings* film trilogy (see Chapter 14). As a result of the films, New Zealand has been marketed as Middle

---

Case Study 4.4. Lord of the Rings (Buchmann *et al.*, 2010).

Films are understood as representations, simulations and contrivances – emblematic of the simulacra and the hyperreal. Added to the cinematographic experiences is the 'real world' of travelling to destinations that have been depicted on screen. The *Lord of the Rings* films are interpretations of a fictional story as well as products of advanced graphic simulations. As they were produced in New Zealand and placed strong emphasis on the landscapes and scenery, the country has become known as Middle Earth and tours themed around the trilogy attract high numbers of tourists. As the study by Buchmann *et al.* (2010) shows, the physical places and social settings (the fellowship of the tour group) are pivotal to understanding tourists' sense of what is and is not an authentic experience. The film tourist as a post-tourist is:

> Quite aware of and able to navigate through the layers of their experience of both New Zealand and 'Middle-Earth' to make judgments, from setting to setting, about the authenticity of their experiences. They navigate the multi-layered construction of the 'reality' they wish to experience – from the fictional books, through the film version of them, the 'making ofs' (short documentaries that 'reveal' the back stage of those versions), through the mix of New Zealand places, film sets (sometimes no longer existent) and fictional places.
>
> (Buchmann *et al.*, 2010)

The experience of the *Lord of the Rings* tourist shows that the experience of New Zealand as Middle Earth reinforces the image of the country being green, unique and the exotic other – coinciding with the original ideas of authenticity being equated with other places and other times – whether real or fictional. As the film tourist also encounter elements of myth and fantasy from film and is able to 're-enact' the film, film tourism experiences also contribute to existential and socially constructed authenticity.

Earth – a fictional country based on the books of Tolkien. Similarly, Romania has adapted the stories of Dracula in its marketing strategies to make the destination more spectacular and, hence, more attractive.

The 'Other' Postmodern Tourism

In contrast to the dominance of media and media images within society, Munt (1994) identified a different movement within tourism and the search for authenticity through 'the emergences of more "individuated" markets (as distinct from mass markets) and the notion of a "specialized" or post-Fordist mode of consumption'. The rise of individual travel is represented as a consumer reaction against being part of mass tourism with its package holidays (Urry, 2000). New forms of travel are offered and consumed, new niches arise (e.g. ecotourism, culture tourism, ethnic tourism) and specialized tour operators emerge that target consumers for these niches. Within tourism market segmentation, tourism undergoes further processes of intellectualization, where holidays are no longer for pure relaxation purposes and tourists grasp opportunities to experience the world through a pseudo-intellectual frame, and professionalization, where work qualification within the tourism industry becomes increasingly important (Munt, 1994).

Key to this argument is the differentiation between tourists and travellers, as already indicated by Boorstin. The search for authenticity becomes the distinguishing feature that differentiates these two categories. Munt primarily refers to the middle class – a class fraction within which less formalized forms of tourism are emerging and these less formalized forms are characterized by an obsessional quest for authenticity (as indicated by MacCannell). The quest for 'Otherness' does not only expresses itself by looking for the 'Other' (other times and other cultures) while on holiday, but also by the fact that the search for 'Otherness' is tied up with the quest for distinction from the mass (Munt, 1994). Again, as the Other is said to be the primitive, exotic and can only be found in premodern societies, the post-tourist seeks it in

less-developed countries or in the past. Exclusiveness, uniqueness, romanticism and relative solitude are the components of tour operators that aim to target these consumers with their marketing of remote destinations and their 'primitiveness' (Munt, 1994). However, these tourists find it difficult to legitimate their experiences spatially, as tourism is a 'touristic tidal wave' (Urry, 2000), a driver of globalization, reaching the remotest places; thus, it is hard to find an unspoilt destination yet to be explored. Although Munt primarily focuses on the middle classes, current tourist types such as the backpacker are a very good example of travellers who seek to differentiate themselves from the masses through their quest for local culture and experiences away from the tourist bubble. 'Tourist' becomes an insult and to these people 'tourism' (not only as an industry, but also as a system or ideology) has negative connotations.

Together with these spatial changes come temporal changes. Postmodern tourism has become increasingly concerned with the quest for nostalgia. The popularity of culture, heritage and countryside tourism owes considerably to the search for the 'Otherness' that is believed to be found in premodernity, hence, in the past. Under the condition of postmodernity, society is concerned with the conservation, representation and recreation of the past and these trends are reflected in tourism.

Museums have been established in order to interpret history, but the methods of interpretation, such as audiovisual displays, animation, or 'living museums', create myths about the past. Other forms of searching for the authenticity of premodern forms in terms of nostalgia direct tourists towards the countryside; tourists are fascinated with the countryside because they have the vision of a 'bucolic vision of an ordered, comforting, peaceful and, above all, deferential past. The countryside has rather rarely been quite like this!' (Thrift, 1989). 'There has been a loss of historical sense of meaning and its replacement with a postmodern nostalgia in which we seek the past through "our own pop images and stereotypes about the past which remain forever out of reach" (Jameson, 1984:118)' (Urry, 2000). Furthermore, 'the past is seen in the way in which we would like to see it, and not the way it was' (Wheeler, 1992; cited in Sharpley, 1999). The authenticity is questioned in these forms of tourism concerned with the past, as it has become a collage of images of different epochs, a pot-pourri of images and only a version of the 'authentic' life.

The Post-tourist and the Death of Authenticity?

Following the postmodern discussion and offering an alternative to the argument that the tourist is in a constant search for authenticity it is argued that not only tourism but also the world is a stage and the post-tourist can delight in the multitude of games to be played (Urry, 2002). Post-tourists are characterized by three different features. First, they do not have to leave their houses in order to see the objects-to-be-seen. This mirrors late ideas of the virtual tourist who views scenes through a frame (i.e. television, the internet) and the availability of media that transmit images into our living room results, so that physical travel is no longer necessary to achieve touristic experiences. The concept of authenticity is challenged here in that the images provided to the 'tourist' via television are only an edited version, but do not involve any interaction or 'authentic' experiences. Secondly, post-tourists are very aware of change, enjoy the multitude of choice available and consider themselves as part of the 'game' (Urry, 2000). Post-tourists are aware of simulacra and the combination of images, signs and reality and seek exactly this as their destination. Third, post-tourists are aware of being tourists and, therefore, being realistic, know that they cannot evade their condition of outsider and know that 'authentic' local entertainment is as socially contrived as the 'ethnic' bar, and that preserving a quaint 'fishing village' depends on the income from tourism. The growth of mass media makes information available to every individual, but instead of ruining the illusion that authenticity can be found somewhere while on holiday, consumers and tourists in contemporary society have become more critical, not only in their search for authenticity, but also towards the forms of tourism and production of tourism products and services.

Further challenges to the understanding of authenticity have been proposed by Bruner (1994). The idea of authenticity presupposes that the original is better than its counter-concept, the copy. If the original is to be found in a premodern period where people seemed to live at ease with themselves (Bruner, 1994), the tourist penetrates this pure original state in the quest for authenticity. The very search destroys the authenticity – it becomes polluted and the tourist destroys what was aimed for.

Referring to the idea of authenticity being socially constructed, Bruner has added to the discussion by asking how people themselves think about objects as authentic and how this thinking is underlined by continuous construction through social processes. Rather than accepting a face value of authenticity, understanding the different meanings and heteroglot nature of authenticity is important. Overlapping social processes with competing voices can relate to the same objects and this is where authority comes into play. Hence, four types of authenticity can be delineated: (i) credible and convincing today; (ii) a complete and immaculate simulation of as it once was; (iii) original, as opposed to a copy; and (iv) authorized and certified by legitimate institutions.

While these ideas reflect the discussions above, Bruner highlighted the point that all ideas about authenticity are created in the present within a continuous process of constructing culture. This leads to two different conclusions. First, as Bruner removes the concept from the object and focuses on the meaning making processes in the present, he echoes Cohen's idea on negotiable authenticity which presupposes that authenticity is no longer seen as a quality of an object, but a cultural value that is constantly created and reinvented in social processes. Authenticity is further challenged as it has an inherent Western ideology. Most discussions, and the chapter here, focus on what Western tourists consider to be authentic. This is coming back to the idea that Western societies are more developed and modernized, hence more contrived and characterized by notions that drive tourists to search for authenticity. As most tourists originate from Western societies and dominate tourism flows, the hegemony of Western thought and ideology is also reflected in the discussions and understanding of authenticity.

Second, if authenticity signifies the pure, unadulterated, original, we could argue that no such thing as authenticity exists. If every culture is constantly changing and, subsequently, cultural products will not cease to change and adapt, there is no basis against which to judge authenticity and hence, nothing is authentic. In contrast to this, Cohen (1988) suggested 'emergent authenticity' in that what is previously inauthentic can become authentic over time. For example, Greenwood's first investigation into the Basque festival first indicated that locals were alienated by the touristification of their culture, but later studies revealed that the locals adapted to these changes. Even Disneyland, although often described as the inauthenticity *per se*, is an inherent part of American culture and can be perceived as an 'authentic' American tradition (Cohen, 1988). Hence, everything is authentic in its own interpretation.

Finally, MacCannell (1999) advanced that the quest for authenticity in tourism fails because of the tourist role. Commercialism and the quest itself result in tourist experiences being inauthentic. According to this perspective, authenticity is only achievable outside the realm of the tourist role. Tourists, no matter how much they try to blend in and adapt to local culture, will always be outsiders and only be able to get a superficial view of local life, even if we distinguish between tourists and travellers.

Future Research

Authenticity in tourism has been well discussed and researched, from the application of authenticity to case studies in cultural and heritage tourism to philosophical and theoretical discussions of the concept. Yet there are still areas for further research.

Most research of authenticity in tourism has focused on the tourist's perspective, the tourist–host relationship and, to a lesser extent, on supply and how the industry manipulates the tourism product to create an illusion of authenticity. While the local community's role is taken into account, it is often limited to a passive role of the victim. However, just as locals play a significant role in creating the tourist experience, they can have an active role in shaping authenticity. What has yet to be researched in more detail is the local's perspective of authenticity, with particular reference to Cohen's (1988) idea of emergent authenticity. Similarly, with the rise of event and festival research, more opportunities for research authenticity within a festival context and the role that local communities play in these festivals are evident (Getz, 1998).

Looking beyond the discipline of tourism and building on the interdisciplinary nature of tourism as an academic subject, it is interesting to note that among historians and within history research the concept of 'invention of tradition' (Hobsbawm, 1983) has received much attention. The discussions of authenticity and invention of tradition have so far been separate, but a closer investigation and comparison of these two concepts may suggest similarities and opportunities to borrow more concepts from each other.

Finally, researching authenticity in the context of sustainability gives further scope for research. As Cohen (2002) discussed the relationship between sustainability, authenticity and equity, he questioned whether 'the quest for authenticity, insofar as it is a significant motive in contemporary tourism, contributes to or detracts from the sustainability of tourist sites, amenities and attractions?' Following a basic argument, while the quest for object- and subject-related authenticity endangers the presence and sustainability of pristine, untouched destinations and existential authenticity could facilitate the task of achieving sustainability in tourism.

Conclusion

As this chapter has outlined the different ideas on authenticity, it has become clear that authenticity in touristic experiences is both an opportunity and a challenge for discussions. On an optimistic level we can use definitions and interpretations to investigate the meaning of authenticity to the different tourism players – the tourist, the local community and the industry. On a more critical level, it can be argued that authenticity has become such a flexible and changing concept that its entire existence is in question.

As our society experiences changing processes in economical, political and especially cultural or social terms there is a shift or break from modernity to postmodernity. The unlimited movement of people across and within national borders has led to a globalized form of tourism, where the most remote cultures can be reached, explored and commodified in order to be sold to tourists. Originally, there were a lot of authentic events, but under the umbrella of postmodernity these have become more and more simulated and thus less authentic. The quest for authenticity has become a frustrated search, as tourists can never be sure whether the object or culture they encounter is authentic. Many cultural products or performances are manufactured for tourism because they are expected to be like that; hence tourists encounter a world of simulations and contrived pseudo-events (Boorstin, 1961; Baudrillard, 1988). However, as Urry (2000) suggested, the post-tourist is aware of the game and plays the game. Furthermore, while conditions of postmodern society may challenge the idea of the authentic tourist experience, recent studies emphasize that authenticity still exists through a wide range of possibilities for social constructions and negotiations (Wang, 1999; Buchmann *et al.*, 2010).

Review Questions

1. To what extent is the idea of authenticity challenged by common stereotypes that we have of cultures?

2. To what extent has the condition of postmodernity challenged ideas of authenticity?

3. Consider your own and other's holiday experiences – how is a local performance or an experience judged in terms of authenticity?

References

Baudrillard, J. (1988) Simulacra and simulations. In: Poster, M. (ed.) *Jean Baudrillard: Selected Writings.* Blackwell, Cambridge, UK, pp. 169–187.

Baudrillard, J. (1993) *Symbolic Exchange and Death.* Sage, London, UK.

Boorstin, D. (1961) *The Image or What Happened to the American Dream.* Penguin Books, Victoria, Australia.

Bruner, E. (1994) Abraham Lincoln as authentic reproduction: a critique of postmodernism. *American Anthropologist* 96, 397–415.

Buchmann, A., Moore, K. and Fisher, D. (2010) Experiencing film tourism – authenticity and fellowship. *Annals of Tourism Research* 37, 229–248.

Cohen, E. (1972) Towards a sociology of international tourism. *Social Research* 39, 64–82.

Cohen, E. (1988) Authenticity and commoditisation in tourism. *Annals of Tourism Research* 15, 371–386.

Cohen, E. (2002) Authenticity, equity and sustainability in tourism. *Journal of Sustainable Tourism* 10, 267–276.

Davis, J. (2001) Commentary: tourism research and social theory – expanding the focus. *Tourism Geographies* 3, 125–134.

Eco, U. (1987) *Travels in Hyperreality.* Picador, London, UK.

Getz, D. (1998) Event tourism and the authenticity dilemma. In: Theobald, W. (ed.) *Global Tourism*, 2nd edn. Butterworth-Heinemann, Oxford, UK.

Goffman, E. (1959) *The Presentation of Self in Everyday Life.* Penguin, London, UK.

Greenwood, D. (1989) Culture by the pound: an anthropological perspective on tourism as cultural commoditization. In: Smith, V. (ed.) *Hosts and Guests – The Anthropology of Tourism*, 2nd edn. University of Pennsylvania Press, Philadelphia, USA, pp. 129–138.

Hobsbawm, E. (1983) *Introduction: Inventing Tradition.* In: Hobsbawm, E. and Ranger, T. (eds) *The Invention of Tradition.* Cambridge University Press, Cambridge, UK.

Iso-Ahola, S. (1982) Toward a social psychological theory of tourism motivation: a rejoinder. *Annals of Tourism Research* 9, 256–262.

MacCannell, D. (1999) *The Tourist – A New Theory of the Leisure Class*, 2nd edn. University of California Press, Berkeley, California.

Munt, I. (1994) The 'other' post-modern tourism: culture, travel and the new middle class. *Theory, Culture and Society* 11, 101–23.

Pearce, P. and Moscardo, G. (1986) The concept of authenticity in tourist experiences. *Journal of Sociology* 22, 121–132.

Pretes, M. (1995) Post-modern tourism – the Santa Claus industry. *Annals of Tourism Research* 22, 1–15.

Rojek, C. (1997) Indexing, dragging and social construction of tourist sights. In: Rojek, C. and Urry, J. (eds) *Touring Cultures – Transformations of Travel and Theory*. Routledge, London, UK, pp. 52–74.

Salamone, F. (1997) Authenticity in tourism – the San Angel Inns. *Annals of Tourism Research* 24, 305–321.

Sharpley, R. (2008) *Tourism, Tourists and Society*, 4th edn. ELM Publications, Huntingdon, UK.

Thrift, N. (1989) Images of social change. In: Hamnett, C., McDowell, L. and Sarre, P. (eds) *The Changing Social Structure*. Sage/Open University, London, UK, pp. 12–42.

Uriely, N. (1997) Theories of modern and post-modern tourism. *Annals of Tourism Research* 24, 982–984.

Urry, J. (2002) *The Tourist Gaze*, 2nd edn. Sage, London, UK.

Wang, N. (1999) Rethinking authenticity in tourism experience. *Annals of Tourism Research* 26, 349–370.

5 The Semiotics of Tourism

Dr Richard Tresidder

Introduction

Although semiotics is well established within tourism studies, the phraseology of semiotics is used as a convenient label for the analysis of the signs and images produced and utilized by the tourism industry. Semiotics may be simply defined as the study of signs and images, and the nature of the tourism as an industry. Through the marketing of tourism, semiotics is heavily reliant on the use of signs and images to add meaning to destinations, to marketing or to explain the destinations or the experience we can expect when we get there. In order to achieve this, the tourism industry and marketers adopt and develop a semiotic language of tourism that is used when promoting and marketing destinations. This language uses certain conventions that signpost our expected experiences and perceptions. For example, in the majority of brochures a beach, if shown, is usually deserted with no sign of people, cars or telegraph poles. This is done for a reason – the emptiness means something to us – as will be discussed later in the chapter. Understanding semiotics and the language of tourism is important as signs and images are used in many aspects of the tourism industry. As such, we need to understand what they mean to people so that we can use the right ones when attempting to transfer a message to the tourist or potential visitor. Semiotics can also be used to analyse texts such as brochures, flyers and travel guides. We do this in order to see how marketers, organizations or governments give meaning and value to their destination or product. It also enables us to witness patterns of words and images so we can see what is identified as significant. For example, in tourism brochures we see certain dominant words such as 'fun' and 'escape' that direct how we should be thinking about the place or event. The most important aspect of semiotics is to recognize how we interpret the signs and images that make up the language of tourism – but as we all come from different cultures and societies, are different sexes and have different interests, we all interpret the semiotics of tourism in different ways. As this chapter later explores, however, there are some elements upon which everyone is agreed.

Semiotics and Tourism

The semiotics of tourism is not a new subject area; it has been developed and discussed by a number of authors who have identified its significance (Uzzell, 1984; Culler, 1988; Dann, 1996a; Hopkins, 1998; Echtner, 1999; Jenkins, 2003; Berger, 2007; Thurlow and Aiello, 2007), while MacCannell (1999) went as far as to state that 'there is a privileged relationship between tourism and semiotics'. Critically, however, although a clear connection exists between tourism and semiotics as an area of study, it has not been developed to the same extent as other fields of critical tourism studies. Further, it is surprising that the area has not been developed to any great extent considering that Crick (1989) defined 'the semiology of tourism' as being one of the three main strands of tourism research. This view is supported by Dann (1996a) who stated 'nowhere ... is a semiotics perspective considered more appropriate than in the analysis of tourism advertising with its culture coded covert connotations, in the study of tourism imagery and in treatment of tourism communication as a discourse of myth'.

For Culler (1988), 'tourism is a practice of considerable cultural and economic importance' and as such it becomes an 'exemplary case for the perception of sign relations' within contemporary society (Culler, 1988). Thus, for Culler, the relationship between semiotics and tourism both 'advances the study of tourism' and 'in turn enriches semiotics in its demonstration that salient features of the social and cultural world are articulated in the quest for experience of signs'. Yet despite the recognition of the importance of semiotics within tourism studies, little theoretical development has taken place in terms of developing semiotics from the purely abstract. The application of semiotics within tourism studies has been theoretically applied as a label for the signs, images and representations and to a certain degree the experiences of tourists. For example, Urry (2001) explained that 'one learns that a thatched cottage with roses around the door represents "ye olde England", or the waves crashing on to rocks signifies "wild, untamed nature" or especially, that a person with a camera draped around his/her neck is clearly a tourist.' Or similarly, as Culler (1988) commented, 'All over the world the unsung armies of semioticians, the tourists, are fanning out in search of the signs of Frenchness, typical Italian behaviour, exemplary Oriental scenes.'

Such statements assume that all tourists are 'amateur semioticians' (Urry, 2001), all interpreting and reading the signs and images presented by the tourism industry within the same manner and searching for the same types of experiences. Although both Culler and Urry refer to tourists as semioticians, the designation of tourists as semioticians is questionable as there is a difference between reading signs in practice and being a semiotician. Yet, even though the signs and images utilized by the tourism industry 'signpost' experience (Jenkins, 2003), the individual interpretation and reading of these signs and images is an individual activity in which we draw from our own backgrounds and experiences. This adds a complexity to the perceived relationship between tourism and semiotics.

It is easy to oversimplify the relationship between semiotics and tourism, as there is a lack of clarity within the definition of semiotics in terms of phraseology, method and definition of what a sign stands for. Smith (2005), undertaking a substantial semiotic analysis of Barcelona, went some way to clarifying terms within tourism studies by examining how Barcelona has been represented in the tourism literature and what these representations mean to tourists prior to visiting the destination. Additionally, Jenkins (2003), in her analysis of the relationship between photographs within travel brochures and backpackers' experiences of destinations in Australia, examined how the signs and images that backpackers saw before they went to the destination impacted upon where they visited and what photographs they took while there. This research found that where there was a strong or dominant image that was used in tourism marketing such as the Sydney Harbour Bridge or the Eiffel Tower in Paris, tourists were drawn to these sites and they would have their photograph taken in front of then to demonstrate that they had been there; the photograph itself would then become a semiotic marker of this excursion. Similarly Hopkins (1998) examined the frequency of certain signs and images within a number of tourism brochures designed for the Lake Huron region of Canada. His findings showed that the brochures centred on certain myths or significant tourist attractions such as the Tower of London in the UK, The Empire State Building in the USA or the Taj Mahal in India. These are elevated to almost a mythical status, but once we go there we are often disappointed as they do not live up to the images seen in brochures or on television. Hopkins (1998) explained this in the following way; 'Imagination and desire fuel place-myths, but familiarity and dashed expectations will dissolve them'. The significance of this is that we give places a semiotic meaning within tourism and people accept these meanings. It informs their decisions to visit, and also defines their expectations upon arrival.

The Tourist as Semiotician

We are all semioticians to various degrees. We are surrounded by signs and images from the moment we get up in the morning until we go to bed. Signs tell us when we can cross the road, which door to use and how we can exit a building. We all understand the meaning of these, and the reason we can do this is because we read them and interpret them. The semiotics of tourism are no different: there is a set of signs and images that surround the concept of tourism that we read and understand, therefore we are all semioticians as we are continually reading and interpreting signs and images. However, the signs and images we interpret do not just have to be pictures or images, they can also be words or colours or a mixture of all three as each changes the way in which we understand the text. Kress and Van Leeuwen (1996) defined this approach to semiotics as 'multimodal social semiotics' and it allows us to try to understand why certain images are used, how they are influenced and how we as consumers interpret them. A good example of this is a set of traffic lights, which is universally recognized. The red light tells drivers to stop (and red carries the connotation of danger), while the green light tells drivers to proceed (and green generally means go and safety). Alternatively, it is possible to argue that traffic lights are ideological and are a means by which those in power (the government) get us to behave how they want. This example highlights the problem with semiotics; that everyone interprets things in different ways, or that not everyone agrees with the meaning and will resist it.

The interpretation of the semiotics of tourism therefore relies upon a number of factors, including the ways that tourists – or potential tourists – understand the signs and images that are used. The interpretation of signs and images will depend on the context in which they are presented, which is usually defined by where the signs and images are presented (the sign vehicle). The medium that carries the message may be a brochure or website and the context of meaning will be directed or defined depending on who has produced it and who it is aimed at. For example, Australian tourism marketing campaigns often use images of aboriginal people in their adverts. In the context of tourism, we understand this as an example of local culture and customs and that the purpose of the campaign is that it is selling us Australia as a destination. If the same image is used in *National Geographic Magazine* then it is clear that its purpose is different – the publication is not a marketing text; it is not trying to sell a holiday, but rather the image will be supporting an academic debate. Different 'sign vehicles' have different locations (focused at different audiences) and can change the meanings of images. As semioticians we understand that these same signs or images can have different meanings depending upon where they are placed and our individual backgrounds.

The role of the individual tourist within the semiotic interpretation process is clearly explained in Fig. 5.1. This demonstrates how the 'circle of representation' can be applied to this process. The model identifies the method by which the individual interprets the signs and images contained within the brochure. The image projected within can be seen to be located within the social area of understanding and meaning (what a specific society thinks of the image), while the perception, negotiation and interpretation of the brochure are located within the sphere of the individual. It is within this sphere that the tourist finds meaning, and as meaning may seem to be located within the individual, the interpretation of the brochure can be seen to create various individual readings. However, the role of the societal view guides and 'signposts' experiences by utilizing various signs and images that have been socially and culturally embedded (e.g. people in the developed world have a very different idea of 'good' living standards to those in the developing world). As a result, a semiotic language of tourism exists that is represented in the form of particular signs and images that come to represent the phenomenon of tourism to the individual. However, although the semiotic language of tourism may be socially and culturally embedded within the individual sphere, the individual traveller negotiates these.

The semiotic language of tourism that underpins contemporary tourism has been historically, socially and culturally constructed

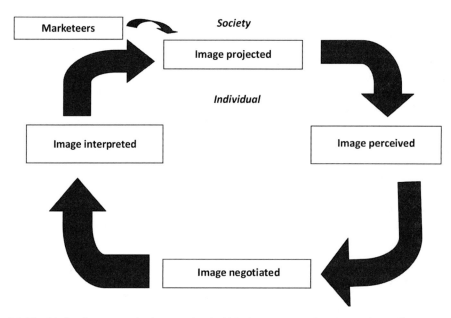

Fig. 5.1. The 'circle of representation' as contained within the semiotics of tourism. (After Hall, 1997.)

into various semiotic signposts that create 'consensus constructs' (Emanuel, 1997) and leads to what can be defined in tourism as 'expected places' (Herbert, 1995; Emanuel, 1997). It is at this point that individuals use prior knowledge, experiences and emotions to interpret and negotiate the signs and images presented to them, thus creating their own understanding of the images. The importance of socially and culturally locating the signs and images within a recognizable construct is fundamental to the interpretation process, as it completes the 'circle of representation' (Jenkins, 2003). In more simplistic terms, unless the interpreter understands or recognizes the significance of the signs and images then the messages cannot be communicated or interpreted. For example, when destinations are being represented the materials will often focus on the environment or culture of the place. These signs and images 'contain a multitude of embedded "analytical" processes' or 'signposts' (Jenkins, 2003) that direct interpretation and meaning, but are further directed by text and the socially and culturally constructed definitions of both tourism as an activity and the place itself.

The text that surrounds the images becomes a reactor, as the 'text directs per-

ception' (Kress and Van Leeuwen, 2001) by creating or reinforcing 'signposts' that direct the reader. For example, in the semiotic reading of a recent Cornish tourism brochure, the initial pages show a deserted rugged cliff scene (text hidden) that is geographically and culturally non-specific and generically anonymous – the picture could represent any number of non-specific destinations around the world. However, the previous page textually directs the reader and as such it can be seen to geographically locate the representation as being in Cornwall, while simultaneously identifying that the representation needs to be contextualized and interpreted within the embedded definition of the tourism brochure as representing various touristic destinations. Thus, the text directs perception while guiding the significance of the landscape geographically, socially and culturally. As a consequence, a conversion process takes place in which meaning is guided by changing perception through various techniques (Davis, 2005) such as the use of text and changes in context. Kress and Van Leeuwen (2001) called this process 'participant relay'. This relay denotes a text–image relationship in which the text extends or reconceptualizes the visual information. Furthermore, the interpretation of narrative images is also guided by the inclusion of what Kress and Van Leeuwen (1996) defined as 'secondary participants'. These participants are not dominant in the text, but become related in other ways or circumstances (Kress and Van Leeuwen, 2001); that is, the 'setting' of the narrative images, thus highlighting the nature both conceptually and narratively within the text. For example, the tourist represented within the brochure may create the vector, but the locals in the background highlight the nature of the relationship between both the host and guest and the position of the tourist within the host–guest cultural relationship.

Tourism, Semiotics and Meaning

The way in which signs and images are constructed gives meaning. For example if we take three letters and arrange them in the order 'ODG' they mean nothing; if they are arranged as 'DOG' they mean something completely different and as 'GOD' they mean something different again. Thus, the order in which we construct the signs and images of tourism changes the meaning and context. For example Dann's (1996a) analysis of the people located within the tourism brochure illustrates the way in which local people are represented within the tourism brochure (see also Nelson, 2005) and provides a good example of these relationships and definitions of subordination and power relations within tourism. This subordination is reinforced by the angle, position or size of the represented participant. This process is illustrated in the SAGA 'Travellers World' brochure, which locates the tourist as guest, being served and entertained by a number of local musicians. This thus represents difference and economic superiority, and is representative of a number of host–guest conventions that are continually utilized within the brochure to mark a differentiation of status. Such semiotic relationships within the semiotics of tourism do not reflect real or natural classifications, but rather imply something. Examples of this can be seen in most tourism marketing and are important in giving significance to the language of tourism. In the Welsh AM/PM television marketing campaign, the representation of

deserted landscapes came to mean something else – not just a deserted landscape, but a place of escape, to find yourself. This theme is also witnessed in Baz Luhrmann's (2009) 'Come Walk About' advertising campaign commissioned by the Australia Tourism Board, in which a clear differentiation of time and space is marked by the tourism process. However, it is important to identify the chains of significance that support and define subordination; these chains are open to manipulation and have a direct relationship to the social and cultural construction of narratives and discourses and the subordination of participants. As a result, the subordination of participants is a direct consequence of social power. As Kress and Van Leeuwen (1996) have stated, signs and images represent 'hierarchies of social power'; thus, the structures as identified within the SAGA brochure 'represent the world in hierarchical order' and critically in which the relationship between the host and guest is identified. In a way, the host is represented as a servant or a cultural attraction and the guest is being waited on, watching for their pleasure. This view is reinforced in Dann's work (1996a), where he identified that the representation of local people in tourism marketing texts often reinforces the power structures that underpin contemporary society and the relationship between the first and third worlds, host and guest, and centre and periphery. Therefore, it is important to recognize that often the signs and images we see also reflect power relations in contemporary tourism.

The Social and Cultural Embedding of Tourism

Through their continual use, signs and images become socially and culturally embedded within a discourse or language of tourism – they become accepted. If we are to represent a beach, we leave it empty; if we are to market France, we use the Eiffel Tower. The use of these types of images and tourism conventions signposts the significance of them and guides or informs the interpretation process. As Robinson and Andersen (2002) stated, tourism is '... defined by setting and meanings that are socially coded and understood within spatial and temporal boundaries.' The embedding of meaning requires a two-stage process to be implemented. First, the practical embedding process is reinforced. For example, within the tourism brochure the meaning is embedded on the first page through the identification and 'sign-posting' (Jenkins, 2003; Urry, 2001) of the medium and the fact that the brochure is marketing or advertising tourism experiences. Second, the position of the viewer and the interaction between producer and viewer builds a relationship (Kress and Van Leeuwen, 1996) within the text by forging a certain significance or emotional attachment to the brochure. For example, in the Cornwall brochure the brochure creates an attachment by offering a place in which the individual can find a form of escape, emotion, hedonism and so on. For Robinson and Andersen (2002), this may be reflected in a psychological reaction to the brochure. Thus, the tourist needs to identify the relationships between the signs and images used and their own experiences. By doing this we become emotionally related to the text. For example, by leaving the image of the beach empty, it allows us to put ourselves into the image. We can imagine ourselves on the deserted sand, with our friends, family or partners; we build a relationship with the text. If the beach was crowded, it would be more difficult to build that relationship.

The Semiotic Language of Tourism

As the interpretation process involves a certain degree of emotional involvement, we need to understand how this is built by the semiotics of tourism. A number of conventions underpin definitions of contemporary tourism, including certain themes and signs that construct the experience of tourism – the semiotic convention of tourism is presented to us as the language of tourism. The first element of the language of tourism involves the semiotic construction of a time and place in which the experience of tourism is located. The social and cultural embedding of tourism offers a time and space within destinations that is removed from everyday lived experience or can be perceived as 'extraordinary' (Urry, 2001).

The semiotic construction of destinations within tourism reinforces the significance of tourism within contemporary society, while simultaneously defining the phenomenon itself – thus, in a way, creating a 'circle of representation' (Jenkins, 2003). The semiotic construction of the landscapes of tourism and definition of the destination establishes a 'configuration' of time, space and power (Jokinen and McKie, 1997), which defines the destination as different from the everyday. The language of tourism uses a particular semiotic language (Culler, 1981; Dann, 1996b; Selby, 1996) that generates an embedded configuration of touristic time and space, which for the purposes of this chapter may be defined as 'sacred'. The reason this phraseology has been chosen is that, first, the sacred as a distinguishing element of time and space can be seen to represent the 'extraordinary' nature of tourism in contemporary society. Second, it enables the recognition of the distinctive time and space as represented within tourism. For Rojek (1995), 'A tourist sight may be defined as a spatial location which is distinguished from everyday life by virtue of its natural, historical or cultural extraordinariness.' It is this configuration of time and space and the extraordinariness of touristic landscapes, as represented within the brochure, that reinforces the binary relationship between the ordinary/everyday and the extraordinary (Urry, 2001). The brochure reinforces and defines this binary opposition (Tresidder, 1999) by semiotically signifying timeless and spaceless representations of destinations, which may be perceived to be 'extraordinary' in comparison to everyday lived experience. This differentiation of time and space in the language of tourism is best explained by adapting Durkheim's (1995) concept of the 'sacred and profane' as a means of expressing the represented differentiation of time and space in the semiotics of tourism.

Interpreting the semiotics of tourism is just one of the means by which the individual frames his/her experiences of the social. Just as Silverstone (1988) envisaged television as a 'ritual frame', there is a cognitive, imaginative and practical space in which everyone can access the things that mark off the social from the private (Couldry, 2001). For example, the tourism brochure constructs a ritual frame that is semiotically composed and marks the distinction between social experience and ordinary experience, and subsequently what may be termed the sacred and the profane. This differentiation is represented in the One&Only 'Resorts' brochure. The campaign reinforces this spaceless/timeless world in which normal working times are replaced with an oppositional definition of time, where the brochure states that 'Between 2 and 3.30 even the statues sleep.' This semiotic approach not only manipulates time and space, but also reinforces the experience (not just through the representation of a deserted landscape) by drawing upon the religious analogy of '... walking on water.' The use of a black and white format emphasizes the temporal liminality of the experience by making the pictures timeless; they could have been taken in the 1950s or 2010. The campaign clearly embeds the signs and images used in the brochure with a conception of differentiation of time and space or alternatively the sacred and profane. The touristic landscapes contained within the One&Only brochure are socially produced and consumed through various social and cultural influences; the brochure has become a semiotic, spatial and temporal social marker for landscape and the individual in which the 'passage into the sacred' is offered.

The sacred or extraordinary status of destinations is reinforced not only by the semiotic language of tourism, but also by the status of the brochure's symbolic authority (Couldry, 2001). For example, the Warner, 'Just for Adults' brochure uses a recurring theme of escape within the campaign. The brochure uses images that offer a deserted landscape apart from the representations of carefully selected tourists. This adoption of deserted landscapes is an element of an embedded 'analytical process' (Kress and Van Leeuwen, 1996) that 'signposts' (Jenkins, 2003) a notion of escape/freedom in which the tourist is freed from the pressures of urban everyday lived experiences, as it is also possible to derive meaning from what is not being shown. This analytical process is further guided by the use of text to reinforce the message that creates a 'reactional process'

between the text and the reader (Kress and Van Leeuwen, 1996), whereby the representation and meaning of the spa is guided by the text which states: 'It's truly a paradise – for the mind, body and soul.' This sentiment is further reinforced by the extended text at the bottom of the page which states; '... Thorsby Hall is not only a celebrated hotel, but also a luxurious spa retreat – a veritable "great escape" where you can unwind ...' This notion of escape continues to inform the 'reactional process' and is reinforced by statements such as: 'As soon as I stepped through the doors, the outside world seemed to melt away.' In the opening paragraph of the third image, the main text states: 'Romance is never far away at picturesque Littlecote House ... This Grade 1 listed Tudor mansion'. As a consequence, the interactive participant is presented with a set of signifiers that offer something 'extraordinary' within the 'sacred sphere of excess' (Caillois, 1988) and which guide the interpretation process.

It is within this discussion that the sacred and profane is a useful analogy for the distinction between the semiotic world of tourism and the ordinary world of everyday lived experience (see Sheldrake, 2001; Nelson, 2005). Durkheim's (1995) account of the sacred and profane helps to identify the particular features of the tourism/ordinary distinction, yet it is not a social fact. However, it can be reasoned that the signs and images contained within the semiotic language of tourism reshape social reality; they mystify the definition of touristic landscapes as being somehow apart from the ordinary. Tourism texts often make a semiotic distinction between time, space and everyday lived experience. What this semiotic language of tourism achieves is the definition of a space that may be defined as sacred through the creation of symbols and a reactional process that relies upon the social and cultural embedding of the concept of tourism within contemporary society.

Escape from your usual world is also a dominant convention in the semiotic language of tourism. The industry offers various forms of escape, but the ability to escape from normal life is a significant motivational factor within tourism. As a consequence, tourism has become elevated to an almost metaphysical level within its language, with the promise of destinations and experiences that will lead to escape (Cohen and Taylor, 1992) and rejuvenation (Krippendorf, 1999). For Turner (1977), tourism fulfils some of the societal and cultural functions traditionally provided by religion; however, the secularization within postindustrial society has left a vacuum or void in everyday life (York, 2001). The implication of these two approaches is that tourism provides a release from the pressures of everyday life and enables the individual to make sense of his/her lived existence (Tresidder, 1999; Sheldrake, 2001). It can be perceived that the interpretation of the signs and images of the tourism enables individuals to be released from their normal social constraints (Krippendorf, 1999) into a place in which they can explore their own identities reflexively (Lash and Urry, 1994; Young, 1999). As stated previously, the tourism brochure creates a ritual frame, 'a cognitive and practical space' (Couldry, 2001) in which the tourist can negotiate the 'social'. The signs and images contained within the language of tourism are seen to represent some form of sacred; however, access relies on the social and cultural acceptance and embedding of the ritual within the social and cultural definitions and location of tourism within contemporary society.

Once of the most significant themes or semiotic conventions within the semiotic language of tourism is the signposting of authenticity, experience and nostalgia (Frow, 1991). These themes are regularly represented in many forms within tourism texts. The signs and images may offer authenticity of emotions, landscape, culture or society, but these representations become defined as 'classificatory image structures' (Kress and Van Leeuwen, 1996) that order and signpost the text in terms of experience and context. These structures come to 'signpost' a realistic time and space in which the 'interactive participant' may find genuine reflexive experiences represented within the brochure. The 'represented participant' or 'place' comes to represent something more than just a geographical entity. These semiotically constructed places of tourism and their associated conceptions of freedom become places that are unique and extraordinary in

comparison with the everyday lived experience. For example, the Thomas Cook 'City Breaks' brochure clearly illustrates the use timeless and spaceless signs and images that semiotically represent some form of heritage, whether natural or cultural. The text 'signposts' the interpretation process by using the words 'heritage' (in the case of Reykjavik) and 'rich diversity of history' (in the case of Lisbon); it directs the reader into a 'classificatory image structure' in which heritage and authenticity are central. This convention is even more explicit in the Warner 'Just for adults' brochure, where the text continually alludes to historical characters such as Nelson and Jane Seymour. Consequently, the signs and images contained within the semiotic language of tourism create a time and space in which roots and heritage are explicitly offered as an alternative to the blurring of boundaries and de-differentiation associated with the postmodern era. These representations build a relationship with the tourist by offering notions of authentic experiences of food, culture, music and even love as a significant part of the language of tourism.

Future Research

Although the semiotics of tourism is recognized as one of the major strands of tourism research, it has not developed to the same extent as other areas. In recent years, however, it has started to become more fashionable as an area of research within tourism studies. This ability to read the signs and images of tourism has genuine implications for tourism management and tourism marketing, for all the reasons discussed within the chapter.

It has been recognized that tourists form an idea of a destination through the images they see in brochures and on websites, television programmes and even in films. When they choose a destination, these images often guide their choices of activities. There are, therefore, strong links with film tourism (Chapter, 14) and with the consequential issues around culture and access (Chapter 12). By paying greater attention to how destinations or attractions are semiotically constructed and represented within various media forms, it is possible to direct tourists' experiences and expectations.

This offers much opportunity for research to consider the ways in which images are accessed, photographed, captured, presented and shared. As the interpretation process is heavily influenced by an individual's social and cultural background, it is also important to replicate this research across various social, cultural and ethnic groups to create an understanding of international semiotic tourism values.

Conclusion

This chapter introduces the semiotics of tourism and more significantly the semiotic language of tourism. The semiotics of tourism plays an important role in contemporary tourism studies. It underpins tourism marketing and raises questions as to how local people and places are represented and interpreted within tourism. Quite often, we do not take the time to understand the images that are put in front of us – just like in the traffic light example used earlier in the chapter, we simply accept that we have to stop. By taking the time to examine and analyse what images are being used in tourism and what they mean, we can understand what

people are looking for, how the language of tourism is constructed and how it can be used. It is also important to ask the question of what is missing, as this is as significant as what is included. Furthermore, it is important to recognize that the meanings or conventions used within the semiotics of tourism draw from a wide range of sources. Therefore, in order to understand the language we need to understand tourism. Semiotics is not an exact science as it involves interpretation and, as such, everyone will interpret things in different ways. However, we can identify elements that we can all agree on, and that is that tourism is about: fun, escape and finding a place in which we can be removed from the pressures of everyday life.

Review Questions

1. Consider a tourism destination that you enjoy and evaluate the semiotics involved in the promotion and representation of that destination.
2. Explain how semiotics can be used within research to evaluate destination image, perception, representation and marketing.
3. Consider your own photographs from places that you have visited. What do they tell you about your role as a semiotician?

References

Berger, A.A. (2007) *Thailand Tourism*. Haworth Press, Philadelphia, Pennsylvania, USA.

Caillois, R. (1988) *Man and the Sacred*. Free Press, Glencoe, Illinois, USA.

Cohen, S. and Taylor, L. (1992) *Escape Attempts: The Theory and Practice of Resistance to Everyday Life*. Routledge, London, UK.

Couldry, N. (2001) *Inside Culture: Re-imaging the Method of Cultural Studies*. Sage, London, UK.

Crick, M. (1989) Representations of sun, sex, sights, savings and servility. *International Tourism in the Social Sciences; Annual, Review of Anthropology*, 18, 307–344.

Culler, J. (1981) Semiotics of tourism. *American Journal of Semiotics*, 1, 127–140.

Culler, J. (1988) *Framing the Sign: Criticism and its Institutions*. Basil Blackwell, Oxford, UK.

Dann, G. (1996a) The people of tourist brochures. In: Selwyn, T. (ed.) *The Tourist Image. Myths and Myth Making in Tourism*. John Wiley and Sons, Chichester, UK, pp. 61–82.

Dann, G. (1996b) *The Language of Tourism: A Sociolinguistic Interpretation*. CAB International, Wallingford, UK.

Davis, J. S. (2005) Representing place: deserted islands and the reproduction of Bikini Atoll. *Annals of the Association of American Geographers* 93, 607–25.

Durkheim, E (1995) *The Elementary Forms of Religious Life* (1912, Trans. Joseph Swain). Harper Collins, London, UK.

Echtner, C. (1999) The semiotic paradigm: implications for tourism research. *Tourism Management*. 20, 47–57

Emanuel, L. (1997) An investigation of visitor and resident place perception of mid Wales. *Leisure Studies* 2001, 199–214.

Frow, J. (1991) Tourism and the Semiotics of Nostalgia. *October* 57, 123–151.

Hall, S. (1997) *Representation: Cultural Representations and Signifying Practices.* Sage and the Open University, London, UK.

Herbert, D. (1995) Heritage as a literary place. In: Herbert, D. (ed.) *Heritage, Tourism and Society.* Mansell, London, UK, pp. 212–221.

Hopkins, J. (1998) Signs of the post-rural: marketing myths of a symbolic countryside. *Geografiska Annaler* 80, 65–81.

Jenkins, O. (2003) Photography and travel brochures: the circle of representation. *Tourism Geographies* 5, 305–328.

Jokinen, E. and McKie, D. (1997) The disorientated tourist: the figuration of the tourist in contemporary cultural critique. In: Rojek, C. and Urry, J. (eds) *Touring Cultures.* Routledge, London, UK, pp. 23–51.

Kress, G. and Van Leeuwen, T. (1996) *Reading Images: The Grammar of Visual Design.* Routledge, London, UK.

Kress, G. and Van Leeuwen, T. (2001) *Multimodal Discourse: The Modes and Media of Contemporary Communication.* Arnold, London, UK.

Krippendorf, J. (1999) *The Holiday Makers.* Heinemann, Oxford, UK.

Lash, S. and Urry, J. (1994) *Economies of Signs and Space.* Sage, London, UK.

MacCannell, D. (1999) *The Tourist: A New Theory of the Leisure Class.* University of California Press, Los Angeles, California.

Nelson, V. (2005) Representation and images of people, place and nature in Grenada's tourism. *Geografiska Annaler B* 87, 131–143.

Robinson, M. and Andersen, H.C. (Eds.) (2002) *Literature and Tourism: Essays in the Reading and Writing of Tourism.* Thomson, London, UK.

Rojek, C. (1995) *Decentring Leisure: Rethinking Leisure Theory. Theory, Culture and Society.* Sage, London, UK.

Selby, M. (1996) Absurdity, phenomenology and place: an existential place marketing project. In: Liu, Z. and Botterill, D. (eds) *Higher Degrees of Pleasure.* Proceedings of the International Conference for Graduate Students of Leisure and Tourism, 15th July 1996. University of Wales Institute, Cardiff, UK, pp. 49–68.

Sheldrake, P. (2001) *Spaces for the Sacred: Place, Memory and Identity.* SCM Press, Cambridge UK.

Silverstone, R. (1988) Television, myth and culture. In: Carey, J. (ed.) *Media, Myths and Narratives.* Sage, Newbury Park, California, pp. 20–47.

Smith, A. (2005) Conceptualizing city image change: the 're-imaging' of Barcelona; *Tourism Geographies* 7, 398–423.

Thurlow, C. and Aiello, G. (2007) National pride, global capital: a social semiotic analysis of transnational visual branding in the airline industry. *Visual Communication* 6, 305–344.

Tresidder, R. (1999) Sacred spaces. In: Crouch, D. (ed.) *Leisure Tourism Geographies: Practices and Geographical Knowledge.* Routledge, London, UK, pp. 137–145.

Turner, V. (1977) *Process, Performance and Pilgrimage: A Study in Comparative Symbology.* Concept Publishing Company, New Delhi, India.

Urry, J. (2001) *The Tourist Gaze: Leisure and Travel in Contemporary Society.* TCS, London, UK.

Uzzell, D. (1984) An alternative structuralist approach to the psychology of tourism marketing. *Annals of Tourism Research,* 11, 87–99.

York, M. (2001) New age commodification and appropriation of spirituality. *Journal of Contemporary Religion* 6, 12–27.

Young, M. (1999) The relationship between place meanings and tourist motivation. *Tourism Geographies* 1, 35–60.

6 Sustainable and Alternative Tourism

Ade Oriade and Mike Evans

Introduction

There is no doubt that sustainable tourism both as a concept and goal is a vital area in tourism management. Sustainability in relation to tourism in a basic sense may be regarded as the application of sustainable development ideas to the tourism sector (Weaver, 2006). Obviously the term is one of the most controversial concepts in the study and management of tourism. However, despite the non-consensus among academics and practitioners on this definition, the majority of writers in the field agree that a combination of effective policy, planning and management decisions is the secret key that unlocks the door to sustainable tourism development. Most of the time ideas that revolve around alternative kinds of tourism as opposed to mass tourism are advocated; even then, this is also controversial as it has been observed in many quarters that all forms of tourism tend towards mass tourism, as discussed in Chapter 1.

Often in the recent past in developing tourism, managers, planners and developers annex and exploit the unique sociocultural, economic and physical environment of a given destination. In modern day tourism, the concept of sustainable tourism has stimulated a prominent concern for equity and fairness. It has been suggested that the majority, if not all, stakeholders should be involved in decision making in order to determine the type and level of development that is acceptable to all. While this is a laudable idea in principle, it has proved to be challenging in practice. Nevertheless, developing tourism is no more the sole decision of a group of technocrats or the benefit of a group of few people who have financial and political interest. At least this is the case in most developed countries; tourism development and decision making in less developed countries is still the domain of a few powerful or privileged people.

Most of the tools and techniques advocated for the achievement of sustainable tourism development have been based on trade-offs and compromises, some of which are examined later in this chapter. Given the multidimensional nature of tourism and the multitude of stakeholders involved in planning, decision making becomes a complex task that requires rigorous assessment of the costs and benefits. In addition, an understanding of market economics and organizational attitudes and realities should not be under-emphasized. It should be noted that this area is not dealt with in this chapter, but is discussed in Chapter 7.

This chapter examines and analyses varying views, issues and prospects for sustainable tourism. Discussion and analysis is structured as follows: discussion of the basis for definitions of sustainable tourism and an analysis of definitional and conceptual issues. This is followed by the creation of understanding the trend of tourism development and the necessity for rethinking the philosophy of past development. The chapter also goes further to examine key theories and ideas and explore a range of management and planning principles associated with sustainable tourism development.

Definitions

The concept of sustainable tourism may be regarded most basically as the application of sustainable development ideas to the tourism sector (Weaver, 2006). The World Commission on Environment and Development (WCED, 1987) described sustainable development as a form of development that 'meets the needs of present without compromising the ability of future generations to meet their own needs'. The application of sustainable development principles to tourism management, according to the English Tourism Council (ETC, 2001), encompasses visitor satisfaction, industry profitability, community acceptance and benefit, as well as environmental conservation. To this end, Swarbrooke (1998) defined sustainable tourism as the 'forms of tourism which meet the needs of tourists, the tourism industry and host communities today without compromising the ability of future generations to meet their own needs'. This definition is in line with most authors' view. It is safe to say that this definition adopts a generalist view; hence it is open to many interpretations. Again, it is safe to say that sustainable tourism has been embraced more as an industry than an ideal.

Early definitions of sustainable tourism placed emphasis on physical environment. To a very large extent it is commonplace to see terms such as ecotourism and green tourism used interchangeably with sustainability. However, the late 1980s and early 1990s witnessed a shift in which the social and cultural dynamics of a destination were closely linked to the concept. A further shift was seen by the last decade of the 20th century, including economic and organizational perspectives in the explanation of the concept (Mason, 2008). In light of this, Inskeep (1991) saw the principle of sustainable tourism as encompassing the management of all resources in a way that economic, social and aesthetic needs can be fulfilled while cultural integrity, essential ecological processes, biological diversity and life support systems are maintained. Mason (2008) interpreted Inskeep's (1991) view of sustainable tourism thus: 'Non-intrusive, non-depleting and renewable, scaled to the particular environment, natural in material make-up and presentation and well integrated into the local physical, social cultural and economic environment.' Although the picture painted by Inskeep (1991) and supported by Mason (2008) is an attractive one, the practicality of the model is questionable.

Tourism Development

The rapid development of tourism, after World War II, into a formidable industry has been argued to be as a result of increases in household income that subsequently afforded families more discretionary income to be spent on leisure. Other factors such as paid holiday, a better educated population that is willing to learn and explore and increased business travel have also been identified. Perhaps the major driver has been acknowledged to advances in technology, most importantly transportation. With increased travel resulting in tourist numbers doubling in most destinations, the World Tourism Organization (WTO, 2010) has reported that international tourist arrivals rose from 534 million in 1995 to 920 million in 2008, before declining to 880 million in 2009 as a result of the deepest economic crisis ever experienced in most parts of the Western world.

The implication of these increased tourist numbers was that destinations had to meet demand with supply, hence the sporadic development of facilities to accommodate growing demand, particularly in the 1980s. Tourism is generally considered to be the provider of a substantial proportion of income required to supplement the primary economy in some countries and the main source in some few others. It has been seen as providing capital investment opportunities for public and private sectors and both generates employment and enhances quality of life within the local community (see Chapter 2 for further discussion).

Alternative forms of Tourism

The term 'alternative tourism' emerged from the ideology that unregulated tourism development will result in undesirable high economic, environmental and sociocultural

Case Study 6.1. Tourism development in Ghana.

Following Ghana's independence on March 6, 1957, the tourism industry emerged. This was regarded as a socioeconomic phenomenon that could be enhanced for the development of the country. Ghana was the first country south of the Sahara to have gained independence. Kwame Nkrumah, the Ghanaian Prime Minister who championed the African emancipation struggles, turned Ghana into a destination for international conferences and meetings for other African and African Americans leaders fighting for freedom and independence. The country subsequently began to attract Europeans and Americans.

The tourism industry has suffered failures in its development since independence, which can be attributed to Ghana's approach to tourism development and its over-zealous attempt to meet the mass tourism demand. Adu-Febiri (1994) conceded that mass tourism as envisaged was inconsistent with the country's low domestic investment and capital accumulation capacity to support the basic tourism infrastructure, untrained and unskilled labour force, indigenous entrepreneurial skills and inexperienced local residents.

Tourism growth started to decline rapidly following the fall of Nkrumah's government when he was deposed in 1966 by a military *coup de état*. The attraction of tourists, foreign capital and investment opportunities became severely constrained due to the country's volatile and unstable governments, with one coup after another until 1992.

Meanwhile, the formal development of tourism in Ghana actually occurred in 1972 after an assessment and evaluation of the country's tourism resources by the Obuan Committee in 1970. The objective of the committee was to identify the potential tourism resources to kick-start a 5-year development plan covering the period 1972–1976.

The late 1980s saw a renewed effort put into tourism. This was given a considerable attention as part of the economic development strategy of Ghana, and has enabled Ghana's tourism to move up to be among the top 20 leading tourism revenue earners in Africa (World Tourism Organization, 1999). Table 6.1 shows a steady increase in the number of international visitor arrivals in Ghana from approximately

Table 6.1. Ghana: international tourist arrivals and average trip travel spend.

Year	Total international arrivals (000s)	Average trip travel spend (US$)
1988	114	482
1989	125	576
1990	146	555
1991	172	686
1992	213	784
1993	257	802
1994	271	841
1995	286	815
1996	305	816
1997	325	818
1998	348	816
1999	373	815
2000	399	838
2001	439	800
2002	483	742
2003	531	780
2004	584	798
2005	429	1949
2006	497	1733
2007	625	1453
2008	670	1541
2009	695	1512

Source: WTTC (2009).

Case Study 6.1. *Continued.*

114,000 in 1988 to about 695,000 in 2009. Average visitor spend has grown steadily from US$482 in 1988 to US$1512 in 2009, albeit with a slight decrease in 2002. In Ghana's economic activities, tourism is ranked as the third largest earner of foreign exchange behind mineral and cocoa exports.

The increase in visitor arrivals and spend can be attributed to the aggressive tourism marketing effort by democratically elected governments since 1992. Ghana Tourism (2008) states that even though there have been significant gains in visitor numbers and increased visitor spend, there are some problematic areas that need immediate attention if Ghana's tourism is to be sustainable. The areas identified are: (i) poor infrastructure (bad road network, especially leading to tourist sites, inadequate supply of water and sewage system, electricity supplies in remote regions); (ii) inadequate positioning and targeting of Ghana's tourism products in the marketplace; (iii) poor internal and external service quality delivery; and (iv) poor business relationships between the public and private sectors and lack of capital investment in the tourism industry.

In view of these problems, the Ghanaian government has initiated a 5-year Strategic Tourism Action Plan, which is to address the negative aspects of tourism development and growth in the country. The aim of the action plan is to hasten growth and make Ghana a serious competitor in Africa's tourism destinations by providing high-quality products and services to tourists within the framework of respect for the Ghana's cultural, historical and environmental heritage. The plan's objectives include: (i) overall improvement of tourism infrastructure; (ii) training and manpower development; (iii) opening up investment avenues; and (iv) improving the tourism product and ensuring standards in facilities at tourist destinations (Ghana Tourism, 2008).

costs. With the realization of the impact of mass tourism and conventional tourism development, many destinations and authors have advocated caution in the scale and pace of tourism development. Alternative tourism may therefore be regarded as an early form of recognition and adoption of sustainability ideals (Weaver, 2006). The term is usually used to describe products and activities that are considered to be more suited to the environment than conventional mass tourism (Fig. 6.1). The following sections present discussions on some forms of

tourism that are thought to be more desirable than conventional mass tourism.

Table 6.2. Broad categories of adventure tourism

Soft	Hard
Noticeable growth	High-cost product
Reduction of risk	Small market volume
Packages	Require advanced or prior
Aimed at broad market	skills
Tend towards mass tourism	Greater individual risks

Adapted from Buckley, 2004.

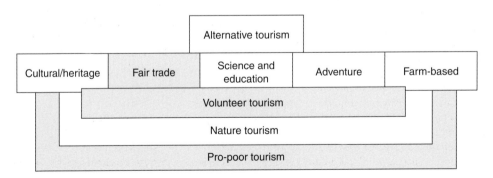

Fig. 6.1. Forms of alternative tourism.

Adventure tourism

The Canadian Tourism Commission (1995; cited in Newsome *et al.*, 2002) has defined adventure tourism as an outdoor leisure activity that takes place in an unusual, exotic, remote or wilderness destination, involves some form of unconventional means of transportation, and tends to be associated with low or high levels of activity. Muller and Cleaver (2000) posited that adventure tourism provides tourists with a relatively high level of sensory stimulation, which is usually achieved through a mixture of physically challenging experiential elements and typical tourist experiences.

Adventure tourism may be on a large (mass tourism safari), medium (rafting) or small (bird-watching) scale in terms of the intensity of the activity and number of tourist involved. There-fore, it may be justifiable to conclude that the environmental sustainability of a given type of adventure tourism will depend on its position on the continuum. Despite this realization, most travel marketers often advertise their products as green irrespective of their position on the scale. This is discussed further in Chapter 11.

Agro-tourism (or agritourism)

Agro-tourism is a long-standing sector of the tourism industry and an important source of diversification for rural economy. This type of tourism makes use of local knowledge and facilities, which mostly are not primarily developed for tourism. It mainly derives its income from agriculture and agro-allied products, such as farming, fishing and forestry practices. It is sometimes referred to as farm-based tourism, although there has been debate about what constitutes these two or each type of tourism. Henderson (2009) submitted that farm tourism can be conceived as a vital constituent of agro-tourism as it relies on farm and farmers in its conceptualization.

While the main argument for the development of farm-based tourism has been economic, there has also been doubt about the extent of the positive economic contribution of this form of tourism (see Oppermann, 1996).

Volunteer tourism

This denotes the type of tourism where travellers, for various reasons, volunteer in an organized manner to undertake a holiday that may involve aiding or reducing material poverty of some group of people within a given society; it may also involve restoration of certain environments or research into aspects of the society or the environment. It often takes place in developing countries and is linked to charitable organizations that recruit their volunteers from developed countries. This form of tourism may also be applicable to academia, for example those in the field of archaeology, history and medicine.

Pro-poor tourism

Pro-poor tourism (PPT) is not a specific product, but an approach to managing the industry in order to alleviate hardship and poverty for poor people, particularly those living in rural and developing areas and who are sometimes seen as 'victims' of tourism. The idea of PPT is to increase the positive impacts of tourism on poor people. It is an approach that aims to encourage the participation of poor people at many points in the industry. It also seeks to increase social benefits accruable from tourism to people who are otherwise deemed to not have had the opportunity to benefit. Charitable organizations in countries in the eastern and southern parts of Africa (e.g. Kenya, Uganda, Namibia) are notable for programmes directed at encouraging PPT. Arguably, any form of tourism can be PPT insofar that the aim is to bring economic benefit to 'marginalized communities'. In essence, one may be tempted to ask the following questions: what about environmental sustainability? What about sociocultural sustainability? What about intergenerational equity?

Fair-trade tourism

Like PPT, fair-trade tourism is not a product. The aim of fair-trade tourism is to address injustices associated with conventional trade in which poor producers suffer in the global market place. Fair trade is seen by many as another initiative that makes some contribution to the sustainability agenda while benefiting from improved image and potential tourism promotion.

The Fairtrade Foundation suggests five goals that have to be met in order to achieve 'Fairtrade Town' status. An example of a Fairtrade Town is Wolfville, Nova Scotia, Canada, which is reputed to be the first Fairtrade Town in the country. The five goals can, for purpose of ease, be referred to as the five Cs: council, commerce, community, common consensus and captains. These goals in a broad sense relate to the following:

- The local council passes a resolution supporting fair trade and agreeing to serve fair-trade products in meetings, offices and cafeteria.
- A range of fair-trade products, at least two, is readily available in the area's retail outlets and served in local catering establishments.
- Fair trade is supported by local workplaces and community organizations and fair-trade products are used whenever possible. A flag-ship employer is a requirement for populations over 100,000.
- Publicity and media coverage are managed to raise awareness and understanding of fair trade across the community.
- A local fair-trade steering group is inaugurated to ensure the Fairtrade Town campaign continues to develop and gain momentum.

Tourism planning models

The realization that every form of tourism brings with it some impacts emphasizes the need for a holistic system approach to assessing tourism impacts and managing the industry. Despite the non-consensus among academics and practitioners on the definitions of sustainable tourism, the majority agree that effective planning is the way forward for tourism to be sustainable. Planning for tourism development at the inception of mass tourism in the 1950s was simplistic, with the sole focus on economic benefit. No doubt with the attendant impacts

associated with the type of development witnessed up to the late 1980s and early 1990s, tourism planning techniques evolved to address changes deemed undesirable and damaging.

Getz (1987) identified planning approaches with their underlining assumptions and view of tourism planning problems. The four broad categories that can be considered as staged development of tourism planning philosophy are as follows:

- Boosterism orientation sees tourism as inher-ently good and as such it should be developed. The predominant view is that cultural and natural resources should be exploited.
- Industry orientation takes tourism as an industry in its own right, hence effort is expended on optimising income. This plan-ning orientation sees tourism as a means to create employment, earn foreign revenue, stimulate regional development and encour-age economic equality.
- Spatial orientation defines development in environmental terms and effort is often concentrated on manipulating travel patterns and visitor flow.
- Community orientation places emphasis on the role of community in the tourism experi-ence.

Further exploration of the individual tourism planning philosophy identified by Getz reveals weakness(es), which can be compensated by one or two other approaches. Hall (2000) suggested a fifth approach, which he termed an integrated approach, where social, environ-mental and economic, as well as cultural and political goals can be achieved.

Visitor management approaches

Central to the philosophy of sustainable tourism is responsible resource use and this informs the basis of most approaches employed in managing visitors or visitors' use of tourism resources. Visitor management has been employed by various levels of agencies and organizations to control visitor flows. Most visitor management approaches are associated with areas of natural beauty or the countryside, and concern for the environmental resources is the main motivating factor for their adoption. One may be tempted to ask the question: what happens to other areas of tourism and forms of resource? Although it can be argued that since the aim of private investors is to attract as many visitors as possible, these approaches are not applicable to most private business that are predominantly mass tourism oriented – a view that the authors of this chapter dissociate from. For tourism generally to be sustainable, approaches for ensuring responsible resource use must cut across all sectors of sustainability, lest particular sectors of the industry be jeopardized.

The ETB (1991 in Mason, 2005) suggested that there are three principal techniques employed in managing visitors:

- Control of visitors number – for example, imposing a limit on the number of visitors that can be allowed on a site at a given time.
- Adaptation of resources to cope with visitor numbers – this is related to protecting tourism resources from 'wear' and 'tear'.
- Modification of visitors' behaviour – this can take the form of enlightenment, education and establishment of code of conduct.

These three techniques are explained here in the following sections: carrying capacity, limit of acceptable change and the recreation opportunity spectrum.

Carrying capacity

This concept is a useful tool in visitor management strategies when used in the context of social, economic and environmental analysis in planning and as a guide in decision making about tourism development and growth. As stated by Coccossis (2008), tourism prospects at a destination may be affected by irreversible damages in social, economic or environmental systems that may be caused by rapid tourism growth. Coccossis (2008) suggested that:

> There should be limits on tourism development (size or intensity) often expressed as crow[d]ing or the maximum number of people who can use a site without causing an unacceptable alteration to the physical environment (natural and man-made) and without an unacceptable decline in the quality of the experience gain by the visitors.

Many attempts have been made to define carrying capacity by different authors such as Middleton and Hawkins (1998), Coccossis and Parpairis (2000) and the WTO. There is a consensus in the definition of carrying capacity among all the aforementioned authors, which proves that the concept itself is being generally accepted. None the less, there is some scepticism and disagreement regarding the practical application of the idea, in particular with regard to its use as a management tool (European Commission, 2002).

A general framework guiding local community, planners and decision makers can be provided through the process of refinancing and implementing tourism carrying capacity and the holistic process of planning sustainable tourism, which are not dissimilar to each other.

The framework tends to consist of policy measures, aiming objectives in respect to tourism development at a destination on the basis of the destination's distinctive characteristics/features respecting local capacities to sustain tourism. Capacity limits for sustainable tourism activity, when set at a destination, must involve a vision about local development and decisions about managing tourism. The best approach is to carry out decision making in the form of democratic community strategic planning initiative that requires the participation of all major actors and the community at large.

The components of carrying capacity involve three basic techniques, dimensions or indicators that can enable managers to confront increasing pressures from tourism development, namely: physical–ecological, sociodemographic and political–economic. All three components are interrelated to some extent, but they should be considered differently with regard to the characteristics and particularities of the destination that provides the basic structure for the development of tourism. These include local resources, the vulnerability of local natural ecosystems, population size, economic structure and cultural and local heritage. In general, the resilience to pressure from tourism depends on the characteristics of the locality. The dynamism, size and structure of the local society, culture and economy are contributing factors that sway the local ability to cope with the pressure of and impacts from tourism.

The type(s) of tourism present at a destination can determine the basic characteristics of tourist behaviour to some extent and the condition of the tourist/local community, tourism/local economy and tourist development/ environmental quality relationships. Motive(s) for visiting a destination, the mode of transport, the frequency and length of stay and activity range of tourists depend heavily on the type of tourism on offer at a destination. In view of this, it is important to consider differences between types of tourists in terms of expectations, attitudes and behaviour, as these influence the pressures and impacts of tourism on a place (European Commission, 2002).

A limit (threshold) in the tourist activity in coastal, protected, rural, mountain or historical destinations should be a concern and priority of local tourism planners and managers. Tourism creates pressures on the natural and cultural environment affecting resources, social structures, cultural patterns, economic activities and land uses in local communities. Real or perceived limits can encourage communities to take actions that can be incorporated within the existing responsibilities and activities of those managing local affairs at the destination level (European Commission, 2002).

The physical–ecological component of the carrying capacity consists of all 'fixed' and 'flexible' aspects of the natural and built cultural environment, as well as infrastructure. The fixed components refer to the capacity of natural systems, and are occasionally expressed as ecological capacity or assimilative capacity. The flexible components refer initially to infrastructure systems and their physical characteristics, for example water supply, sewerage, electricity, transportation, social amenities such as postal and telecommunication services, health services, law and order services, banks, shops and other services.

According to the European Commission (2002), the level of capacity for the components can be set in terms of the following:

- Acceptable level of congestion or density in key areas/spatial units such as parks, museums, city streets and so on.
- Maximum acceptable loss of natural resources (e.g. water, land) without significant degradation of ecosystem functions, biodiversity or loss of species.
- Acceptable level of air, water and noise pollution on the basis of tolerance or the assimilative capacity of local ecosystems.
- Intensity of use of transport infrastructure, facilities and services.
- Use and congestion of utility facilities and services of water supply, electric power, waste management of sewage and solid waste collection, treatment and disposal and telecommunications.
- Adequate availability of other community facilities and services such as those related to public health and safety, housing and community services.

The next tourism carrying capacity to be considered is the sociodemographic component. This looks at those social aspects that are important to local communities, because of their strong relationship with the presence and growth of tourism at a destination. Social and demographic matters such as available manpower or trained personnel and sociocultural issues such as the sense of identity of the local community or the tourist experience must be scrutinized carefully in order to balance the levels of tolerance of the host population as well as the quality of experience received by visitors to a destination.

The European Commission (2002) expresses the levels of capacity for the components in the terms of the following:

- Number of tourists and tourist/recreation activity types that can be absorbed without affecting the sense of identity, lifestyle, social patterns and activities of host communities.
- Level and type of tourism that does not alter significantly local culture in direct or indirect ways in terms of arts, crafts, belief systems, ceremonies, customs and traditions.
- Level of tourism that will not be resented by local population or pre-empt their use of services and amenities.
- Level of tourism (number of visitors and compatibility of types of activities) in an area without unacceptable decline of experience of visitors.

Political–economic tourism carrying capacity is the last component to consider. This component refers to the impacts of tourism on the local economic structure and activities, not withstanding competition with other business sectors. The European Commission (2002) considers political–economic parameters as an expression of divergence in values and attitudes within the local community in relation to tourism. The levels of capacity for the components are therefore expressed in terms of: (i) level of specialization in tourism; (ii) loss of human labour in other sectors due to tourism attraction; (iii) revenue from tourism distribution issues at local level; and (iv) level of tourism employment in relation to local human resources.

There is a general consensus that the need for developing and utilizing tourism carrying capacity tools that facilitate planners and decision makers in their efforts to control tourism development is growing. Eagles *et al.* (2002) stated that there are four main strategic approaches in visitor management that can be used to reduce the negative impacts of visitors at a destination. These are as follows:

1. Managing the supply of tourism or visitor opportunities (e.g. by increasing the space available or the time available to accommodate more users).
2. Managing the demand for visitation (e.g. through restrictions of length of stay, the total numbers, or type of use).
3. Managing the resource capabilities to handle use (e.g. through hardening the site or specific locations, or developing facilities).
4. Managing the impact of use (e.g. reducing the negative impact of use by modifying the type of use, or dispensing or concentrating use).

Limit of acceptable change

Limit of acceptable change is a framework that encourages identification of the level of acceptable resource use; emphasis is always placed on the conditions desired in the area rather than on how much change the area can tolerate. It requires a political decision about what is acceptable, hence it has the advantage of empowering and involving members of the host community in deciding how much tourism should be developed. In other words they can, to some extent, give permission as to the degree engagement in tourism will affect them. 'The value judgements made about acceptable levels of change reflect philosophical, emotional, spiritual, experience-based and economic response' (Newsome *et al.*, 2002). However, destination managers are confronted with resolving conflicts or differences that may result from diverse opinions as different individual stakeholders or groups come with varying aspirations and expectations, which of course have to be effectively managed.

Recreation opportunity spectrum

In this approach, the emphasis is on identifying areas of distinct characteristics and subsequently assigning differing levels and types of recreational activities to them in order to minimize strain on only one area. The idea is to provide a wide range of opportunities in terms of experiences that visitors to a given area are seeking. To this end, the recreation opportunity spectrum helps to achieve two principal objectives: (i) mitigation of adverse effects on the physical environment; and (ii) enhancement of the tourist experience. The distinct areas that are identified are referred to as 'opportunity class'; Newsome *et al.* (2002) have submitted that nowadays, the word 'zone' is used.

Management tools such as zoning may be used effectively in protected areas, since their special status allows the definition and delimitation of zones where protection, conservation and limitations in the various uses are imposed. Visitor management strategies adopted by the aforementioned researchers may be applied to tourism carrying capacity measurement and implementation.

Collaboration

The nature of the tourist destination is another vital factor in sustainable tourism development and management. A destination as a geographic location can be defined at various levels of aggregation, taking into account the mixture of differing types of organizations and groups of people. Often the organizations and people in question include more than those who primarily offer tourism products and services. To this end, value is created and delivered to visitors by a myriad of interacting and interdependent differing units. For instance, a tourist on holiday will have to stay in some sort of accommodation, serviced or unserviced; eat in restaurants and cafe; engage in leisure activities, which may be indoor or outdoor; and visit places of interest using one form of transport or another at the destination. Usually, these services and products are provided by several organizations. In the case of this hypothetical tourist, provision of unsatisfactory service by one provider may detract from the overall holiday experience.

Around the world, participants in search for sustainable tourism include government at all levels (national, regional and local); non-governmental organizations such as Tourism Concern, Friends of the Earth, the World Travel and Tourism Council (WTTC) and the World Leisure Organization; small- to large-sized tour operators; independent and international chains of hotels; and other stakeholders involved in tourism. Each of these groups makes decisions affecting part of the entire tourism system; however, the breadth of control needed to achieve sustainability is generally beyond the individual stakeholder acting in isolation.

The essence of sustainable development is to ensure a good quality of life through the provision of the basic needs of society. The WTO (2001), however, defines sustainability in tourism literature as 'Development that meets the needs of the today's tourists and the host region while protecting and enhancing opportunities for the future.' It is envisaged as leading to the management of all resources in such a way that economic, social and aesthetic needs can be fulfilled while maintaining cultural integrity, essential ecology processes, biological diversity and life support systems.

These two definitions have identified four different stakeholder groups in sustainable tourism: the present tourists, the present host community, the future tourist and the future host community. Therefore, all of these groups have a legitimate interest in tourism development in their community because they can affect or be affected by the tourism business as a whole. Other major stakeholders are central and local government, the private sector, international organizations, public/private initiatives and traditional chiefs/community heads.

Mayers and Vermeulen (2005) developed stakeholder influence mapping (Fig. 6.2), a tool recommended for the examination and pictorial representation of the relative power and influence exhibited by stakeholders in decision making. In testing the tool, they examined the UK international development policy for a period of 8 years (1997–2005) and a further predictive 5 years of policy implementation. It was found that the position of some stakeholders changed on the map for various reasons such as war and conflict, trade agreements, globalization and a host of other factors. Mainly the central government remained most influential, while the common man on the street remained uninfluential, partly as a result of non-consultation.

The host community can be classified as stakeholders with low power or less influence on decision making, but have high interest in the tourism business and its consequential actions. Nevertheless, they will make their concerns obvious and may be able to influence the powerful stakeholders and affect their behaviour if their interest is not considered in a suitable manner or if there is a negative impact on their quality of life. It is therefore recommended that the local community is consulted and kept abreast with decisions and the development of tourism activities in that community. Private investors and local and central governments are in the category of stakeholders with high power and high interest, who are involved in managing the tourism products and also have the power to superimpose their own plan or agenda in a tourist destination operation in a given territory or region.

As stated previously in this chapter, the tourism industry is multifaceted and fragmented in nature and with a wide range of stakeholders at both national and local levels, all having a role in the formation and implementation of sustainable tourism policies and strategies. All stakeholders must be encouraged to express their views and concerns freely and their interests should be taken into account; governments must embark on consultative processes in the formulation and implementation of

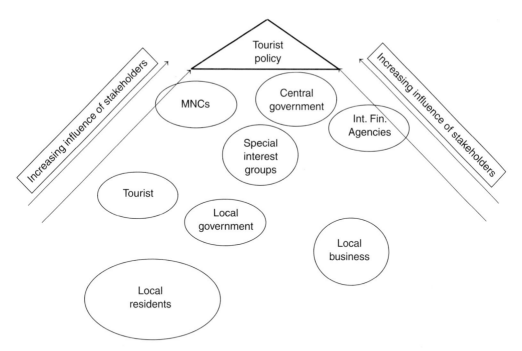

Fig. 6.2. Stakeholder influence map. (Adapted from Mayers and Vermeulen, 2005.) MNCs, multinational companies; Int. Fin Agencies, International Finance Agencies.

tourism policies. Communication in developing countries may be problematic due to the remoteness of some areas and the lack of telecommunication networks; however, this can be overcome through effective communication from the central to the regional and local levels by the use of conventional communication methods (e.g. forums, meetings and workshops). This approach will limit the top-down communication methods, policies and decision-making systems that minimize the opportunity for local people to participate in decisions concerning sustainable tourism planning and development in developing countries.

Stakeholders' perspectives and concerns in tourism planning and development (Table 6.3) must be carefully analysed and incorporated at the design stage of any attraction or destination management. Primarily, the perceptions and attitudes of residents towards tourism and tourists must be assessed at the planning stages before successful sustainable tourism can be

Table 6.3. Conflicts of interest among stakeholders.

Stakeholder	Primary expectation	Secondary expectation
Investors	Financial return	Added value
Employees	Increased wages/salaries	Work satisfaction
Service providers	Competitiveness	Goodwill
Suppliers	Payment	Long-term relationships
Local residents	Safety and security	Contribution to community
Tourists	Supply of service	Quality
Government	Compliance	Improved competitiveness
Special interest groups	Conservation and preservation	Equity and fairness

Adapted from Lynch, 1997.

developed. Successful tourism must engage the host community in a direct and meaningful participation in the planning and decision-making processes at the very early stages. Any tourism development must promote a sense of ownership in the community. Traditionally, the aim of tourism planners is how to attract visitors by increasing visitor numbers and developing the infrastructure that is required for the destination to achieve this. It is generally assumed that the more people visit a destination, the more people from the community will benefit. However, in some instances this is not the case as major developments may have a huge negative impact on the destination. Therefore, sustainable tourism requires the support of local residents, effective management and use of resources for the proper conservation, protection and use of land and the environment, as well as for the benefit of all stakeholders.

It should be noted that collaboration is not a panacea to achieving sustainable tourism, but it has its benefits. The potential benefits of collaboration and partnerships in tourism are as follows:

- Introduction of changes and improvements as a result of the contributions of a range of stakeholders.
- A likely increase in the social acceptance of policies.
- Working together may improve cooperation, understanding and mutual respect.
- Innovation and effectiveness may increase through the sharing of ideas and benchmarking.
- Likely increase in commitment.
- Development of skills.
- Pooling of resources to achieve economies of scale and efficiency.
- Sensitivity of policy to local values and residents' expectations.
- Broadening of the local economic and social base.

In the same vein, as much as collaboration may be beneficial, its implementation may also be very problematic. Barriers to achieving successes in collaboration and partnership initiatives in tourism include the following:

- Limited or no awareness of benefits of collaborative initiatives.
- Lack of access to collaborative opportunities.
- Reluctance to trust potential partners, particularly if they are competitors.
- Communication problems.
- Partners are likely to focus on and advance their individual organizational goal/interest.

Mason (2008) also highlighted potential problems of collaboration and partnership in tourism:

- Possibility of paying lip service to an issue.
- Possibility of under-resourcing collaborative efforts, both in materials and personnel.
- Stakeholders with lesser power may be excluded and alienated.
- Varying vested interest of multiple stakeholders may block innovation.
- Complexity of engaging diverse stakeholders in policy making.
- Effects of fragmented decision making on implementation.
- Creation of power blocks.

Sustainable Livelihoods

Sustainable tourism, in many quarters, is considered as the promised cure for alleviating all the problems of negative tourism impacts by ensuring the long-term viability of a destination and improving the quality of life of its local residents. Due to conceptual and practical deficiencies that have hampered the application of the sustainable tourism ideal, particularly in the area of socioeconomic prosperity of local people in both tourism and tourism-related businesses, a number of authors (see for example Tao and Wall, 2009) have suggested the concept of 'sustainable livelihood' as an alternative approach to achieve socioeconomic prosperity.

According to Wilson and Boyle (2006), there is a wide area of interest in the potential of inter-organizational relationships and collaboration in the management of heritage sites, notwithstanding participation of local communities over the last 30 years in the creation of benefits that could not be realized otherwise by organizations operating on their own.

Case Study 6.2. Elmina.

Elmina's history dates back to 1470, when Portuguese explorers discovered gold along the West African coast. Due to the proximity of the goldfields and its strategic location, Elmina became the centre of the West African gold business. The Portuguese founded a castle 'Sao Jorge' (St George) to protect the gold-rich lands in 1482. When the castle was completed in 1486 the town was raised to the status of a 'city'. However, in 1637, the Dutch took control of Elmina by defeating the Portuguese. They then expanded the castle to its present structure, reflecting the enormous wealth that gold and slavery had brought to the city. At the height of the slave trade in the 17th century, Elmina became the focal distribution point before slaves were shipped to America.

The castles in Elmina attract approximately 100,000 tourists annually, 70,000 of which are foreign tourists (Arthur and Mensah, 2006). With the steady growth in visitor numbers, private investors have noticed the potential of Elmina as a tourist destination and started investing in the supply side of tourism in the form of hotels with good-quality restaurants. Arthur and Mensah, however, argue that in spite of the economic potential of the heritage monuments and increased visitor numbers, the locals have not benefited from tourism-related employment opportunities. Living standards in Elmina are so low that this is reflected in the community and the environment. The thriving fishing harbour has become dilapidated with silt and pollution, the beaches are covered with waste, the city's drainage system is poor and basic road, telecommunication and electricity infrastructures are either broken or inadequate. There are huge constraints on health care and education opportunities, with a subsequent impact on living standards of the residents.

Arthur and Mensah (2006) stated that Elmina is in dire need of an overhaul and that the Elmina District Assembly cannot do the overhaul on its own. Therefore, help is required from potential partners in the private sector, community and educational institutions, in addition to support from the central government and to a larger extent international agencies.

Complexity in relation to the interdisciplinary nature of conservation, tourism and visitor access management prompted UNESCO (1998) to suggest that heritage site management must be integrative and proactive by involving key stakeholders; the use of inter-organizational relationships and collaboration could also be helpful in protecting sites from conflicting uses and inappropriate development. UNESCO (1998) provided for 'the participation of local people in the nomination process' with the view of securing shared responsibility for the care of inscribed sites in paragraph 14 of its guidelines on World Heritage Sites management. UNESCO's suggestion was backed by Bryson (2004), who stated that the management of World Heritage Sites is within the remit of 'inter-organizational domain', meaning the public and private sectors, non-profit organizations and local communities must collaborate to achieve a common goal.

Wilson and Boyle (2006) referred to the World Heritage Congress in 2002, which identified the need for a formal structure for participation and collaboration between the public and private sectors to provide a solid grounding in planning work that involves or integrates the voices of the various stakeholders in any situation. The formal structure should include well-established regulatory powers and working partnerships between public and private organizations for any heritage site to be planned and managed effectively (Middleton and Hawkins, 1998). The relationship between the different sectors and the environment within which the tourism industry operates is not self-generating; it needs direction, and sustainability can only be achieved on a collaborative basis.

Corporate Social Responsibility

With reference to the World Bank's (2007) definition of corporate social responsibility (CSR), which states that '[CSR] is the commitment of businesses to contribute to sustainable economic development, working with employees, their families, local community and society at large to improve the quality of life – in ways that are both good for business and good for development', it can be deduced that the concept of CSR – if embedded at the planning and development stage of sustainable m, communicated effectively and involv- all stakeholders – may play a vital role in tributing to successful tourism management and help avoid any future conflict among stakeholders. Incorporating the principles and practices in the areas of business ethics, corporate citizenship and sustainability or the stakeholders' view of both the supply-side and demand-side of the tourism industry through the use of effective communication (which must take place at all levels between and amongst the different stakeholders) will create common ground and understanding of some of the sustainability issues and the potential of CSR to enhance business viability and longevity. The tourism industry could use community-based organisations and non-governmental organisations at local levels as intermediaries to promote a local interpretation of the CSR framework. Creating a clear and univocal understanding of what CSR means might maximize the participation of local communities, in particular small and micro businesses (WTO, World Bank and USAID 2006).

Communication in the CSR concept must be in appropriate language that can be understood by all stakeholders. This is essential to help tourism organizations and tourists understand and adopt relevant environmental and social sustainable standards and systems such as environmental management systems, fair trade and community relations. It can also create better relationships among large tourism operators, local communities and small- to medium-size enterprises, allowing the development of better and more successful partnerships.

Current Research and Debates

As mentioned earlier, there is lack of consensus regarding the definition and meaning of the concept of sustainable tourism. It must be noted that there has never been a shortage of efforts and attempts to provide better understanding. However, Gunn and Turgut (2002), in reference to the various attempts made, submitted that most contributions to the explanation and definition of sustainable tourism add more confusion than clarity. The debate is wide-

ranging and the direction of any given argument is, obviously, dependent on the values of each stakeholder.

Although sustainable tourism is a valid area of study, going by the number of academic journals and magnitude of research seen over the years, it remains a heavily contested concept. It is generally acknowledged that its focal point is the wise use of resources, but the way in which 'wise use' is articulated is dependent upon the values of various stakeholders. This varied value base has no doubt contributed to the myriad of debates and studies witnessed in this field over the years.

The concept of sustainability has become an important field of academic research in tourism planning and development. Areas of research in this field are as varied as its definition. One can identify a wide range of research focuses, which include visitors' experiences and management, conservation and resource management, collaboration and community participation, transport in tourism development and planning and policy development and assessment. Others include the development of indicators for sustainability, local economic sustainability and livelihood, resident–tourist relationships and tourist behaviour. However, the two major themes that have featured prominently in sustainability discussions are economic and environmental sustainability. The following two sections explore these two areas in detail.

Economic overview

The tourism industry comprises a vast range of economic activities and is considered the only major service sector in which developing countries do record trade surpluses year on year. It is also an important source of employment, albeit with poor wages paid to employees, creation of unskilled labour and encouragement of migration from poor rural areas. Tourism may be considered as a sector that contributes significantly towards the empowerment of women and provides jobs for the unskilled local labour force, therefore alleviating poverty. However, McLaren (2003) stated that many researchers are sceptical about the magnitude of the local economic impact inherited from the tourism industry in developing countries. The main focus is the perceived multiplier effect, which suggests that earnings from tourism will flow through transactions of workers into the local economy, neglecting the fact that benefits from the industry are unevenly distributed and even made worse through internal and external economic leakages (McLaren, 2003). Ownership of the main components of tourism (transportation, accommodation and procurement of tourists) tends to be dominated by foreign companies and influences the extent of economic leakages through repatriation of tourism revenue in the form of profits, income and imports.

Sharpley (2000) argued that, apart from inequalities in benefits distribution, there are also socioeconomic inequities in developing countries brought about by the control and influence exerted by powerful economic and political players in tourism, which inevitably places local entrepreneurs at a major disadvantage. McLaren (2003) opined that in many developing countries, promised job opportunities in tourism have never been realized and when there are jobs, they tend to be temporary, menial and low wage, as compared to other comparable occupations. Moreover, most middle and top management positions are occupied by foreigners, with little or no opportunity for locals to move up.

In most developing countries, local people or entrepreneurs are denied access to the tourism market because of the enclave forms of tourism. Tourists are sometimes advised that it is not safe to interact with the local community; therefore, tourists tend to confine themselves to their hotels. With the advent of 'all-inclusive' package holidays, this makes it even more difficult for local traders to sell to tourists. For tourism to be sustainable in a competitive world market there is a need to operate in ways that enable local people to have better access to tourism and minimize leakages, and implement strategies that add value to livelihoods through employment and small-business development, strive to encourage projects that contribute to local economy and not just national economy, maintain natural and cultural assets and develop plans to control negative social impacts.

The growth rate of tourism must be controlled and, finally, all stakeholders must be involved in decision-making processes.

Environmental overview

Besides the economic benefits for many countries, regions and communities generated from the activities of the tourism sector, there must be a cautious approach in expanding the sector rapidly due to adverse environmental and sociocultural impacts.

Depletion of natural resources and environmental degradation associated with tourism activities can pose serious problems in tourism regions. Management of natural resources to reverse damage done to the environment can be very challenging for governments, especially in developing countries and regions. Therefore, implementation of effective environmental management and visitor management strategies for protecting natural resources and local ecosystems is necessary to control tourism expansion (Neto, 2002).

Tourism also exerts undue pressure on cultural and heritage resources. These attract tourists, and as such there is a strong case for their protection, conservation and enhancement. Heritage destinations experience many pressures. Tourist flows and uncontrolled tourist development may affect the architectural character of a historic town and hence create conflicts between the host community and other stakeholders. Land-use conflicts, access to local resources and services and costs of living can all adversely impact quality of life.

The adverse impacts of tourism include pressure on natural resources – that is, pressure on the availability and prices of resources consumed by local residents. Consequently, without careful land-use planning and tourism development, natural landscapes can be threatened by loss of wetlands and soil erosion. The expansion of coastal and ocean tourism activities can threaten coral reefs and disturb marine aquatic life. Furthermore, pollution and waste generation is a major problem for many developing countries and regions that are unable to treat waste materials properly. Improper disposal of untreated waste may contribute to the reduction of or damage to coral reefs and other marine resources, consequently discouraging tourism and damaging future local tourist businesses and fisheries.

Unarguably, tourism involves travelling. The mode of transport may be a combination of road, land, sea or air. Land and sea travel play a major role in bringing tourists into many hard-to-reach areas (Bredenhann and Wickens, 2004), but the majority of tourists travel by air. With the prediction of the WTO (2001) that long-haul air travel between world regions is set to grow rapidly to remote destinations and countries at the development stage of tourism, airlines are therefore deemed major contributors to air pollution. 'The economic and social benefits of increasing tourist mobility have, however, created a major sustainability dilemma' (Becken, 2006). Traffic congestion, noise and air pollution, accidents, greenhouse gas emissions, resource depletion and other environmental problems are attributed to the negative impacts from tourist transport. With all the negative impacts of tourist transport on the environment, it is no coincidence that the WTO (2003) has been attracted to the global issues on the contribution made by tourist transport to the anthropogenic emissions of greenhouse gases, and the ever-increasing fears about global climate change and its consequences for tourism and for the future of the planet.

Future Research

Tourism and related services can have both negative and positive impacts on sustainable tourism development. In one aspect, they can stimulate economic growth, which is to a great extent needed in developing countries for the provision of vital resources for protecting the environment and promoting conservation of natural and cultural heritage. On the other side of the coin, tourism can have tremendous negative impacts on local communities in the form of inequalities in employment, unfair distribution of benefits and uncontrolled developments that gravely affect the social and physical environment.

The negative effects appear to be greater among developing countries and poorer segments of society. Developing countries are, therefore, faced with huge challenges in creating appropriate policies and strategies that enhance sustainable tourism planning and development while staying within the remit of international obligations on trade.

This calls for further research on the effects of mass tourism promotion, liberalization in tourism, service provision in developing countries and the implementation of safety valves such as schedule limitations, public welfare protection, quality of life, visitor experience and a balance between the economic benefits of tourism among all stakeholders. Effective visitor management tools such as tourism carrying capacity and zoning need to be considered.

In the developed countries of the world, the CSR concept is not new in other business sectors. In the tourism sector, however, the principles and practices are only mentioned in the ecotourism movement and within hospitality. It is therefore recommended that future research is intensified in this area to assess the impact on all the different stakeholders and at all levels of planning and developing sustainable tourism.

Conclusion

Sustainable tourism is an accepted paradigm, although complex and besieged with controversies. Its focus is on meeting the needs and wants of the host community, satisfying the demands of tourists and the tourism industry, and safeguarding the environmental resource base for tourism.

Sustainable tourism management requires careful consideration. A long-term and holistic planning perspective is necessitated by the diverse nature of tourism and the relationship between tourist activities and the environment. In order to provide the necessary resources for visitor management, a systematic approach, standardized collection of visitor data and knowledge-based planning approach are needed to protect areas that can impact on natural and cultural resources and the quality of the visitor experience.

While the sustainable tourism development concept and principles have been well instituted in the Western developed world, less developed countries are still grappling with the basic art of sustainability and are mostly not closely linking the concept to destinations' social and cultural dynamics, by error or omission. Often the focus is on economic sustainability which is, most of the time, not achievable as a result of developing countries' fragile economic structure, low bargaining power and limited expertise in the field.

Review Questions

1. Conduct a literature search and extract at least five different definitions of the concept of sustainable tourism. Conduct a critique of these definitions and choose one that you think describes the concept appropriately.

2. Evaluate the role that communication can play in designing and implementing sustainable tourism strategies and projects in your country.

3. What is meant by corporate social responsibility? How can its incorporation in business activities by tourism suppliers enhance the quality of life of local residents at a tourist destination?

4. Evaluate the overall benefits that sustainable tourism can bring to the local community in Elmina.

References

Adu-Febiri, F. (1994) *Tourism and Ghana's Development Process: Problems of and Prospects for Creating a Viable "Post-industrial" Service Industry in a Non-industrial Society.* University of British Colombia, British Columbia, Canada.

Arthur, S.N.A and Mensah, J.V (2006) Urban management and heritage tourism for sustainable development. *Management of Environmental Quality: an International Journal* 17, 299–312.

Becken, S. (2006) Tourism and transport: the sustainability dilemma. *Journal of Sustainable Tourism* 14, 113–116.

Bredenhann, J. and Wickens, E. (2004) Tourism routes as a tool for the economic development of rural areas – vibrant hope or impossible dream? *Tourism Management* 15, 13–22.

Bryson, J.M. (2004) *Strategic Planning for Public and Non-Profit Organizations*, 3rd edn. Jossey-Bass, San Francisco, California.

Buckley, R. (2004) Skilled commercial adventure: the edge of tourism. In: Singh, T.V. (ed.) *New Horizons in Tourism: Strange Experience and Strange Practices*. CAB International, Wallingford, UK, pp. 37–48.

Byrd, E.T. (2007) Stakeholder in sustainable tourism development and their roles: applying stakeholder theory to sustainable tourism development. *Tourism Review* 62, 6–13.

Coccossis, H. (2008) Cultural heritage, local resources and sustainable tourism. *International Journal Services Technology and Management* 10, 8–14.

Coccossis, H.N. and Parpairis, A. (2000) Tourism and the environment – some observations on the concept of carrying capacity. In: Briassoulis, H. and van der Straaten, J. (eds) *Tourism and the Environment. Regional, Economic, Cultural and Policy Issues*. Kluwer Academic, London, UK, pp. 91–106.

Eagles, P., McCool, S.F. and Hayes, C. (2002) *Sustainable Tourism in Protected Areas: Guidelines for Planning and Management*. IUCN Gland, Switzerland and Cambridge, UK.

ETC (2001) *A Time for Action: A Strategy for Sustainable Tourism in England*. English Tourism Council, London, UK.

European Commision (2002) *Defining, Measuring and Evaluating Carrying Capacity in European Tourism Destinations*. B4–3040/2000/294577/MAR/D2. Athens, Greece.

Getz, D. (1987) Tourism planning and research: traditions, models and future. Proceedings of the Australian Travel Research Workshop, 5–6 November, Bunbury, Western Australia.

Ghana Tourism (2008) Castles – Ghana Tourist Homepage. Available from: http://www.touringghana.co/castles/index.asp. Accessed 22 February, 2010.

Gunn, C.A. and Turgut V. (2002) *Tourism Planning: Basic, Concepts and Cases*, 4th edn. Routledge, New York.

Hall, C.M. (2000) *Tourism Planning: Policies, Processes and Relationship*. Pearson Education, Harlow, UK.

Henderson, J.C. (2009) Agro-tourism in unlikely destinations: a study of Singapore. *Managing Leisure* 14, 258–268.

Inskeep, E. (1991) *Tourism Planning: An Integrated and Sustainable Development Approach*. Van Nostrand Reinhold, New York.

Lynch, R. (1997) *Corporate Strategy*. Pitman Publishing, London, UK.

Mason, P. (2005) Visitor management in protected areas: from 'hard' to 'soft' approaches? *Current Issues in Tourism* 8, 181–194.

Mason, P. (2008) *Tourism Impacts, Planning and Management*. Butterworth-Heinemann, Oxford, UK.

Mayers, J. and Vermeulen, S. (2005) *Stakeholder Influence Mapping*. International Institute for Environment and Development. Available from: http://www.policy-powertools.org/Tools/Understanding/docs/stakeholder_influence_mapping_tool_english.pdf. Accessed 22 March, 2010.

McLaren, D. (2003) *Rethinking Tourism and Ecotravel*, 2nd edn. Kumarian Press, West Hartford, CT.

Middleton, T.C. and Hawkins, R. (1998) *Sustainable Tourism: A Marketing Perspective*. Butterworth Heinemann, Oxford, UK.

Muller, T.E. and Cleaver, M. (2000) Targeting the CANZUS baby boomer explorer and adventurer segments. *Journal of Vacation Marketing* 6, 154–169.

Neto, F. (2002) Sustainable Tourism, Environmental Protection and Natural Resource Management: Paradise on Earth? International Colloquium on Regional Governance and Sustainable Development in Tourism-Driven Economies, United Nations. Cancun, Mexico, 20–22 February, 2002.

Newsome, D., Moore, S. and Dowling, R.K. (2002) *Natural Area Tourism: Ecology, Impact and Management*. Channel View Publications, Clevedon, UK.

Oppermann, M. (1996) Holidays on the farm: a case study of German hosts and guests. *Journal of Travel Research* 34, 63–67.

Sharpley, R. (2000) Tourism and sustainable development: exploring the theoretical divide. *Journal of Sustainable Tourism* 8, 1–19.

Swarbrooke, J. (1998) *Sustainable Tourism Management*. CAB International, Wallingford, UK.

UNESCO (1998) *Convention Concerning the Protection of the World Cultural and Natural Heritage. Report of the 22nd Session*. World Heritage Committee, Kyoto, Japan.

Tao, T.C.H. and Wall, G. (2009) Tourism as a sustainable livelihood strategy. *Tourism Management* 30, 90–98.

WCED (1987) *Our Common Future*. Oxford University Press, Oxford, UK.

Weaver, D. (2006) *Sustainable Tourism: Theory and Practice*. Butterworth-Heinemann, Oxford, UK.

Wilson, L.A and Boyle, E. (2006) Interorganisational collaboration at UK World Heritage Sites. *Leadership and Organisation Development Journal* 27, 501–523.

World Bank (2007) *Corporate Social Responsibility and Corporate Citizenship in the Arad World*. Cairo, Egypt.

WTO (1999) *Tourism Market Trends: Africa 1998–1999*. World Tourism Organization Commission for Africa, Madrid, Spain.

WTO (2001) Guide for local authorities on developing sustainable tourism Madrid. World Tourism Organization, Madrid, Spain.

WTO (2003) *Proceedings of the International Conference on Climate Change and Tourism. Djerba, Tunisia*. World Tourism Organization, Madrid, Spain.

WTO (2010) 2009 International Tourism Results and Prospects for 2010, UNWTO news conference. Available from: http://www.unwto.org/pdf/Barometro_1_2010_en.pdf. Accessed July 1, 2010. World Tourism Organization, Madrid, Spain.

WTO, World Bank and USAID (2006) *Communication and Sustainable Tourism: Proceedings of the Global E- Conference and Summer Speaker Series on the Role of Development Communication in Sustainable Tourism. WTO, World Bank and USAID*.

WTTC (2009) Ghana: International Arrivals and Average Trip Spend. Available from: http://www.wttc.org/eng/Tourism_Research/Tourism_Impact_Data_and Forecast Tool. World Travel and Tourism Council, London, UK.

7 Community Tourism

Peter Robinson and Peter Wiltshier

Introduction

Community tourism evolves from one of two perspectives. Either the community has a vision of how their place of work or their home can be a destination and the way in which this is connected to the potential for community development, or the community gains the net impacts of their proximity to a major tourist destination. These may be positive, such as the increased popularity and economic growth enjoyed in places such as Whitby as a result of the association with Dracula and the various television programmes that have been filmed there.

However, the benefits of tourism are not always passed on to the communities where the impacts of tourism are felt. Bladon in Oxfordshire, UK, is one such example. This small village, located on the edge of the Blenheim Palace estate (a World Heritage Site) has a typical village church and graveyard, which includes the burial place of Sir Winston Churchill. Despite huge interest from coach parties and individual visitors, tourism has brought little benefit to this community, which has seen the closure of pubs and the total loss of the village shop and post office. Here, there is clear capacity to benefit from tourism.

Similarly, there are other places where the community has a strong identity and is known for its traditions and festivals. An example is Wirksworth in the Peak District (a UK National Park). Wirksworth has a long established and very popular arts festival, yet for many years there was no clear link between this single event and the wider benefit that could be derived from

a clear and cohesive approach to tourism development.

In essence community-based tourism (CBT) is based upon a useful combination of resources, resources plus strategy, values, vision and sufficient projects with resources to be implemented and developed. This chapter explores these issues from a developmental perspective, and considers how tourism can become a part of the community and the ways in which it can contribute to economic growth and social cohesion, explained through both theoretical perspectives and case studies.

A Historical Perspective

Since the dawn of the jet age and affordable mass transportation, communities have been able to enjoy greater benefits from an increased number of visitors – invited and uninvited – as transport, accommodation, food and drink and modest entertainment have become more accessible to a wider range of consumers.

At the same time, especially in the UK since European Economic Community accession in 1973, communities in rural locations have recognized that an increased share of their income is now derived from services such as tourism and not from traditional commercial activities such as farming and manufacturing.

It is this decline in primary activities such as farming and manufacturing, and an increase in the delivery of services such as tourism and technology, that has led communities to slowly recognize that their values, vision, goals and strategies for community development are more dependent on a healthy mix of tourism and other forms of service delivery.

CBT development is therefore dependent on adequate supplies of goods and services developed for and within the host community. This must be coupled to a shared set of values and vision developed over a period of time with stakeholders in that community and public sector resources for ongoing maintenance of sustainable and responsible tourism that has been devised by community residents and business owners under shared social, economic and environmental factors.

Definitions

France (1997) offered insight into the approach and the nature of community tourism as an alternative management approach, describing it as 'A type of tourism run by and for the local community. It may be alternative in character... or may cater for larger numbers and have more in common with aspects of mass tourism [it can even] be associated with organised packages and even coach travel'. She went on to provide a useful historic contextualization, noting that in 1991 the Department for the Environment identified that among the guiding principles it proposed for sustainable development, it is implicit that such initiatives would only be successful if there was a 'movement towards integration of the physical environment, the cultural environment (host community) and the tourist ... future planning of tourism [requires effort] to incorporate community representation into the planning process'. However there is also recognition within this that it will be difficult to achieve because of the problem of 'defining the true meaning of community because of its diversity and complexity of social construction', which makes 'universal agreement of such wide representations of interests ... difficult'.

A further definition offered by Mathieson and Wall (2006) 'refers to enhancement, at the local level, of the capability to participate in the development process. Opportunities should be provided for local participation in tourism, both directly through investment in and employment in tourist businesses as well as in supporting activities such as agriculture and craft industries'. It is these relationships that need to

be understood. Shaw and William (2004) recognized that communities 'may resist or embrace, or simply be overwhelmed by, the influences of the tourists. These host–guest relationships are central to tourism experiences and tourism impacts'.

Tourism concern (Shaw and William, 2004) suggests tourism should involve the following:

- Be run with the involvement and consent of local communities, which of course links directly with the ideas of community participation.
- Be in a position to share profits 'fairly' with the local community.
- Involve communities rather than individuals.

There is, however, a range of limiting factors (Murphy, 1985; Jenkins, 1993; Beech and Chadwick, 2006):

- Nature of politics and degree of political literacy and understanding.
- Nature of tourism and tourism issues.
- Perception of tourism and history of involvement in tourism.
- Attitudes of the media.
- Apathy among citizens.
- Cost in relation to time and money.
- Increase in decision-making time with community involvement.
- Ensuring fair opportunities for representation from the whole community.
- Lack of understanding of complex planning issues and processes.

For any community participation to be effective, Shaw and William (2004) highlighted that it is essential to integrate 'local community needs and ways of life with tourism developments to avoid the problems and conflicts associated with erosion of local cultures'. These ideals of community tourism 'are increasingly part of the state and [non-governmental organization] agendas billed under "community tourism" or "sustainable tourism"'.

Community Capital

This chapter develops the theme of shared socioeconomic and environmental factors under the umbrella of good sustainable practices, which are explored in all of the case studies, identifying inputs and outcomes that deliver a return to the host community. That return is comprised of socioeconomic and environmental benefits to both host and visitor and a measurable, long-term improvement in the capital invested in the relationship between host and visitor. This capital has at least two components: one is the inventory of goods and services owned and developed within the community by the community (residents, businesses, groups, charities and other stakeholders; discussed later) and the second is the social capital owned in common by the community. Social capital can be perceived as identifiable from other forms of capital, infrastructure or regional enterprises and social services. The social capital is held in equal shares by residents and business owners within the community and is derived from education, skills, knowledge, esteem, recognition and health, all of which are attributable to the benefits that tourism brings to the destination.

Supply Issues

Inherent in the successful and sustainable development of CBT is the view that scarce resources need to be managed effectively to maximize the return on the deployment and management of commercial activity, including services management and tourism. Tourism development is therefore seen as a historical process of structural changes that are essentially driven by innovation and embedding new forms or organization and management. The conceptual view of tourism is as a driver of economic development using innovation-driven qualitative change through the introduction of new combinations of political freedom, economic facilities, social opportunities, transparency guarantees and security (Schumpeter, 1943; Sen, 2006).

A successful CBT regime is dependent on maximizing a return on the economic and social investment in tourism compared to a range of alternative, or substituted, goods and services using existing and planned resources available.

A decision support process and system is useful in identifying whether tourism is an appropriate and sustainable commercial activity for the destination. The elements of a decision support process required to determine the likelihood that tourism is an appropriate and sustainable option comprise a resource audit, skills audit of community residents and business owners, inventory of components of competitive advantage, evolving community satisfaction indicators, legacy of sociopolitical structures, supportive legislation, quality of life indicators and impact analysis.

Case Study 7.1. Linking communities through tourism.

West Oxfordshire, branded as 'The Oxfordshire Cotswolds', is characterized by the historic market town of Witney and the famous village of Burford, with its steep hill and golden stone buildings, acting as a mecca for tourists. It is wealthy area, close to the M40 and within the London commuter belt. It has a low population and is distinctly rural. Most communities are based around small villages, many on the main routes into the district, but others are hidden away off the beaten track. Traditional villages in this area still retain their manor house, church and pub, and in some cases a village shop. However, the appeal of these villages has led to many houses being bought as second homes or holiday cottages and the traditional community has been degraded. This has led to a breakdown in community spirit and the apparent wealth of the area also hides pockets of deprivation; rural deprivation is much harder to identify than it is in urban areas. In response to this, the local authority has worked hard to include these villages within the tourism product, focusing on walking trails and cycle routes, linked to places to stop and eat, and highlighting specific features that are worth visiting such as churches, village pubs, quaint tea rooms and attractive architecture. This is an effective way of bringing additional tourism into these rural backwaters and while this may exacerbate the appeal of second homes it does, at least, encourage people to spend money in local pubs, make donations to churches and discover another dimension of the destination.

The Role of the Small- and Medium-sized Enterprise

Most communities working within the framework of CBT comprise small- and medium-sized enterprises (SMEs). The success of CBT, therefore, is predicated on successful socioeconomic capital development and return on investment to compare the destination against a basket of comparable community-based sustainable examples to identify the nature of successful CBT in practice. This benchmarking is currently the only way to measure success. Globally, tourism is a series of complex and highly interdependent organizations linked to provide core and ancillary services for consumers. These organizations are typically SMEs, characterized by the scale of operations. SMEs have few employees, are often built around the family, tend to specialize in some aspect of services for visitors, usually have specialist skills and are ultimately focused on delivering specific goods and services to the visitor. This is illustrated by Case Study 7.2.

SMEs typically build business and resources around the goodwill of the family or the owner-operator. The disadvantages of the small scale of operation of SMEs are as follows:

Case Study 7.2. Wirksworth.

The pretty post-industrial heritage town of Wirksworth is located on the south-east boundary of the Peak District National Park, which was established in 1951 and is now the busiest national park in Britain and second most visited in the world. In the late 1970s with the demise of quarrying and mining in the district, the local council and parish decided to bid for public funds to restore the town's fine Georgian architecture and ultimately ensure Wirksworth would become a great place to live and work.

Mining has been associated with Wirksworth since Roman times and the town stands at what was once the core of the lead mining industry in England. The town has a fine collection of Georgian market-town vernacular architecture and Richard Arkwright's Mill at Cromford, the heart of the Industrial Revolution, and the Derwent Valley Mills World Heritage Site are located adjacent. In addition to the Wirksworth Festival, visitor attractions include the Wirksworth Heritage Centre, the Ecclesbourne Valley Railway, the National Stone Centre and the Cromford to High Peak Trail, as well as Carsington Water, a reservoir owned and operated by Severn Trent Water. All of these attractions and the festival have the potential to deliver 100,000 visitors each year to the town and create further employment in related services. Unfortunately some related negative factors emerged as researchers engaged in dialogue with stakeholders. Power elites, nimbyism, low levels of cross-sectoral interest between organizations, disagreement over sectoral and spatial development agendas, competition for public funding and finally the complete absence of any sector-specific or integrated implementation planning are notable, but certainly not unique to Wirksworth.

Central to this regeneration is a community-led organization, New Opportunities for Wirksworth (NOW!). NOW! is an organization run by and for local people, under the name of the Wirksworth Regeneration Board. It has articulated a tourism vision and mission statement that incorporates a strategy for tourism development that, in its own words, is designed to be 'a framework for Tourism Development which can operate at strategic level, as a tool for funding applications and for ensuring clear aims and objectives for businesses and residents in Wirksworth'. By the end of the 1980s the townspeople had undertaken reviews to address and reverse trends in economic decline and social deprivation, with a view to funding heritage building conservation that would retain the historic character of Wirksworth and focus on an improved local economy (Michell *et al.*, 1989). In 2002 a further report (Davies, 2002) was commissioned by the town council and funded through the East Midlands Development Agency. This report identified that further research into developing tourism and retail, the arts and education would be desirable from the perspective of local solutions for local problems and scoping of clusters to support regeneration was recommended. Over two decades a range of stakeholders from the arts, tourism, retail and services sectors, initially under a civic trust umbrella and funded through local government grants, considered various pathways to regeneration. Initial work focused on community consultation, resource provision (usually defined in this context as experts and their advice) and tended towards the unofficial rather than the official (Michell *et al.*, 1989). As Foley and Martin observed in 2000, governments have traditionally underestimated the practical problems at the local level: patchy support to endogenous policy creation, capacity concerns from the local community, effectiveness of disseminated experiences and lessons learned, low skill levels and lack of time resources provided by local and central government to the regeneration project.

- The difficulty in parallel development of resources and skills required to manage complex relationships with suppliers and consumers.
- Time needed to up-skill.
- Limited time and opportunities to reflect on the success of the current activity.
- Reduced purchasing power and negotiation for maximizing return on the investment because of scale.
- Limited control over product development.
- Legacy issues and inheritance of the business through succession planning.

Forecasting

Without doubt, the sustainability component of CBT is based around decision making informed by all of the relevant factors in social, economic and environmental development. To successfully manage the business now and into the future requires the business owner to be able to measure how well CBT is managed now and positioned in relation to a basket of other competing organizations and relative to the supply chain (vertical, horizontal and diagonal). Generally, there is a focus on three types of collaboration: vertical relationships, horizontal relationships and diagonal relationships. A vertical relationship can exist between suppliers and buyers – in Case Study 7.2, between a heritage tour operator, an accommodation provider and a transportation provider. We witness contemporary challenges and success in modern supply chain literature through the deliberate creation of collaborative strategic partnerships with select partners. Horizontal relationships occur between competing companies selling similar products or services, for example two competing coach tour operators. Diagonal relationships represent relationships that develop in different industries and sectors (Fyall and Spyriadis, 2003; Von Friedrichs Grängsjö, 2003).

To compete sustainably, a business must accumulate and articulate a range of analytical tools in planning for the future. These comprise a broad range of datasets, expert opinions and macro-economic scenario plans. At first glance these forecasting tools appear daunting to the

owner-operator of an SME. What can be simplified and made accessible to SMEs is a tool kit that empowers the owner-operator to comprehend strategic forecasting issues while simultaneously reinforcing or adapting, due to changes in the social, economic and physical environment, the values, mission and vision in contemporary CBT.

The toolkit comprises public and private perspectives on CBT, the contribution of the public sector, local or regional government best practices, sources of funding required for SMEs to develop their services, a review of employment and business creation statistics and other items required to attract inward investment and confidence from the supply chain. This chapter now looks at these issues as they contribute to a successful forecasting toolkit.

Public Sector Input

The public sector, typically represented by local government regeneration, plays an essential role in the delivery of CBT because of the intrinsic relationship between planning, development and economic growth derived from tourism. This is, however, often a contested issue because of the sensitive balance between growth and development and the need to retain community spirit. The primary point of contest, though, is the misunderstanding that often arises between community stakeholders and the local authority. The community can easily identify and will frequently comment on poor-quality public sector services, but often the relationship to ensure stakeholder buy-in does not exist. For example, a review of the economics of market towns is undertaken by the local government to inform development and regeneration, but the outcome does not drive product or service development by relevant stakeholders within that community. If understanding is created between both sides of the argument it becomes easier to explain, for example, what support the community needs and to work with the local authority to improve public toilets, develop tourist information resources and improve interpretation and signposting within the community.

There are generally clear lines of responsibility for the public sector and often these are prioritized through statutory (legal) requirements first, such as street cleaning, parking enforcement, litter and highway maintenance, and then the other duties that contribute to tourism. These may include planting flowers, installing street furniture and providing tourist information.

Additional debates exist within these developmental frameworks, such as charging for parking, provision of public transport and timings of roadworks and maintenance so as to not interfere with the tourist trade.

However, while a community investigating CBT may complain that not enough is done to support it in the public sector, other communities – those suffering the effects of overcrowding and capacity – may look to the local authority to ease pressure on their community through increased parking charges, greater parking enforcement or even admission charges, which can then be used to enhance and improve facilities.

These issues are not just relevant to rural destinations, with major urban centres investigating and implementing congestion charges (London and Durham, UK), improved public transport infrastructure (London and the Eurostar service between London and Paris) and increased intra-urban bus capacity. Furthermore, major cities are also investing in better interpretation and signage to direct tourists and manage their movements.

The key benefits that are derived in all these areas are shared across the community. As a result, they offer a shared benefit to both visitors and the local community.

Business Support Systems

In the UK, funding for tourism development is usually devolved to the regional government body, where it is managed through two tandem organizations and processes: the tourism board and the business development agency. To benefit from the business support system CBT acknowledges dual sources of funding, including match funding. Match funding supports service and product development by the acquisition of project funding, such as provided by Leader Plus, usually sourced via the regional government's coffers, and strategic development funding, often sourced through organizations such as Business Link, which can support sustainable capacity and organizational growth.

It is important that SMEs recognize the dual development opportunity that public sector funding offers in terms of strategic, long-term organizational goals as well as project funding, shorter-term 'pump-priming' and funding designed to support specific activity to broaden the base of the SME operationally. In short, business support systems help the SME to become part of a lobby for better sustainable business, provide a coherent, if not quite 'one-stop' shop approach to acquiring support and help owner-operators in their inevitable struggle to meet minimum performance standards and compliance with both industry and consumer expectations at the same time through understanding the need for baseline uniform standards in operations and promotion. Examples of dual funding and match funding activity are shown in Case Study 7.3.

Research and Information

A variety of sources must be used by owner operators and communities to determine appropriate sustainable pathways for tourism development. As observers have noted, there is a need for multidisciplinary and interdisciplinary approaches to developing sustainable CBT. Partnerships require effective understanding and skills in managing supply chain and distribution resources for sustainable approaches to development. Mathieson and Wall (2006), identified that 'communities are not homogenous, there are uneven power distributions, a multiplicity of stakeholders that are involved, different degrees of experience and tourism, a lack of desire to be involved ... a political and administrative history ... that is not conducive to such processes'.

Researchers commonly use public sources of data on employment, income, demographics and business ownership, creation and wealth distribution. In the UK, these datasets are available from the Office of National Statistics,

Case Study 7.3. Inverclyde Tourism Group.

Inverclyde is described by the local authority as the 'export capital of the world'. It is situated to the west of Glasgow and describes the area that borders the south side of the River Clyde, which is historically a major shipbuilding area, and includes the towns and villages of Gourock, Greenock, Port Glasgow, Wemyss Bay, Kilmacolm and Inverkip. In recent years the shipbuilding industry has declined, leading to a rise in unemployment. Amid the context of this decline there are a number of tourist attractions and facilities, including Newark Castle and the Clyde Muirshiel Regional Park. The area also has a small number of hotels and is close to both Glasgow and the tourist honeypots around the Trossachs and Loch Lomond, together with ferry crossings to the southerly Scottish islands of Bute and Great Cumbrae. It is also within a 30-minute drive of many Ayrshire attractions.

As a result the area has considerable tourism growth potential. Alongside this is a £400m public/private initiative, Riverside Inverclyde, which aims to regenerate the riverfront with new harbour and marine developments and residential, office and industrial space being created close to existing urban centres.

The close proximity to Glasgow, itself the recipient of considerable regeneration and rebranding since the early 1990s, has led to the increasing popularity of Greenock as a port of call for many UK cruises. Historically a weak infrastructure and no formal tourist information centre have meant that those disembarking have generally had little guidance and have headed out of the area to Glasgow, Loch Lomond or further afield.

In 2001, a group of friends created the Inverclyde Tourist Group as a voluntary organization to welcome cruise visitors, provide information and offer guided tours of Inverclyde. The group today numbers 50 members, has a formal organizational structure and uses facilities provided by Clydeport, which manages the harbour facilities. They provide multiple services to cruise visitors, including an individual welcome for each passenger, a welcome from a piper, the opportunity to meet Hamish the Inflatable Scotsman, tourist information, transport plans to reach destinations further from the coast and, most importantly, tours of the Inverclyde area and riverside, which has much to offer in terms of historical narratives, but requires good guiding to bring the history to life (Fig. 7.1). Cruises also receive a farewell from a Scottish pipe band as the ship departs.

In addition, the group is actively involved in community activities and education projects, striving to retain cruise visitors in the area by offering free local coach tours and encouraging passengers to remain within Greenock to benefit the local economy. The work of the group has had such a positive impact that it has received funding for training, marketing activities and promotional materials and benefits from strong positive relationships with the local media.

Although the community is still coming to terms with the loss of the traditional manufacturing industries, it are starting to welcome potential positive impacts of urban renewal under the auspices of Riverside Inverclyde in addition to investment from service-sector businesses such as T Mobile and RBS. A new theatre is under construction at the waterfront. The local council has revised its tourism strategy.

(Case study provided by Ann Macleod, Inverclyde Tourist Group; http://www.inverclydetouristgroup.co.uk)

Fig. 7.1. Images from Inverclyde.

the Official Labour Market Statistics. In addition, various tourism-related datasets should be consulted in preparing for sustainable CBT. These include the following:

- Tourism information systems: actual demand by number of arrivals, number of nights, period, origin of arrivals, purpose of trip, accommodation, final destination and combined purposes, origin and accommodation. These data are usually collected annually through random sampling.
- Quantitative data: expenditure per person and per family, expenditure per category, combination expenditure and other items. These data are collected every 3–4 years by random and targeted sampling.
- Demographic profiling and market research: family size, age, profession, method of booking, transport, repeat, information gathering, activities, evaluation. These data are every 3–4 years by sampling.
- Qualitative data: potential demand can be identified through consumption and supply trends, awareness, new markets, image and competitors. These data are collected every 3 years through a variety of desk research and focus groups.
- Tourism satellite accounts: these offer regional and national data:
  - tourism consumption by product and type of visitor (domestic, inbound, outbound, internal tourism consumed);
  - production accounts of tourism industries;
  - domestic demand;
  - employment;
  - gross fixed capital created;
  - tourism collective consumption; and
  - aggregate datasets – numbers of international visitors, number of nights, number of businesses.
- Marketplace surveys:
  - Mintel data;
  - international passenger surveys;
  - UK Tourism survey;
  - UK Day Visits survey; and
  - National Opinion Poll Holiday Survey.

Stakeholders

CBT relies on a wide range of stakeholders to facilitate the creation of tourism products. Effective stakeholder management also defines roles and responsibilities within communities. This can be achieved through a stakeholder analysis (Fig. 7.2), which identifies who has the most significant levels of interest and influence in the CBT.

Having identified the roles of the stakeholders, it is possible to assign tasks or identify responsibilities for the delivery of different elements of the CBT. So, if parking is an issue then a strategy or action plan should identify the local authority as the body responsible for this. When incorporated into a strategic framework, tasks can be given significance, timescales and ownership.

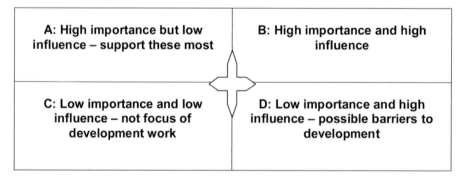

Fig. 7.2. Matrix of stakeholder analysis.

Case Study 7.4. Tourism orientation and competence: the example of the Chatham Islands of New Zealand.

The Chatham Islands are the most remote continuously inhabited islands of New Zealand. The island group has a declining population, which is estimated to be 750 people and falling. The group lies in the Southern Ocean some 800 kilometres to the east of New Zealand. This remoteness has led to the development of both a homogenous identity among the Chatham Island inhabitants, in that they identify as 'Chatham Islanders', and a more heterogeneous identity based on indigenous background. On the Chathams, two large groups vie for the position of being the first people. They are the Moriori, an early subgroup of the New Zealand Maori and the original people of the islands. The Moriori were followed by European sealers and whalers, and finally, in 1840, by a vicious Maori invasion that decimated the peaceful Moriori, then the majority on the islands. The Maori group claim to be the people of the land as the Maori are recognized as the original settlers of New Zealand – of which the Chatham group is part (King and Morrison, 1990). This has, in the past, created much tension and confusion while the Moriori and Maori play out their differences. Recognizing the need to generate both sympathy and funding, the Moriori have organized into a powerful political lobby. This has resulted in the establishment of a Moriori Marae, which occupies prime land overlooking Waitangi Bay.

The isolation of the islands has also led to development of a unique system of governance, which in some respects has not always been to the islands' benefit. This unique solution will form part of the following discussion regarding tourism competence. It is the very isolation, and the desire to experience something considered authentic that has attracted visitors to the islands in the last 5 years (Olsen, 2002; Bellingham and Cardow, 2005). Indeed, a desire to experience a wilderness is an attraction for a great number of visitors to New Zealand. In a wider context, tourism is vital to the continuing economic development of New Zealand. Figures provided by the Ministry of Tourism suggest that tourism is a NZ$17.5 billion industry that contributes 9% of New Zealand gross domestic product and employs 176,000 full-time equivalents or 9.8% of the total workforce. These figures place tourism and tourism activities in New Zealand as the largest income earner for the country, just ahead of agriculture. On the Chatham Islands, however, tourism as a tool for sustainable economic development has been very slow to be recognized. Part of this lack of traction has to with the inherent tourism orientation of the islanders, and part has to do with systemic tourism competence on the Chathams in that, on the islands at least, fishing, not tourism, has historically been seen as the tool for sustainable economic development. The growing awareness that fishing is declining has only in the last 5 years led some on the islands to shift their focus towards the emergent tourism industry (Wiltshier and Cardow, 2001; Bellingham and Cardow, 2005; Cardow and Wiltshier, 2006).

From small beginnings in 2001 to an acceptance of tourism in 2005, various tourism operators on the Chathams have grouped together to form a visitor industry group. This industry group comprises operators of the only two hotels on the island and a mixture of motel operators, bed and breakfast operators and activity providers. The visitor industry group has branded the experience a visitor receives on the islands as 'life on the edge'. Although the industry group has a brand, it is divided as to what that brand actually means and its members have not in the past worked cooperatively to provide a tourism product. For example, both of the hotel operators operate their own rental car facility and provide their own guides. This is a situation replicated by the motel operators. In addition, there has been reluctance within the Chatham Islands' tourism community to cooperatively offer their products by way of joint marketing opportunities. Cai (2002) suggested that one way in which a remote location can begin to utilize tourism as a tool for economic development is to cooperatively brand the destination. For this to happen, Cai suggested that all actors involved in the tourism industry must both buy into the 'brand' as opposed to a destination name and act cooperatively in order to secure the economic advantages that spring from such a collective image (Cai, 2002). However, for the tourism operators on the Chatham's, despite having a brand it would appear that it is economic life on the edge of profitability.

Entrepreneurship

Recent research tends to suggest that CBT is successful when approached in an entrepreneurial way, with a leader in the community driving the project forwards. It appears to work less effectively where the input and driver of change come from outside the community, through the public sector or project staff. The stakeholders within communities exchange knowledge informally and develop a single identity, shared values and knowledge through problem solving, mutual work and everyday interactions. In an organization there are visible communities of practice and some that are not easily detectible since the members keep changing. Internalized knowledge is exchanged directly and implicit knowledge is embedded in community values, identity, brand and image and everyday performance is connected through a specific context in tourism and regeneration. Project staff develop communities of practice and act as moderators whose responsibility is to direct the community towards outcomes. Important individuals may be members of different communities and also act as 'boundary spanners' across such divides and help knowledge move between these communities.

Partnership and Networks

Tourism is by its very nature multilayered, complex and multidisciplinary. CBT requires operators and public and private sector interests to work collaboratively to ensure success in the highly competitive destination marketplace. 'Individuals, organisations and firms are not isolated, independent actors separately contributing their piece to the total value created for customers; they are parts of value chains and networks through which value is co-created and co-delivered' (March and Wilkinson, 2009). For the SME, that means investment in membership of relevant organizations, such as the destination management partnership, the regional tourism organisation and the regional marketing organisation as a minimum. Subscription is the normal route to membership, with some partnerships being maintained for a few hundred pounds each year on subscription.

Other partnerships demand a larger investment in terms of time, such as the local chamber of commerce, business round table or other professional organization in tourism. The latter organizations may include the Institute of Travel and Tourism, the Tourism Management Institute or other national organization that provide resources and appropriate training and skills updates at nominal charges. Membership of these professional organizations can usually be maintained for a few hundred pounds on annual subscription.

Of course, the added advantage of membership of regional and national organizations is both acknowledgement of minimum performance standards by the SME and its staff and benchmarking the quality of service provision in an often highly competitive market environment. It is also important to identify that membership of informal organizations, such as the local chamber of commerce or a local action group, can lead to pre-empting the competition in new projects and development funding through access to public sector policy initiatives and documents. This can also facilitate shared marketing and publicity and contribute to shared costs, reducing the burden on individual organizations and creating a strong and identifiable brand for the community destination. In addition, shared buying power for gifts and local produce can enhance economies of scale between businesses working in synergy.

Demand issues

In operating in free-market conditions, the CBT operator will be highly influenced by and subject to vagaries in market conditions in both the home market and international demand. Political and sociocultural changes have proven to be hugely important in the sustainability and success of SMEs in tourism. In 2001, foot-and-mouth disease outbreaks set many SMEs back in terms of profits and business growth for up to 5 years as a result of the restricted movement of people in rural Britain. This was further influenced in the international market by the rise of factions linked to terrorism in the global market place and security concerns impacting on the free and ready movement of visitors between North America, Asia and Europe. This highlights the need for CBT and SMEs to recognize the fluidity of demand, including the waning of demand in times of political strife and as a result of health and safety issues well beyond the ready control of the individual operator or the destination marketing organization itself. This strengthens the argument for collaborative working. This can also be linked into the retailing of local products, local foods and fair trade produce.

The second issue is to be mindful of the consumer as an individual. The cult of self, of the individual and how tourism can support self-actualization – the achievement of which differentiates the individual in our complex postmodern society – is nirvana, and the role that CBT plays as 'Shangri La' as the consumer moves towards a coordinated personal development and somewhat hedonistic self-centred image of consumption becomes important for the owner-operator. Issues that emerge from self-centredness in consumption include differentiation of services and products by the target market. The case studies described in this chapter delve into how operators are able to mimic personal development achievement and ways in which CBT can be differentiated to meet the needs of increasingly discerning consumers.

Resources

Core components of a sustainable model of CBT can be identified for owner-operators concerning supply, demand, product distribution and exceeding consumers' expectations. Central to these are: (i) sales promotion intermediaries, usually travel agents or tour operators; (ii) technology for inventory control, supporting distribution and communicating with consumers and supply chain organizations; (iii) data collection for product development and collection of consumer feedback, monitoring of activity and product and service evaluation; and (iv) developing a network of volunteers and charitable trusts and societies to support product development and provide networks and partnerships.

The skills, aptitudes and approaches required for managing a complex series of operations and multisectoral partnerships within communities can present a challenge to communities. Often it is the hospitality and tourism entrepreneurs within those communities who represent success in small- to medium-sized business operations. Skills and aptitudes required in these owners and operators in CBT include innovative thinking, motivation skills, positive attitude, lateral thinking, self-confidence, creativity, intellectual ability, coordinating skills, foresight, intelligence, intuition, leadership skills, analytical thinking, communication skills and judgement (after Carson *et al.*, 1995; cited in Morrison *et al.*, 1999).

> The importance of knowledge as one of, and perhaps, the driver of innovation, productivity and competitiveness in tourism. Tacit knowledge is particularly important in terms of competitiveness, but this is also relatively sticky. It is possible to identify those general characteristics which facilitate tacit knowledge transfer, such as multiple networks, across space and sectors, openness and cosmopolitanism.
>
> (Shaw and Williams, 2009).

Future Research

> The array of studies on residents' perceptions of tourism, along with the application of various conceptual frameworks ... all point to the importance of increased community participation ... the conceptual frameworks for such participation have been partially constructed in abstract terms, while more specific frameworks tend to have been disproportionately researched in the context of eco-tourism developments in fragile environments. The shift from theory to practice remains a major issue in community tourism planning in all types of environments.
>
> (Beech and Chadwick, 2006)

The multidisciplinary nature of tourism studies in higher education institutions has helped to end the dominance of travel and tourism management as a single-discipline outcome predicated upon skills and knowledge of an idiosyncratic nature of traditional management and operations within travel and tourism. Graduates can now identify and articulate arguments for the regeneration of communities using a knowledge-based and problem-solving approach largely drawn from sociology,

8 Rural Tourism

Dr Helen Farrell and Sheila Russell

Introduction and Key Concepts

It is helpful to define what is meant by 'rural' and to also explain the scope and nature of 'countryside', where rural tourism takes place. In Europe, the countryside is comprised of rural areas that have been transformed extensively by human activities associated with the land. Elsewhere, the countryside is distinct from wilderness, which may not have seen such levels of human influence. Activities such as clearing woodland to plant crops and herd animals have been taking place since prehistoric times, and help to define the countryside as a modified landscape. Further common acts of countryside modification include the planting of forestry and hedgerows and the building of paths, roads, bridges, dams and walls. These activities have created a rural landscape that is neither wild nor urban, and that is appreciated for its picturesque scenery.

Before the 18th century, rural life was the only known existence (urbanization was a consequence of the technologies and systems developed through the Industrial Revolution). Rural life took many forms throughout Europe, from the landed estates of the rich to small-scale peasantry. Rural land was under the ownership of a limited number of powerful individuals and groups such as the church, royal families and the aristocracy. Peasants were those who worked the land and paid taxes and rent to the landowners. The result was a landscape that was partly in active use for agriculture, partly common grazing and partly landscaped for aesthetic purposes. Cities developed through the 18th, 19th and 20th centuries, but it was not until the late 1840s that there was any sense of the need to provide the thousands of factory workers (who had migrated to the city for work) with formal holidays. Once Thomas Cook pioneered mass travel, facilitated by the railway, the rights of workers and the need to reward workers was widely recognized (prior to this only a few industrial pioneers provided much in the way of a philanthropic approach to people management). As cities began to dominate the countryside economically, people started to long for the simpler, more wholesome way of life in tune with the seasons, to be found in the countryside (Taylor, 1994; Berghoff, 2002) and so developed a romantic, nostalgic sense of 'what we have lost.' It was in this period that the National Trust emerged. Founded in 1895, its aim was to preserve and allow access to cultural and natural heritage, including areas of rural land. Several decades later, however, access to the countryside had grown into a much more contentious issue that culminated in the mass trespass on Kinder Scout in the Pennines in 1932. At this time, walkers were denied access to areas of countryside by law. The mass trespass served to highlight this issue and is credited with being the trigger that prompted the formation of the UK's National Parks.

Case Study 8.1. Uluru-Kata Tjuta National Park.

Uluru-Kata Tjuta National Park was made an UNESCO World Heritage Site in 1987 for the following reasons:

1. It is an outstanding example representing significant ongoing geological processes, biological evolution and humanity's interaction with the natural environment.
2. It contains unique, rare or superlative natural phenomena, formations or features or areas of exceptional natural beauty, such as superlative examples of most important ecosystems to people, natural features, sweeping vistas covered by natural vegetation and exceptional combinations of natural or cultural elements.

Formerly called Uluru (Ayers Rock) National Park, the park is traditionally owned by the Anangu Aboriginal people, who have looked after this land for tens of thousands of years. The Australian government has put measures in place to acknowledge and celebrate the importance of this park to the Anangu people and developed a range of walks and a cultural centre to help visitors interpret and understand the Anangu culture, land, nature and science of the area. Visitors receive a unique experience at the park and gain an insight into how the park is managed according to traditional Anangu cultural practices.

In 1975, Australia was the first country in the world to enact specific legislation to protect World Heritage areas, thus ensuring that ownership of the park will remain with the Anangu people, their culture is protected and the park cannot become government property or be subject to control under any foreign power or other international organization. The World Heritage Convention aims globally to do the following:

- Promote co-operation among nations to protect worldwide heritage that is of such international value that its conservation is a concern for all people.
- Commit signatory nations to help in the identification, protection, conservation and presentation of World Heritage properties.
- Encourage signatory nations, with international assistance where appropriate, to 'adopt a general policy that aims to give the cultural and natural heritage function in the life of the community and to integrate the protection of that heritage into comprehensive planning programs'.
- Oblige signatory nations to refrain from 'any deliberate measures which might damage directly or indirectly the cultural and natural heritage' and to 'take the appropriate legal, scientific, technical, administrative and financial measures' necessary for its protection.

In 1994, Uluru-Kata Tjuta National Park became the second property in the world to be listed as a cultural landscape as it fulfils the following criteria: (i) a cultural landscape representing the combined work of nature and of man, manifesting the interaction between humankind and its natural environment; and (ii) an associative landscape having powerful religious, artistic and cultural associations of the natural element.

Following its listing, annual visitor numbers to the park reached 400,000 in 2000. The ongoing challenges to conserve the park for future generations while addressing the needs and impacts of ever-increasing visitor numbers continue, while the increase in tourism will continue to provide regional and national economic benefits.

Rural Tourism

Contemporary urban attitudes to the country-side are often based on a romantic notion of rural life. Indeed, some of the best known poetry, music and art in Western society from the last two centuries feature themes of nostalgia for a disappearing countryside (Ousby, 1990; Berghoff, 2002; Murdoch, 2003). The Romantic Movement of the late 18th and early 19th centuries was based largely on this impression. Even today there tends to be a desire to retain some of that belief that the countryside represents some lost, golden age of the 'pastoral' (Taylor, 1994).

Rural areas became idealized in this way as urbanization increased, agriculture modernized and landscapes changed (Murdoch, 2003). It is

Case Study 8.2. Rural tourists in Spain.

Rural tourism is not a large sector of the Spanish tourism offering and it is relatively underdeveloped as a result. It remains considerably less diverse a product than can be found elsewhere in rural Europe, and has grown more slowly than elsewhere, too. However, Spanish rural tourism is expanding in agricultural regions as a means to address the over-concentration of tourism on the coasts in the sun, sea and sand sector. It is primarily farm-based and therefore family-run, although there are also increasing numbers of urban-incomers setting up rural tourism businesses.

Development of rural tourism has not been helped by a lack of marketing (Cánoves *et al.*, 2004) and recognition for the sector from national and regional government. Promotion of rural tourism has therefore mainly taken place at local level and has not been well coordinated in the recent past (Pearce, 1997). There is, however, a demand for rural tourism in Spain and it comes mainly from domestic tourists. It is most popular with those who have only recently moved away from the countryside (Hoggart and Paniagua, 2001). In this case, tourism takes the form of visiting friends and relatives (VFR) (Yagüe Perales, 2002).

It is difficult to acquire accurate secondary data on rural tourism in Spain. The definition of 'rural' varies from one autonomous region to another, and data are therefore not fully comparable (Barke, 2004; Cánoves *et al.*, 2004). It is also not common for rural tourism establishments to register with regional or national tourism bodies, meaning they are excluded from official records (Barke, 2004). Additionally, Spanish official literature on rural tourism tended, until the 1980s, to define rural tourism quite narrowly as farm tourism, therefore missing out other forms of tourism activity in the countryside (Barke, 2004).

Despite all of the above, we do know that the rural tourism sector in Spain has been growing and that substantial developments took place in the 1990s. In the period 1996–1999 alone, there was an 83% increase in rural tourism accommodation availability (Cánoves *et al.*, 2004). Most of this development centred on the regions of Castilla-La Mancha, Extremadura and Castilla-León (Barke, 2004). These were also the regions facing the highest rates of rural depopulation (Barke, 2004).

As mentioned, the domestic market is the main source of tourists, and this is partly because of recent rural depopulation. Many urban Spaniards retain close family ties to rural areas (Barke, 2004). While this creates a loyal market of repeat visitors to the areas where friends and family remain (Barke, 2004), it also means that marketing, promotion and information availability take less significance. VFR-type tourists typically do not use these, and rely far more on personal knowledge and experience or tips gained through word of mouth.

arguable that the admiration for nature that is evident in much of the art mentioned above is based partly on a collective sense of guilt for the changes imposed on the countryside.

Sociological Influences

In society today there is evidence that our lives have become far more secular. The value of leisure has significantly increased as people work longer hours and have less leisure time, greater awareness, education and knowledge of the world, more affordable travel and increased technology. All of these factors contribute to the need to find or create a connection with the countryside, and rural tourism serves as a way to escape the mundane and find breathing space through exploration of the countryside.

The increase in heritage tourism (see also Chapter 13) has brought about an increase in the desire to know the 'story' of places and people, stories that would have been held in oral tradition but again have been lost through increased mobility. This desire can be seen in the rise in the popularity of and demand for authentic, artisan products, heritage foods, arts, crafts and pastimes, highlighting a need to connect with ancient traditions and ways (Dallen and Boyd, 2006).

In response to the increased appetite for these local products and services (see also the discussion around slow tourism in Chapter 9), a number of phenomena have occurred:

- There is an increase in sales of 'traditional' and 'authentic' products from developing countries being purchased by Western tourists or being imported to the developed world.

- Within Europe, several European Regional Development-funded initiatives have been set up to harness demand by bringing together producers, retailers and small businesses who are producing and selling items that enhance the uniqueness of a rural area and are made locally using traditional ingredients or raw materials and by traditional methods, with an aim to promote these businesses to tourists and locals alike.
- Festivals and events have also responded to these desires to enhance authenticity and 'local identity' within the experience of the event.

The interest in rural customs and accompanying products is thriving. Part of this renewed interest in our sociocultural heritage has led to an interest in the origins of food. Combined with an increased awareness of health and healthy eating, this has led to a greater demand from consumers keen to understand where their food comes from and a need to reconnect with the countryside through what they eat. This concept is supported by the increase in the popularity of celebrity chefs, many of whom have wholeheartedly embraced the 'local foods' concept. This has brought about changes in what we eat and a real interest in where food comes from and how it is produced.

Rural Tourism and Food Tourism

The UK's Department for Environment, Food and Rural Affairs (DEFRA) is the government department responsible for policy and regulations regarding the environment, food and rural affairs. DEFRA helps to protect the regional identity of particular foods associated with a particular area, which helps the local economy. DEFRA (2002) defines 'regional food' in England as 'food or drink produced within a particular geographical area that is marketed as coming from that area. However it may be sold within or outside that area'. Regional food is perceived to have a distinctive quality because of the area in which or by the method in which it is produced.

People today are far more concerned with how their food is produced than they were 10 years ago and there has been a surge in the number of people growing their own food and getting back to basics; a far cry from the convenience foods that have dominated the food landscape for a number of years. A keynote report (Mintel, 2009) outlined a trend in the 'good life' and anticipated that people would start to look more for life's simple pleasures as part of their process of reconnection with the countryside and an understanding of nature. Part of this process has led to a revival in traditional methods of farming and organic production and many more people are interested in buying organic produce or produce that has been grown or reared in an ethical, responsible manner with an emphasis on methods that protect the environment and ensure animal welfare. The Food Industry Sustainable Strategy developed by DEFRA in 2006 was designed to ensure best practice in all stages of the food chain and to ensure that economic benefits are not at the expense of the environment and are not likely to disadvantage future generations living in rural destinations.

This is just one example, but globally it is leading to a new type of rural tourism – 'food tourism' – with food festivals, events and farmers' markets adding to the range of activities that are enjoyed by visitors keen to take home a taste of the countryside they have visited. By taking something home, tourists take away a connection with the place they visited – something to remind themselves of the place, but also something that is 'from' the place, produced in and therefore infused with the 'localness' of the area (see also Chapter 17).

The Ministry of Agriculture, Fisheries and Food and the Countryside Agency report 'Tourists Attitudes towards Regional and Local Foods' (Enteleca Research and Consultancy, 2004) reported that 42% of tourists claim they actively look for specialties with a 'local identity' and 34% look for local produce. The report identified the following:

- There is a significant tourist market for local foods and meals based on local ingredients.
- The cooking, freshness and quality of ingredients are key factors that create

Case Study 8.3. Developing rural tourism in the Republic of Ireland.

The Irish tourist board promotes the Republic of Ireland's rural tourism offering online. It links heritage, culture and landscape themes in this promotional activity. Themes of peace and tranquillity, the green landscape, historic sites and traditional culture are all played upon. The Irish language and Irish traditional music are attractions for international and domestic tourists alike, with many domestic Irish visitors to the west of Ireland in particular, travelling for the purpose of studying the Irish language in a Gaeltacht (Irish-speaking) area.

Rural tourism is promoted by the government of Ireland as a tool for rural development. Ireland is a rural country where 40% of the population lives in towns and villages of less than 1,500 people (the Irish definition of rural) (Hall *et al.*, 2005). These settlements are small by international standards (the UK commonly defines rural areas as towns and villages with fewer than 10,000 inhabitants) and are reflective of the small size of the total population of the Republic of Ireland.

Substantial developments in Irish rural tourism took place in the late 1980s and early 1990s, with government funding for small-scale accommodation. However, development tended to be piecemeal and *ad hoc* (Gilbert, 1993). The result is that Irish rural tourism provision is patchy and based on small-scale private businesses.

Although previously more accurately described as 'agritourism,' tourism today is less connected to the land and is typically rural tourism. Rural tourism currently is mainly seasonal, small-scale and based on the appearance of the landscape (Hegarty and Przezborska, 2005). Rural tourism business success is based more on local distinctiveness and less on the size of the business (Cawley and Marsat, 2007).

Development is also hindered by poor infrastructure and unfavourable exchange rates for international visitors (Hall *et al.*, 2005; Hegarty and Przezborska, 2005). Central government's role is to provide promotional materials, financial support and funding allocation, as well as policy and planning guidance (Hall *et al.*, 2005). The institutions involved in promoting Irish rural tourism are outlined in Table 8.1 below:

Table 8.1. Supporting rural tourism in Ireland.

Level	Name	Role(s)
International	LEADER[a] programme	Main source of funds for small-scale rural tourism infrastructure projects and promotion
International	Tourism Ireland	Promotes Ireland as a tourism destination overseas
National	FÁS[b]	Training and employment agencies in all sectors
National	Department of Tourism, Culture and Sport	Sets tourism policy
National	Department of Community, Equality and Gaeltacht Affairs	Administers LEADER programme Sets rural policy, therefore rural tourism policy
National	Department of the Environment, Heritage and Local Government and Department of Communications, Energy and Natural Resources	Environmental protection and development of tourism infrastructure
National	Fáilte Ireland	Domestic tourist board: promotional and funding roles; regulates accommodation; provides training
Regional	Development commissions	Coordinate and fund rural tourism
Regional	NUTS2[c] regional assemblies	Monitor EU investment
Regional	Tourism authorities	Coordinate and promote tourism activity at a regional scale
Regional	Údarás na Gaeltachta	Administers development of Gaeltacht areas
County	Local authorities (county and city councils)	Regulate physical development
County	Tourism committees	Report to regional tourism authorities

[a] Liaison Entre Actions de Développement de l'Economie Rurale, meaning 'Links between the rural economy and development actions'.
[b] Foras Áiseanna Saothair, the national training and employment authority in the Republic of Ireland.
[c] Nomenclature of territorial units for statistics for member states in the EU (in French, nomenclature d'unités territoriales statistiques).
Source: Cawley and Marsat, 2007.

excellent experiences for people, along with the use of local produce and local specialities.

- Many people perceive that local ingredients make an essential contribution to the quality of the meal and the taste of the food.
- There is a widely held perception that purchase of local foods assists the local economy (82%) and the local environment (65%).

Recent research reinforces this idea and shows that purchasing local food has a significant impact on the rural economy. Findings show that almost two thirds of visitors buy local food (Enteleca Research and Consultancy, 2004) and highlight the importance of understanding spending patterns in rural tourism for practitioners working in the industry. Evidence has indicated that visitors spending the highest amounts on local food are more than likely to have collected a high level of information before their trip. Spending on promotion therefore has real and tangible benefits, provided that the marketing campaign emphasizes the qualities of local foods that are attractive to consumers. For example, the authenticity and traditional character of the local food products and the producers should be framed in the relevant countryside lifestyle (Skuras *et al.*, 2006). This highlights the relevance and need for the tourism industry to aim 'local' themes effectively to the relevant sociodemographic groups, but also supports the work that is done by many of the regional food groups that have been established. Research has shown that consumers will seek out local food products and the level of spending increases for consumers who have already purchased these products on a previous trip. Once familiar with local products, consumers will then search for these same products or their equivalents when back home (Skuras *et al.*, 2006). With this is mind, the opportunity for rural food producers to market their produce through the internet becomes a viable reality.

Much of the nostalgic appeal of the countryside can be traced to its loss and the increasing pressure on those areas of rural land that remain. Today's countryside is subject to multiple uses and therefore multiple pressures,

which include tourism but also changing agricultural practices, changes in government and policies on rural affairs, out-migration and the loss of community structures (Murdoch, 2003). Recent changes such as increasing retirement migration into the countryside and the use of rural villages as dormitory settlements for larges towns and cities have influenced the ways in which rural society is organized (Halfacree, 2007). Tourism, therefore, represents only one of many activities taking place in this complex environment.

Rural tourism is, of course, not a single activity but a range of possible activities. These can be categorized as active pursuits such as walking and cycling; creative industries such as dry stone walling; celebrations of the past such as heritage sites and museums; nature tourism activities; adventure tourism; festivals and events; sports; attractions; and accommodation. All of these are discussed in detail in other chapters within this book.

With this increase in activity, there is inevitably a dramatic increase in the number of visitors going to the countryside. As a result, special measures have been put in place to protect the environment and in particular National Parks, which were set up 60 years ago to conserve the countryside in some of the most visited areas. The influx of such huge visitor numbers impacts in many ways. The pollution from the sheer number of cars pouring into the area, particularly on weekends, is an obvious problem, along with the direct impacts of visitors, including erosion, litter and noise pollution. Many areas in the countryside are protected (in the UK these include National Parks, National Nature Reserves, Sites of Special Scientific Interest, Nature Reserves and Areas of Outstanding Natural Beauty), but access has to be maintained because of networks of footpaths and the impacts of legislation such as the Countryside Rights of Way Act. (This is a UK Act of Parliament that came into force on the 30th November 2000 and allows access to previously limited areas in England and Wales. The Act implements the 'Right to Roam' in certain upland, uncultivated areas and is the realization of the aims of the Ramblers Association by providing greater access to the countryside.) National Parks have an obligation

---

Case Study 8.4. Food from the Peak District.

The Food from the Peak District initiative was created to promote and support small- to medium-size rural businesses that are using the uniqueness of the Peak District environment to promote and enhance the products they are creating. Currently funded by the Peak District National Park Authority's Live and Work Rural programme, previously the New Environmental Economy (see Case Study 8.5) the scheme was set up to promote and encourage the use of locally sourced produce by food producers and end users such as pubs, hotels, restaurants and bed and breakfasts in and around the Peak District.

To give this some national context it should be noted that in 2004 there were some 3,500 non-farm businesses employing 24,300 people (Lindsay, 2004). These figures do not include the number of working farms or their employees. Some 11% of businesses and 13% of jobs are in the hotel and restaurant sector, with 9% of businesses and 20% of all jobs in manufacturing. Around 80% of the business population is classified as small or micro-business, with many operating as sole traders or with fewer than five employees, meaning they do not usually qualify for mainstream business support or financial assistance.

To date, the scheme has over 100 members ranging from Michelin-starred hotels to organic beef farmers, artisan chocolatiers and village tearooms. All members sign up to a set of criteria that reflect the principles of the Food from the Peak District initiative, as outlined in the Environmental Quality Mark (see Case Study 8.5) as follows:

- Honesty, transparency, traceability, accountability.
- Working towards sourcing as much produce as locally as possible.
- Collaboration not competition.
- Building on what already exists in a complementary way.
- Working to protect and enhance the distinctiveness of the local culture and the local environment.
- Supporting the local economy by using local products and services where possible.
- Minimal packaging.
- Bringing producers and consumers together to learn from each other.

The initiative has established a brand to identify to consumers that they comply with the above principles and to add value to the food producers and food-using businesses that are committed to providing a product or service that enhances the uniqueness of the Peak District environment. Many researchers claim several benefits are derived from the provision of locally sourced foods to the tourism market, including environmental benefits such as the reduction of food miles, packaging and waste, to social and economic benefits through boosting the rural economy and the creation of 'iconic' products (Sims, 2009b).

Members pay an annual membership fee and benefit from a variety of promotional activities such as inclusion in an annual food guide and on a website, networking opportunities, specialist training opportunities, events and access to the group logo and branding. The group also acts as an information signposting service through its knowledge of the Peak District food sector and acknowledges that education and creation and promotion of links between food producers and food-using businesses is essential to its survival (SQW, 2006). This concept is reinforced by the research undertaken by Green and Dougherty (2009) into culinary tourism.

Funding has been secured until 2011, when the group will need to be fully self-sustainable and able to continue to grow without any public sector funding. The challenge now for this group is to become fully sustainable and to grow its membership base while continuing to uphold the principles underpinning its foundations.

---

to protect the fabric of the area and its sociocultural aspects, while also providing an accessible network of footpaths to accommodate visitors, who bring a much needed economic boost to the local community. This juxtaposition brings about a number of conflicts of interest as National Parks seek to retain the environment for visitors, wildlife and those that live and work there. Through programmes of guided walks, well-maintained footpaths and support for small local businesses that provide accommodation, refreshments and activities for visitors, National Parks are effectively minimizing the negative effects of rural tourism. There are, however, other negative impacts of rural tourism that it is important to explore.

Case Study 8.5. Environmental Quality Mark.

A raft of EU-funded initiatives has been created nationwide to enhance and protect the environment in which we live and promote sustainable development in rural areas of Europe, while addressing economic, social and environmental concerns. One such example is that of the New Environmental Economy, a Peak District initiative that was led by the Peak District National Park Authority from 2003 to 2008 with the aim of supporting small, local businesses and projects that showed social, economic and environmental benefits to the Peak District environment. The scheme provided grants and support for business start-ups and also funded the Environmental Quality Mark (EQM) scheme and the Foods from the Peak District initiative (see Case Study 8.4). The following objectives were set for the successful running of the New Environmental Economy:

- Use the high-quality landscape as a unifying theme between agriculture, tourism and arts and crafts, and to develop the local economy.
- Encourage the development of new products using local resources.
- Improve integration between tourism, agriculture and arts and crafts.
- Stimulate formal collaboration between business and the public sector.
- Expand existing jobs and create new local jobs with a variety of skills (and improve the local skills base).
- Stimulate 'Pride in the Peak' as an instrument for environmental management and improvement.
- Develop public funding support mechanisms to encourage the development of the Peak District economy.
- Create a single mechanism to provide advice to local businesses.

The EQM addresses these environmental objectives and awards businesses that have made special efforts to conserve the natural environment of the Peak District. The award is a certification mark and can only be awarded to businesses that demonstrate that they actively support good environmental practices within the Peak District National Park. It is the first environmental award of its kind in England and continues to grow, with 88 businesses currently holding the award. To qualify for the mark, businesses have to achieve high standards of care for the environment in all aspects of their management practice including the following:

- Conservation of the Peak District National Park.
- Use of locally grown and made products and services.
- Use of environmentally friendly products.
- Efficient use of energy and water.
- Minimization of waste by reducing, reusing and recycling.
- Provision of environmental information to customers.

Award holders include: producers of environmentally friendly food, arts and crafts; farms that conserve wildlife habitats, archaeology and iconic Peak District landscape; and bed and breakfasts, shops and cafes that sell local, ethically produced goods and services.

Award holders are able to use the accredited 'mark' on their promotional materials and websites and feature on the Peak District National Park Authority's website; they are also promoted in leaflets and at shows and events. Other benefits also include access to advice and support for environmental issues and networking opportunities with like-minded businesses, producers, suppliers and outlets (SQW 2006).

Impacts of Rural Tourism

The ways in which tourism inserts itself into rural life and the rural economy are complex, and tourists' perceptions of rurality can be very different from those of local residents (Murdoch, 2003). The interaction of tourism and other rural activities is one of the most important aspects to consider here, and is key when attempting to understand the impacts of rural tourism.

Case Study 8.6. Supporting rural tourism in India.

India offers many examples of small-scale, community-based rural tourism. The Government of India's Ministry of Tourism has been working with the UN Development Assistance Framework in order to develop a number of new rural tourism projects throughout the country. Details can be found online at http://www.exploreruralindia.org. This national rural tourism scheme (RTS) comprises 31 rural sites to date.

Although supported by national government and the UN Development Program, there is a strong grassroots element to the Indian rural tourism projects included in the RTS. Community involvement is facilitated by local non-governmental organizations (NGOs), which work on capacity building and greater inclusion of target groups (typically local women, low-income groups and unemployed youth). These groups' involvement in rural tourism is supported through various forms of skills development, which are offered in their home villages. However, before training can be offered and before the tourism projects can begin, the community must be consulted. The RTS is based on the concept of endogenous tourism, which is aimed at generating local income and improving quality of life. Central to this is community ownership and action, and one of the first steps when preparing for a new local tourism project is to conduct a participatory rural appraisal. This process, normally facilitated by an NGO, enables the community to create a 'vision' for the project that incorporates its needs.

Rural tourism projects under the RTS are based on local culture, arts and crafts. Endogenous tourism's attraction lies in the local community and visitors' interactions with members of this community. In the heritage village of Samode, near Jaipur, Rajasthan, the local NGO provides training in health and hygiene, hospitality, language skills and handicrafts. Marketing materials such as brochures have been translated into French, German, English, Spanish and Swedish. In 2006 80% of visitors to Samode were from France, so French language training for tour guides, shopkeepers and host families was particularly important.

Similar training takes place at other rural sites within the RTS. Women are targeted for training in many cases; typically, they are illiterate and have no regular income. Training in arts and crafts to create products marketable to tourists is therefore deemed most appropriate, while the some women are also offered training in the preparation of traditional food. Younger men are given training in tour guiding. They receive an officially endorsed certificate on successful completion of the course. It should be noted that rural people would previously have been employed in agriculture and would not usually have the skills to produce good-quality, saleable arts and crafts.

In regions such as Kerala, where endogenous tourism takes the form of agritourism, more locally specific training is available. In this case, organic cultivation, the rearing of various livestock animals, waste management and composting training are included alongside courses in hospitality and tour guiding.

Living and working in rural areas

Those living and working in areas with high levels of rural tourism are undoubtedly affected in many ways. Areas with high visitor figures tend to see an increase in the cost of homes (as many are bought as second homes, retirement properties and holiday cottages), making it increasingly difficult for those born and raised in the area to continue to live there. The average house price in these areas is driven up and those buying second homes and retirement properties have a higher disposable income. The area becomes more desirable and as a result house prices climb, leaving local people unable to buy a house in these areas. This results in an ageing population and an increase in the number of older people moving into the area. This has resulted in a public sector drive to encourage and support local business start-ups to improve opportunities for younger generations to stay in the local area, rather than move away to find cheaper homes and lower living costs.

Many businesses in areas with high levels of rural tourism rely on the tourist trade for their income and can suffer out of season. Destination management organizations (DMOs), local councils and community programmes all realize the importance of extending the tourist season and offering festivals, events and other activities outside of the traditional summer season, focusing on shoulder months to encourage year-round income from tourism to improve opportunities for small businesses to generate year-round income, especially those that are totally reliant on the tourism industry. Research shows that every £1 spent in local businesses leads to £10 being spent in the local economy (Ward and Lewis, 2002).

Conflict and contested values

Another impact of rural tourism is the conflict that can occur between local residents, local councils and National Parks. Although there is a clear need to conserve the environment, this can cause conflict with local residents' applications for planning permission, particularly in areas with conservation-area status. Some residents find this even prevents them from diversifying into tourism, while in other areas such policy is totally at odds with environmental best practice, curtailing the use of solar panels and any other structures that could impact upon the appearance of the area. It can also prove to be expensive to maintain a property in these areas as building materials and style must be in keeping with the heritage

and structures already in place. It is often a requirement to replace like for like, which can cause bad feeling and perceived inconvenience for those living in the area.

The Popularity of the Countryside

There are numerous possible explanations as to why the countryside is a popular tourism destination and how this popularity has been maintained over many years, seemingly avoiding the decline of coastal tourism or the impacts on cities of fickle and changing tourist tastes. Rural tourism has a very long history in Europe in general, and its popularity is based partly on the idyllic images illustrated in Fig. 8.1 (Garrod *et al.*, 2006). Current marketing and promotional materials still play on this today. This image is reinforced by the contrasting poor image of urban areas, which are portrayed in the media as sites of crime and of poor or unhealthy environments.

Rural tourism is fashionable among the wealthier socioeconomic groups, especially

Fig. 8.1. The rural idyll: the Peak District National Park, UK.

ownership of second homes or future retirement homes in the country. Rural areas are therefore aspirational destinations (Curry, 2001).

Marketing Rural Tourism

The way in which rural activities are marketed is changing and becoming further segmented. Destination management organizations (DMOs) no longer place their marketing emphasis on traditional, generic tourism activities such as sightseeing and shopping, which have formed the basis of earlier marketing campaigns. Rather, they now include 'special interest tourism' (McKercher *et al.*, 2008), which has been described as the 'hub around which the total travel experience is planned and developed' (Hall and Weiler, 1992). The countryside is no longer sold just as a place to relax, enjoy local produce, walk and cycle, but for adventure, adrenaline sports and other niche activities.

It is important to understand the decision-making processes and motivational factors involved in rural tourism to develop a strong approach to marketing. Much research has been carried out by DMOs to establish the reason why people travel, but it can be argued that much of this research is flawed as it relies on secondary analysis of activity questions in departing visitor surveys. This method only shows us what visitors do once they arrive in a destination and then attempts to form a tenuous link between actions and motives, which can result in some visitors being classified as cultural tourists because they made a visit to a country house, museum or theatre. This does not take into account the fact that visitors will probably engage in many different activities and experiences and the research does not underpin the actual reason why a trip was made to the museum in the first instance (McKercher *et al.*, 2008).

A study carried out by McKercher *et al.* (2008) sought to establish whether Hong Kong could be classed as a culinary destination and attempted to address the imbalance in earlier research. By adopting a broader holistic approach, they enabled the findings to be placed in context rather than viewed from a narrow perspective that can result in misleading results and too great a segmentation. Their findings concluded that food is embedded in the tourism offer and fits into the mass market alongside other activities, such as sightseeing and shopping, that are associated with the chosen destination.

The research (McKercher *et al.*, 2008) demonstrates the risk evident in examining a potential special interest activity out of context of where it fits in the destination's broader product mix. It is important to bear this in mind when analysing motivational factors and the chosen activities of visitors in destinations to ensure that a broad perspective is maintained.

Another growing element of the broader product mix is the increase in availability and frequency of various leisure opportunities now available in rural areas. These leisure opportunities need not be specifically rural in nature – for example, many extreme sports are more widely available in rural areas – but it is the availability of land and space that makes these activities possible (Curry, 2001), often combined with natural features such as cliffs, hills and rivers, reducing costs for the operators of these businesses.

Marketing by DMOs has evolved to reflect this change in the demographics of the visitor to the countryside and is now targeting young, urban professionals to engage them in the numerous outdoor pursuits available, from rock climbing to horse riding and paragliding. This new type of marketing is a far cry from the type of visitor and demographic groups that have been traditionally targeted as the countryside becomes more accessible, offering something for everyone.

Special festival and short-break packages now reflect new themes within tourism and are aimed at new sociodemographic groups. For many years, the typical visitor to the countryside was over 45 years old and marketing emphasized local arts, crafts, foods and festivals. Demographics showed this type of visitor to be interested in local food and drink, culture, walking and nature. The face of rural tourism is changing and we are now seeing more marketing and activities aimed at young, urban professionals. While new activities are promoted and encouraged, there is also a demand and a clearly defined need to look after the countryside that makes the destination so attractive in the first place.

Case Study 8.7. 'Mind the Gap'.

The Summer 2009 'Mind the Gap' campaign by Visit Peak District in partnership with East Midlands Trains targeted visitors from London and the south east with colourful posters portraying Peak District scenes in a bid to attract tourists away from the cities and into the countryside of the Peaks. The campaign utilized the London Underground, using posters to target young, urban professional commuters, normally urged to 'mind the gap' when commuting, to explore the Peak District. It cleverly contrasted the urban environment with the rural landscape of the Peak District using imagery. The campaign cost £50,000 and ran from July to the end of 2009 and aimed to improve accessibility to visitors by showing that 'the gap' is closing between London and the Peak District and Derbyshire, both in cost and journey time. The poster campaign was reinforced by leaflets and advertising in London newspapers and was supported by special offers on train tickets and two-for-one tickets to visitor attractions, making the success of the campaign easily measurable through ticket sales and those taking up the special offers. The campaign built on the trend in 'stay-cations', whereby more UK residents are holidaying within the UK. Furthermore, it provided value breaks to encourage commuters to head north by train, which also had environmental benefits by encouraging holiday makers to leave their cars at home.

Along with this increase in activities and differentiation between the type of person and social groups taking an interest in rural tourism come the negative impacts that these activities can place on the local environment. Although it is well known that tourism can bring economic prosperity to a destination, there is a growing awareness of the importance of finding a balance between the number of visitors, range of activities and accommodation available so that the pressure caused by high visitor numbers has minimal negative impacts on the destination (Picard, 1995; Shaw and Williams, 2002).

Many rural areas now identify that these impacts are not just economic, but also social, cultural and environmental. They have, therefore, sought to address the balance through the creation of tourism products and services that enhance the uniqueness of the destination in question (Sims, 2009a). Today the market has evolved to showcase the many leisure activities that are available for the varying market sectors as well as highlighting the 'green' qualities of local businesses and accommodation providers, which are increasingly being recognized and acknowledged through accreditation to various schemes. It would appear that these 'green' credentials are actively sought and many businesses are now using these benchmarks to give them a marketing edge. The creation and development of 'iconic' products can also be used to brand a region and offer opportunities for further tourism development. Many tourists are now selecting accommodation, not just on location and quality standards, but also by the owners' commitment to looking after the environment.

Future Research

There is clear potential for further research into rural tourism. It will be obvious from your reading of this chapter that there is a paucity of research into rural tourism in the developing world, although the Indian examples are promising. There is also potential for research into some of the increasingly specialized forms of rural tourism such as food tourism and other niche products. Given the raft of many European Regional Development-funded initiatives, local food tourism is likely to continue to expand as a means of boosting local economies, ensuring the survival of rural food producers and protecting the local landscape for years to come (see also Chapter 9 on slow tourism and Chapter 17 on gastronomy). The complex relationship between rural and urban and the blurring boundaries between these spaces are of interest in sociological and economic terms in general, and tourism should be seen as part of this relationship. Urbanization and rural countermigration are topics that are appearing in the tourism literature now and are likely to attract further interest in the future. Finally, a shift in focus away from the zoned, single-use approach to land management in the countryside and towards the multifunctionality that sustainable development demands will be an interesting area to investigate further.

Conclusion

This chapter started with an introduction that outlined what is meant by 'rural' in the case of rural tourism. Our interpretation of rural land has changed over time and also varies depending on the location, but it is not to be confused with wilderness and is definitely not an extension of the city.

Rural tourism is not a new phenomenon and the chapter mentioned some of the early attractions for rural tourists, based on a romantic image of an unspoilt space. The discussion was then brought up to date, with mention of the sociological influences on rural tourism today. This includes tourists' changing lifestyles – they value their limited leisure time, are more knowledgeable and better educated than ever before and live in a fast-paced, modern world. The countryside therefore appeals as a tourism destination because of its perceived authenticity, tradition and slower pace. Two examples were listed here: food tourism and the growing interest in local produce and quality, and the National Parks and outdoor active tourism.

The impacts of rural tourism and ways in which it interacts with other rural activities were also considered. Some of these impacts included the rising house prices and costs of living in rural areas that are popular destinations for visitors. This led to a discussion of the popularity of rural tourism and the marketing of it. The creation of niche products and the increasing diversification of rural tourism were mentioned. The Peak District's 'Mind the Gap' campaign on the London Underground was given as an example of a targeted marketing programme.

The case studies gave brief insights into specific examples. In Spain, the focus shifted onto the rural tourists – who, in this case, were most likely to be domestic tourists participating in VFR-type tourism (Case Study 8.2). The Irish case study (Case Study 8.3) illustrated the development process from agritourism to a more diverse product, while the Case Study 8.4 concentrated on a very specific form of tourism – food tourism in the Peak District. The EQM in the Peak District (Case Study 8.5) is aimed at promoting a more environmentally aware attitude in business and among consumers. Government support, with the aid of international organizations and NGOs was highlighted in the Indian rural tourism case study (Case Study 8.6). In this case, brand new community-based endogenous tourism projects were the focus, and the need for training and preparation for tourism was identified.

Review Questions

1. Why is it important to consider the history of rural tourism development when looking at today's trends?

2. Consider the example of the Republic of Ireland. Critically evaluate the challenges that the rural tourism industry faces as it moves away from agritourism to a more diverse form.

3. Critically assess why Spanish rural tourism has been late in developing, compared to northern European examples.

4. Consider how the 'Food from the Peak District' initiative can develop new routes to market and improve supply chain activity within the group.

5. Consider other contemporary forms of marketing and media that could be used to promote the 'Food from the Peak District' initiative (Case Study 8.4).

References

Barke, M. (2004) Rural tourism in Spain. *International Journal of Tourism Research* 6, 137–149.

Berghoff, H. (2002) *The Making of Modern Tourism. The Cultural History of the British Experience, 1600–2000.* Palgrave, Basingstoke, UK.

Cánoves, G., Villarino, M., Priestley, G.K. and Blanco, A. (2004) Rural tourism in Spain: an analysis of recent evolution. *Geoforum* 35, 755–769.

Cawley, M. and Marsat, J.B. (2007) Promoting integrated rural tourism: comparative perspectives on institutional networking in France and Ireland. *Tourism Geographies* 9, 405–420.

Curry, N. (2001) Access for outdoor recreation in England and Wales: production, consumption and markets. *Journal of Sustainable Tourism* 9, 400-416.

DEFRA (2002) *The Strategy for Sustainable Farming and Food: Facing the Future.* Department for Environment, Food and Rural Affairs, London, UK.

DEFRA (2006) *Food Industry Sustainability Strategy.* Department for Environment, Food and Rural Affairs, London, UK.

Enteleca Research and Consultancy (2004) *Tourists' Attitudes towards Regional and Local Foods.* Ministry of Agriculture, Fisheries and Food and Countryside Agency, London, UK.

Garrod, B., Wornell, R. and Youell, R. (2006) Re-conceptualising rural resources as countryside capital: the case of rural tourism. *Journal of Rural Studies* 22, 117–128.

Gilbert, D.C. (1993) Issues in appropriate rural tourism development for southern Ireland. *Leisure Studies* 12, 137–146.

Green, G.P. and Dougherty, M.L. (2009) Localizing linkages for food and tourism: culinary tourism as a community development strategy. *Community Development* 39, 148–158.

Halfacree, K. (2007) Trial by space for a 'radical rural': introducing alternative localities, representations and lives. *Journal of Rural Studies* 23, 125–141.

Hall, D.R., Kirkpatrick, I. and Mitchell, M. (2005) *Rural Tourism and Sustainable Business.* Channel View Publications, Clevedon, UK.

Hegarty, C. and Przezborska, L. (2005) Rural and agri-tourism as a tool for reorganising rural areas in old and new member states – a comparison study of Ireland and Poland. *International Journal of Tourism Research* 7, 63–77.

Hoggart, K. and Paniagua, A. (2001) The restructuring of rural Spain? *Journal of Rural Studies* 17, 63–80.

Lindsay, C (2004) *State of the Labour Market, 2004 Report.* Office for National Statistics Labour Market Division, London, UK.

McKercher, B., Okumus, F. and Okumus, B. (2008) Food tourism as a viable market segment: it's all how you cook the numbers! *Journal of Travel and Tourism Marketing* 25, 137–148.

Mintel (2009) Mintel Trend Report 2009. Available from: http://http://www.mintel.com. Accessed July 14, 2010.

Murdoch, J. (2003) *The Differentiated Countryside.* Routledge, London, UK.

Ousby, I. (1990) *The Englishman's England Taste, Travel and the Rise of Tourism.* Cambridge University Press, Cambridge, UK.

Pearce, D. (1997) Tourism and the autonomous communities in Spain. *Annals of Tourism Research* 24, 156–177.

Picard, M. (1995) Cultural heritage and tourist capital: cultural tourism in Bali. In: Lanfant, M.F., Allcock, J.B. and Brunner, E.M. (eds) *International Tourism: Identity and Change.* Sage, London, UK, pp. 44–66.

Shaw, G. and Williams, A. (2002) *Critical Issues in Tourism: A Geographical Perspective.* Blackwell, Oxford, UK.

Sims, R. (2009a) Putting place on the menu: the negotiation of locality in UK food tourism, from production to consumption. *Journal of Rural Studies* 26, 105–115.

Sims, R. (2009b) Food, place and authenticity: local food and the sustainable tourism experience. *Journal of Sustainable Tourism* 17, 321—336.

Skuras, D., Dimara, E. and Petrou A. (2006) Rural tourism and visitors' expenditures for local food products. *Regional Studies* 40, 769–779.

SQW (2006) *Evaluation of the New Environmental Economy Programme Final Report.* SQW Ltd, Cambridge, UK.

Taylor, J. (1994) *A Dream of England Landscape, Photography and the Tourist's Imagination.* Manchester University Press, Manchester, UK.

Ward, B. and Lewis, J. (2002) *Plugging the Leaks.* New Economics Foundation, London, UK.

Yagüe Perales, R.M. (2002) Rural tourism in Spain. *Annals of Tourism Research* 29, 1101–1110.

9 Slow Food, Slow Cities and Slow Tourism

Sine Heitmann, Peter Robinson and Ghislaine Povey

Introduction

The Slow Food movement is a non-profit, eco-gastronomic, member-supported organization that was founded in 1989 to counteract fast food and fast life, the disappearance of local food traditions and people's dwindling interest in the food they eat, where it comes from, how it tastes and how our food choices affect the rest of the world (Slow Food, 2010). A further development of Slow Food is the Slow City movement, which builds on the ideas of Slow Food but extends the philosophy to cities and destinations. Following on from the Slow Food and Slow City movements, Slow Tourism has evolved as an extension of this philosophy to encompass travel and tourism activities. There is very little research on Slow Tourism, but nevertheless there is a growing interest in this concept. Slow tourism can be discussed from a consumer behaviour, marketing or sustainable tourism perspective. While relatively new in its idea, a range of existing tourism theories and concepts can be adapted to fit the Slow Tourism ethos. This chapter will outline the origins and key ideas of both the Slow Food and Slow City movements, as well as related concepts such as fair trade, before conceptualizing Slow Tourism and the scope of research and discussion this concept provides.

Slow Food – The Origins of the movement

The Slow Food movement originated in Bra, a small city in the north west of Italy, alongside the Langhe wine district and near to the Alba tourist region. During the 1970s, Bra was characterized by small, independent businesses and farms, who were struggling with encroaching industrialization and a number of strong, predominantly politically left-wing social groups, which were popular because of a fierce allegiance to local cultural identity and a determination not to let the area become a victim of the monoculture of industrialization. One particular group (the Free and Praiseworthy Association of the Friends of Barolo) had an unusual perspicacity for the time as they aimed to preserve and promote the food and wines of the region, particularly home-made and traditional wines and dishes. Despite the fact that tasting food and drinks was not a fashionable pursuit, the group organized wine and food tastings, taught visitors how to best to enjoy their products and, having created a market for their products, set up mail-order businesses supplying them worldwide (Petrini, 2001). This was the birthplace of a new business model that has begun to establish itself in the food industry (Nosi and Zanni, 2004), where the view of industrial, mass-produced food being the most preferred consumer choice has given way to a growing preference for seasonal, local and traditionally made products.

During an anti-McDonald's protest in Rome 1986 the term 'Slow Food' was coined as a rallying call for those who wanted to halt the invasion of standardized, Americanized 'fast food' (and culture) into the heart of Rome. A second influence on the formation of the movement was the death of 19 Italians who drank cheap wine that had been mixed with methanol. In reaction to these events, Carlos Petrini formed the embryonic Slow Food movement, which was officially launched in December 1989 in Paris. Since then the movement has gone from strength to strength, and now has 100,000 members from 132 countries worldwide (SlowFood, 2010).

Slow food is part of a movement for change that advocates sustainable, less greedy and slow life. For the movement, food is central to everyday life. If we were only able to eat Slow Food, if fast food restaurants and supermarket ready-meals did not exist, then our whole lifestyle would have to change. Meals would have to be cooked, time to do this would have to be found and families would have to work together to get their food. It could change the entire way that we live in industrialized countries (Petrini, 2001). Our very relationships with some commodities could be completely changed, and Slow Food has catalysed regeneration in regions where local food products are recognized and valued for their unique contribution to taste (Hall, 2006).

Slow food is philosophically centred on the rights of all citizens to enjoy clean (unpolluted), fairly traded food that has been sustainably produced with consideration for all stakeholders, including the animals being eaten and the planet itself. It has a mission to enhance the taste education of all citizens of the world and to develop links between all the stakeholders in the production and consumption of food. Within the Slow Food movement there are some key structures. First is the Foundation for Biodiversity, which uses the Ark of Taste, a repository for a wide range of diverse species of edible plant and animals that are protected in their traditional home environments by 'guardians'. This promotes a system of preserving traditional biodiversity, not just in terms of the genetic DNA of food plants and animals, but also in the traditional methods of production and culture of consumption. Within the Ark of Taste are the 'presidia'. A presidium is a group that specifically focuses on an individual product to ensure its preservation. This group works to help the product to retain its authenticity while engaging with the modern food environment with support in production and marketing to ensure economic viability. The

Foundation for Biodiversity also supports Tierra Madre events, which bring together food communities from all over the world to discuss how to preserve traditional foods and to form networks for support and trade. Secondly, the Slow Food movement promotes food education largely through 'convivium'. A convivia is a group of interested people in an area who host food tastings, dinners and other events that help local people to learn about food and taste. These convivia are another way to help networks form, often between consumers and producers. More formal educational institutions can also join these links through membership and, when invited, lead '*salon degustation*' or taste workshops. Other activities include helping schools to set up school gardens and helping children to learn about taste.

Underpinning this movement is the breaking of the link between food and price. Industrialization reduces cost in that economies of scale can be gained from mass production. This is often, unfortunately, accompanied by a loss of quality and the introduction of inhumane treatment of the environment and the animals involved. Petrini (2001) asserts that it is important that consumers learn to value quality and understand that to get that quality they may have to pay a higher price. The Slow Food movement proposes a market mechanism that is local and self-supporting, and eliminates the need for industrial food (Pietrykowski, 2004).

Slow food and gastro-tourism

Historically there has been a strong recognition of the opportunities that local food presents to maximizing the multiplier effect in tourism destinations (Robinson, 2008a). This growth in interest in local products linked to their regional or local heritage is valuable for the tourism industry, and has for many years been supplemented by what actually appear to be many of the components of Slow Food and Slow Cities, in urban, semi-rural and rural environments. Since its identification as a food on the verge of extinction, the traditional form of pork fat (lardo di Colonnata) has made the tiny Italian town of Colonnato a mecca for culinary tourism. It has helped the region function from the demise of traditional industries and stage an economic recovery (Leitch, 2003). According to Fogarty (2003), in 2003 there were 'over 390 farmers markets and the calendar year is once again filled with local food festivals, agricultural shows, weekly and monthly fresh produce markets'. In addition, there were 17 Slow Food convivia defined by 'incredible diversity that reflects local distinctiveness of their regions ... helping communities to rediscover their landscapes and culinary treasures and are giving value to producers'. Not all of these farmers markets were related to the Slow Food movement, and many just saw the opportunities presented by growing interest in regional fair as a commercial opportunity. The market also serves 'social sustainability' by maintaining a sense of belonging and ownership and building local consciousness for the connection between quality of life and the availability of services and products that are locally produced and sold (Mayer and Knox, 2006). Further advantages of these local markets are that they can address negative impacts of leakage and homogenization of the produce sold (Robinson, 2008a).

Food has always been clearly linked to politics, and indeed to many historical revolutions (Leitch, 2003). For example the French Revolution in 1789 was sparked at least in part by Marie-Antoinette's lack of sympathy to bread shortages. Early academic predictions were that these protest movements were unlikely to have an impact on the food industry (Jones *et al.*, 2003), but they have entered the debate arena and there has been growth in new campaigns to return to local, seasonal, humane food production techniques, and away from factory farming and fishing.

Whether it was actually the spark that lit the flame of the worldwide protest movement against the industrialization of food (initially) and life itself (latterly) or just part of a wider zeitgeist, the Slow Food movement has established itself as having a significant role in the current global food environment from both supply and consumption aspects. The Italian origin of the movement reflects the Italian culture, in which food and wine are integral. Furthermore, eating is a driving force that also serves as a means to encourage social networks and relations and, of course, food is vital for employment and trade. These three areas highlight the centrality of food in everyday life and are therefore the basis on which not only the Slow Food movement is based, but also from which the Slow City movement takes its guiding principles.

Slow Cities

The Slow City, Cittàslow or Città Lenta movement is a spin-off of the Slow Food movement. It has variously been defined as an urban social movement and a model for local governance (Pink, 2008). The Slow City movement seeks to extend the Slow Food movement's philosophy to all aspects of urban living, providing an agenda of local distinctiveness and urban development. While having a political anti-globalization message, it distinguishes itself from other protest groups as globalization is used for positive purposes, exploiting global communication potential for the promotion of food and cultural differences and fostering networks and transnational cooperation.

Formed in 1999 in Italy, this non-governmental organization has spread across 10 countries and awarded certification to more than 100 cities worldwide. Most of these are located in the Tuscan and Umbrian regions of Italy, but other European cities have also joined (e.g. Waldkirch, Hersbrück and Schwarzenbrück in Germany; Levanger and Sokndal in Norway; Ludlow, Diss, Mold and Aylsham in the UK) as well as towns in Australia and South Korea (Cittàslow, 2006a). For a town to become a member, the population must number less than 50,000 and comply with a list of criteria covering the six pillars of environmental policies, infrastructural policies, technologies and facilities for urban quality, safeguarding autochthonous production, hospitality and awareness (Table 9.1). The Slow City charter contains 55 pledges or criteria and provides detailed guidelines on requirements for Slow City status. Regular assessment of the adherence to charter guidelines is carried out once Slow City status has been awarded (Cittàslow, 2006b).

The Slow Food and Slow City movements encourage a change of mindset and philosophy

Table 9.1. The six pillars of Slow City certification.

Pillar	Examples
Environmental policies	Air-quality control, waste management, light pollution control, alternative energy sources
	Compliance with environmental legislation, adoption of environmental management systems
Infrastructural policies	Urban planning and transport measures – reduction of traffic, improvement of parks, restoration of old buildings
Technologies and facilities for urban quality	Urban design that bans neon signs
Safeguarding autochthonous production	Banning fast food outlets, promoting local markets, support for local products, development of organic agriculture
Hospitality	Supporting conviviality through local cultural events and the establishment of convivia, increase local gastronomic traditions
Awareness	Education programmes for both locals and visitors
	Taste education in schools, creation of school gardens
	Skill sharing and skill building in farming techniques, food preparation and crafts
	Code of Conduct

and a reevaluation of changes that modern society has brought. Technological advances have resulted in time savings and as a consequence modern society is characterized by fast living and a constant fast-forward motion by which people are often overscheduled, busy, task orientated and stressed. Consequently, connections and connectedness are argued to be lost. The preservation of local and cultural heritage as well the integration of local production and support of independent businesses are some of the key issues for a Slow City. Impacts of commercialization and the development of mass tourism is discouraged and avoided, and there is extensive concern for the local environment by promoting sustainable travel modes. From a supply-side perspective, this may be further enhanced through the development of tourism capital within communities, manifest through community-based tourism projects (see Chapter 7) and the use of other local facilities such as religious buildings and leisure facilities. A convivium is the basic structural unit and is required to be an open group with its activities and events not simply limited to members (statutes the limit minimum and maximum numbers). The direct participation of private companies in convivia is not permitted, but otherwise each convivium is free to organize its own agenda of activities and initiate supporting links with local producers.

Convivia also play an important role in the larger projects in their own regions as sponsors or nominators (Parkins and Craig, 2006).

Following Slow Food and Slow Cities, the movement has been extended further to other aspects of society and living. The Slow Movement (see http://www.slowmovement. com) provides ideas on how the concept of slow can be applied to education, books, money and living. How the concept is adapted to travelling and tourism will be outlined further below; however, central to all of these applications is addressing the issue of time poverty and fast solutions by encouraging more thorough connections to people, places and life.

Slow Tourism

Building from the ideas of the Slow Movement, the same principles and philosophy can be easily applied to tourism. Central to the meaning and concept of Slow Tourism is the shift in focus from achieving a quantity and volume of experiences while on holiday towards the quality of (generally fewer) experiences. It is a form of tourism that respects local cultures, history and environment and values social responsibility while celebrating diversity and connecting people (tourists with other tourists and with host communities); it is characterized

---

Case Study 9.1. Cittaslow in the UK.

Ludlow's bid to become a Slow City came about as a result of a public meeting organized by the town's local Agenda 21 group. Thirty people attended this first discussion. After a meeting with Cittaslow in London, the group pressed ahead with the application, supported by the Chamber of Trade and Commerce and the town and district councils. On November 24, 2003, Ludlow became the UK's first Cittaslow.

Numerous organizations are now actively involved in Cittaslow Ludlow, including local wildlife trusts, Age Concern, youth groups, women's institutes and business groups. The project is closely linked to the Ludlow Marches Slow Food Convivium, demonstrating how these two concepts can be joined together effectively.

Since 2003 a number of other UK Towns have also become Cittaslow members, including Aylsham, Diss, Mold, Perth, Berwick-upon-Tweed, Cockermouth, Linlithgow and Sturminster Newton.

Within this listing, Mold was the first Welsh town to become part of the movement and the impact of Cittaslow has been evidenced through some of the work and activities that have taken place since. Within the scheme in Mold there are three subgroups: environmental policy, space and place (infrastructure), and local produce and community.

Future aims of the Mold movement include an assessment of the opportunities for Mold to become a carbon-neutral community, while previous projects include the creation of a local producers' directory, a farmers' and producers' forum, promotion of the diversity of local produce and a monthly Cittaslow market stall. Other work includes a survey of public benches and an assessment of future transport requirements and opportunities to develop and promote local heritage.

---

by the enjoyment of discovery, learning and sharing. This 'slowing' of the pace of a holiday provides opportunities to interact and connect with local people and places on a deeper level. This facilitates a more detailed exploration of the cultural environment in which the holiday is taking place and results in a more rewarding and memorable experience for the participants.

Slow Tourism can be considered from several different perspectives. The first central element of tourism activity is the necessity for transport and travel to a new place. In the slow scenario, this represents a move away from long-haul, airline-focused travel (which reaches many destinations very quickly) towards alternative forms of travel. Not only does Slow Tourism require a change in travel behaviour and transport choice, but also the supply perspectives linked to the choice of transport. Second, the slow philosophy shares common characteristics with sustainable tourism. Therefore, Slow Tourism needs to be discussed in the context of tourism development and sustainability. Third, Slow Tourism as a product requires a discussion on the value that the label 'slow' attaches to a product or a service. Hence there are marketing implications, which are discussed later in this chapter. Finally, we need to establish who the Slow Tourist is and highlight ideas on how slow fits in with theories of consumer behaviour.

Travel is addressed separately as it is, arguably, separate from tourism – unlike accommodation provision, which, to fit the slow philosophy, tends to relate to people staying in self-catering accommodation and more often than not buying food in local shops and integrating themselves further into the local community. It may be more popularly manifest through camping and particularly through the recent increase in high-quality camping in wigwams, with kitchens and other facilities more akin to those that would be found in a building (luxury or 'glam' camping has recently been named 'glamping'). The opportunity to stay in self-catering facilities allows the traveller to become more integrated into the community, partake of community services, visit local hostelries and purchase local produce. It moves away from the idea of the 'resort' or the 'holiday park' (which are conversely noisy and exciting, with fast food and instant entertainment) and seeks to offer a more traditional lifestyle that may bring with it many benefits to the local community. Such benefits are precluded by the inclusive nature of resort-type facilities, which prevents local interaction and stymies the potential economic benefits for local communities.

Slow Tourism activities while on holiday do not differ much from other types of tourism, but again the key characteristics of engagement, immersion and slowness are central to the experiential philosophy of 'slow' that requires more integration, research and lingering within the environment to acquire more knowledge and form stronger memories. Not all attractions are designed to offer this experience and many are forced to offer 'fast' tourism because of their popularity and consequent pressure to manage high visitor volumes. Arguably, then, while Slow Tourists are likely to engage with any type of attraction, the smaller 'hidden gems' are likely to be the most rewarding.

Slow Travel

The primary idea of slow travel is its relationship and connection with culture and the opportunities it offers for visitors to become a part of a local community, often using local services, and travelling slowly enough to enjoy more detailed aspects of the places that they pass through. It removes the notion of 'must-see attractions' and the need to 'fit as much in as possible', but avoids the idea that a tourist sits on a beach for a week doing very little. Instead, it represents a very different experience that includes some of the must-see places, but seen more purely through their relationship with their host community.

If we consider Slow Tourism and apply it to transport, one key observation here is the move away from airline travel and the use of slow transport or forms of transportation that fit the slow philosophy. Air transport is considered to be an epitome of globalization and hence an antidote to slowness. Instead, Slow Tourism requires the use of slower and more environmentally friendly forms of transport. Furthermore, within destinations, public or local transport should be used in order to encourage the closer connection with locals and local culture. As Slow Tourism is also characterized by a more active engagement, hiking and cycling are tourism activities that fit the concept as these forms of transportation encourage the tourist to engage more with the destination, landscape and local environment.

Slow travel is clearly exemplified in the example of narrowboats or heritage railways where these are part of the tourism infrastructure, but they represent a mode of travel that is relatively polluting for the environment. By contrast, travel that follows the true nature of the slow concept – traditional and low-impact (e.g. horse-drawn carts) – still exists in some parts of the world, not just for the benefit of tourists but as a necessity for the community. The Island of Sark (UK Channel Islands) is one example, representing a deliberate decision by the islanders to focus on traditional forms of transport. This is the opposite of the situation in some countries, such as rural Romania, where horse-drawn carts may be the only form of transport available because of the economic conditions. Whether this contributes to the experience of tourism in those countries is arguable, although most likely the majority of travellers see this as part of the authentic nature of the destination. This idea, of course, derives from its polar opposite of fast-moving commuter trains and busy stations and instead looks back to a reflective and quieter past.

The Slow Tourist

Not much research has yet been done on the Slow Tourist, which is not surprising given the recency of the idea. Nevertheless, looking at the theories of consumer behaviour and tourism motivation discussed in Chapter 3, we can apply these to the slow themes of food, travel, tourism and lifestyle.

Slow food appeals to those gastro-tourists who are motivated by the desire to acquire social capital, as well as those who are motivated by a love of good food. Appreciation of food and the development of taste are attributes of cultural capital and can be flaunted by these tourists upon their return home as part of their habitus or lifestyle (Bourdieu, 1984). These models of food and drink consumption enhance identity and are intrinsic to an individual's class, prestige and status (Pietrykowski, 2004).

While it is a criticism of Slow Food that it is firmly positioned in the concept that models itself on European culture and lifestyle – which is somewhat exclusive of non-European, urban working classes – it is the preserve of the educated and travelled (Gaytan, 2003). The implication of this is that those interested are likely to be interested in gastro-tourism, and due to their status have sufficient resources to participate and then purchase goods when they return to their homes. Slow Food events however, such as Terra Madre, have been a catalyst for people to travel from all over the world. Convivia members, who are often not the typical gastro-tourists and come from diverse non-European backgrounds, are regular delegates at these events.

On the one hand, Slow Tourists share characteristics with the generic tourist types. On the other hand, they do not fit one type. For example, a Slow Tourist could be argued to be a venturer as he/she seeks to engage with the local culture and learn about local heritage while using local transport and facilities. Yet, in the case of the Slow Tourist, the criticism of Plog's geographical focus applies, as the aversion to long-haul travel and the centrality of exciting, adventurous experiences while on holiday seems to be in direct conflict with the slow philosophy. Consequently, the Slow Tourist only partly fits the model of Cohen's drifter and explorer, while also sharing personality traits more akin to the mass tourist. The Slow Tourist might rely on holiday rentals and home-from-home environments in terms of accommodation, but is very independent and flexible in planning experiences as this facilitates unique insights into the host culture and local environments. Furthermore, central to Slow Tourism is to follow the natural rhythm of things and pay more attention to local aspects of life off the beaten track. Yet, as the Slow Tourist is less likely to travel far and is not found in long-haul destinations, the host environment resembles more similarly the tourist's home environment and there is not much of a culture shock.

Of course, taking geographical distance as a deciding factor is too simplistic, and if long-haul travel is taken out of the equation, Slow Tourists will still populate long-haul destinations. While a plane might have brought the tourist to a destination, the Slow Tourist may still engage in tourism activities that reflect the slow philosophy. Backpackers serve as a good example here: they are found in long-haul destinations, but make extensive use of local facilities and seek engagement with local people to add to their experiences. Similarly, volunteer tourists can be considered Slow Tourists, travelling to developing countries in Africa, Asia or Latin America where they stay in one area and take part in local life while helping the local community.

Apart from the tourist typologies, Slow Tourism motivation can make use of generic tourism motivation theories. Given that Slow Tourism originates from the Slow Food movement, the appreciation of local food and taste is central to the Slow Tourism experience and the food (including its production process) can be considered a pull factor. Accordingly, Slow Tourism mainly caters for physical motivators. This is further evidenced through the avoidance of stress and noisy environments and a focus on activities that engage body and spirit (e.g. hiking, cycling). However, as the Slow Tourist is also keen on learning about local culture, cultural factors play a central role in motivation and local culture and heritage are further pull factors. Furthermore, if the Slow Tourist is seeking to understand the places he/ she visits, or is seeking to develop new skills through learning the language or taking a cooking course, personal development is another motivator. Again, volunteer tourists share the ideas of Slow Tourists in that they are helping the local community and thereby satisfying their achievement and development needs. Here, the slow philosophy and the concept of slow is not such a strong pull factor as it caters for some of the tourist's needs and there are considerable overlaps with regard to satisfaction of higher-level needs. Therefore, slowness may also function as a push factor. If we consider the Slow Tourist's background, the travel career ladder could also give scope for analysis – assuming that many people do most long-haul travelling during their younger years, the more senior traveller looks for more comfort and less adventure, reflecting at least a little of the idea of the Slow Tourist.

In addition, authenticity is another concept that can be applied to the Slow Tourist experience. While the locals refer to the 'soul of the town' and local heritage (Nilsson *et al.*, 2007), Slow Tourists focus on immersion in local life and an understanding of the places they visit beyond their initial tourist offer. Hence, authenticity becomes a focal point for the Slow Tourist and much of the experience is driven by the search for authenticity. Indeed, much of the slow philosophy resembles the idea of authenticity. The central idea of slow travelling is not a new concept as it is very much what Boorstin (1961) laments in his discussion on the lost art of travel (see Chapter 4). At this point, we could pick up the discussion of traveller versus tourist, in that the Slow Tourist can be described as a traveller who rejects the tourism infrastructure with Western amenities, commodified products, standardized services and the focus on consumption. Nevertheless, just as the discussions surrounding tourist types and motivation can be reiterated here, likening the Slow Tourist to a more sensitive traveller gives room for discussion surrounding mass and niche tourism (see Chapter 1) as well as the individual nature of each tourist (see Chapter 3).

Slow Tourism as a marketing tool

The Slow Food and Slow City movements are not directly aimed at tourism (despite reference being made to hospitality in the charters) and thus are not about tourism or destination marketing. However, they can influence local tourism in two ways. First, they can have an influence on destination development; and second, the brand 'Slow' can bring a quality reputation with it (Nilsson *et al.*, 2007). Subsequently, Slow Tourism and its associates, Slow Food and Slow City, can make use of the label 'slow' to attract quality tourists and quality tourism development.

Tourism development, according to the slow philosophy, brings together processes guided by a slow ideology that influence the quality of a destination's appearance and environment, as well as its public image. In terms of destination-specific resources, the attractions mainly build on cultural heritage such as historical buildings, pedestrian streets, street markets and gastronomy. While the focus is more on the supply side and less on the demand side, marketing has not been explored by any Slow Cities yet – this omission might be intentional in order to avoid too much tourism, or due to a lack of skills. Nevertheless, the concept indirectly influences segmentation.

The consumer's interest is a distinctive point in Slow Food, Slow Cities and subsequently Slow Tourism, which already results in one possible segmentation of the market – quality products and services aimed at the (environmentally or culturally) conscious consumer. Furthermore, the close link between Slow City and Slow Food influences Slow Tourism and potential marketing activities through a common brand identity that can benefit any slow products and services. Food is most publicly visible aspect of most towns' events and both Slow Cities and Slow Tourism can benefit from a well-known brand among a relatively large group of people interested in gastronomy. Hence, a second consumer market is the gastronomic tourist and tours themed around Slow Food. Referring back to the potential background of Slow Tourists, Nilsson *et al.* (2007) observed a substantial number of older tourists in Slow Cities, which suggests that this is a market segment to which the concept of slow is appealing. As the Slow Movement rejects homogenization in the form of chain stores and mass tourism in favour of supporting local producers and independent businesses, economies of scale do not apply and prices are fair, but higher. Consequently, Slow Cities as tourism destinations will never have a wide appeal among lower-income groups. While a wealthier clientele certainly brings low-impact but high-quality money into these areas, Nilsson *et al.* (2007) have warned that there is a risk of increased social segmentation and gentrification, which may have a negative impact on the local community.

Besides external marketing, the concept of slow is also a useful internal marketing tool. The movement is guided by an integrated set of thoughts that requires the involvement of the local community and partnerships, and further involves changes in lifestyle, values and attitude – not only towards the concept of slow, but also towards tourism. As locals are an important part of creating an appealing atmosphere for tourists and tourists' feedback in turn can lead to an appreciation of local culture and heritage among locals, it thereby encourages local involvement in tourism and a strengthening of the local identity (Nilsson *et al.*, 2007).

Case Study 9.2. Hersbrück and Waldkirch, Germany (adapted from Mayer and Knox, 2006).

A study by Mayer and Knox (2006) highlights how two German Slow Cities have adopted programs, policies, and activities to exhibit a strong emphasis on connecting the three Es (economy, environment and equity). Hersbruck has created income opportunities for local residents and regional and community economic development through strong coalitions between farmers, city government and small businesses, which all work together to protect traditional pasture land. Networks of local farmers sell their products directly from the farm, and regional fairs of local products are held yearly in a different village in the region. Protection programs also focus on heritage apple trees and organic produce made from local fruit trees and pasturelands, which are marketed regionally. This extends to the use of local produce in traditional region-specific dishes in restaurants, thus extending the links through the supply chain within the hospitality sector. In addition, local cooking schools teach children how to prepare and serve food as well as educating them about food and taste. This ensures that the next generation acquires skills and knowledge about local traditions and further enhances the connection between food and locality and territory. Finally, another local group has been formed to discuss and implement better uses of local woods and the promotion of local wood varieties for alternative energy production, house building and furniture. All of these projects highlight how Hersbruck's efforts can connect environmental protection with community economic development by building on local distinctiveness and the revival and protection of local traditions in a forward-looking way.

Waldkirch represents a good example of how a city can underpin its economy with consideration for the socioeconomic well-being of its community members and promotion of social sustainability. Through a project called 'Red House', a house – formerly used for homeless people and where the public space served as a car junk yard – was renovated and is now a multifunctional community place that offers local employment opportunities. It now houses a social worker office, a community kitchen, a weekly farmers' market in the front of the house, a second-hand shop and various service-oriented activities (e.g. garden work, couriers, moving services). Since its opening and through its various associated programs, crime and vandalism has been reduced and residents of all ages and ethnic groups have built stronger social networks. In addition, Waldkirch emphasizes the protection and creation of social sustainability in other areas; for example, through the main farmers' market in the prominent central square, which offers locals, vendors and visitors an opportunity for social interaction and produces increased identification as well as a strong sense of place. Waldkirch aims to rebuild a sense of local community through projects and programs that build local consciousness for the quality of life, the availability of locally produced and sold services and products, locality sensitive lifestyle, and food production and consumption, as well as the security of local jobs.

These two German Slow Cities illustrate the possibilities of implementing an alternative urban development agenda by focusing on the connections between economy, environment and equity. The strategies focus on community economic stability, asset specificity and economic localism – thereby following the guidelines as set out by the Slow City philosophy. However, crucial to the success of both cities is that the strategies had been implemented before they became certified as Slow Cities. The Slow City certification adds an official stamp of approval to the efforts that were already underway. In addition, political circumstances have increased the readiness to adopt alternative strategies; both towns have social-democratic mayors who have served for a long time and gained the trust of the residents. The high number of civic organizations already present resulted in the towns already having a strong sense of community. In addition, both towns have favourable economic conditions as they are located near successful larger cities and have a strong small business community that plays an active leading role in the Slow City movement.

---

investment required for businesses to be accredited. Butler (1998) observed that 'thinking globally and acting locally will work only if local actions are part of an integrated holistic approach and include solutions to past problems [and, therefore, sustainability] cannot be tackled in isolation, spatially, economically or temporally ... the past holds the key to the future'.

While Slow Food and Slow Tourism can be adapted in many destinations, only a few of these will fit into the category of Slow City (an urban area with a population of less than 50,000). These ambiguities, finite numbers and limits may create more barriers to inclusion than incentives to join. There has been growing interest in America, but the urban structure and sociocultural patterns are different from those in Europe.

Having discussed Slow Cities within the context of sustainability, the discussion invariably leads to criticism of the term for exactly this reason. The lack of a consensus on definitions of sustainability and sustainable tourism has led to various interpretations, depending on the individual, local or national ideology that influences the policies created for the purpose of sustainable (tourism) development. This is reinforced by arguments that sustainability is a political rather than a technical or scientific construct. However, this is arguably where Slow Tourism can address the issue. As mentioned above, the Slow City charter provides a detailed, yet holistic approach that irons out potential points of concern with its clear philosophy and ideological guidelines. Just as sustainability is a contested concept (as it refers to a balanced approach or wise use of resources, but the way in which balance or wise use is defined will depend upon the values of various stakeholders; Hall, 2008), the Slow City concept can also potentially become the subject of argument. However, where Slow Tourism may have an advantage above other measures of sustainability is its potential for internationalization, as it is able to apply the same standards to its members wherever they are located in the world. By contrast, the ethical, environmental and economic aspects of sustainable management will differ in different countries based upon political motivations, structure and development needs, and the action encouraged by Agenda 21 is exclusively local.

Future Research

As identified at the start of this chapter, the idea of Slow Tourism and its associated concepts are new; subsequently, there is much still to research. The opportunities to investigate the phenomenon of Slow Tourism and slow travel are vast because so little has yet been researched.

There are debates around the motivations for and benefits of involvement, levels of support and participation and the adoption of 'slow' as an element of community-based tourism. None of the towns involved in the movement has been involved in any in-depth or longitudinal surveys and little has been done to assess the economic impacts of the Slow Movement.

There is also much to study around the label of 'slow' and what it really means to various stakeholders, its role within and outside of sustainable tourism development and its role within consumer motivation. Current research suggests that the next decade will witness a move away from purchasing goods to spending more on experiences, and experience will become of far greater value to many travellers.

Like Slow Tourism, slow travel is a new concept and will probably grow in both its academic research base and its popularity as a product if 'slow' also becomes a more widely accepted product base and viable service. From a demand perspective, much research has been carried out into sustainable tourist behaviour; however the role of the Slow Tourist still begs further investigation in order to establish whether the philosophical underpinnings, as proposed in this chapter, present a different view of the tourist.

Conclusion

This chapter has provided an overview of the three concepts of Slow Food, Slow Cities and Slow Tourism. While the Slow Food movement has attracted many followers and is considerably well known, Slow City is still struggling to survive as a viable concept. Independent of their popularity, both movements present new approaches to long standing issues within contemporary society. Applying and extending the two movements to tourism, this chapter has sought to apply the slow concept within a tourism context by offering insights into how tourism destinations, businesses and consumers can be guided by a shift in the underlying principles and philosophy of 'slow'.

Just as the Slow Food and Slow City movements oppose fast food and globalization, Slow Tourism can be considered to be the antidote to mass tourism and the subsequent

Case Study 9.3. 'Streets for All'.

Another movement that has seen a significant growth in popularity in the UK is a rebellion against signage and enforceable street furniture such as bollards and bins. This movement has arisen from an interest in the historic value and nature of the traditional street scene. This is best exemplified through well-preserved Georgian towns with architecture and street views that are worthy of note, but suffer a blight of poles, posts, signs, furniture and other items that have become necessary. By contrast, that same town with these items removed starts to return to its true historical appearance, creating the type of environment that suits the Slow Movement.

In some instances this signage is necessary and useful, but then the focus is on the characterization and appropriateness of signage so it doesn't detract from the quality and sense of place, but adds to it through the use of historic design features (Fig. 9.1).

In the early part of the millennium this issue started to concern English Heritage, England's public sector body responsible for heritage. In response, English Heritage produced a set of streetscape manuals, 'Streets for All', that stipulated how streets and street furniture can be better managed. Each document addresses the systems required to reduce clutter, coordinate design and reinforce local character.

The documents consider the nature of ground surfaces, pavement colours, historic kerbstones and street furniture such as barriers, lighting and colours, and suggests designing streets to minimize the need for street furniture such as bollards. Coloured tarmac should be avoided and consideration of future maintenance also needs to be built into any design plans. Coordination is also required between the local authorities responsible for roads and planning to ensure a joined-up approach to urban development and restructuring.

In towns where these methods have been adopted, this has often required special permission to demarcate parking areas with different signage and the installation of structures such as wooden posts, road narrowing and coloured flagstones to demarcate pedestrian crossings. The results have been very popular with local communities and the improvements have benefited the context of the town and, therefore, the experience and authenticity for tourists.

Fig. 9.1. Original features and related modern additions in the streetscape of Ironbridge, UK.

mass tourism development and commodification of local culture to cater for mass tourists. This does not mean that Slow Tourism can be considered niche tourism. Instead, it is suggested here that the meaning of slow is applied to destination management, business operations and consumer behaviour to create a change of status quo to oppose existing tourism ontologies. The viability and success of this paradigm shift is yet to be proven, but may be possible.

Review Questions

1. Develop an evaluative response to the concept of 'slow' as a tool for sustainable tourism management.
2. What other elements of the tourist experience could be described or packaged as slow? How would these enhance the slow experience?
3. Debate this question: is Slow Tourism a viable approach or 'old wine in new bottles'?

References

Boorstin, D (1961) *The image or what happened to the American Dream.* Penguin Books, VIC, Australia.

Bourdieu, P. (1984) *Distinction.* Harvard University Press, Cambridge, Massachusetts.

Butler, R. (1998) Sustainable tourism – looking backwards in order to progress? In: Hall, C.M. and Lew, A. (eds) *Sustainable Tourism.* Addison Wesley Longman, Harlow, UK, pp. 25–34.

Cittàslow (2006a) Slow for a better life, Cittàslow – Reze internazionale delle città del buon vivere. Available from: http://www.cittaslow.net/sezioni/Rete%20Internazionale/pagine.asp?idn=1234. Accessed 4th June, 2008.

Cittàslow (2006b) Cittaslow International Charter, Cittàslow – Reze internazionale delle città del buon vivere. Available from: http://www.cittaslow.net/sezioni/Rete%20Internazionale/pagine.asp?idn=1384. Accessed 4th June, 2008.

Fogarty, W. (2003) *Slow Food UK in Slow Food Agricola Editore – Bra (Cn).* Slow Food, London, UK.

Gaytan, M. (2003) *Globalizing the Local: Slow Food and the Collective Imaginary.* American Sociological Association, Atlanta, Georgia.

Hall, C.M. (2008) *Tourism Planning – Policies, Processes and Relationships,* 2nd edn. Pearson Education, Harlow, UK.

Hall, M.C. (2006) Introduction. Culinary tourism and regional development: from Slow Food to Slow Tourism? *Tourism Review International* 9, 303–305.

Heitmann, S. and Robinson, P. (2009) Slow cities – the Emperor's new clothes or (another) solution for sustainable tourism management? BAM Conference, Brighton, 15–17th September, 2009.

Jones, P., Shears, P., Hillier, D., Comfort, D. and Lowell, J. (2003) Return to traditional values? A case study of Slow Food. *British Food Journal* 105, 297–304.

Leitch, A. (2003) Slow food and the politics of pork fat. *Ethnos* 68, 437–462.

Knox, P. (2005) Creating ordinary places: Slow Cities in a fast world. *Journal of Urban Design* 10, 1–11.

Mayer, H. and Knox, P. (2006) Slow cities – sustainable places in a fast world. *Journal of Urban Affairs* 28, 321–334.

Nilsson, J.H., Svard, A.C., Widarsson, A. and Wirell, T. (2007) 'Slow' destination marketing in small Italian towns, Paper presented to the 16th Nordic Symposium in Tourism and Hospitality Research, Helsingborg, 2007.

Nosi, C. and Zanni, L. (2004) Moving from 'typical products' to 'food-related services': the Slow Food case as a new business paradigm. *British Food Journal* 106, 779–792.

Parkins, W. and Craig, G. (2006) *Slow Living.* Berg, Oxford, UK.

Petrini, C. (2001) *Slow Food: The Case for Taste.* Columbia University Press, New York.

Pietrykowski, B. (2004) You are what you eat: the social economy of the Slow Food movement. *Review of Social Economy* LXII, 307–321.

Pink, S. (2008) Sense and sustainability: the case of the Slow City movement. *Local Environment* 13, 99–106.

Radstrom, S. (2005) An urban identity movement rooted in the sustainability of place: a case study of Slow Cities and their application in rural Manitoba. Master's dissertation, University of Manitoba, Manitoba, Canada.

Robinson, P. (2008a) Local food – an opportunity for tourism. *Tourism Insights,* February, available at: http://www.insights.org.uk/articleitem.aspx?title=Local+Food+%E2%80%93+an+Opportunity+for+Tourism; accessed 3rd November 2010.

Robinson, P. (2008b) The Case for Community-Led Tourism. Leisure Studies Association Conference. Liverpool John Moore's University 8–11th July, 2008.

Slow Food (2010) Definition of Slow Food. Available from: http://www.slowfood.com. Accessed May 29, 2010.

10 Events, Festivals and the Arts

Gemma Gelder and Peter Robinson

Introduction

This chapter introduces and defines events, festivals and the arts, which are inextricably linked to tourist activity and interest. The purpose of this chapter is to highlight and understand the role and contribution of these concepts and the key themes that emerge. The chapter is divided into three sections for convenience based on each individual discipline; however, it must be noted that the three concepts do interlink and are not discussed in isolation. Events, festivals and the arts have a tourism connection and a range of local and international case studies and examples used throughout the chapter illustrate the relationships between them, especially their ability to draw large audiences both local or from a great distance, the latter of which usually results in an overnight stay.

The events industry, including festivals, the arts, meetings, incentives, conferences, exhibitions, sports and a range of other activities, has witnessed significant growth over the last two decades, and today makes a significant contribution to business- and leisure-related tourism. This growth has also been reflected in education, with a host of events-related courses being developed and a significant increase in research in the events sector.

Events today, be they local or international, are central to our culture, more perhaps than ever before. Increased leisure time and discretionary spending have led to an abundance of public events, celebrations and entertainment. Governments now support and promote events as part of their strategies for economic development, nation building and destination marketing. Festivals and events are viewed as a new form of tourism that attract thousands of visitors (and thus tourist income) and encourage economic prosperity, development and regeneration.

A Historical Perspective

Events have long played an important part in human society and were originally a celebration of ceremony and rituals. In the contemporary world several major events still revolve around periods in the Christian calendar such as Christmas and Easter, in addition to Halloween and patriotic celebrations. In can be argued therefore that special events are historically embedded in the social fabric of day-to-day life, but in modern times we are often so used to special events that we do not always see them in this context. This indicates the difficulty for students of event-related disciplines to fully understand the true extent of these activities, their variety, their role and how they operate.

Since the mid 1990s, much of the focus of events and festivals has been on attracting tourists due to the additional economic benefits they bring to a community or place. Many events that people take for granted today, however, have been taking place in one form or another for hundreds of years. These include fairs, festivals, sporting events, exhibitions and other forms of public celebration. Examples include the Lord Mayor's Show, which originated in 1215, and the Olympic Games, which date back thousands of years. Over the last 100 years, the Olympic Games has become the biggest sporting and cultural event in the world. Although there are some long-established festivals such as the Three Choirs Festival (the oldest surviving non-competitive music festival in the world, dating back to 1715), the majority have appeared since around the 1960s onwards. This period is particularly notable for factors that shaped events as they appear today.

Rogers (2003) in Bowdin *et al.* (2006) points out that the 1960s witnessed significant investment in infrastructure that supported conferences, meetings and related events. This period also saw the rapid increase of events celebrating different cultures, such as the Notting Hill Carnival established in 1964, and the appearance of a number of popular music festivals, including the Bath Blues Festival (1969) the Pilton Festival (1970, now the prestigious Glastonbury Festival) and the Isle of Wight Festival (1968, 1969 and 1970). The 1970 Isle of Wight Festival is believed to be the largest ever UK music festival, with over 600,000 people attending (Bowdin *et al.*, 2006). It became a free show as the organizers fought a losing battle to keep control over admissions to the sprawling event. Sections of fence around the arena were broken down and people poured in. This illustrated the need for event professionals to organize and control such events.

The 1970s and 1980s witnessed the building of a range of multipurpose venues, including the National Exhibition Centre (NEC) in Birmingham (1976) and the Brighton Centre (1977). These continue to cater for numerous events and exhibitions. The 1980s saw a rapid increase in the use of spectator sports for corporate hospitality, with international sporting events such as the Open Golf Championship, Wimbledon and Royal Ascot still popular today. The 1980s also saw expansion in the number of arts and culture-related events due to increased funding from the Arts Council and regional arts boards. Links with local authorities increased as they recognized the huge role these play in tourism and urban regeneration.

Throughout the 20th century and into the new millennium, the UK enjoyed major success in hosting an array of international events, including winning the bid to hold the Olympic Games in 2012. Over the years the pace of development has rapidly increased to include a number of multipurpose indoor arenas in large cities such as Birmingham, Manchester and Cardiff, plus the launch of ExCeL, a £300 million international events venue, in London in 2000. Major events are continuing to be held through 21st century, with increasing recognition that they go beyond mere entertainment. This brief outline of the history of modern events, although primarily related to the UK, has been replicated in most post-industrial societies (Bowdin *et al.*, 2006). The emergence of an events industry in Australia, for example, only really occurred in the mid-1990s and the title 'events management' was first used as late as 1986 (Yeoman *et al.*, 2004). Events are now a growing phenomenon worldwide and continue to play a dominant role in society, fulfilling a basic human need.

Events

Before exploring the notion of events in more detail it is important to provide some context and a framework to clarify the shape and scope of the sector. As some have contended, there are as many definitions of events as there are texts. Getz (2005) noted, however, that a principle applying to all events is they are temporary and that 'every such event is unique stemming from the blend of management, program, setting and people'. Shone and Parry (2004) said, 'Special events are that phenomenon arising from those non-routine occasions which have leisure, cultural, personal or organizational objectives set apart from the normal activity of daily life, whose purpose is to enlighten, celebrate, entertain or challenge the experience of a group of people.'

Douglas *et al.* (2001) referred to events 'for people to come together to celebrate, to demonstrate, to worship, to honour, to remember, to socialise ...' while Allen *et al.* (2008) said they are 'specific rituals ... or celebrations that are consciously planned and created to mark special occasions' and that it is 'impossible to provide a definition that includes all varieties [of events]'. From a tourism context, Jago and Shaw (1998) suggested six core attributes of events and stated that special events should: (i) attract tourists or tourism development; (ii) be of limited duration; (iii) be one-off or of infrequent occurrence; (iv) raise the awareness, image or profile of a region; (v) offer a social experience; and (vi) be out of the ordinary. In their summary definition of a special event, they drew these together in defining an event as 'a one-time or infrequently occurring event of limited duration that provides the consumer with a leisure and social opportunity beyond everyday experience. Such events, which attract, or have the potential to attract, tourists, are often held to raise the profile, image or awareness of a region' (Jago and Shaw, 1998).

Events can also be categorized or grouped on the basis of size or type (Fig. 10.1). The largest events are called mega events and are generally targeted towards international markets. They usually occur after competitive bidding and can have an effect on the whole

community or nation and have worldwide implications. Examples include the Olympic Games, Commonwealth Games and FIFA World Cup. According to Getz (2007), these are 'by way of their size or significance ... those that yield extraordinarily high levels of tourism, media coverage, prestige, or economic impact for the host community, venue or organization'.

Hallmark events are those that have played a major role in international and national tourism marketing strategies. Their primary function is to provide a host community with the opportunity to secure high prominence in the tourism market place. Events and their host destinations become inseparable in the minds of consumers and provide widespread recognition and awareness. Ritchie (1984) defined them as 'Major one time or recurring events of limited duration, developed primarily to enhance awareness, appeal and profitability of a tourism destination in the short term or long term. Such events rely for their success on uniqueness,

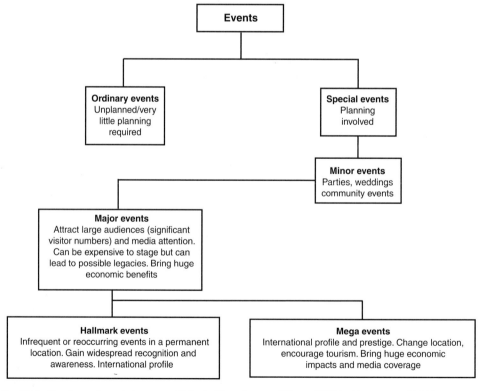

Fig. 10.1. Typology of events by scope. (Adapted from Jago and Shaw, 1998 in Masterman, 2004.)

status, or timely significance to create interest and attract attention.'

Examples of hallmark events include the Melbourne Cup, Adelaide Festival of Arts, Tour de France and Rio Carnival. Classic examples from the UK include Wimbledon, the Glastonbury Festival, the Notting Hill Carnival and the Grand National.

By their size and scale, major events can attract significant visitor numbers and media coverage, as well as generating considerable tourism revenue and economic benefits. Many top international sporting championships fit into this category (Bowdin *et al.*, 2006) and are increasingly being sought after by national sporting organizations and governments in the competitive world of international major events. Examples include the Open Golf Championship and the Australian Tennis Open. Other non-sporting examples that fit into this category include arts festivals that bring people together to celebrate their local area or the musical *Phantom of the Opera* in London, which attracts thousands of international visitors a year.

Most events, however, fall into the category of minor events. These include anything from parties to celebrations and meetings to weddings. Most community, social, fundraising and charity events fall into this category. Many of these are planned and delivered to raise awareness or money and are organized by volunteers. Both in private and public, people like to mark, celebrate and rejoice the important occasions in their lives and remember milestones. Local governments often support such events as part of their community and cultural development strategies as they can encourage community participation in sports, arts-related activities and so on, and produce a range of benefits including pride in the community, a sense of belonging and promotion of cultural awareness and diversity (see Chapter 7).

Events in tourism

Events serve many purposes, including celebration, entertainment for locals and provision of recreational activity in and out of season for visitors. They help promote a destination and attract tourism, which leads to economic prosperity and development, including regeneration. Media coverage generated by events can contribute towards creating a positive destination image in the tourism marketplace. Events and festivals are seen as a tool for raising awareness and as a catalyst in promoting a destination and attracting tourists. The image of a destination can be enhanced or damaged by the success or failure of a festival or event.

Event tourism has been defined by Getz and Wicks (1993) as 'the systematic planning, development and marketing of festivals and special events as tourist attractions, catalysts, and image builders'. Enhancement of consumers' awareness of a destination is a common reason that destinations seek to host events

According to Morgan and Pritchard (2004), it is difficult to visit a major city without being confronted by an impressive list of sporting and cultural events that compete to capture the attention of tourists. The events add to the city's range of tourist attractions and they often actively seek media coverage as a promotional strategy, hoping that more people will be encouraged to visit the city in the future. Thus, events and tourism have become intrinsically linked. One significant element of this relationship is the way in which images associated with an event may be transferred to the destination. In this way, the destination brand may be strengthened, enhanced or changed.

The 2002 Commonwealth Games in Manchester witnessed significant tourism during and after the event. The games generated significant media coverage worldwide (Maunsell, 2004), which had a considerable beneficial impact on tourism for the city through improved awareness and perceptions of Manchester as a visitor destination. Furthermore, a post-games study revealed that an additional £46 million was spent in the region during and after the games. In addition, the games acted as an additional stimulant for the expansion of hospitality facilities in Manchester and the city centre now has a greater capacity to host additional events such as business conferences, major entertainment events (e.g. pop concerts) and major sporting events (e.g. national and international championships) (Maunsell, 2004).

Business events in tourism

Business tourism is a sector of the wider tourism industry and includes meetings, incentives, conferences and exhibitions. These industries are sometimes grouped as discretionary business tourism, MICE. It is an increasingly important part of the tourism industry since it is often of high value and earns hoteliers, caterers and transport companies significant income. The Business Tourism Partnership (2005) has suggested that conferences, exhibitions, incentive travel, corporate hospitality and business travel combined account for 28% of overseas visitors in the UK and 29% of all inbound tourism earnings. This equates to an estimated tourism income worth £20 billion.

Business tourism stimulates future inward investment as business people see the attractions of a destination while travelling on business or to attend a conference, exhibition or incentive, and then return to establish business operations there. They can also become unpaid 'ambassadors' for a destination by communicating to colleagues and others their positive impressions and favourable experiences about a particular destination. Business tourism also complements the leisure tourism sector, relying on much of the same physical infrastructure and bringing business to destinations such as seaside resorts that would otherwise be dependent upon a

relatively short summer season for their economic health and prosperity. In many destinations, such as Brighton in the UK, major conference centres have been developed. The Brighton seafront, partly as a result of the success of the world-famous Brighton Centre, is home to numerous hotel chains and independents. Even facilities designed purely for the events sector, such as the NEC in Birmingham, have been catalysts for hotel developments that now serve the leisure sector as well. In Birmingham this is demonstrated by many of the world-famous events held at the NEC, such as Crufts, alongside trade exhibitions and conferences.

Investments in business tourism facilities lead to the regeneration of urban and inner-city areas, as evidenced by cities such as Birmingham, Belfast, Cardiff, Glasgow and Manchester. Opportunities to host major events – such as the Commonwealth Games (Manchester) or those associated with becoming a European Capital of Culture (Glasgow) – also support major regeneration projects. Many of the investments in a destination's infrastructure designed primarily for the business tourist (e.g. hotels, transport and communication facilities, restaurants, attractions and amenities, even conference auditoria) provide benefits that can also be enjoyed by leisure visitors and local residents.

Case Study 10.1. Multiuse venues offer a host of tourism opportunities (courtesy of Harriet Crowe).

Many theatres now market themselves as multipurpose venues, providing combinations of live entertainment, corporate and private events, and activities for local communities. The Brighton Centre is one of the largest multipurpose venues in the south of England and a thriving business within the local economy and the industry as a whole. Primarily providing a variety of productions and conferences, for which people travel considerable distances, the Brighton Centre demonstrates the possibility for venues to grow into successful businesses as a result of developing their facilities. The number of venues expanding their facilities is increasing, with many now also providing theatres, function spaces and community activities.

The Cresset, another multipurpose venue located in Peterborough, England, demonstrates an understanding of the importance of the local community. The Cresset hosts a wide range of community activities, involving all ages within the surrounding areas. The business is now established as a contributor to the local community and, therefore, the local economy. This in turn ensures the venue's place as a key stakeholder within both the community and the economy.

By making a contribution to the surrounding community and local economy, a business can increase its success. If the business continues to maintain and develop facilities it can sustain or even increase revenue, and subsequently maintain its financial contribution to the local economy. In some cases, such venues can even aid regeneration in surrounding areas.

Audience motivation

Another major part of event tourism is the investigation of a visitor's motivation to attend special events or festivals. Motivation controls behaviour and is usually regarded as having two aspects: it energizes behaviour and directs it towards a goal (see Chapter 3). According to Crompton and McKay (1997), motivation is conceptualized as a dynamic process of internal psychological factors (needs and wants) that generates a state of tension and equilibrium through satisfying the needs. A motive is an internal factor that arouses, directs, and integrates a person's behaviour. Thus a decision to visit an event or festival is a directed action that is triggered by the desire to meet a need.

According to Moutinho in Nicholson and Pearce (2001) motivation 'is a state of need, a condition that exerts a "push" on the individual towards certain types of action that are seen as likely to bring satisfaction'. Crompton (2003) pointed out that a primary goal for staging festivals and events is to create an attraction that offers visitors the potential for satisfying experiences. Satisfaction refers to the quality of a visitor's experience, which is defined as the realization of desired intrinsic outcomes.

One of the key theories of motivation in establishing why people attend festivals and events is conceptually grounded on both the escape-seeking dichotomy and the push–pull model. Escaping is 'the desire to leave the everyday environment behind oneself'; while seeking is 'the desire to obtain psychological (intrinsic) rewards through travel in a contrasting (new or old) environment'. (Iso-Ahola, 1982 in Crompton and McKay, 1997) suggested that a tourist:

> may escape the personal world (i.e., personal troubles, problems, difficulties and failures) and/or the interpersonal world (i.e., co-workers, family members, relatives, friends and neighbours) and he may seek personal rewards (e.g., feelings of mastery, learning about other cultures, rest and relaxation, recharge and getting renewed, ego-enhancement and prestige) and/or interpersonal rewards.

This concept is very similar to the push (escape) and pull (seeking) forces that were proposed by Crompton (1979). In this theory,

push factors (e.g. escapism, curiosity) propel us towards an event, while pull factors (e.g. aspects of the events such as music or artists playing) draw us to an event. Yoon and Uysal (2005) stated that push motivations are more related to internal or emotional aspects and can be seen as the desire for escape, rest and relaxation, prestige, adventure, social interaction and excitement. Pull motivations, on the other hand, are connected to external, situational or cognitive aspects and are inspired by a destination's attractiveness, recreation facilities, cultural attractions, entertainment and natural scenery. The push–pull framework provides a useful approach for examining the motivations underlying tourist and visitation behaviour.

Festivals

In the past couple of decades, festivals have been one of the fastest growing sectors of the world leisure industry. Allen *et al.* (2002) pointed out that festivals are an important expression of human activity that contribute much to our social and cultural life and that they are also increasingly linked to generating business activity and providing income for their host communities. Festivals are attractive to communities looking to address issues of civic design, local pride and identity, heritage, conservation, urban renewal, employment generation, investment and economic development. The word 'festival' can be applied to many activities, but essentially they are special events in which there may be a particular theme or concentration of activities over a set period of time.

Festivals can take many forms – ranging from music, including rock, pop, jazz and folk, to cultural and wine festivals – and their scale and scope can vary from an audience of a few hundred to several thousand. There have been strong uplifts in festival attendance in the last decade due to the emergence of a plethora of major festivals. A large number of festivals are located in rural or coastal parts of the country and in areas that are already attractive to tourists because of their heritage or natural scenery. They have become a pervasive feature of our culture and constitute a vital and growing component of the events industry.

Festivals and tourism

The nature and size of festivals ranges greatly. The Notting Hill Carnival in London, for example, is an annual event that attracts up to 2 million people over two consecutive days. The Adelaide Arts Festival, one of the largest multi-arts festivals in the world, attracted a 600,000-strong audience in 2008 and exceeded box office targets to achieve more than AU$2.5 million in ticket sales. Total income from the festival and its associated events reached nearly AU$6 million (Adelaide Festival, n.d.). In the UK, the music festivals of Glastonbury, Leeds, Reading and the V-Festival are all well-known examples in relation to economic impact and tourism value – the world-famous Glastonbury Festival impacts on the worldwide economy to the tune of more than £73 million (Bakers Associates, 2008). Even festivals that operate on a much smaller scale, such as the Big Chill, Creamfields and Latitude, also make a positive contribution to the economy.

Festivals frequently use unconventional buildings such as stately homes (V-Festival), churches (Rheingau Musik Festival in Germany), museums, art galleries and market halls, or can resort to temporary buildings such as marquees. Although some festivals are not established with tourist audiences in mind, their very nature, destination, range of performers and productions in one place over a short period of time, usually in the summer months, encourages audiences from a wide catchment area. Festivals provide an opportunity for local communities to develop and share their culture, which creates a sense of shared values and beliefs held by the individuals in a local community and provides an opportunity for members of the community to exchange experiences and information. Festivals provide the tourist with the opportunity to see how local communities celebrate their culture and this affects community development. It also helps visitors to interact with the host community and helps local people to meet their leisure needs. The consequence of this process may be tourism development that is in keeping with community wishes and, therefore, more authentic (see Chapter 4). It may thus be satisfying to residents and visitors, and sustainable over the longer term.

Positive and negative impacts of festival tourism

If a festival is successful in attracting tourist audiences and non-locals it is usually considered favourably (Fig. 10.2). Positive impacts may include the following:

- Both direct and indirect audience spending by tourists into an area. According to Shone and Parry (2004), the indirect effects on local businesses, services, infrastructure and environment are extremely significant.
- A festival can create good publicity and a good image for the area, including repeat visitation at non-festival times and encouragement by word of mouth for other non-related businesses to locate in the area (inward investment).
- Opportunities can be created for community development and environmental enhancement, in addition to the more obvious benefit of income generation.

There are, however a number of potential problems associated with festival tourism:

- Hughes (2000) argued that not all festivals are an addition to an area and that some visitors may have visited anyway.
- Regular visitors to the area may be put off by the festival tourists; hence, they are only being replaced with little or no addition to overall numbers.
- The influx of additional tourists results in a change in community infrastructure to serve the needs of festival visitors so that, as festivals grow and begin to make stronger links outside the locality, local entrepreneurs are likely to become 'resentful'. Consequently, the economic benefits of the festival become less significant (O'Sullivan and Jackson, 2002).
- Not every festival is well received by host communities. An influx of visitors can alienate the local community and may have a knock-on effect in terms of traffic congestion, crime and vandalism, resulting in irritation and resentment from the host community.

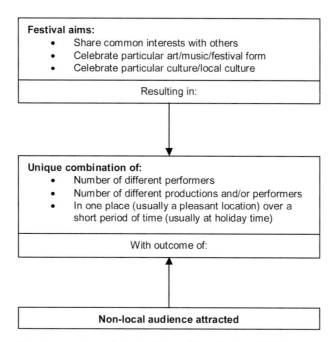

Fig. 10.2. Features that attract tourists to festivals. (Adapted from Hughes, 2000.)

The Arts

The arts are seen as an integral part of celebrating a country's culture or history and are often closely associated with festivals and events (e.g. Adelaide Arts Festival, San Francisco International Arts Festival). Today 'the arts' encompasses a wide collection of activities such as contemporary arts, dance, popular music and visual arts. Traditionally the term 'arts' refers to works and activities such as classical music, opera, ballet, theatre, paintings and sculpture. This list is by no means comprehensive, but does introduce the concept of the arts. It can be argued that it is difficult to actually interpret what art is and that ultimately it is a matter of opinion. According to Tusa (1999), however, the arts are associated with refinement and as being something more than the ordinary man or woman could either produce or appreciate without effort, education and training. The arts are regarded as the work of talented people; they represent the highest levels of human creative ability and are created because of a 'love of the arts' and not as a primarily commercial activity.

The arts are important in society because they bring enjoyment and pleasure, offer a fresh and different perspective, and stimulate and enrich our lives. The arts can also meet some deep needs by helping us to be more creative, communicate, make our mark, find our voice and make sense of the world around us. 'Great art inspires us, brings us together and teaches us about ourselves and the world around us. In short, it makes life better' (Arts Council, 2008).

However, the point where art becomes tourism relies upon accessibility (see Chapter 12). Until art is accessible, it plays no role in the public elements of arts development. It is this aspect of the arts that encourages the public sector to invest in arts development for the benefit of local communities directly (through participation, civic pride and regeneration) and indirectly through tourism. Many international governments have set up bodies through which they finance the arts; examples are Arts Council England, the Australian Council for the Arts, the Canada Council for the Arts, Creative New Zealand and the US National Endowment for the Arts. These bodies all operate on similar principles and have similar objectives, which are

Case Study 10.2. Peter-and-Paul Festival, Bretten (Germany) (Heitmann and David, 2010).

The Peter-and-Paul Festival in Bretten, Germany, is an annual heritage festival during which the local community celebrates the history of its city. Over the years, the festival has attracted up to 125,000 visitors. The main focus is on the medieval history, and a range of activities and smaller events that showcase medieval aspects take place over the 4 days of the festival. These include jugglers, music performances, plays, medieval dances and much more. Most of these are performed by local entertainment and theatre groups, but some outside groups are invited to perform as well. None of these groups receives money, but each collects 'tips' from the audience afterwards. The highlights of the festival are the parade of all participating groups, the firework show and the re-enactment of a battle that took place in 1504.

One of the key parts of the festival is some 3000 locals who wear medieval dress and form groups with specific medieval themes, such as archers, shepherds, lancers, gypsies and many more. Of more than 50 groups most are locals, but several international medieval-interest groups (from Poland, Italy and the UK) are invited to camp during the festival. Each group sets up a camp in which members of the group spend most of their time cooking, socializing or displaying their newly acquired skills to visitors and fellow locals.

Visitors are not allowed in the camps, but are allowed to glimpse into the camps and observe activities. Only those in a medieval dress are allowed access to the camps, and while locals welcome visitors to observe, the separation between locals and visitors is very strict. Comments from participants include 'Sometimes you do feel like an exhibit' and 'If I am in the camp they don't disturb me. I mean there must be some parts, where tourists are not allowed to go.' The medieval dress plays a very important role as these locals explain: 'We do not dress up or put on costumes, we say we want to live our history. To us, it is not a carnival, or a costume party, that is why we say vestments and not costumes.' 'I don't feel costumed; I felt good right from the beginning, because it is practical and comfortable, not like carnival.' 'That gives a feeling of closeness and openness.' 'When I went to the dance, it was weird to see people without vestments, you feel uncomfortable. In the camps it is cosier.'

Fig. 10.3. Images from the Peter-and-Paul Festival, Bretten, Germany. (Pictures © Sine Heitmann.)

to encourage 'excellence' in the arts, new art forms and the widest access to and participation in the arts.

Public art

The term 'public art' refers to the work of art in any form of media that has been planned and executed with the specific intention of being sited or staged in the public domain, usually outside and accessible to all. The term is sometimes also applied to include any art that is exhibited in a public space, including publicly accessible buildings. Sometimes this art is simple and straightforward, traditionally taking the form of statues of famous people or memorials to notable events. It can also be used to soften, enhance or make interesting the appearance of everyday items such as street lighting, park benches and public buildings. Public art may also be designed to be challenging and controversial, while at other times it is just there to complement new buildings or redevelopments, brighten up stonework and public spaces or be funny, different or unique.

Public art in this context can take many forms, from the purpose-built gallery that displays a range of art to retail art galleries or art in public spaces. It is interesting to note that in the case of galleries, the building itself is often of artistic architectural merit or designed for another purpose that is of such architectural interest that it is considered to be artistic and is an attraction in its own right.

The Arts Council England (2008) describes three key aspects of developing public art:

- Developmental activities: commission, installation, investment, collaboration, participation, exhibition, performance, intervention, dialogue or theoretical indication.
- Role of public art: architectural collaboration, urban design, social responsibility, cultural regeneration and sustainability.
- Regeneration: public art has a 'cultural function' through architectural branding and signature buildings, gateways and landmark features, and art interventions are now an indispensable part of any city's cultural and architectural identity.

Sharp *et al.* (2005) suggested that public art can contribute to local distinctiveness, attract investment, boost cultural tourism, enhance land values, create employment, increase use of urban space and reduce vandalism. However, the arts typically suffer from problems of under-funding and under-valorization. Governments frequently take a rather tokenistic approach to the arts, exploiting their economic and social potential without adequate reinvestment and support. More research and evaluation is therefore needed to prove the true worth of the arts to the process of regeneration (unfortunately, often a time-consuming, difficult and expensive process).

Given the costs associated with art installation, and the time involved in planning and development, it is essential that any public sector investment demonstrates links to social and economic development. The roles of public art, according to Robinson (2009), can be summarized as follows:

- Providing links to the past, which may include a focus on traditional industries or a commemoration of 'famous' locals (e.g. sculptures at St Pancras railway station and Aldeburgh, Suffolk).
- Providing a vision of the future, to inspire local communities, investors and visitors (e.g. Antony Gormley's 'Angel of the North').
- Enhancing the current offer and image of a destination (e.g. Cardiff Bay, Wales).
- To form an attraction in its own right (e.g. Gormley's 'Another Place' and street artists in York).
- Complementing the natural environment (e.g. artist-designed benches, bridges and interpretation panels).
- Involving local communities in the design and development of artwork to enhance civic pride and local ownership (e.g. community tapestries, posters and mosaics).

The challenge of public arts

Although the use of public art contributes to tourism activity and regeneration and can enhance a destination's image, it is important to highlight the main issues that may arise with artwork and give consideration to how these issues are to be managed. Public art needs to be maintained by either the local authority or the artist, and in either case the funding body must be able to understand the long-term maintenance needs. All too often public art is commissioned with no thought given to long-term maintenance issues. The result is that damage, vandalism, dirt and simple deterioration are often left unrepaired. The original asset is devalued and the reputations of all those involved is placed at risk.

Public art is an asset for the community in which it stands. It brings visual quality, interest and identity to places that might not otherwise possess them, and as with any other asset it should be a matter of principle that works of art are cared for into the long-term future.

> If the artwork requires specialist care and maintenance then these costs and requirements need to be understood. It should be made clear within contracts if the artist is responsible for the long-term care of artwork and where this is a requirement then costs should be built in so that the artist is paid to carry out this management.
>
> (Robinson, 2009)

Other issues include negative discernment and publicity. Some artwork developments have

Case Study 10.3. Another Place (Antony Gormley).

Internationally acclaimed artist Antony Gormley chose Crosby Beach, Liverpool, to showcase his work 'Another Place'. Another Place is a huge installation that consists of 100 cast-iron, life-size figures, moulded from the artist's own body in the style that has become synonymous with his work, and spread along 3 km of the foreshore (Fig. 10.4). Previously the work was shown at Cuxhaven in Germany, Stavanger in Norway and De Panne in Belgium. In 2006 it was expected to move to New York, but there was a controversial proposal to retain the work in Liverpool and that is where it will now permanently remain.

The artwork was brought to the area by the South Sefton Development Trust, a new organization set up by South Sefton Partnership to continue its regeneration work in the area. The officials in Sefton worked hard to include the local people of Merseyside in the project, with consultation evenings before the project began. The 'Sefton Extended Schools Project' now helps local schools to make use of the fantastic opportunity of having a famous artwork on their doorstep by organizing trips to the beach as well as projects for use in lessons such as art, history, drama and literacy.

Another Place is seen as a poetic response to the individual and universal sentiments associated with emigration, including sadness at leaving and the hope of a new future in another place (Sefton Council, n.d.). On close inspection, the figures are vague in detail and rusty, punctured with several plug holes where iron was poured in the casting process. There is no real protectionist management in place; as the beach changes shape, the statues become buried in the sand and are subject to natural degeneration. Furthermore, people are encouraged to dress the sculptures up and have fun with them.

Antony Gormley's work has already brought thousands of visitors to the area and a huge amount of interest. Large numbers of people – including families and school parties – visit the beach to see the statues. The work has undoubtedly raised the profile of Merseyside due to its extensive coverage in both the press and broadcast media.

Fig. 10.4. 'Another Place' by Antony Gormley. (Pictures © Peter Robinson.)

been plagued by budget problems, delays and controversy, which can attract news coverage and media attention. The infamous 'concrete cows' in Milton Keynes are a prime example, where publicity ranged from commendation to comedic shambles. The cows have made the news for vandalism that has included painting pyjamas on them, subjecting them to BSE graffiti and adding concrete 'cow pats'. Tony Dennett, Director of the Sculptors' Society of Ireland, observed 'Where public art really fails is not where there is negative publicity but rather where there is indifference' (Public Art South West, 2008). It can be argued that even negative publicity is good for a destination and as long as the artwork draws attention to a place then it has fulfilled its role in raising the profile of a particular destination.

Security is also a key consideration, and while anything that is large and made of steel or concrete is unlikely to be stolen, smaller artworks are at risk of theft. Outdoor and rural artworks are also at high risk of vandalism and theft. CCTV may be one deterrent, but is not always practicable or appropriate. Alternatives include the provision of legal 'graffiti walls' for local artists and the younger generation to use, the involvement of the local community at the earliest stages of commissioning and the creation of community workshops with the artist as a part of the project. This gives ownership of the art back to the community and thus it is less likely to be damaged or vandalized. The impact of public art on a community is priceless and immeasurable and once experienced it only adds to the appreciation. In some instances though, such as the Milton Keynes' cows, and Antony Gormley's figures, humorous vandalism only serves to add to the artwork and to continually raise its profile.

Street art

Street art is any art that is developed in public, outdoor spaces. It can include traditional graffiti, stencil graffiti, sticker art, video projection, flash mobbing and street installations. Street art also extends to street performances such as dancing, juggling and human statues. London's Covent Garden is particularly associated with the latter, where it has been transformed into a tourist zone of specialist shops, stalls and cafés and is regularly animated by fire-eaters, jugglers, human statues and the like, who contribute to attracting tourists.

Typically, the term 'street art' or the more specific 'post-graffiti' is used to distinguish contemporary public-space artwork from territorial graffiti, vandalism and corporate art. The movement began in the late 1960s with anonymous spray-can art in New York and Philadelphia, and has since grown into a cross-cultural phenomenon. Stunning and vibrant artwork can be found on buildings, sidewalks, street signs and other surfaces in cities from New York to London to Barcelona. Unlike graffiti, where the work is intended to make sense to a peer group, street art is open to

everyone to understand, to be liked, loved, hated, judged or simply ignored (Mathieson and Tapies, 2009).

While practically every large city in the world, and some of the larger regional towns, host some form of street art or graffiti, a few locations are considered to harbour forerunners of particular mediums or foster a pioneering street art culture in general. Such locations often attract internationally known street artists, who travel to these locations to exhibit their works as well encourage visitors to a particular area. Berlin, Germany, for example, has attracted attention from international street artists since the reunification of the city, making it one of Europe's street art strongholds. Bizarre post-communist locations, cheap rents and ramshackle buildings have given rise to a vibrant street art scene. London, UK, has become one of the most pro-graffiti cities in the world. Although officially condemned and heavily enforced, street art has a huge following and in many ways is embraced by the public. Melbourne, Australia, is home to one of the world's most active and diverse street art cultures, including pioneers in the stencil medium. Works are supported and preserved by local councils. Key locations within the city include Brunswick, Carlton, Fitzroy, Northcote, and the city centre, including the famous Hosier Lane. São Paulo, Brazil, is generally viewed as one of the capitals of street art, particularly murals. The lively and colourful atmosphere of the city is reflected in the street art scene, which quickly evolved into one of the biggest and best in the world, drawing many artists from around the world to collaborate. New York City, USA, is considered the home of modern graffiti and the city has a thriving street art scene. Finally, Stavanger, Norway, is host to the annual Nuart Festival, one of Europe's leading events dedicated to promoting street art.

It is clear that the emergence of street art has redefined what art can be. Some cities, such as Barcelona, encourage this type of art form from an early age and are making it part of their tourism offer. Street art is the artistic phenomenon of our times and is proof of how vibrant the art scene can be, with the hundreds of brilliant practitioners who have emerged in the field.

Arts in regeneration

Arts and cultural projects have played an increasingly important role in British urban regeneration since the mid 1980s; however, the focus has shifted over the years to the capability of arts activity in supporting community-led renewal, rather than on capital projects. It has been highlighted that:

> Public Art can play an important role in providing an attractive, high quality environment and in helping to build a new community. Public Art can provide a focal point, enhanced sense of place and delight for local residents. To provide added value, the process associated with commissioning the artwork can involve local communities, help build local pride, and help foster social cohesion and community cohesion.
>
> (English Partnerships, 2005)

These are all components of regeneration and the links between public art and regeneration are comprehensive. This is also supported by Hastings Borough Council (2005), which stated that art 'contributes to social health and well-being by placing a sense of value on individual citizens and by provoking thought and an awareness of the world around them. It elevates and enriches the simple experience of being in a place. This shared experience in public spaces in turn fosters social interaction'.

Hastings Borough Council (2005) similarly summarized the role of public art as a catalyst for regeneration:

> Public Art is an important tool for creating successful communities and places. It has a role to play in public business and residential areas. The past decade has seen a renaissance of activity and interest in public art that has been driven by a new urban regeneration agenda. The message is clear: public art aids urban regeneration and has the unique ability to bring together social, economic and physical aspects of urban improvement.

Some key issues need to be considered in the planning of public art as part of regeneration projects, especially given the costs of all aspects of its development. The most important deliberation is the overall purpose of the proposed artwork. Identifying the aim and vision for a particular area is essential as this will outline the ways in which public art can be best designed and managed to ensure it fits with broader aims and objectives. Community involvement is paramount when art is used in housing estates, for example. Public art helps define an entire community's identity and can reveal the unique character of a specific neighbourhood – it is a unifying force. In business districts art may be sponsored by private organizations, while in tourist areas it most certainly needs to fulfil the roles of linking heritage to the future and broadening the traditional audience. Public art is a major investment. If it is not well planned then public contempt may never allow an installation to achieve its stated aims or purpose.

Arts and architecture

Architecture plays an important part in encouraging tourism, as can be seen from the following examples. Modern architecture can be viewed as a valid publicity tool in attracting visitors to a particular area or destination, for

---

Case Study 10.4. The Avenue of the Arts.

Over the last 20 years, cultural, economic and political elites in Philadelphia (Pennsylvania, USA) have been developing a cultural district, the 'Avenue of the Arts'. This is a 1 mile block of performing arts venues, hotels, restaurants and office buildings. Diverse leaders from the government, arts and business sectors have worked together to implement this cultural district in the hope of using cultural amenities as tools for generating tourism and reviving a declining downtown area. Statistically, the Avenue of the Arts is the longest, widest, busiest street in the region and it operates at both the street level and underground. It unifies a wide range of different neighbourhoods and bridges both the historic and the new. Moreover, the Avenue is home to over 50 of the city's most important institutions dedicated to arts and culture, education and hospitality, while also becoming known as a place to stay, dine and shop (Smith, 2006). A recent economic impact study (Econsult, 2007) showed that in 2006 an estimated US$424 million was generated for the region by activities on the Avenue of the Arts, with an estimated US$150 million in total earnings, supporting approximately 6,000 jobs.

example the inclusion of modern architecture and sculptural forms used as landmarks in the redevelopment of Cardiff Bay, Wales. There may be a requirement for new infrastructural developments, such as transport and accommodation, especially if landmark buildings or 'mega-events' are not located centrally. Opportunities to increase length of stay, destination awareness and expenditure may be needed. Cities such as Bilbao in Spain struggled in the initial stages of regeneration and tourism development, despite the apparent 'success' of the Guggenheim Museum, as there was little else for tourists to see or do once they had visited this one attraction. The Guggenheim Museum is now an internationally renowned art museum and one of the most significant architectural icons of the 20th century, and an ever-growing institution devoted to the art of the 20th century and beyond. This use of architecture as an art form is now commonplace throughout regeneration schemes. A further example is the redevelopment of St Pancras Station in London as part of the High Speed 1 project (Fig. 10.5).

Buildings themselves can be tourist attractions in their own right. It is becoming more common to have organized tours around theatres and back-stage areas. This appears to be the case for new, distinctive or famous buildings. The Kodak Theatre, renowned for hosting the Oscars in Los Angeles, receives additional income from its theatre tours. The Theatre Royal in London's Drury Lane, which dates back to 1663, also advertises

Fig. 10.5. St Pancras Station platform. (Pictures © Peter Robinson.)

behind-the-scenes tours led by professional actors. The significance and appeal of many theatres is reflected in the fact that they have been identified as having particular architectural or historical importance (Hughes, 2000).

Future Research

Due to the rapid growth of events since the early 2000s, and as seen from the Isle of Wight Festival in 1970, the need for event professionals is paramount. We are now seeing an emergent, distinct and dynamic industry accompanied by associations, development of education programmes and increasing government involvement. In the early years of the industry the field was dominated by a large number of volunteers (Bowdin *et al.*, 2006). Those events managers who obtained paid positions came from a variety of related disciplines, drawing on their knowledge gained from that discipline and skills learnt on the job. Many came from allied areas such as theatre and entertainment, audiovisual production or film, and adapted their skills to events. A key development was education and training at a number of levels, which arose to meet the needs of a professional industry. Alongside the emergence of professional qualifications, the Association for Events Management Education was set up in 2004 in order to further develop education in events and to support and raise the profile of the events discipline by sharing education and best practice. It has become apparent that events management in the contemporary world requires trained staff, specialism and professional expertise.

It is evident that the rapid growth of events has led to the formation of a distinct professional industry with its own associations, practitioners, resources and a range of qualifications and academic texts. Events have become an essential element of contemporary life, linked inseparably with tourism promotion, government strategies and corporate marketing. Despite this emergence, events are generally an under-researched area and to date there is no national or international measure of the size, scope or value of the events sector. Unlike in many industries, it is almost impossible to quantify in monetary terms how much events are actually worth as an industry because of the sheer range of events, from mega international events such as the Olympic Games to local weddings and music festivals. Furthermore, events are so varied and so very different that there are a multitude of areas of possible research.

Bowdin *et al.* (2006) pointed out that much event research is still dispersed over a wide range of journals from allied fields, notably tourism and sports management, and some key topics remain under-researched.

Event and festival research is continuing to expand. It is providing valuable insights into the behaviour of events and a better understanding of the events management processes and outcomes, but still has a long way to go. For future research, a combination of quantitative and qualitative data is needed in order to generate more complete and unbiased information. Most studies in the field of events focus on economic impacts; more future research is needed from social and cultural perspectives. Furthermore, Gelder and Robinson (2009) highlighted that festivals and events should no longer be considered just as tourism offerings but also as recreation, and that multiple motivations come into play in event attendance. Most theories associated with event attendance and motivations are from the field of tourism and in some instances sport. This suggests that as the event industry is becoming more prominent and distinct, the need for event theories is growing.

The arts also deserve further attention as an area of research. Specific attention needs to be given to the management and use of street art as a form of tourism activity and the way in which it contributes to the image of a tourism destination. Likewise, static public arts also need to be considered from both a community and tourist perspective, and the semiotics that exist between specific art works and destination perceptions are also of note. Art is such a key element of society and of the way tourism spaces are shaped and used that there is much scope to address the use of arts within tourism frameworks. The nature of temporary exhibitions, the role of art as an attraction and the way that it is now adopted in the private sector (e.g. through displays in the grounds of stately homes open to the public) have heavily influenced the role of art in society.

Conclusion

Events, including festivals and the arts, can perform a powerful role in society and have existed throughout the history of mankind in all times and all cultures. They generate huge amounts of tourism in an area, promote destinations and encourage regeneration and economic prosperity. This chapter has discussed each concept individually, although it is evident there are interrelationships between them.

Events seem to be central to our culture today as perhaps never before. They can be categorized by size and scope, ranging from mega events to major, hallmark and minor events. They can also be classified by form or content, including festivals, sporting events and MICE. From a tourism perspective they have a number of key attributes: they attract tourists or tourism development; they can help extend the tourism season; they are of limited duration; they are a one-off or infrequent occurrence; they raise awareness or help (re)create the image or profile of a region; they attract media attention; they have a large economic impact; and they are out of the ordinary or unique. A major trend worldwide over the past decade has been the growth and expansion of the events industry. Having emerged as an industry in its own right through the 1990s, the events industry continues to grow, fuelled by economic growth and increases in leisure spending. Events have become an essential element of contemporary life, linked inseparably with tourism promotion, government strategies and corporate marketing.

This chapter also examined festivals, of which there is now a plethora across different themes, as a form of tourism. Their very nature – the range of performers, productions and ancillary services in one place over a short period of time – encourages audiences from a wide catchment area. In addition, many festivals are located in rural or coastal parts of the country and in areas attractive to tourists because of their heritage or natural beauty. Festivals celebrate a sense of place and provide a vehicle for communities to host visitors to share in activities as representations of community-agreed values, interests and aspirations. The impacts of festivals are often considered favourably, although it must be recognized that the influx of tourists to an area is not always positively received. Festivals are now embedded into our culture and continue to be a dominant and growing component of the dynamic event industry.

The arts are also seen by the tourist industry as having potential to attract tourists. They can be the sole or main attraction and are important factors in visiting a destination. The arts are associated with the highest levels of human creativity and the work of gifted people, who are often involved for reasons that are non-monetary. The arts encompass a wide collection of activities and the difficulty remains in their actual interpretation. The arts have been singled out by governments for many years. This is largely accounted for by the view that art is 'special' – the embodiment of human achievement – and thus deserves to be encouraged and to survive. This chapter highlighted that although art contributes greatly to tourism activity and regeneration, there are issues with artwork that require consideration and sound management.

The events industry is promising, young and dynamic, and is supported by an increasing body of knowledge, education, research and industry professionals. This chapter has hopefully contributed to a better understanding of how events, festivals and the arts enrich our lives and encourage tourism. It has also underlined some of the potential management challenges.

Review Questions

1. Identify an event in your region that has the capacity to be a hallmark event. Give reasons for placing it in this category and an evaluation of the factors that need to be further developed to deliver an event of an appropriate scale.

2. Analyse the ways in which events can be used to encourage tourism and the role they play in branding a destination.

3. Evaluate the use of public arts in the area where you live. Assess the ways in which public art is managed and developed, and the reasons for its installation.

References

Adelaide Festival (n.d.) History of the Adelaide Festival of Arts. Available from: http://www.adelaidefestival.com.au/servlet/Web?s=2290869andaction=changePageandpageID=792949593. Accessed 10 March, 2010.

Allen, J., O'Toole, W., McDonnell, I. and Harris, R. (2002) *Festival and Special Event Management*, 3rd edn. Wiley, Milton, UK.

Allen, J., O'Toole, W., Harris, R. and McDonnell, I. (2008) *Festival and Special Event Management*, 4th edn. Wiley, Milton, UK.

Arts Council (2008) Great art for everyone. Available from: http://www.artscouncil.org.uk/publication_archive/great-art-for-everyone-2008–2011. Accessed 3 February, 2010.

Bakers Associates (2008) Glastonbury Festivals 2007 economic impact assessment. Available from: http://www.mendip.gov.uk/Documents/Finaland20ReportLOWRES.pdf. Accessed 10 March, 2010.

Bowdin, G., Allen, J., O'Toole, W., Harris, R. and McDonnell, I. (2006) *Events Management*, 2nd edn. Elsevier, Oxford, UK.

Business Tourism Partnership (2005) *Business Tourism Leads the Way*. Business Tourism Partnership, London, UK.

Crompton, J. (1979) Motivations for pleasure vacation. *Annals of Tourism Research* 6, 408–424.

Crompton, J. (2003) Adapting Herzberg: a conceptualization of the effects of hygiene and motivator attributes on perceptions of event quality. *Journal of Travel Research* 41, 305–310.

Crompton, J. and McKay, S.L. (1997) Motives of visitors attending festival events. *Annals of Tourism Research* 24, 425–439.

Douglas, N., Douglas, N. and Derrett, R. (2001) *Special Interest Tourism*. John Wiley and Sons, Chichester, UK.

Econsult (2007) Avenue of the arts economic impact study. Available from: http://www.avenueofthearts.org/about_facts.asp. Accessed 3 February, 2010.

English Partnerships (2005) *Creativity in the Coalfields*. English Partnerships, Warrington, UK.

Gelder, G. and Robinson, P. (2009) A critical comparative study of visitor motivations for attending music festivals: a case study of Glastonbury and V Festival. *Event Management* 13, 181–196.

Getz, D. (2005) *Event Management and Event Tourism*. Cognizant Communication Corporation, New York.

Getz, D. (2007) *Event Studies: Theory, Research and Policy for Planned Events*. Butterworth Heinemann, Oxford, UK.

Getz, D. and Wicks, B. (1993) Editorial. *Festival Management and Event Tourism* 1, 1–3.

Hastings Borough Council (2005) *A Strategy for Developing Public Arts in Hastings*. Hastings Borough Council Regeneration and Planning Division, Hastings, UK.

Heitmann, S. and David, L. (2010) Sustainability and event management. In: Robinson, P., Wale, D. and Dickson, G. (eds) *Event Management*. CAB International, Wallingford, UK, pp. 181–200.

Hughes, H. (2000) *Arts, Entertainment and Tourism*. Butterworth Heinemann, Oxford, UK.

Jago, L.K. and Shaw, R.N. (1998) A conceptual and differential framework. *Festival Management and Event Tourism* 5, 21–32.

Masterman, G. (2004) *Strategic Sports Event Management: An International Approach*. Elsevier, Oxford, UK.

Mathieson, E. and Tapies, X.A. (2009) *Street Artists: The Complete Guide*. Graffito, London, UK.

Maunsell, F. (2004) Commonwealth Games Benefit Study: Final Report. Available from: http://www.nwda.co.uk/pdf/CGamesReport.pdf. Accessed 4 March, 2010.

Morgan, N. and Pritchard, A. (2004) *Destination Branding: Creating the Unique Destination Proposition*, 2nd edn. Elsevier Butterworth-Heinemann, Oxford, UK.

Nicholson, R. and Pearce, D.G. (2001) Why do people attend events: a comparative analysis of visitor motivations at four South Island events. *Journal of Travel Research* 39, 449–460.

O'Sullivan, D. and Jackson, M.J. (2002) Festival tourism: a contributor to sustainable local economic development? *Journal of Sustainable Tourism* 10, 325–342.

Public Art South West (2008) Viewpoints. Available from: http://www.publicartonline.org.uk/resources/viewpoints. Accessed 5 March, 2010.

Ritchie, J. (1984) Assessing the impact of hallmark events: conceptual and research issues. *Journal of Travel Research* 23, 2–11.

Robinson, P. (2009) *Public Art and Regeneration in Insights.* VisitBritain, London, UK.

Sefton Council (n.d.) Antony Gormley's 'Another Place'. Available from: http://www.sefton.gov.uk/Default.aspx?page=6216. Accessed 16 March, 2010.

Sharp, J, Pollock, V. and Paddison, R. (2005) Just art for a just city: public art and social inclusion in urban regeneration. *Urban Studies* 42, 1001–1023.

Smith, M.K. (2006) *Tourism Culture and Regeneration.* CAB International, Wallingford, UK.

Tusa, J. (1999) *Art Matters: Reflecting on Culture.* Methuen, London, UK.

Yeoman, I., Robertson, M., Ali-Knight, J., Drummond, S. and McMahon-Beattie, U. (2004) *Festival and Events Management – An International Arts and Culture Perspective.* Elsevier Butterworth Heinemann, Oxford, UK.

Yoon, Y. and Uysal, M. (2005) An examination of the effects of motivation and satisfaction on destination loyalty: a structural model. *Tourism Management* 26, 45–56.

11 Sport and Adventure Tourism

Christine Roberts

_____

This chapter provides an understanding of sport and adventure tourism as a subcategory of mainstream tourism. The chapter begins with an appreciation of 'sport' and 'tourism' as separate entities, combined to form a new and exciting phenomenon; with 'adventure' emerging as a result of the industry's zestful and heterogeneous nature.

In order to fully understand the diversity of sport and adventure tourism alongside its interrelations, challenges and future opportunities (both in business and academia), this chapter provides an overview of the industry, depicting specific typologies of sport and adventure tourism. The sport and adventure tourist is then explored, including profiles, motivations and behaviours. From here, an exploration into market size, trends and providers emerges, with an emphasis on industry strengths, weaknesses, opportunities and threats. This is followed by industrial impacts from the macro and micro environments that shape the sport and adventure tourism phenomenon as it stands today. An exploration into such aspects allows industry professionals and students of this subject to hold a greater appreciation and understanding of the industry, sustaining its importance, potential and growth.

Introduction

Sport-associated travel is a multifaceted leisure phenomenon that has grown significantly over the last 30 years, birthing the emergence of adventure tourism as a key feature. Types of sport tourism include passive, active and

nostalgic formations, with adventure tourism as a subcategory of mainstream sport tourism, usually falling into the 'active' category. While the industry holds well in terms of longevity, the focus of academic inquiry is a more recent feature. Therefore, our current knowledge of sport and adventure tourism is growing yet incomplete; changes in politics, social behaviour and economic activity further transgress the current body of knowledge, adding scope for further exploration.

Working Definitions

For the purposes of appreciating the size and heterogeneity of the industry, a working definition of sport and adventure tourism is needed. On its own, the realm of sport holds a different meaning to different groups of society. This is also true for the realm of adventure and that of tourism. An appreciation of these differentiated meanings, therefore, demonstrates the challenges of attempting to classify such a dynamic industry. For the purposes of providing a better understanding of the industry and frameworks for research, a breakdown of the definitions for 'sport', 'tourism' and 'sport and adventure tourism' as a whole will now be attempted.

Sport

There is no single definition for sport; the phenomenon is multifaceted and interpretations vastly differ. Variations in the description of sport emerge due to a variety of factors, but mainly due to: (i) the element of competitiveness; and (ii) the level of physicality. Many authors support the need for a winner and loser, while others question such a necessity. Similarly, while some authors dictate the inclusion of physicality for an activity to be classified as a sport, others refute such notions. None the less, most authors agree that sport is a microcosm of society, exhibiting characteristics of social politics found in almost all societal settings. Frey and Eitzen (1991) described sport as:

> structured conflict and competitiveness in controlled settings ... rules are formal, generalizable, and enforced by formal regulatory bodies (e.g. National Collegiate Athletic Association-NCAA); the outcome is serious for individuals and organizations not actually participating in the physical activity, and winning (the outcome) is more important than participation (the process).

This definition reflects desired inequalities based on the demonstration of superior levels of skill and physicality. Winners are separated from losers and the drive for elitism is not only desirable but of supreme importance. However, left-wing idealisms for sport, namely 'sport for all' policies, discern that sport is a fundamental right for all and offer numerous benefits to society. Policies for equal access and encouraged participation have loosened the idealism of sport as an institutionalized, competitive domain, transforming it into an entity that houses 'all forms of physical activity, which through casual or organized participation, aim at improving physical fitness and mental well-being, forming social relationships, or obtaining results in competition at all levels' (Council of Europe, 2001). This definition neglects the inclusion of competitiveness and elitism. Instead, the act of participation as a beneficial activity is prominent. Therefore, activities that do not necessitate a winner and loser (e.g. dancing) could be categorized as a sport. Both definitions, therefore, assume some level of physicality involved; however, there are numerous activities, namely snooker, darts, chess and fishing, that invoke limited physical effort yet meet all other criteria as dictated by popular sport definitions. For the purposes of this chapter, therefore, a combination of

varying levels of competition and physicality will be considered relevant to the definition of sport, as it is believed that the extensive scope of activities that either require or refute the need for winners and losers, elitism and ranging levels of physical exertion have all driven forward the size and vastness of sport and adventure tourism within today's society.

Sport and adventure tourism

As demonstrated, difficulties are experienced in defining sport and tourism as separate entities. Understandably, therefore, a combination of the two proves equally taxing. In addition to the previously explored definitional variance is the challenge of placing emphasis within either the realm of sport or that of tourism. When separate, each discipline prevails as a dominant feature of both industry and academia. When combined, however, the power of domination is interchangeable across these two fields, proving to be fluid and complex in nature. To ascertain the field of dominance, motives for participation must first be understood. It should, therefore, be queried as to whether the primary motive for participation derives from the desire to be involved within a sport (whereby tourism is a secondary component) or whether the act of tourism provides the principal motivation for participation and subsequent involvement in sport is purely incidental. Simply put, does the participant travel for the purposes of engagement within sport, or is the involvement in sport merely a consequential feature of the participant's stronger desire to travel? As a result of this uncertainty, academics have compiled slightly differentiated definitions: a sport-focused (sport tourist) definition may be 'a temporary visitor staying at least 24 hours in the event area and whose primary purpose is to participate in a sports event with the area being a secondary attraction' (Nogawa *et al.*, 1996), whereas a travel-focused (tourism sport) definition is 'persons travelling to and/or staying in places outside their usual environment and participating in, actively or passively, a competitive or recreational sport as a secondary activity (Gammon and Robinson, 2003).

The aspect of adventure is a more recently observed phenomenon, falling into a subcategory of tourism, whereby sport may or may not be included. For example, travelling to a destination for the purposes of rock climbing constitutes as 'sport adventure tourism', whereas an activity such as backpacking constitutes adventure travel, but is not overly sport-based. It is important to draw this distinction between the inclusions of 'sport' and 'adventure', as they are very different subjects yet may be dually applied to the same activity. The Ministry of Commerce (1996), New Zealand, define adventure tourism as 'commercially operated activities involving a combination of adventure and excitement pursued in an outdoor environment'. For an activity to be deemed 'adventurous', qualifying elements need to be in place involving perception of risk, excitement, newness and discovery. Participants voluntarily put themselves in a situation where they believe they are taking a step into the unknown; a place where they will face challenges and gain something valuable from the experience (Swarbrooke *et al.*, 2003). The concept of 'adventure' entails the inclusion of action. Therefore, active recreation involving physical, intellectual or emotional involvement is assumed but not always present. Again, definitions are problematic in that individuals experience and describe adventure differently; while an activity may be described as adventurous by one individual, others may disagree.

Definitional challenges of sport and adventure tourism are born from individual descriptions of sport, tourism and adventure, alongside descriptions of these entities when combined. Naturally, these definitions need some amount of unity in order to provide scope for frameworks of research. On a wider spectrum, these challenges also affect providers in terms of whether responsibility for governance lies within councils for sport or tourism boards, thus encompassing contrasting policy issues. Regardless of the chosen definition, sport and tourism are now inextricably linked, leading to the new development of sporting opportunities through tourism and, equally, tourism opportunities through sport. As explored in later sections, sport and adventure tourism is subcategorized by the nature of participation, namely 'active'

forms, whereby the individual actively participates in a sport, and 'passive' forms, where the individual passively participates through means of spectatorship. Definitions can be further subcategorized dependent on the nature of involvement or level of activity. As shown in Fig. 11.1, sport tourism falls into two camps: 'hard' and 'soft'. Gammon and Robinson (2003) proclaimed that when referring to sport tourism, 'hard' forms involve high-level competition in sporting events such as Wimbledon or the Olympics, whereas 'soft' forms refer to active recreational activities such as fun runs or cycling events. Soft forms also encompass spectatorship – a lucrative component of the sport tourism industry. For tourism sports, the 'hard' forms refer to holiday-makers who choose holiday locations that offer sports and activities as a secondary component to the travel experience. 'Soft' forms of tourism sports refer to a visitor's incidental participation in sport. Adventure travel is also defined with similar categories. 'Hard' adventure travel generally encompasses risk, physicality and challenge within unknown territories, whereas 'soft' adventure travel requires less physical effort and a minimal sense of danger. Both forms of adventure, however, involve an intimate experience with the environment and culture of the destination (Swarbrooke *et al.*, 2003).

When participating in hard adventure travel, participants should be prepared for all weather conditions, sleeping arrangements and dietary restrictions. Examples include climbing expeditions, arduous treks, hang-gliding, rock climbing, white-water kayaking, and wilderness survival. Soft adventure travel encompasses activities with less physical risk and lower physically demanding involvement; participants will generally have less experience as the activity is less demanding. Trips of this nature generally offer more in terms of convenience, such as sleeping and travel arrangements. Examples include horseback riding, rafting, canoeing, cross-country skiing, surfing and walking tours.

Industry Overview

While academic research into the field of sport and adventure tourism has emerged relatively

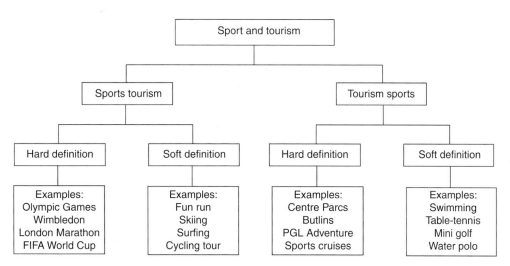

Fig. 11.1. Hard and soft forms of sport tourism. (Adapted from Gammon and Robinson, 2003.)

recently, sport-related travel has been observed for centuries. Travelling with a specific purpose to participate or view a sports event can be traced back as early as the Ancient Greek Olympic Games in 776 BC (Hudson, 2003). Today, sport and adventure tourism has reached phenomenal heights globally, with mass participation in holiday sports, both actively and passively. As key marketing initiatives and media attention grows, ever more individuals are immersed into the sport and adventure tourism phenomena. Improvements in mass education have demonstrated the health and recreational benefits of active involvement, further increasing participation rates. Travel operators and other travel-related providers often market their products alongside the provision of sport or adventure-based activities, such as hotels promoting their facilities due to the inclusion of sports provision or stating their close proximity to hallmark stadiums. Examples such as these demonstrate how the product of tourism can be enhanced by the inclusion of sport-based commodities.

Vast increases in the provision and popularity of spectator-driven tourist opportunities have become apparent. Travel and short-term stay within a destination far from home for the sole purpose of passive participation within a chosen sport prove lucrative, particularly for mega events such as the Olympics, the Wimble-don Tennis Championships and the Tour de France. Participation is increased where the popularity and scale of the sport are strong, such as football – a globally significant sport that hosts mega events such as the FIFA World Cup. Incrementally, more attempts have been made to bring sport into general society, such as increased running events through local community areas and skateboarding based in inner-city areas, whereby active and passive participation is sought not only by local residents but also the travelling sport enthusiast. The sheer size, value and interest in sport and adventure tourism have driven academic intrigue. At present, sport and adventure themes are not only written about as subcategories within tourism literature, but as hybrid phenomena in their own right, born from sport and tourism, forming a new field of research. Academic journals are now publishing within this significant area, namely, *The Journal of Sport and Tourism* and the *Journal of Hospitality, Leisure, Sport and Tourism Education*. Sport and tourism are solely interrelated; sport benefits tourism just as much as tourism benefits sport. While it is true that in some areas, changes in today's economic climate and adaptations of international markets have stunted sport and adventure tourism activity, such changes have forced the industry to adapt and evolve, leaving more choice and exciting possibilities for the sport and adventure tourist.

Typologies of Sport and Adventure Tourism

Early work within the field of sport and adventure tourism typologies made the distinction between active and passive participation. From here, frameworks for the study of sport tourism have advanced to subcategorize more specific components of the industry. Sport tourism generally falls into the very broad camps of: (i) passive/event tourism, whereby tourists visit a sports event for the purposes of spectating; (ii) active tourism, whereby the tourist physically participates in the sport, and; (iii) nostalgic tourism, referencing the tourist who visits a destination for the purpose of paying homage to a person or event. There is, however, some fluidity between these three components as it is possible for a tourist to engage in more than one activity during the same trip. For example, an individual vacationing for the primary purpose of spectating at sport events may also choose to visit a hallmark stadium in the surrounding area. Sport tourism supply comes with much variation and is generally referred to as the typologies of sport tourism. One of the first presented models of sport tourism typologies subcategorized resorts, vacations, sports museums, multi-sport festivals and sports facilities as typologies (Redmond, 1991). The Sport Tourism International Council (STIC) built upon this work by presenting a framework of five typologies, namely attractions, resorts, cruises, tours and events (Hinch and Higham, 2001). These categories are further subcategorized by theme-inclusions, such as adventure (further subcategorized as soft and hard forms), health and fitness, and leisure. Other models attempt to define and confine more specific aspects of sport and adventure tourism. Linking in the realm of health, Hall (1992) devised a framework that plots the level of activity against the level of competitiveness to derive a nine-category matrix (Fig. 11.2).

This framework is particularly useful as it identifies activities undertaken for the purposes of recreation from those of competitiveness, while still incorporating the traditional typological distinction of active and passive sport and adventure tourism modalities.

Participant profiles

By creating a definitive typography of sport and adventure tourists, it is believed that industries are better equipped with the knowledge to attract and sustain business with target markets. Academics also classify tourists for purposes of research, observing and predicting behaviours and motivations in order to inform frameworks for future application.

Traditionally, the typified sport tourist will be white, male and middle class. This profile of participation closely follows that of sport in general. Understanding this trend is fairly simple; first, the socialized manifestation of male dominance within the sporting world has always been apparent – a trend that has inevitably filtered into sport and adventure tourism. Second, from our understanding of class dominance throughout the history of sport tourism, alongside the exclusivity,

	Less active $\longrightarrow$ More active		
Non-competitive	**Health tourism** Health voyages, spas	**Health tourism** Health and fitness retreats	**Health tourism** Snowboarding, horse-riding
	Adventure travel Sailing, off-road driving	**Tourism activities** (Containing components of health, sport and adventure) cycling, abseiling	**Adventure travel** Climbing, wind surfing
Competitive	**Sport tourism** Spectating, snooker	**Sport tourism** Curling, golf	**Sport tourism** Triathlon, marathon running

Fig. 11.2. Hall's (1992) model of adventure, health and sports tourism.

stereotyping and elitism present in sport, it is not surprising that sport tourism is also dominated by the financially privileged. While many advances have been made in terms of sport tourism accessibility, cheaper travel options and increased interest, demand for sport and adventure tourism is still largely compiled of the traditional participant profile. That said, changes are occurring, particularly in terms of increasing female participation. This is largely due to changing gender roles, dual-income families, delayed marriages and births, lower birth rates in general and increased female empowerment. In addition, increased female participation may be due to strategic marketing initiatives; while it is likely that tour operators choose to adopt strategies that target their primary market (i.e. the white middle-class male), others have clearly recognized the female 'gap', seeing this as an opportunity to attract custom in other key areas. In addition, cost-friendly excursions are now also present, aiming to attract lower-income individuals. Profiles, however, can be far more sophisticated than the generalization of colour, sex and class; the

collation of participation statistics and market trends can all contribute to profiling the sport and adventure tourist, thus providing key marketing information and, to an extent, informing future forecast models and matrices of participant behaviour. Reeves (2000, in Hinch and Higham, 2004) provided such a matrix (Table 11.1), depicting patterns based the importance of decision making, reasons for participation, the likelihood of travelling with others or independently, levels of importance in the activities and variations in spending.

The matrix uses levels of participation, namely incidental, sporadic, occasional, regular, dedicated or driven. These profiles demonstrate that higher levels of participation place more importance on decision-making aspects such as the choice of location and length of stay. These individuals consider sport participation to be the primary motive for the trip, and generally participate individually or in groups. Conversely, incidental participants are less particular regarding decisions, participating out of duty to others. They are more likely to travel within their family unit and spend far less.

Table 11.1. Sport tourism visitor profiles.

Type	Decision making	Participation	Non-participation	Group profile	Lifestyle	Spending
Incidental	Unimportant	Out of duty	Not relaxing, holiday-like	Family	Sport is significant	Minimal
Sporadic	Relatively important	If convenient	Easily contained/ put off	Friends and family	Non-essential	Minimal except for 'one-off's
Occasional	Sometimes determining	Welcome addition to tourist experience	Other commitments	Often individual, especially business tourists	Conspicuous consumption	High on occasions
Regular	Important	Significant part of enjoyment	Money or time become prohibitive	Group or individual	Important	Considerable
Dedicated	Very important	Central to experience	Due to unforeseen barriers	Individuals and groups of the like-minded	Defining element	Extremely high and consistent
Driven	Very important, but little autonomy	Sole reason	Through injury or fear of it	Elite groups or solitary	The profession	Extremely high, but funded by others

Source: Reeves (2000) in Hinch and Higham (2004).

Motivation

As described within earlier sections of this chapter, people have been historically compelled to travel for the singular purpose of sport. Choices in consumption are based on intricate motivations relating to either or both of 'tourist' and 'sport' motivators (Robinson and Gammon, 2004). These are likely to be differentiated by each specific sport or activity. For example, a group of sports fans travelling to a major football tournament may well be motivated by aspects of socialization, ritual fan behaviour and patronage as well as the match itself, while individuals participating in a snowboarding trip are likely to be motivated by factors relating to being out of their comfort zone, sense of adventure and physicality of the activity.

In the early works of Crompton (1979) it was stated that tourists are largely homogeneous in their motives for travel. These general findings pointed towards the motivation occurring from a desire of escapism, self-exploration, relaxation, prestige, regression, enhancement of kinship relations and social interaction (Gibson, 2004). However, today's trends demonstrate far greater diversity in motivations for tourist activities. Crompton later added culture, novelty and education as additional motives, which may direct destination choices. Berlyne (1960) theorized that decisions made to participate in or avoid an activity are largely based on preferred levels of arousal, deeming this supposition the 'concept of optimum stimulation'. Berlyne proposed that individuals select or avoid activities, environments or situations according to their desired level of stimulation. Therefore, individuals seeking adventure and excitement are likely to choose activities or environments that fulfil their need for high-level stimulation, such as parachute-jumping or rock-climbing. These activities provide the thrill, perception of danger and physical effort to fulfil needs, whereas those seeking low-level stimulation may choose activities such as hiking or cycling. Individuals, however, cannot necessarily be typecast to a particular level of desired arousal; they may wish for high-stimulation activities on one occasion and low-stimulation activities on another, depending on mood, life stage and a variety of other psychological and physiological factors. Therefore, individuals should not be typecast to particular activities as participation is interchangeable. Many other motivational theories have been transferred from mainstream tourism to the specific avenue of sport tourism; for example, McIntosh *et al.* (1995) identified four travel motivators that could be applied to sport-related travel:

- Physical motivators – directly related to physical needs such as self-improvement through fitness participation.
- Cultural motivators – referring to traditions and heritage such as halls of fame.
- Interpersonal motivators – referring to prospective social activity among those with similar interests.
- Status and prestige motivators – desired by particular individuals attracted by high-profile destinations or events.

More dominant tourism theories refer to push and pull factors. Push factors refer to socio-psychological needs that an individual experiences that form the motivation to travel to a destination and participate in a sport, whereas pull factors refer to the attraction of the destination or sport itself as the primary motive for participation. Underlying this theory is the notion that needs underpin all behaviourisms, embedded in primitive physiological and socio-psychological desires. During sport and adventure tourism participation, some needs are satisfied while others are not, possibly explaining why the same individual may chose to be an active sport tourist on one occasion and an event sport tourist on the next (Gibson, 2004). For the athlete participant, the mastery of skill is essentially important, while for the spectator participant, the display of skill-mastery and discipline exhibited becomes the need, forming the conception of perfection and a worthy lifestyle. For the thrill-seeking tourist, commonly termed the 'adrenalin-junkie', the motivation to 'push the boundaries' and the thrill of the initial experience is capable of satisfying the psychological need for adventure and perceived danger, yet a repeated experience (where the activity is no longer new) may produce a lesser thrill, thus creating the need for a newer, more daring experience. This notion demonstrates that it may not be lucrative overall for researchers to use needs to forecast types of activities, but rather to link personalities that are motivated to fulfil similar needs (see Chapter 3).

The Market

Tourism is one of the world's biggest industries, with a subsection termed 'special interest tourism'. Sport tourism is a significant niche section of that industry. As stated earlier, sport tourism itself is heterogeneous and therefore offers a diverse range of niche markets for its participants (broadly named active, passive and nostalgic classifications), with adventure tourism as a subcategory (usually) of active sport tourism.

A UK market report conducted by Mintel (2008) concluded that leading travel provider, TUI, has around 400,000 customers annually within its activity sector alone, which includes sailing, inland waterways, adventure travel and 'experiential' escorted luxury tours. The report estimated that 10.2 million breaks were taken in 2007 (netting a volume growth of 17.2% since 2003), meaning that activity-based holidays easily outperform all other sectors within the travel market. The report continued that activity-based holidays accounted for £4.2 billion out of the £5.2 billion market total (Mintel, 2008).

Market trends

Mintel's (2008) market report stated that over half of all active holiday-makers ventured out to their chosen destinations with friends or family, whereas over one-third travelled as a couple. One in six travelled through facilitation with an organization, such as a corporate entity, sports club or educational institution. Through governmental initiatives and dispersing trends within Westernized countries, a climate of health and fitness is now prevailing as a major component of the leisure economy, particularly among higher-income groups. The trend to experience adventure in exciting new destinations and 'try something different' is a high influencer of increased adventure travel (Mintel, 2008). When travel is to new and unusual destinations, the tourist's focus is more likely to be on the destination itself, yet when travelling to more mainstream destinations, tour operators attract business through the inclusion of sport and adventure activities such as white-water rafting, kayaking or cycling expeditions. While the industry is largely dominated by male counterparts, trends in the market are showing a significant increase in the participation of females aged 20–44 years, particularly with the inclusion of soft adventure travel, where relaxing, leisurely activities are popularized. Of all special interest holidays, those centred on active participation such as walking, trekking, hiking or rambling are the most popular, accounting for one-third of the market, with extreme sports boasting the fastest-growing segments (Mintel, 2008). Another significant growth area is virtual sport tourism, whereby video games, fantasy sports and virtual reality form another variety of passive involvement. As this is a rather new development, there is little research in this area.

Market providers

While sport tourism is widely adopted throughout the world, major participating countries are Malaysia, the USA, China, Ireland, Thailand, Korea, Nepal, Barbados, Brunei, Portugal and Australia (Higham, 2005). Major tour operators include TUI, alongside other large, independent, overseas operators such as GAP Adventures and Intrepid Travel. In addition, Abercrombie & Kent are major players in terms of luxury or tailor-made adventure tourism. From here, the market branches into a plethora of smaller operators, often with a specific destination, activity or specialized expertise as the mainframe of their business (Mintel, 2008).

Analysing the market

A compilation of data surrounding market trends, visitor profiles and industrial impacts, combined with a strategic overview of the market, will provide businesses with the tools needed to develop a competitive advantage.

Strategic overview may be obtained through use of a SWOT analysis. SWOT is a strategic planning method that analyses the 'strengths, weaknesses, opportunities and threats' of a business or venture. SWOT ensures a suitable method of reviewing the strategy, position and direction of a company or business venture to ensure effective decision-making. A SWOT analysis (Table 11.2) highlights key issues within the sport and adventure tourism industry in need of consideration.

Industry impacts

All forms of sport and adventure tourism have some level of impact upon the internal and external environment of which they operate. Sport tourism activities generate enormous economic reverberations, alongside the social/cultural and intellectual repercussions of tourism. An assessment of these impacts can be made through the adoption of the PESTEL framework. This method of inquiry aims to

Table 11.2. SWOT (strengths, weaknesses, opportunities and threats) analysis of the sport adventure tourism industry.

Strengths	Weaknesses
Nationwide health and fitness obsession: all sport participation has increased, naturally leading into sport tourism. Government pushes for health reinforce such vacations. Sedentary workers in the knowledge economy show desire for 're-embodiment' through soft adventure travel	*Inactivity holidays*: polarization of tourists preferring sedentary holidays and those choosing activity
Increased activity at home: this trend feeds seamlessly into activity holidays	*Identity of adventure travel*: the growth of mainstream and luxury travel providers, alongside provision of soft adventure travel, continues to dilute the distinctiveness and attractiveness of adventure holidays, thus, lessening the 'adventure' image
Increases in soft adventure travel: trends moving beyond traditional backpacker to mature, sophisticated markets. Desire for long-haul, grassroots, authenticity, slow and eco tourism within hot destinations	*Overreliance on group travel format*: while group travel will appeal to some, others may be deterred by the prospect of travelling with strangers
Revitalization of domestic markets: potential of sport to re-energize tired beach holidays	*Seasonality*: issues surrounding the cyclic nature of tourist supply/demand forced by seasonality

Opportunities	Threats
Specialist activity provision: barriers to entry are low for holiday providers offering specialized sports/adventure components	*Independent travel*: threats prevail in Europe for tourists to generate their own sport/adventure tourism plans, particularly in walking and snow sports
Further revitalization of domestic markets: room for continued provision of sport and activities to increase appeal of short breaks, school and corporate packages	*Fuel price hikes*: air passenger duty changes in 2009 add to financial pressures during times of recession
Building on health trends: holiday providers can push stress release through sport and adventure pursuits, alongside marketing their products as health- and fitness-promoting to kick start well-being	*Greening societies*: eco travel guilt threatens long-haul travel markets
Linking sport with education: strong commercial potential exists for mind/body products in the schools sector	*Competition*: growth of regionally specific operators building on location strengths and super-niche operators poses a threat to larger operators. Consumers have more choice in terms of activities, destination and price. Operators, therefore, have less 'edge'
Soft adventure travel trends: large growth potential in soft adventure travel with contrasting elements such as gastronomy, nature/cultural discovery and relaxation	

Adapted from Mintel, 2008.

identify the political, economic, social, technological, environmental and legal impacts of a particular phenomenon. For the purposes of meeting this chapter's objectives, an analysis of the political, social, economic and environmental impacts will now be explored.

impacts reside in cases where the host nation fails to generate a legacy and instead triggers massive debts (e.g., the 1980 Olympic Games in Lake Placid, New York) or fails to generate interest, such as the poor attendance figures at the New Orleans Olympic Games.

Political impacts

Political impacts are rife within forms of sport and adventure tourism, but particularly within mega events (event sport tourism) such as the Olympics. Exposure of the host city through worldwide television coverage and other forms of media attention all contribute to a nation's symbolic step onto the world stage. The media almost always describe the hosting of such an event as a being positive, making reference to the many associated benefits to local communities. More importantly, however, is the strong political message conveyed by the host nation, both internally and externally. For example, the 1936 Olympic Games in Berlin, Germany, came about at a time of political turmoil with the onslaught of the Nazi regime. The message portrayed to the rest of the world was that of supremacy, dominance and power. Political messages conveyed more internally within a host nation include the benefits of fitness and athleticism and encourage healthy lifestyles. This is particularly useful to surrounding communities left with the potential to use state-of-the-art sports facilities. Other significant political messages have aimed to attract business to the host nation and contribute towards globalization in terms of the removal of cultural differences. The latter is particularly relevant to the Olympics as the message of unity is symbolically conveyed through the use of emblems such as the five-ringed logo, representing the union of the five continents, the Olympic hymn, forming a statement of peace, and the lit torch, symbolizing continuity through time and space (Guttmann, 2002).

While these impacts are generally positive, there have been numerous instances where the political ramifications were largely negative. With the entire world watching, mega events are an optimal time for the intrusion of protests and even terrorism. Other negative political

Social impacts

All forms of tourism impact on host communities, again both positively and negatively. As a global phenomenon, sport attracts mass spectatorship and active participation, all bringing forth the subcultural attributes of that sport. Generally, researchers focus on the economic impacts of such an attraction, hence research in this area is limited. Social impacts may be described as 'the manner in which tourism and travel affect changes in the collective and individual value systems, behaviour patterns, community structures, lifestyle and quality of life' (Hall, 1992). Social impacts are generally viewed as short-term effects to host communities, whereas cultural impacts are long-term in nature, based on the changes of the host nation's social relationships, norms and standards (Ohmann *et al.*, 2006). Therefore, most studies in this area focus on the more identifiable social impacts of sport tourism. Various authors have documented the range of impacts of events, with some deliberation as to the overall effect being positive or negative, or even both. Table 11.3 shows the positive and negative impacts of event sport tourism identified by Fredline (2005).

In addition to Fredline's findings, Higham (1999) identified further negative social impacts such as crowding, local community displacement and disruptions to normal life. As a microcosm of society, each individual sport carries with it certain cultural behaviours, attitudes and rituals. These behaviours are not restricted to the athletes themselves, but also to their spectating fans. For example, hooliganism, drinking, crime and nationalism are all observed traits within football fans, having an extensively negative impact on host nations. This reputation for hooliganism is not only damaging to host communities but also provokes a negative and embarrassing image of the hooligan's home

Table 11.3. Fredline's (2005) positive and negative impacts of event sport tourism.

Positive	Negative
Sense of pride	Rowdiness
Self-actualization	Fan delinquency
Entertainment, community and family cohesion	Nationalistic prejudice as a result of team competition and interaction with host communities
Opportunity to witness the effects of health- and fitness-bound lifestyles	Decreased well-being and quality of life as a consequence of perceived loss of control within the local environment

Adapted from Ohmann *et al.*, 2006.

country. On a more positive note, Hall (2004) highlighted the magnitude of a resident's increased quality of life due to the event's role in urban rejuvenation, supply of new sports facilities, architecture and newly generated image. These factors positively influence community pride, togetherness and social cohesion (see also Chapter 10).

Economic impacts

Similar to the social impacts, sport and adventure tourism also have positive and negative repercussions on local and national economies. The increased provision of sport and adventure provision brings mass tourism, resulting in financial gains directly to the attraction itself and also indirectly to local businesses such as restaurants, hotels and other amenities. Incidental visitation to surrounding businesses unrelated to tourism may also increase. Moreover, raising the profile of such destinations attracts new business, some directly relating to a particular sport tourism attraction (e.g. merchandisers of sports equipment, memorabilia and smaller sport activity supply chains) and other unrelated businesses that simply benefit from their location within particular tourist destinations. Undoubtedly, the growth of new business contributes to the local economy, with the added benefit of increasing demand for employment.

However, local residents are largely susceptible to the negative economic impacts of sport and adventure tourism attractions. There have been numerous documented incidences of forced relocation of residents due to the manner in which these attractions raise the area's profile. Increased housing and market prices, rent and taxation are all typified results of area reconstruction stimulated by sport tourism provision, particularly with the inclusion of prolific events such as the Olympics. This effect can be seen before, during and after the event itself. In the case of the 2000 Sydney Olympics, soaring costs of living were observed immediately following the announcement of the destination as future host for the prestigious event.

Environmental impacts

The effects that sport and adventure tourism have on the environment are generally negative, with some outlets being guiltier than others; the detrimental environmental impacts of ski resorts have been well established and largely researched. The clearing of trees, building of ski huts and marking out of ski runs all contribute to increased carbon emissions and waste. Other problems are associated with increased traffic flow to the attraction, the expansion of built-up areas and construction and use of ski runs, alongside the production of waste in the process. Many similar effects are seen in golf tourism, whereby deforestation and disruptions to the landscape are consequences of economic gains. Skiing, golf and many forms of sport tourism attractions are still dominated by the affluent – a social class with more access to methods of private transportation such as the use of cars. This means that air pollution is often as apparent in ski and golf resorts as that experienced within urban areas. Naturally, this leads to additional consequences in terms of soil and vegetation; the pollution poisons the ground, thereby increasing the risk of numerous health hazards and premature ageing (Weiss *et al.*, 1998).

Noise pollution is another result of increased traffic flow to tourist destinations. In addition, light pollution occurs due to increased illumination within these areas. However, the disruptions experienced by local residents are far greater than those of excess light and noise. As has already been discussed, successful sport tourism destinations are likely to attract new businesses to the area. While such endeavours offer economic benefits, they also lead to space shortages as locations become transformed into tourist centres. This further attracts people to the destination, leading to overpopulation in a now built-up area, forcing ever more construction to support increasing demands for housing, which in turn results in the loss of more natural land. Moreover, the onslaught of construction over natural land causes damage to the local wildlife. While environmental laws have emerged prohibiting any further building or expansion on such areas, as well as many resort operators adopting changes in urban peripheries to reduce traffic and air pollution, the damage may have already been done. The desecration of vegetation and wildlife is, in some cases, irreversible. The delicate nature of the earth's ecosystems must not be underestimated. The development of ski slopes has also lessened agricultural output, which in turn reduces surface water after rainfall (Weiss *et al.*, 1998), affecting agricultural livelihoods and thus reversing some of the economic benefits of the attraction itself.

Future Research

Increasing environmental pressure clashing with economic costs forces the need for greater research and innovation that works towards enhanced sustainable development. While this chapter has unravelled many advances in this area, most sport and adventure attractions and destinations still produce excessive waste, carbon emissions and other environmental pollutants either directly (e.g. the construction of facilities) or indirectly (e.g. participants' methods of travel to the destination).

The exploration of the market demonstrates changing patterns of consumption, whereby the trends for participation are in a state of evolution. Tour operators need to adapt to the changing profile of increased consumption from female markets (particularly in the realm of soft adventure travel) without alienating the mainstream population. This may be more difficult than merely changing marketing tactics as research on motivation demonstrates that in the case of adventure tourism, the participant needs to credit the

---

Case Study 11.1: Vallée Blanche Ski Resort, French Alpines.

Vallée Blanche has been operating since 1989, offering ski and small-scale snowboarding facilities, alongside a canteen. While business has always been steady, the continued growth of providers has begun saturating the market, allowing customers more choice in consumption and thus weakening demand at Vallée Blanche. In order to remain competitive, Vallée Blanche intends to rejuvenate its tired facilities, aiming to become a more attractive resort, thus appealing to recognized growth areas such as female and family markets, while also expanding demand for snowboarding within mainstream participation. Plans for reconstruction include enhanced hospitality provision, including restaurant and hotel facilities. These are intended to form part of the package deal and (based on key market findings) will be more likely to attract custom. Furthermore, due to limited public transport to the destination, increases in car-parking facilities are also required. In order to combat the downside of seasonality through the warmer months, Vallée Blanche will increase its use of artificial snow generated from water in nearby lakes. The environmental downside of such ventures is that increased water consumption reduces the growth of grass and flowers during the summer, alongside damages to vegetation of nearby farming communities. Plans to reconstruct facilities in order to become more attractive to customers will inevitably increase waste and other pollutants. In addition, the increased volume of customers will increases demands on local communities in terms of population, noise, congestion and vehicle emissions. Despite their image, the Alpines support a very fragile ecosystem that is likely to suffer the consequences of ski developments. However, for Vallée Blanche to keep pace with local competition, it must match the products offered and gain a competitive edge.

experience as exciting, challenging, exclusive and with perceived danger. Once the experience is no longer distinguished in such a way, tourists will chose new adventures to fulfil their needs. As demonstrated within the SWOT analysis, when more people engage in the activity, the perception of 'adventure' is lessened. This underlying weakness needs to be addressed.

Research is also needed surrounding newly emerging areas of sport and adventure tourism, such as virtual sport tourism and the loss of health-inducing active qualities. At the opposite end of the spectrum is the onslaught of extreme sport tourism, whereby thrill seekers are continually pushing the boundaries of the experience towards greater adrenaline-fuelled danger. This contemporary phenomenon requires more attention in terms of how such activities contrast with many well-established motivational theories. A continuation of adventure tourism also raises the question as to the extent of the incurred danger and where the limits lie, alongside issues surrounding the activity provider's social responsibility.

Conclusion

The chapter has considered the broad nature of sport and tourism as separate entities and how the very definitional difficulties contribute towards policy and governance issues. The chapter provided an overview of the industry, before undertaking an analysis of sport and adventure tourists, including their profile, behaviourisms and motivations. Finally, the chapter analysed the market in terms of size, trends and providers, alongside internal and external issues affecting suppliers, and providing the information key to attaining competitive advantage.

Review Questions

1. What are the benefits of profiling sport and adventure tourist participants? How would you categorize individuals?

2. Review the tourism-adapted motivational theories within this chapter. Highlight some of the key weaknesses when applying these to segments of sport and adventure tourists.

3. Highlight current participant trends within the industry. Using this information, suggest ways in which operators could adjust their products to meet changes in demand.

4. Revisit the sport and adventure tourism SWOT analysis. How might travel operators neutralize the weaknesses within the industry to gain competitive advantage?

References

Berlyne, D. (1960) *Conflict, Arousal and Curiosity*. McGraw-Hill, New York.

Council of Europe (2001) *The European Sports Charter (Revised)*. Council of Europe, Brussels.

Crompton, J. (1979) Motivations for pleasure vacation. *Annals of Tourism Research* 6, 408–424.

Fredline, E. (2005) Host and guest relations and sport tourism. *Sport, Culture and Society* 8, 263–279.

Frey, J. and Eitzen, D. (1991) Sport and society. *Annual Review of Sociology* 17, 503–522.

Gammon, S. and Robinson, T. (2003) Sport and tourism: a conceptual framework. *Journal of Sport Tourism* 8, 21–26.

Gibson, H. (2004) Moving beyond the 'what is and who' of sport tourism to understanding 'why'. *Journal of Sport Tourism* 9, 247–265.

Guttmann, A. (2002) *The Olympics: A History of the Modern Games*, 2nd edn. University of Illinois Press, Illinois, USA.

Hall, C. (1992) Adventure, sport and health tourism. In: Weiler and Hall (eds) *Special Interest Tourism*. Belhaven, London, UK, pp. 141–158.

Hall, M. (2004) Sport tourism and urban regeneration. In Ritchie B. and Adair, D. (eds) *Sport Tourism: Interrelationships, Impacts and Issues*. Channelview Publications, Clevedon, UK.

Higham, J. (1999) Sport as an avenue of tourism development: an analysis of the positive and negative impacts of sport tourism. *Current Issues in Tourism* 2, 82–90.

Higham, J. (2005) *Sport Tourism Destinations: Issues, Opportunities and Analysis.* Butterworth-Heinemann, Burlington, Massachusetts, USA.

Hinch, T. and Higham, J. (2001) Sport tourism: a framework for research. *International Journals of Tourism Research* 3, 45–58.

Hinch, T. and Higham, J. (2004) *Sport Tourism Development.* Channel View Publications, Clevedon, UK.

Hudson, S. (2003) *Sport and Adventure Tourism.* The Haworth Press, Binghampton, UK.

Leiper, N. (1981) Towards a cohesive curriculum in tourism: the case for a distinct discipline. *Annals of Tourism Research* 8, 69–74.

McIntosh, R., Goeldner, C. and Ritchie, J. (1995) *Tourism: Principles, Practices and Philosophies.* Wiley, New York.

Ministry of Commerce (1996) *Safety Management in the Adventure Tourism Industry: Voluntary and Regulatory Approaches.* Ministry of Commerce, Wellington, New Zealand.

Mintel (2008) *Activity/Special Interest Holidays UK.* Mintel, London, UK.

Nogawa, H., Yamaguchi, Y. and Hagi, Y. (1996) An empirical research study on Japanese sport tourism in sport-for-all events: case studies of a single-night event and a multiple-night event. *Journal of Travel Research* 35, 46–54.

Ohmann, S., Jones, I. and Wilkes, K. (2006) The perceived social impacts of the 2006 World Cup on Munich residents. *Journal of Sport and Tourism* 11, 129–152.

Redmond, G. (1991) Changing styles of sports tourism: industry/consumer interactions in Canada, the USA and Europe. In: Sinclair, M.T. and Stabler, M.J. (eds) *The Tourism Industry: An International Analysis.* CAB International, Wallingford, UK, pp. 107–120.

Robinson, T. and Gammon, S. (2004) A question of primary and secondary motives: revisiting and applying the sport tourism framework. *Journal of Sport Tourism* 9, 221–233.

Swarbrooke, J., Beard, C., Leckie S. and Pomfret, G. (2003) *Adventure Tourism: The New Frontier.* Butterworth-Heinemann, Burlington, Massachusetts, USA.

Theobald, W. (1998) *Global Tourism,* 3rd edn. Elsevier, Burlington, Massachusetts, USA.

Weiss, O., Norden, G. and Hilscher, P. (1998) Ski tourism and environmental problems. *International Review for the Sociology of Sport* 33, 367–379.

12 Cultural Tourism and Accessibility

Geoff Shirt

Introduction

According to Kroeber and Kluckholn researching in the early 1950s, there were 164 different meanings of the word 'culture'; an English word derived from the Latin *cultura*, which simply means 'to cultivate'. If one were to speak to a scientist about culture, the response would almost certainly be that it is associated with bacteria and will be found growing in the bottom of a Petri dish. Ask a nutritionist and a different response would be forthcoming; perhaps suggesting it to be an ingredient in the process of cheese making. Neither suggestion is particularly helpful to those in the social sciences, although even here there are several possible interpretations that are wide of the mark. The mind of an art critic would almost certainly be drawn to the fine arts; to be *cultured* may be to have studied and to appreciate paintings, know of the key sculptors on the world stage, attend the opera or ballet on a regular basis and quote Shakespeare at cocktail parties with aristocracy. Culture *per se* then might be perceived as elitist or at least accessible to a minority audience. None of the above examples is particularly helpful to the study of tourism management, where widest participation is often sought, although all of them may need to be appreciated by the tourism professional in certain situations.

Beginning with a short résumé from around the point where present society has evolved, it is possible perhaps, to identify the areas, critical success factors and future interests of cultural tourism. Those studying culture from the perspective of tourism should appreciate the researchers of the 20th century, who shaped and polarized study areas under the umbrella term and concept of anthropology (the study of humanity). As might be expected, several types of anthropology were identified, which are typically classified into four groups: cultural or social anthropology, archaeology, linguistic anthropology and biological/physical anthropology. It is perhaps the first of these that is of most interest to the tourism student.

Cultural anthropology has two meanings. The first is the human capacity to classify and represent experiences with symbols while acting imaginatively and creatively. In Africa, a rain-dance may be most readily be associated with this perception. In other geographical locations, it is perhaps (but decreasingly) with a culinary delight that the link is made. The second is the distinct ways in which local people living in different parts of the world are classified (often but not exclusively by themselves) and represent their lifestyle using events, rituals, festivals and other experiences. In terms of tourism, cultural tourism has a tendency to be backward-looking; seeking to 'ground' a community's social identity in the past, wishing to pass this on to future generations, both local residents and visiting guests alike.

Cultural Tourism

According to Richardson and Fluker (2004), cultural tourism embraces both the study of events and rituals passed down through the generations and the wider forms of lifestyle and folk heritage. It is experiential tourism involved

Case Study 12.1. Shrovetide football.

The exact origins of the annual Shrovetide football game in Ashbourne, Derbyshire, have been lost, but the game is generally accepted to go back to the first millennium. Certainly it existed and was a significant event in 1349; we know this because King Edward III tried to ban it, claiming it interfered with his archery practice. Indeed, it retains strong royal connections: the Prince of Wales (later to become King Edward VIII) 'turned the ball up' in 1928, with Prince Charles repeating the role in 2003.

The 'game' is played over two 8-hour periods; the first on Shrove Tuesday and the second on Ash Wednesday. It comprises two teams of players who must be locally born. One team is named the Up'ards and the other the Down'ards, with the distinction being as to which side of the River Henmore the players were born. The aim is to carry the cork-filled ball (historically thought to be a head taken from an execution) to the opposing team's goal, rugby-scrum fashion. There is no given number of team members, but frequently over a thousand take part devoid of any accepted dress code. Two stone goals stand 3 miles apart on opposite sides of the town. Between them the playing surface includes grass fields, the river bed and street tarmac. Sons follow fathers, who followed their own fathers into the team.

The event attracts great interest, both at home and abroad, bringing hundreds of spectators who either wish they were or are quietly pleased they were not born in the environs. Not every shopkeeper is so positive about the event; their shops are virtually under siege for 2 days. As a result, many place barricades across their windows and doors to prevent an often over-exuberant army of brawling youths entering their shops in a glass-shattering fashion.

Fig. 12.1. Shrovetide 2010. Activity in the river Henmore, as ball is temporarily hidden from view. (Picture © http://www.mylimephotography.co.uk.)

with and stimulated by a great variety of things – the performing arts, visual arts, festivals, cuisines, history and experiencing nostalgia and other ways of life. Nostalgia appears to be an increasingly important element of cultural tourism but, as will be seen, perhaps nostalgia is not necessarily what it used to be. As culture is experiential, it is accordingly often intangible. Culture itself then may perhaps not be smelt, touched or tasted – a measure of tangibility is invariably provided through the existence of events, cuisine and artefacts.

Returning to the word culture, society has coined several adjectives that are essential for the complete understanding of the phrase 'cultural tourism'. While high culture may give rise to a form of tourism that focuses upon museums, opera houses, stately homes and galleries, those same venues may be adjacent to buildings and arenas for low and popular culture. A stay in Amsterdam may include a visit to the Rijksmuseum to view Van Gogh's masterpieces, but would any trip to Amsterdam be complete without a few minutes in a brown bar or a walk through the red-light district? On occasions, the same venue might host a Gilbert and Sullivan opera on a Friday and a Beatles tribute band the following night!

Invariably the phrase 'heritage tourism' appears alongside that of culture, as the two are often inseparably linked although they are definitely not the same. Heritage tourism relates to the historical artefacts such as buildings and monuments, which may or may not be viewed within the context of any culture. For instance, the Taj Mahal may be visited and admired without any understanding of the tensions that exist between an Islamic trust, known as the Sunni Waqf Board, and the Indian government. The 'heritage industry' is the phrase used to describe the commercialization of historic attractions for the purposes of tourism development (Page and Connell, 2009).

Terms associated with cultural tourism

To fully understand the term 'cultural tourism', it is essential to appreciate that the tourist will often be a significant part of the experience. The background and context of the tourist will almost certainly determine the success factors and how future word of mouth promotion is affected. The following list may further assist with the consideration of cultural tourism.

According to Weaver and Lawson (2010), 'cultural events' are attractions that occur over a fixed period of time in one or more locations and are more constructed than natural. They include historical commemorations, world fairs, sporting events and festivals. The theory is closely linked to that of 'cultural commodification': the term given to the packaging of cultural events for sale (Richardson and Fluker, 2004). It could be that certain events are linked together, such as the Edinburgh Festival, which has a clear schedule of cultural events that take place over a very short period of time. How such events are packaged in terms of cost, length and location may have an impact upon their success. The crucial factor appears to be fitting them into the tourist's time frame or staging them in an arena to suit the tourist, rather than the intrinsic characteristics of the event itself. This may cause some authenticity issues that may or may not impact upon the perceived value to the customer (see Chapter 4).

'Cultural sites' are geographically fixed attractions that may be more constructed than natural and can be classified into prehistoric, historical, contemporary and economic, with specialized recreational and retail subcategories

---

Case Study 12.2. Liverpool: 2008 European Capital of Culture.

Birmingham, Bristol, Liverpool, Newcastle, Norwich and Oxford were all shortlisted as contenders to become the 2008 European Capital of Culture. Hitherto unprecedented amounts of government and EU funding were to be made available to the winner; this eventually becoming Liverpool. Where better to seek out cultural tourism than in this city that already contained a staggering amount of cultural heritage of both an architectural and anthropological nature.

It is unique in that no other city in England contains two cathedrals – one for the Anglican Church built around 1900 and a Roman Catholic building to cater for the high numbers of Irish Catholics that arrived in the city following the Great Potato Famine around 1850. Liverpool has a great shipbuilding heritage and strong links with the Titanic. This was the ship's home port and although she never visited the city, that has not stopped a Titanic Museum being created. The Albert Docks are centrally located within the city and provide the largest group of grade 1 listed buildings in the UK; these are listed as being of exceedingly high architectural importance. They are now home for the Tate Gallery, the International Slavery Museum and The Beatles Story Museum to name but three. Along Waterloo Road stand the entrance gateways to the plethora of docks that established Liverpool as a ship-building city. These do not have names, rather different symbols such as an eagle, a spherical ball or the head of an animal. Such was the lack of literacy among the new recruits to the workforce, they were simply told to enter by a specific symbol that would lead to the correct dock and shipyard. No other city in England can boast such a strong connection with popular culture. Few cities either can boast to be home to such a pair of consistently high achievers in the world of football. Several hundred examples of high, low and popular culture may be found cheek by jowl within the same street or location within the city.

Fig. 12.2. Petra: this city, built upon earlier settlements by the Nabataeans in the 7th century, remained unknown to the Western World until 1812. Made famous by the film *Indiana Jones and the Last Crusade*, this street carved entirely out of the red sandstone is truly awe inspiring and unique. (Picture © Geoff Shirt.)

(Fig. 12.2) (Weaver and Lawson, 2010). They may provide the arena for cultural events such as re-enactments or glorified car-boot sales!

'Cultural history' is the name given to the oral and written history of a specific group within a particular society or location. The consideration of a significant tour of South America may involve a considerable amount of background reading if maximum benefit from the trip is to result.

According to Hall (2005), 'cultural homogenization/consumerism' is the 'result of capitalist pressure upon a society or grouping that cause global sameness, either in terms of expectation or interpretation'. The complete failure of a culture to *survive* in an *original* form may itself be quite unlikely, although it is likely that most cultures will be undergoing a process of adaptation to a new environment driven by capitalist, industrial modernity (Fig. 12.3). However, homogenization of consumption or production is by no means certain or indeed unwelcomed.

The concept of homogenization/consumerism may be linked to the 'demonstration effect'

(Wall and Matheison, 2006). This is characterized as the disruptive role of tourism when tourists draw the attention of lifestyle discrepancies to the local community; one that has similar sociocultural aspirations. Local governments may argue that such encounters stimulate the host in a positive way, using demonstration effect as a means of enhancing personal expectations locally. Most commonly, however, this is unsubstantiated and the effect is detrimental to the image of the area, as symbols of affluence on parade invariably become targets for theft and associated crime.

'Cultural capital' is a sociological concept first articulated by Pierre Bourdieu during the 1960s (Richards, 2007). Bourdieu stated that every individual will appreciate what is being viewed on the basis of their previous exposure or background. In essence he suggested that, for instance, someone would be more appreciative of a Monet painting if they knew something about the artist, his life and his other works than if the viewer had not received this insight. Everyone has a unique cultural capital because everyone's family, educational

Fig. 12.3. Pizza Hut in Tel Aviv. Pizza Hut often employs a number of Muslims in an attempt to avoid contravening strict Jewish employment laws that prevent observant Jews from working on Shabbat, Friday evenings and Saturday. (Picture © Geoff Shirt.)

opportunities, interests and professional ambitions are different. Those who have studied fine art, according to Bourdieu, will take something different away from a visit to a museum containing paintings than someone who has not (Richards, 2007). For this reason, many cultural tourism providers will try to build experiences from a common point of understanding by 'artificially educating' their visitors. An example of this can be found at Auschwitz in Poland, where a short visual presentation is given in a large plain hall, using a series of monochrome photographs and commentary in several languages to convey the sombre nature of the 'attraction'. In sharp contrast to this, the Tourist Information Centre in Bern, Switzerland, uses a warm, much smaller room to present a three-dimensional historical evolution of the city with animation and graphics and, at appropriate times, even the smell of burning buildings and gun smoke!

The desired outcome is the same; an opportunity for the visitor to have a more informed eye on what they will shortly witness.

According to Page and Connell (2009), 'cultural baggage' is the term given to the beliefs, values and behaviour modes that tourists take with them on holiday. It will be noted here that once again it is not the cultural tourism that is the focus, rather the tourist. If, for instance, it is the cultural norm of the visitor to seek entertainment at a weekend, there may be an unspoken expectation of what is available to him/her on holiday. This may also be used in connection with the fact that many go on holiday for a specific purpose – to be entertained, educated or to simply relax. Knowledge of this may be helpful in advance, although, in reality, it just means the experience may not be one that 'ticks every box' for every visitor. This may be linked to 'cultural brokerage', which refers to the bridge between the host community and visitor. This bridge is essentially the level of effort the providers have taken to discover the precise motivational factors of their guests.

In many cases, cultural tourists looking for originality and authenticity are drawn to sites and events that are not 'presented', where they can see the unspoilt, unstaged nature of a community's culture. Such sites are becoming increasingly rare, due in no small part to the ever-widening coverage of satellite and the internet. Such cultures would be the Amish community in America's Mid West and several Jewish communities around the world. Such is the size of these communities that more than one mobile phone manufacturer provides handsets built without access to the internet – not simply with this facility disconnected, but remanufactured to prevent any subsequent modification being made. Such are the lengths certain cultures go to in order to avoid the 'evils' of this 21st century world. Not all cultures can afford to go to these lengths!

Case Study 12.3. Mea Shearim, Jerusalem.

Mea Shearim was founded in 1874 by five ultra-Orthodox Jews wishing to escape the increasingly crowded old city of Jerusalem. It became one of the first communities to be set up outside the famous city walls. Today, it is home to many thousands of such Jews. Many residents are so ultra-Orthodox Jewish fundamentalists that they are referred to as 'ultra ultras'.

The 'Quarter' represents a living museum, where residents have preserved the traditional ways of life that existed for centuries among ultra-Orthodox Jews in the ghettos of Northern and Eastern Europe. They live and dress in the same sombre style as their European ancestors, with televisions, mobile telephones and computers all taboo and forbidden. Their centuries-old ways flourish because they see change as evil. Houses are small and shabby (Fig. 12.4). The residents have little privacy, with about a third living more than three to a room. Children are raised so as to minimize the impact of the outside world. A child's upbringing is so strict that many have never seen Jaffa Road (the main thoroughfare to the old city that lies just 500 yards away) or a non-religious neighbourhood. Strict, authoritarian education is the primary tool for instilling values in their young, with children spending most of their time in school on a curriculum devoted almost exclusively to religious studies.

This provides for a perfect cultural experience when visiting the City of Peace, but visitors should beware. Over the years, tourist groups have been stoned and driven out as it is felt by residents that such numbers of camera-clicking, foreign-speaking intruders arriving together present a real threat to their lifestyle. The message from the community is clear: spend time in our streets and money in our shops, but come as individuals and couples, not groups. An individual walking down the street will almost certainly step off the pavement to allow a resident pushing a pram to remain on her path. A group of tourists will almost certainly cause the opposite to occur. 'Observe but do not change our community life.'

Fig. 12.4. Mea Shearim. One of the typical houses within the district, 'run-down' by Western standards. To the left is one of the several signs that discourage entry of tourist groups. (Picture © Geoff Shirt.)

Summarizing Culture and Cultural Tourism

Culture is a living representation of the way certain societies live or have lived their lives. As such, one's culture holds great fascination to others and often offers a significant opportunity for cultural tourism activity. Where a past culture is being considered, tourism is invariably assisted by historic artefacts and may be assisted by a growth in heritage tourism.

Access

The word 'access' is both a noun and verb. Accordingly, a definition contains reference to both and each is relevant in the context of this study. Several meanings of the word are of particular interest and relevance: (i) entree: the right to enter; (ii) the right to obtain or make use of or take advantage of a way of entering or leaving; (iii) reach or gain access to; and (iv) the act of approaching or entering.

In the context of leisure, tourism and recreation, both forms of the word are present and invariably relate to the rural environment, the countryside. Looking more closely at the first two definitions, it will be noted that both contain the word 'right'. It would be foolish, however, to pretend that access is an *uncontested* right, as will be investigated later. Suffice to say at this stage, access has been one of the most controversial and misunderstood concepts for the past 80 years and a short history lesson is a helpful starting point.

Access within a historical context

Six hundred years ago, the English countryside was a very different place to what we see today. The landscape was made up of vast forest, moorland, arable crops and common land; the last correctly inferring ownership was available to all. Indeed, the whole concept of ownership was foreign to most Britons; the rural environment was a place of subsistence living and lifestyle. Paradoxically, today's visitor is often drawn to the countryside as it represents a natural, unspoilt environment, but in truth the majority of it is as manmade as the city.

During the Tudor period, things began to change as demand for English wool within Europe outstripped supply and landlords turned their arable lands over to sheep and often extended their farms by unilaterally claimed common grazing. Henry VIII added an additional dimension with his propensity for travelling the country and partaking of his favourite outdoor pleasure and pastime: deer hunting. Large areas of both grassland and woodland continued to be 'enclosed', which essentially excluded the wider population from entering to make a subsistence living from grazing cattle, selling wood for fuel, catching rabbits for the pot and trapping venison for sale.

Around 250 years ago, the Enclosure Movement took firm hold. Paradoxically, it became responsible for both the increased appeal and reduction of 'available' countryside. The 'chequer-board' farmed countryside began to emerge that the public find so attractive today; an exclusive landscape that had been fully inclusive and truly accessible by all only two centuries earlier. The Enclosure Acts and subsequent game laws introduced during the 1870s effectively further restricted access to 'open' countryside, thus depriving many families of their livelihoods and access to their traditional homeland.

The following passage takes a particularly UK view; a more global perspective is provided later in the chapter.

From Satanic Mills to the Elysian Fields

Mill-owners were the next 'agents of change' to affect social habits within the countryside, arguably exacerbating the 'problem' by encouraging outdoor recreation. In an attempt to find adequate recompense for poor working conditions, 'wakes weeks' and charabanc outings were initiated to promote the mass movement of employees, often to the countryside to find 'fresh air'. Ironically, and in spite of the best efforts by noted philanthropists such as Miss Octavia Hill, Sir Robert Hunter and Canon Hardwicke Rawnsley (all founder members of The National Trust), those driving the industrial revolution continued to remove land, often used previously for recreational purposes, from the public domain at an alarming rate.

Other stimuli were to affect demand for recreation in the countryside before the end of the 19th century. In 1865, a group of individuals formed the Commons Preservation Society, which became the first pressure group to lobby for access to the countryside. The society's formation assisted the parliament of the day in designating the first bank holiday in 1871. This act (known as the 1871 Act), theoretically at least, encouraged the use of time to be set aside for leisure by everyone. But the Commons Preservation Society saw a main purpose of the Act as to save the countryside for the learned scholar, thus largely excluding working men and women. Its early members included such well-known members of the Arts and Crafts Movement such as William Morris, social reformers such as John Ruskin and the poet William Wordsworth who, among others, promoted and reinforced links with the Romantic Movement. Poetry, literature, music and paintings had already begun to promote the countryside in a way that appealed strongly to the educated person. Indeed, so powerful was the 'high-brow' rural image they put forward that it has become engraved upon the subconscious mind of today's visitor. The subsequent 'removal process' has presented postmodern countryside planners wishing to promote policies of 'a countryside for all' with perhaps the most difficult psychological barrier imaginable. Albeit coming from different directions, by the end of the 19th century and the early part of the 20th century several pressure groups were lobbying the government.

Their common aim was to highlight the direct relationship between continued industrialization, decreasing levels of rural accessibility and the effects of social exclusion upon the national workforce.

In an attempt to restore the balance and represent their own interests, landowners formed their own groups – ones invariably associated with limiting access (Table 12.1). Although the first 'Access to the Mountains' Bill was put before Parliament in 1884, it was not until 1939 that the first bill reached the statute books. The main reason for the delay was the high proportion of landowners and aristocracy within the British parliamentary system, particularly in the House of Lords, who stood to lose most. The 1939 Access to the Mountains Act suffered the same fate as previous attempts and was never implemented due to the outbreak of World War II. But pressure was building upon the establishment.

Post-war pressure

The formation of the Ramblers Federation in 1930 preceded the mass trespass at Kinder Scout by 2 years and its stance on this event paradoxically led to the formation of the Ramblers Association 5 years later. The Federation was primarily a lobbying organization, while those aligning with the Ramblers Association or 'The Ramblers', to give them their better known title, demanded direct action. However, as strong the desire for recreation was

Table 12.1. The formation of organized recreation and access groups.

Name of club or association	Year formed
The Commons and Open Spaces Preservation Society	1865
The Hayfield and Kinder Scout Ancient Footpaths Association	1876
The Cyclists' Touring Club	1878
The National Trust	1895
The Camping and Caravanning Club	1901
The Caravan Club	1907
The British Association for Shooting and Conservation	1908
The Youth Hostel Association	1930
The Ramblers Federation	1930
The British Field Sports Society	1930
The Ramblers Association	1935
The Standing Committee on National Parks	1936

Case Study 12.4. The mass trespass of 1932.

Credited with establishing the network of UK National Parks, the mass trespass of 1932 was a deliberate act of civil disobedience. Undertaken on land owned by the Duke of Devonshire, it attempted to prove the weakness and inequality of contemporary English law. For generations, serious hikers had felt excluded and been denied the opportunity to walk over open land that they regarded as being stolen from their ancestors 500 years earlier.

The event was well publicized and attracted thousands of walkers, each willing to break the law if necessary to facilitate the outcome of a countryside that was inclusive for all. While not farmed as such, the moorland was used for raising game. The shooting of pheasant and grouse was seen then, as now, as exclusive to the aristocracy and a privileged few. Not unsurprisingly due to the level of media attention given to the trespass, several hundred gamekeepers and members of the police force were in attendance and five almost token arrests were made.

The mass trespass had the desired far-reaching outcome and within 20 years the first National Park, which included Kinder Scout, was established (Fig. 12.5). Eventually, changes in the law would allow all citizens access to public footpaths (and bridleways and byways), regardless of whether they crossed private land. The phrase 'right to roam' was extremely evocative during the 1990s at a time when the Labour government was in opposition to Margaret Thatcher's and later John Major's governments. When Tony Blair headed the New Labour government in 1997, this was a key promise in the manifesto and was partially fulfilled in the Countryside Rights of Way Act that was taken through Parliament in 2000.

Fig. 12.5. Moorlands Centre, a new facility provided by the Peak District National Park Authority in 2006 at Edale. The building is a mere stone's throw from Kinder Scout and the official start of the longest national trail in England, the Pennine Way. (Picture © Geoff Shirt.)

in the immediate pre-war period, successive committees set up to investigate the issues took as their yardstick conservation issues rather than recreation.

Lobbying by conservation bodies, rather than pressure from recreation groups, led Ramsey McDonald to set up a committee in 1929 to explore the possibility of adapting the American National Park template as a concept for the UK. For the next 20 years, subsequent committees analysed and revised proposals. On each occasion, the need for conservation held centre stage while recreation and leisure issues played a much lesser role.

But for the outbreak of and eventual victory in World War II, our famous countryside might have had a very different face. Between 1918 and 1945, the 'land question', as it became known, centred around the desire of the Labour government to nationalize all private land in order to address a wide range of progressive issues, including protecting the special role of agriculture in society; increasing agricultural productivity by encouraging labour back to the land through smallholdings and resettlement; and generally reversing the deterioration of rural life. Note, however, that the words recreation and leisure do not appear in the rationale. The war-time agricultural executive committees had effectively demonstrated the benefits of state intervention as an alternative to the state ownership.

The Scott Report published in 1942 was a brave attempt to find a compromise; brave in what it proposed and also in that it was released while hostilities against Nazi Germany were at their height. At its heart was the need to bring the rural environment within the scope of planning law and it took initial, delicate steps into the sensitive area of town and country planning. But to many would-be users, the countryside was escape, was freedom, was theirs. To them the phrase 'countryside planning' was an oxymoron.

By 1945, Labour had come to recognize that land nationalization was an irrelevance compared to the immediate problem of post-war food shortages. Such compromises might have damaged their relationship with the farmers in the drive for increased productivity. Accordingly, the recreational issue remained on the back burner. But this was not to be. Along with the return of the troops who had fought so valiantly for the protection of their 'green and pleasant land' came a desire to explore and enjoy it through recreational activities.

The 1949 National Parks and Access to The Countryside Act was designed to encourage the provision of public enjoyment in National Parks, arranging access agreements and orders for 'open' country and allowed the compulsory purchase of land for recreation and access. This, together with a requirement for local authorities to survey and map rights of way meant that long-distance routes could be established.

Furthermore, the Countryside Code was introduced.

Responding to a continually changing environment and increased public pressure, the 1968 Countryside Act was passed with the following powers and finally began to take account of recreational use of the countryside.

- The Countryside Commission was formed to have recreational and access duties over the whole of the countryside. This body was subsequently absorbed into Natural England.
- Country parks, picnic sites and transit camping sites were introduced through grant aid, by public authorities and private individuals.
- Finance for access agreements and access orders was extended beyond National Parks and areas of outstanding beauty.
- The definition of 'open' country was extended to include woodland, rivers and canals.
- Highway authorities introduced a comprehensive sign-posting of rights of way.

Several other Acts have been introduced since 1968, with specific aims focused upon providing additional access. The first of these was the 1981 Wildlife and Countryside Act, which updated definitive maps and management agreements for usable access. The Act was amended in 1985 to task National Park Authorities to produce access maps. Ploughing of rights of way was prohibited in the 1990 Rights of Way Act, which also made it illegal to place any obstructions in the way. That same year, the Environmental Protection Act gave limited access to some areas of water industry land, followed a year later by the Water Resources Act, which prohibited all water companies from restricting access.

Not contained within any Act of Parliament itself, something known as the Sandford Principle was created in 1974 (Sandford, 1974). The principle was named after Lord Sandford, who sat on a committee that sought to find and define the line between the importance of recreation and conservation. This principle states that wherever the two issues came in tension, conservation must take priority with the concept of 'carrying capacity' being a key tool in this decision. In local situations, a subjective view was taken by managers as to the number of visitors that could be present at one time before irreparable ecological damage would result. Current debates suggest that historically, managers have drawn this line too early and 'over-protected' the natural environment to the detriment of the nation's health and recreational need. Moreover, the whole concept of carrying capacity has been called into question. Evidence has demonstrated that specific areas, even tourist 'hotspots', can accommodate much higher visitor numbers than allowed for short periods (such as bank holidays), yet on other occasions such as after prolonged rain, damage is caused below this figure. Others state that even if the concept is not flawed, the establishment of the figure shows that it must be exceeded to be found – by which time damage has inevitably been done.

Few contemporary observers would argue with the statement made by Curry (1994) that 'access is synonymous with conflict'. Indeed, his sentiments were endorsed on both sides of the academic and political debate by the National Farmers Union and the Association of National Park Authorities. However, the statement is over-simplistic, misleading and prejudicial for the following reasons:

- It infers a psychological image with 'landed gentry' on one side of the fence and downtrodden members of the deprived working classes on the other. If 'access' is applied to grouse shooting, for example, these lines may be considerably blurred.

- It introduces the dangerous concept of stereotyping opposing groups.
- It infers that the financial interests of the landowner are put at risk by the recreational activities of walkers, for which there is little evidence.

By 1998 and the 6-month period of consultation over, what appeared to be at the heart of the matter was an almost tangible and fundamental lack of trust towards others and their opposing views (DETR, 1998; Mercer, 1998). On the one side, landowners felt contempt towards any visitors, who were perceived at best as unwanted trespassers and at worst as potential vandals. On the other side, there was a (perhaps) widespread sense that civil liberties had become eroded to an unacceptable level. This mistrust was not a modern phenomenon, but one with a long history that could be traced back almost 200 years to the period when 'enclosures' began to appear. For over 40 years prior to 1998, National Park planners had striven hard to increase the area that visitors could access in the countryside. Gains were often made via voluntary agreements although, in truth, many of these were bought with financial incentives.

National parks around the world

The International Union for Conservation of Nature (IUCN) was founded in October 1948 as

---

Case Study 12.5. Carrying capacity at Dovedale.

Dovedale is situated just inside the southern section of the Peak District National Park (PDNP). Although it is only 8 miles in length, it is one of the most popular walks. During a footpath count in Dovedale on a typical August Sunday in 1990, nearly 4,500 walkers were counted on the Staffordshire bank of the river and over 3,500 on the Derbyshire bank. The enormous popularity of the Dovedale area and the pressures brought by the many thousands of pairs of feet has caused serious problems of congestion and erosion. The PDNP Authority attempts to manage numbers by the availability and size of car parking.

In the late 1980s, one enterprising landowner decided that on fine days during the summer season he would open up an adjacent field in order to provide additional income for his farm business. Before long, this activity came to the notice of the PDNP Authority who, seeing the damage potential by exceeding the carrying capacity, approached the farmer and asked him not to continue putting the dale at risk. He refused. Insistent that the carrying capacity must not be exceeded, the PDNP Authority used its powers of compulsory purchase invested upon local government and bought the land from the reluctant vendor. The farmer continues to farm the land albeit through a rental agreement, leaving the task of tourism management to the professionals.

the International Union for the Protection of Nature following an international conference in Fontainebleau, France. Its remit is to 'help the world find pragmatic solutions to its most pressing environment and development challenges' (IUCN, 2010). It supports scientific research projects and manages field projects all over the world. Critically, however, it is held in high esteem by governments, non-governmental organizations, UN agencies, companies and local communities, and accordingly assists with the development and implementation of policy, laws and best practice. Indeed, the IUCN is the world's oldest and largest global environmental network, with a democratic membership union assisting more than 1,000 governments and non-governmental organizations, engaging over 11,000 volunteer scientists in more than 160 countries.

Maintaining biodiversity is central to the IUCN's mission. By demonstrating how bio-diversity is fundamental to addressing some of the world's greatest challenges, the IUCN promotes action on tackling climate change, develops rationales for achieving sustainable energy, gives guidance on improving human well-being and shares expertise on how to build a green economy. One of the key instruments in its toolkit is valuing and establishing protected spaces: 'The world's protected areas are the greatest legacy we can leave to future generations – to ensure that our descendants have access to nature and all the material and spiritual wealth that it represents.'

The IUCN define a protected area as: 'an area of land and/or sea especially dedicated to the protection and maintenance of biological diversity, and of natural and associated cultural resources, and managed through legal or other effective means.' It categorizes protected areas by management objective and has identified six distinct categories of protected areas:

1. Strict nature reserve/wilderness area: a protected area managed mainly for the science of wilderness protection.
2. National park: a protected area managed mainly for ecosystem protection and recreation.
3. Natural park: a protected area managed mainly for conservation of specific natural features.

4. Habitat/species management area: a protected area managed mainly for conservation through management intervention.
5. Protected landscape/seascape: a protected area managed mainly for landscape/seascape protection and recreation.
6. Managed resource protected area: a protected area managed mainly for the sustainable use of natural ecosystems.

According to the above classification, classification 2 uses the phrase 'National Park'. It should be noted that UK National Parks do not fit either descriptor, and are more correctly described as category 5. That they retain the 'National Park' designation is perhaps partially due to the fact that the IUCN came into existence simultaneously with the first UK park. Another explanation may be that the word 'national' instils a sense of ownership within the population.

The world had 30,000 protected areas by the year 2000, covered over 13,250,000 square kilometres of the land surface of the world – approximately the size of India and China combined! This represents a tremendous invest-ment by the countries of the world to protect biological diversity for future generations. A much smaller proportion of the world's seas (barely 1%) are protected.

Protected areas perform many functions. They are essential for conserving biodiversity and for delivering vital ecosystem services, such as protecting watersheds and soils and shielding human communities from natural disasters (IUCN, 2010). Many protected areas are crucial to local communities, especially indigenous peoples who depend upon a sustainable supply of resources. Protected areas provide an arena where people can get a sense of peace in a busy world. They can invigorate the human spirit and challenge the senses. Protected landscapes may also encapsulate important cultural values, with some reflecting sustainable good practice. Furthermore, they are important for research and education and contribute significantly to local and regional economies, especially through tourism and related activities. The Convention on Biological Diversity calls on contracting parties to develop systems of protected areas, so their importance can scarcely be overstated.

The World Commission on Protected Areas, part of the IUCN, notes that protected areas face many challenges, such as external threats associated with pollution and climate change, irresponsible tourism, infrastructure development and ever-increasing demands for land and water resources. Moreover, many protected areas lack political support and have inadequate financial and other resources.

National parks and other protected places are found in most countries around the world and are characterized by the great diversity found in each. Essentially this is to be expected, as for an area to attain this status it must have some unique characteristic or (generally) naturally occurring resource. Many national parks contain multiple attractions. In the case of the Fuji-Hakone-Izu National Park in Japan, the park contains the volcano Mount Fuji, Shiraito Falls, the Atami Hot Springs, Lake Kawaguchi, the Izu Islands, the Aokigahara Forest and numerous historic buildings and temples. The park was originally designated in 1936 and extended in 1950, and has become the most visited national park in the world. Over 100 million visits are made annually, due in part to its vast land and sea area and in part to its proximity to the city of Tokyo, which is just 60 miles away from the volcano.

Although perhaps best known for its trademark volcano, the national park holds geographical, cultural and spiritual significance. Mount Fuji certainly attracts tens of thousands of pilgrims to its temples and religious sites, but it would be wrong to suggest that it is the most sacred mountain in Japan. Rather, Mount Fuji has become famous as a national symbol because it is the highest peak in the country (12,388 feet) and one of the most symmetrical volcano cones in the world. But it does have an ancient body of myths regarding its divine origins, resident deities and spiritual powers. The beautiful peak has been venerated as the home of a fire god, later the dwelling of a Shinto goddess of flowing trees and the home of Dainichi Nyorai, the Buddha of All-Illuminating Wisdom (Hadfield, 2001).

At the base of the mountain is Aokigahara Forest, a dense area that is, according to folklore and legend, haunted by demons and ghosts. In the 19th century, poor families abandoned very young children and their elderly relatives here

and a century later it has become the world's second most popular suicide location (after the Golden Gate Bridge in San Francisco) (The Independent, 2000). Since the 1950s more than 500 people have lost their lives in the forest, mostly through suicide. Recent increases have prompted local officials to erect signs that attempt to convince potential suicides to re-think their plans. A growing issue concerns tourism activity within the forest. Due to the dense forest and rugged inaccessibility, the forest has also attracted thrill seekers. An increasing number of these adventure tourists mark their travelled routes by leaving coloured plastic tapes behind, raising concerns for the forest's ecosystem (Okado, 2008).

Globally, there appears to be no consensus or standard as to admission charges to national parks. In the USA there is often a vehicle and occupant charge, although the entry booths may not be manned during low-season periods. This off-peak 'bonus' may paradoxically be at traditionally high-season periods elsewhere in the country, as is the case during June to August in the Evergreen National Park in Florida. Visitors arriving between these months will certainly not be devoid of a welcome; the swarming mosquitoes are always willing to greet the few visitors taking advantage of the free entry! In Poland, the Tatra National Park contains the Morskie Oko lake, which is completely frozen in winter. Here a variable entry charge is levied depending upon the season. In Israel, there are occasional days when all visitors are allowed to enter parks free of charge. In sharp contrast to this, UK National Parks are prevented from charging any fee at any time because the 1949 National Parks and Access to The Countryside Act dictates that all National Parks in the UK are free, to fulfil the 'second purpose' of promoting opportunities for understanding and enjoyment. National Park authorities do, however, often charge for car parking. Being government agencies and therefore not allowed to make a profit on any activity that they undertake, all profits are ploughed back into infrastructure maintenance.

Accessibility

It can quite naturally be seen that if access is the act of entering, accessibility is the ease of

---

Case Study 12.6. The Everglades National Park.

For many, an essential activity when visiting the Everglades is a trip out in an airboat. Taken at face value, the short trip appears to be the most unsustainable use of petroleum 'gas' available. The boat owners disagree.

There are many thousands square miles of inaccessible islands within the Everglades, many cut off by a very shallow depth of water and reed-beds. The depth is so shallow, in fact, that an outboard board motor would act as a plough and a conventional propeller would become tangled in seconds. Airboats skim the surface and have the potential to take tourists deep into the home of the wild alligator. Each trip undoubtedly disturbs the lifestyle and habits of alligators, but a licence is only provided on the basis of the operator having several distinct routes that leave areas undisturbed for several weeks or even months at a time. Because visitors rarely return without having seen, learned about and indeed stopped alongside several of these magnificent amphibians, there is a belief that they enjoy the human interaction. There is little doubt they would probably enjoy the experience more if the visitors jumped in for an even closer encounter!

---

doing so. While there is some element of truth here, accessibility is much more to do with the interpretation of the disability discrimination legislation. Politically correct language suggests mainstream society does not see anyone in terms of levels of disability, but rather how facilities can be made more accessible. It would be entirely wrong therefore to speak of ethnic minorities in terms of accessibility, unless of course the group in question has a disability! With this in mind, it is inappropriate to consider accessibility only in relation to access to the rural environment, rather across the whole spectrum of tourism. In terms of heritage tourism, the issues would surround physical access to areas and automatic doors, whereas at any visitor attraction the importance of an assistant and guide speaking clearly could not be higher for someone who relies on lip-reading.

There are two important and allied concepts to bear in mind as this chapter concludes, both of which are very relevant in the study of cultural tourism, accessing the countryside and indeed most other forms of tourism, too. These are universal design and social inclusion.

Universal design

Universal design is the phrase given to the concept that if the needs and requirements of people with disabilities are taken into account at the design stage, the cost of including them is generally no more than 1% of the total build cost. The figure for making adaptations to existing buildings is obviously much higher (Fig. 12.6). The costs associated with heritage tourism, where the buildings were almost certainly constructed several centuries ago for a purpose other than tourism, can often be considerable and may even be thought exorbitant or prohibitive. Universal design should accordingly be at the heart of all new facilities at the earliest stage.

Social inclusion and exclusion

Social inclusion and social exclusion are two phrases that are frequently misunderstood within tourism management. The theory here suggests that if improvements are made for a group of individuals with a disability, there is a high likelihood that these improvements will benefit an additional group or groups of visitors. Conversely, if they are not made, this may reduce the enjoyment of another group of able-bodied visitors. Consider the case of automatic doors. The rationale for installing them in a building is to comply with the Disability Discrimination Act, but parents with pushchairs and shoppers with heavy bags greatly benefit from this provision. This may influence the positive feedback at a facility that frequently attracts such visitors. Likewise, the visual displays found on all London Transport underground trains assist both deaf and hearing travellers alike. Disability is much too large an area to consider within this chapter, but there is a final thought to consider. There is a theory that suggests there is no such distinction between able-bodied and disabled people; society as a whole is 'temporarily abled'. It is perhaps a sobering thought that as aging runs its natural course, *everyone* becomes less mobile, suffers failing sight and can hear less well.

Fig. 12.6. Yardenit baptismal site. Due to the high number of Christian pilgrims seeking to be baptized in the Jordan, the Israeli government have built this 'hard' site that, while not pretending to be authentic, is situated on one of short stretches of the river where the water flows naturally. Note the covered chute to the left where people with physical disabilities may be lowered into the water in a specially adapted wheelchair. (Picture © Geoff Shirt.)

In general terms, the word 'access' refers to the rural environment; one that can rarely be accurately described as natural. It has historically been linked to the evocative phrase 'right to roam' and been dramatically increased, some would say *improved*, over the past 10 years. Calls for extending access further are matched by those stating 'enough is enough'. Both are now minority views drowned out by the voices of those promoting a reasonable level of physical exercise. Much remains to be done in attracting wider participation in a countryside that is fit for and accessible to the British public, (Mosaic National Parks, 2009).

Future Research

The area of culture and cultural tourism has grown since the early 2000s perhaps more than any other area of tourism. It is over a similar timeframe that the discipline of events manage-

ment has become identified and accordingly where much contemporary research on culture and its artefacts will be found. There is, for instance, a thin line between where the Shrovetide Football event should be studied – from an events or tourism school. The links between access and culture appear to be growing stronger and are providing many texts and theories linked with, and symbiotic to, the needs of tourism management, and identifying opportunities to research both of these areas, but and arguably more importantly, there is an ongoing need to understand the barriers that limit access to different social and socio-cultural groups.

Conclusion

It will have become obvious that although culture and access are distinct concepts and entities in their own right, there are numerous areas where they are at one with one another. For instance, a considerable cultural change has occurred within the rural community that accepts, indeed welcomes, the urban visitor into their life – especially when and where the host can gain financially from the social exchange. In many parts of the world the physical evidence of culture, the built artefacts, need to be accessed in order to obtain maximum benefit for the visitor. It will also be noted that access needs to be undertaken with a responsible attitude that has sustainability at its heart. Thankfully, acculturalization is not an automatic result of access, although if it is not to occur, access must be managed and monitored carefully by both professionals and community representatives.

Review Questions

1. Consider the challenges surrounding the commodification of cultural tourism against the backdrop of our global satellite society. Is it possible to have culturally specific destinations that retain a unique selling point to an increasingly global audience?

2. Consider instances where local planning law may have overly protected the environment to the detriment of recreational usage. Identify similar destinations to Kenya's Masai Mara National Park, where the Masai tribe has been removed to provide an environment entirely given over to wildlife.

3. Consider how a local cultural attraction or national government has addressed the need to be both non-discriminatory and socially inclusive. In the 2010 World Cup for example, young black children and female teenagers were used extensively for marketing; something very unlikely to have occurred 20 years ago. How central and crucial do you believe this use of black children and young girls was to the message being communicated?

References

Curry, N. (1994) *Countryside Recreation, Access and Land Use Planning.* E. and F.N. Spon, London, UK.

DETR (1998) *Access to the Countryside in England and Wales: A Consultation Paper.* Department of the Environment, Transport and the Regions, London, UK.

Hadfield, P. (2001) Japan struggles with soaring death toll in Suicide Forest. *The Telegraph.* Available from: http://www.telegraph.co.uk/news/main.jhtml?xml=/news/2000/11/05/waoki05.xml. Accessed April 1, 2010.

Hall, M. (2005) *Tourism; Rethinking the Social Science of Mobility.* Prentice Hall, Upper Saddle River, New Jersey, USA.

IUCN (2010) About IUCN. Available from: http://www.iucn.org/about. Accessed July 14, 2010.

The Independent (2000) *Japan's Harvest of Death.* Available from: http://www.independent.co.uk/news/world/asia/japans-harvest-of-death-635356. Accessed July 20, 2010.

Mercer, I. (1998) *Second Draft in Response to the Department of Environment, Transport and the Regions Consultation Paper on Voluntary Access to the Countryside.* Association of National Park Authorities, Morehamptstead, UK.

Mosaic National Parks (2009) *Building Links between Ethnic Communities and National Parks.* Campaign for National Parks, London, UK.

Okado, Y. (2008) *Intruders tangle 'suicide forest' with tape.* Available from: http://www.asahi.com/english/Herald-asahi/TKY200805020328.html. Accessed April 1, 2010.

Page, S. and Connell, J. (2009) *Tourism: A Modern Synthesis.* Thomson, London, UK.

Richards, G. (2007) *Cultural Tourism: Global and Local Perspectives.* Haworth Press, Binghampton, New York.

Richardson and Fluker (2004) *Understanding and Managing Tourism.* Pearson Education Australia, Frenchs Forest, New South Wales, Australia.

Sandford, L. (1974) *Report of the National Parks Policies Review Committee.* HMSO, London, UK.

Wall, G. and Matheison, A. (2006) *Tourism Change, Impacts and Opportunities.* Pearson Prentice Hall, Harlow, UK.

Weaver, D. and Lawson, L. (2010) *Tourism Management.* Wiley, Milton, Queensland, Australia.

13 Heritage Tourism

Carol Southall and Peter Robinson

Introduction

Heritage, according to the UN Educational, Scientific and Cultural Organization (UNESCO, 2010), is our legacy from the past, what we live with today and what we pass on to future generations. Much of the tourism industry around the world is based upon cultural heritage and many of the most important places are open to the public. As Deacon (2004, p. 317) observed, 'heritage and tourism appear to be strange bedfellows.' And yet, there is increasing evidence of their coupling around the globe. Research around Robben Island (Hede, 2007) identified the contested and politicized nature of the management, conservation and interpretation of heritage sites.

McMorran (2008) observed that 'The Renaissance, the Industrial Revolution, urbanization, two world wars and recently amplified globalization have all inspired nostalgia for lost or vanishing architecture, ways of life and social values', which manifests itself as heritage. English Heritage (2003) explained that this is important because 'we know that people value the historic environment, derive enormous benefits and satisfaction from it, and are concerned when it is neglected', but also observed that 'in order to ensure that the historic environment is adequately represented in the allocation of resources we need to be able to quantify the values that it generates'.

What is clear is that, for many tourists, cultural heritage is a significant component of their holiday. This is supported by Evans (2004), who observed that 'the sun, sea and sand offer alone has, as elsewhere, begun to wane in Cancun, even with the promotion of sports tourism (e.g. scuba diving), and most tourism packages now include trips to the archaeological zones of the ancient Mayan sites of Chichen Itza, Tulum and Uxmal'. Whatever the reason for this, and in whatever capacity, destinations are becoming increasingly aware of the importance of maximizing their heritage potential, sometimes to the detriment of that heritage.

Defining Heritage

Many definitions of heritage make reference, either directly or indirectly, to aspects of or the notion of culture, as indeed many definitions of culture make reference to heritage. The European Travel Commission (in VisitBritain, 2010) includes heritage sites in its definition of cultural attractions.

There are numerous definitions of heritage, many of which, as noted, incorporate reference to the concept of culture. It is, however, important to consider the difference between heritage and culture (see Chapter 12) in order to be able to focus more clearly on the heritage tourism concept that is fundamental to this chapter. It is proposed that where heritage tourism often refers to visiting places of historical interest and significance such as castles, monuments and museums, cultural tourism involves participation in and experience of those activities, rituals and routines by which a community is defined. Cultural tourism, argued Dallen and Boyd (2003), 'goes beyond the visitation of sites and monuments, to

© CAB International 2011. *Research Themes for Tourism*
(eds P. Robinson, S. Heitmann and P.U.C. Dieke)

include consuming the way of life of places visited.' Both cultural tourism and heritage tourism are experiential tourism in that they involve personal involvement and stimulation, whether in the sense of feeling part of a place's history or being involved in or stimulated by cultural activities such as festivals and performing arts (Hall and Zeppel, 1990, cited in Dallen and Boyd, 2003).

Heritage has been defined by Tilden (1996, cited in Goulding, 1998) as 'an activity which aims to reveal meanings and relationships as an art, and revelations based upon information whose aim is not instruction but provocation'. Schouten (1995) said 'Heritage is history processed through mythology, ideology, nationalism, local pride, romantic ideas or just plain marketing, into a commodity'. Both identified the idea of the commodification of history to create a product for tourism consumption.

Furthermore, heritage tourism has been described by Pedersen (2002) as embracing 'both eco-tourism and cultural tourism, with an emphasis on conservation and cultural heritage', reflecting the significant debate that has seen the scope of cultural heritage evolve from the monuments, groups of buildings and sites set out in the World Heritage Convention to now include cultural landscapes and intangible heritage.

Clearly there are many differing definitions of heritage. According to Hardy (1988, cited in Dallen and Boyd, 2003), however, 'Most researchers accept that heritage is linked to the past, that it represents some sort of inheritance to be passed down to current and future generations, both in terms of cultural traditions and physical artefacts'. Dallen and Boyd (2003) also discussed the idea of selective heritage, whereby society 'filters heritage through a value system that undoubtedly changes over time and space, and across society.' Thus, they argued 'heritage is not simply the past, but the modern-day use of elements of the past.'

Heritage tourism, then, for the purposes of this chapter, may be simply defined as visits to and experiences of places of historical importance and significance. This is a broad definition that incorporates the tangible and intangible nature of the heritage product. Whether tangible or intangible, heritage tourism is an essential component of the tourism concept as it is interwoven into the fabric of the tourism experience and covers a breadth of attractions. These include the following:

- Industrial archaeology (e.g. Ironbridge Gorge World Heritage Site, UK, and the Big Pit National Coal Museum, Blaenavon, Wales).
- Stately homes (e.g. Chatsworth, UK).
- Art galleries (e.g. The Louvre, France, and Rijksmuseum, The Netherlands).
- Battlefields (e.g. The Somme and Agincourt, France, and Bannockburn, Stirling, Scotland).
- Castles (e.g. Warwick Castle, UK, and Neuschwanstein Castle, Bavaria, Germany).
- Cathedrals (e.g. York Minster, UK, and Cologne Cathedral, Germany).
- Historic waterways (e.g. British canals and the Canal du Midi, France).
- Ancient sites (e.g. Mam Tor Hillfort, UK, and the Acropolis, Greece).
- Prehistoric sites (e.g. Stonehenge, UK, and Lascaux Caves, France).
- Museums (e.g. Natural History Museum, London, UK, and The Prado Museum, Madrid, Spain).

Swarbrooke (2001) explored the notion of heritage ownership, explaining that most heritage sites and attractions fall under public and voluntary sector ownership. This is mainly due to the fact that they share similar motivations for ownership and operation, which include conservation and education as well as visitor management (Swarbrooke, 2001). Indeed, in part due to the drive towards sustainability, the ownership of heritage sites and attractions is often a contested issue, with many arguing that stakeholder cooperation and collaboration is key to the survival of heritage sites and attractions and that 'cooperation can create situations where a wider range of tourism attractions are made available to visitors, as well as ensuring higher rates of success for specific types of attractions' (Dallen and Boyd, 2003). In addition, 'cooperation, collaboration and partnership (e.g. between private, public and voluntary ownership and between places) have become more prominent [as] partnerships have the potential to promote the principles and practices of sustainable development' (Dallen and Boyd, 2003). Many heritage resources overlap both in terms of boundaries and, in some cases, ownership (Boyd and Timothy, 2001, cited in Dallen and Boyd, 2003). In such cases, cooperation is required to maintain an effective balance between conservation, the interests of owners and the local community, and the benefits of tourism.

The exclusion of local communities from their own heritage is also an issue in consideration of heritage 'ownership'. Wall and Black (2004) discussed the less-than-adequate representation of and respect for local community views in the management and planning of Indonesian heritage sites:

> The tendency to adopt top-down, rational, comprehensive planning procedures has resulted in the disenfranchisement of local people whose ancestors have lived with and been the guardians of the sites, sometimes for centuries. This process has tended to ... [exclude] people from their own heritage.
>
> (Wall and Black, 2004)

Heritage and Culture

Both heritage and culture are synonymous with the concept of inheritance and the passage of time. Indeed, it is difficult to focus on heritage without also acknowledging the culture within which it prevails, and which impacts upon both its presence and its operation; the two are firmly interwoven. According to the Nation Brands Index, developed by Simon Anholt in 2005 to measure the image and reputation of the world's nations in terms of six key dimensions of national competence (exports, governance, culture, people, tourism and immigration and investment), France, Italy and the UK are in first, second and fourth place respectively with their relatively balanced cultural brands that span cultural heritage, sport and contemporary culture (Anholt-Gfk Roper, 2009). The rich cultural heritage of developing countries such as China and India assures that they rank highly in the cultural heritage aspect of the 2009 index. The cultural aspect of the Nation Brands Index combines perceptions of a country's heritage as well as contemporary culture such as music, art and literature and a country's excellence in sport.

According to VisitBritain (2010), research indicates that almost 60% of people from 20 countries consider history and culture to be strong influences on their choice of destination. Thus it is imperative that any focus on heritage tourism should be underpinned throughout by the recognition of its vital role within the tourism system and the interrelated nature of heritage tourism and other significant components of the tourism destination region.

Clearly, heritage tourism defines much tourist activity across the world, because it encompasses most cultural attractions and defines the characteristics of nearly all tourist destinations. It is, therefore, essential that the continued management of these destinations is focused upon long-term planning and designed for a balanced approach to financial, environmental and sociocultural sustainability. The heritage sector is most commonly and formally recognized internationally through UNESCO World Heritage Sites (WHS). These sites are considered to be of international significance, and include Australia's Sydney Opera House, Austria's Schönbrunn Palace, Cambodia's Angkor and the UK's Tower of London. It is also synonymous with brands such as The National Trust, which although English in origin enjoys a working relationship with numerous other 'national trusts' around the globe.

The heritage sector provides numerous challenges. Sustainability is of paramount importance and a number of debates remain around this issue. Fyall and Garrod (1998) argued that:

> Heritage and sustainability share a common theme of inheritance [where] heritage tourism is, as an economic activity, predicated on the use of inherited environmental and socio-cultural assets in order to attract visitors [and] sustainability requires that those assets are carefully managed to ensure that future generations inherit a resource base that is sufficient to support their needs and wants.

It is, of course, essential that heritage is preserved and managed for the future, but to preserve in aspic and to prevent access is a pointless exercise because why save heritage if not to share it with a wide audience and use it as a tool for education? Conversely though, without effective management over-use, over-crowding and poor education will quickly diminish both the physical and educative uses of a site. This is supported by the European Travel Council (2005), which argued that 'The World Heritage List – developed by UNESCO with the intention of defining and conserving world heritage – can have the opposite effect due to the growing popularity of the heritage sites on the list.' It is important to strike a balance between the negative effect of too little tourism on cultural heritage, resulting in lack of aware-ness, decay and insufficient financial resources for maintenance, and too much tourism, potentially resulting in vandalism and misuse.

Management and Access

The management of and access to heritage sites has increasingly come under scrutiny in recent years. Undoubtedly heritage resources require effective management and preservation due to the fact that they are irreplaceable (Dallen and Boyd, 2003). The concepts of management and sustainability are often linked, and it is import-ant to recognize that strategic planning for heritage sites should include recognition of the need for sustainable practice (Dallen and Boyd, 2003). In addition, in the case of heritage site management '[s]trategic zoning and phasing should support sustainable tourism to achieve an equitable distribution of wealth and the preservation of ... cultural and natural resources' (Wager, 1995).

'Questions of ownership, access and management of heritage sites and collections, although increasingly raised by indigenous groups and their vocal leaders, seldom feature in tourism promotion and planning or in strategies for community and local economic development' (Evans, 2004). Much of this is due to the fact that heritage sites are often funded by Western organizations, mainly from Europe and North America.

World Heritage

According to UNESCO (2010), the organization 'seek[s] to encourage the identification, protection and preservation of cultural and natural heritage around the world considered to be of outstanding value to humanity'. UNESCO's World Heritage Mission is as follows:

- To encourage countries to sign the World Heritage Convention and to ensure the protection of their natural and cultural heritage.
- To encourage States Parties (countries that have adhered to the World Heritage Convention) to the Convention to nominate sites within their national territory for inclusion on the World Heritage List.
- To encourage States Parties to establish management plans and set up reporting systems on the state of conservation of their WHS.
- To help States Parties safeguard World Heritage properties by providing technical assistance and professional training.
- To provide emergency assistance for WHS in immediate danger.
- To support States Parties' public awareness-building activities for World Heritage conservation.
- To encourage participation of the local population in the preservation of their cultural and natural heritage.
- To encourage international cooperation in the conservation of our world's cultural and natural heritage.

UNESCO is keen for WHS to contribute in a meaningful way to the life of their local communities, while also being preserved and protected for future generations. However, WHS have become so popular as tourist attractions that many scholars now describe World Heritage status as a 'brand' while others speak of it as an authenticity stamp for the heritage tourist or a 'trademark'. If the significance that allowed a site to gain World Heritage status is to be maintained, and WHS are to remain accessible to current and future generations, then managing tourism activity in a sensitive and sustainable is a critical issue.

Current research suggests that many WHS operators are failing to manage their sites (or the consequential economic and social sustain-ability) in a consistent way, with some sites considered to be at risk and others failing to deliver an effective legacy within host communities. One condition of inscription on the World Heritage Cultural List is the application of zoning and legislation to manage sites, which, according to Wager (1995) may include 'site plans; a marketing strategy; a legal framework; regulations; a system of effective administration; financing structures; a programme for staff training; and arrangements for public participation'. This is especially true as the simple fact that WHS status is granted has an impact on the importance of the site as 'must-see' place for tourists to visit.

Public access can also mean very different things, and may refer to simply being able to see an historic site through to opportunities for education and active involvement in conservation. Relationships exist between heritage and volunteering, and the growth of volunteering as part of the serious leisure movement. Access is also defined by the nature of the site (discussed in further detail in Chapter 12).

Many research issues revolve around these management challenges. Consider first a 'do not touch' sign positioned on an antique chair.

Well-intentioned though it is, it is also an unfriendly sign, a negative message that suits the needs of conservators worried about historic fabrics but that attracts the antipathy of front-facing staff keen to provide a visitor welcome. Of course there are compromises – the provision of extra seating for visitors (although often in marked contrast to a historic interior) or more sensitive touches such as placing a rope across the chair. Other attractions may take the opposite approach and allow visitors to sit on and touch everything within reach, placing items for preservation beyond arms reach with ropes, barriers and covers.

Throughout the heritage sector there is a constant debate between the two management specialisms that exist. On one side are the conservators, keen to preserve everything because restoration is costly and results in no original items. On the other side are the business-facing parts of the business, which recognize the need to welcome visitors, perhaps sometimes to the cost of historic furniture.

There are two other key areas to consider in discussions around management and access.

Case Study 13.1. Ironbridge Gorge.

Ironbridge Gorge in Shropshire is a WHS that tells the story of the Industrial Revolution from what is believed to be the birthplace of the revolution. Despite the fact that this claim has been contested by numerous other destinations, the 'attraction', which comprises 10 museums and numerous other sites, also represents breadth of access issues.

The main museum sites are traditional museums (including the Museum of Iron, the Jackfield Tile Museum, the Coalport China Museum, the Museum of The Gorge and the Tollhouse) with hand-on exhibits, items in display cases and a range of interpretive techniques. This philosophy changes at Broseley Pipeworks, where visitors are encouraged to experience the site as if the last workers have just left – this site having not been abandoned until the 1950s. In addition the area is littered with industrial heritage, mainly comprising disused and defunct kilns, many in a ruinous state but sufficiently stabilized that they are safe to explore. Other kilns – the ones where, for example, the iron bridge was cast – are protected in weatherproof buildings with access managed by designated walkways and viewing platforms.

At the Blists Hill Victorian Town in Ironbridge, an entire Victorian town is recreated on a historic iron- and brick-making site, with costumed interpretation, traditional crafts in action, fairground rides and ruins of industrial relics. In contrast to the other museums on the site, visitors are encouraged to touch, feel and experience heritage more closely. Taking this one stage further Enginuity, the newest of the attractions, provides a full range of hands-on activities aimed at children to explain the principles of science and engineering that were first pioneered in the Gorge.

This case study exemplifies the very different management requirements at each of these sites, despite one overall management committee. This deliberate approach is designed to offer different types of accessibility and experience to visitors, but also means that management is challenging. Curatorial responsibilities at the Coalport China Museum, home to rare and priceless artefacts, is very different to the care and management needed at a site where everything is a hands-on experiment. The management challenge is not about restoring the past, but managing the equipment to minimize damage and failure that could impact negatively on the visitor experience.

First, there has been a growth in interest in social history and famous historic celebrities, and many sites now mark out the homes of deceased notables with blue plaques (in the UK) and other devices to celebrate 'birthplaces', 'homes of', and places where the 'first 'x' happened'. Many of these houses are now privately owned and not every home owner wants to have a queue of tourists taking photographs of their property, peering in through windows or knocking on the door. But this is set against a backdrop of the importance of celebrating this heritage.

Education, edutainment and interpretation

Tourism often relies on interpretive material in order to enhance the heritage experience and enable accessibility of heritage (Hede, 2007). Such material may include guided tours, as in the case of a castle or stately home; audiotapes, through which visitors are instructed on the historical context of a site or artefact; brochures and guidebooks, often obtained at additional cost to the entry fee (where applied); and consoles, which allow the visitor to interact with the heritage experience, often by selecting answers to questions, pressing buttons to illuminate specific aspects of a site or artefact or watching and interacting with a short film or documentary. According to Hede (2007), the development of interpretive material is time consuming. In addition, decisions must be made regarding the narrative of any interpretive material, such as what and how a story should be told.

The formalization of education from the 1980s onwards provided heritage attractions with specific educational themes that they could use and adapt to meet the needs of school visits. Many attractions now offer outreach schemes, which may include taking handling collections into schools and offering workshop days and drama performances.

'Edutainment' emerged during the 1990s as a way to make education fun. The term was synonymous with hand-on attractions such as Techniquest and was focused on the education sector and families. At the same time the public sector also recognized that in its role as owner and provider of access to cultural heritage, it was important to make experiences fun. Technology in the 1990s rather limited this to hands-on experiments, easy-to-read signage and costumed talks and video. In recent years, however, the huge growth in technologies such as podcasts, supported by broadening access to high-speed internet, has meant that heritage can be interpreted in many different ways to meet the needs of various audiences.

Whose heritage?

The question of whose heritage is commonly asked. The altruistic view is that heritage is a shared resource that belongs to the widest community who can benefit from it. According to UNESCO (2010), 'World Heritage Sites belong to all the peoples of the world, irrespective of the territory on which they are located.' It can be argued, therefore, that heritage sites should be free to visit – and they frequently are in the public sector. However, there is a growing number of heritage-related attractions and many would collapse within months without the correct care and attention, all of which comes at a cost. With the public sector insisting that heritage is managed and maintained (through planning controls such as listing in the UK), many heritage attractions have to charge admission fees and act as businesses in order to pay for the maintenance of attractions, and equally important, the interpretation, research and presentation of those attractions.

An admission charge is not just an income-generation tool, but also a visitor management tool. The fragile nature of many historic buildings makes it impossible to allow unlimited admission and a charge goes some way to limiting visitor numbers. In instances where even this is not enough of a deterrent, timed and pre-booked ticket systems are also used.

It is of course one thing to charge people to visit a castle or battlefield, but what of religious heritage? Many cathedrals are open to the public, but charge an admission fee. There is inevitable debate around this approach to income generation and the need to provide free access to spaces where people may not be tourists, but pilgrims.

Case Study 13.2. Charging for cathedrals and free entry to national museums.

Cathedrals and churches are an integral part of Britain's national heritage and a major draw for international visitors. According to VisitBritain (2010), 'Churches are an important part of the British tourism product [and many] people will visit a church while on holiday'. Reasons for doing so are likely to include: architectural and historical interest; pilgrimage importance; insight into the life of the local community; musical or theatrical productions, such as brass band concerts or religious plays; exhibitions and festivals; impulse (on passing); part of another activity; personal or family connections (e.g. where grandparents were married); connection with a famous person (e.g. St. Mary's in Scarborough, where Anne Brontë is buried).

With such importance placed on cathedrals and churches it is not surprising that they have become an integral part of Britain's tourism offering. Significant controversy, however, has been caused in recent years in relation to the decision by a number of Britain's cathedrals to charge admission fees to visitors. Interestingly, according to *The Telegraph* (Chartres, 2007), many people believe that cathedrals such as St Paul's in London and York Minster are state funded and that the Church of England is financially able to maintain all churches across the country falling under its remit. While the state may finance the maintenance of religious buildings in other European countries, there is little in the way of similar assistance provided in Britain. In fact, a significant amount of the money required by churches and cathedrals for maintenance is generated by worshippers and local communities. What is clear, argued *The Telegraph* (Chartres, 2007), is that this situation is 'unsustainable'.

In contrast, national museums in Britain have been free since 2001 and, according to ePolitix.com (2009), 'since free admission was introduced in 2001 visits to previously charging national museums and galleries have more than doubled, from 7.2 million [in 2000] to 16 million [in 2008].' The most visited cultural heritage attraction in Britain in 2008 was the British Museum, which attracted almost six million visitors. As a result of the free-entry scheme 'Some privately run museums (which are not part of the free entry scheme) have experienced consequential drop in visitor numbers' (VisitBritain, 2010).

Allocation of state maintenance and support is a contentious issue and for many cathedrals and churches, having to impose admission fees is not a decision taken lightly. The potential to generate significant revenue from admission fees is impossible to ignore, particularly in times of recession when financial support from worshippers and local communities may be limited. Where alternatives include restrictions or even church closure, except for services, it is clear that charging is the only viable option. 'Charging for entry has become a regrettable necessity because it is right that the community's treasury of art and architecture is accessible and properly presented for visitors from home and abroad' (Chartres, 2007). While the government has devised a scheme to refund VAT payments on repairs to listed places of worship and English Heritage has worked to raise awareness of the issue, there remains a necessity to impose admission charges to churches and cathedrals, simply to safeguard against closure (Chartres, 2007).

Heritage stakeholders

Stakeholder participation is considered to be a vital tool in effective heritage management. In her study of sustainability at six WHSs, Landorf (2009) concluded that 'WHSs are not actively planning and managing the economic and social sustainability dimensions in the same way they are managing the environmental sustainability dimension ... [and that] ... A significant factor in this is the level of stakeholder participation in the planning process'. Landorf (2009) argued that early stakeholder involvement in the planning process both educates stakeholders and offers a sense of ownership.

Swarbrooke (2001) argued that local communities should have a say in the stories that are told about their community, should it be the subject of an attraction. Evans (2004) explored the impact of WHS status on the involvement of stakeholders in Mexican tourism, describing communities 'whose collective heritage is used for symbolic economic purposes, but who are marginalized in its interpretation and governance'.

Authenticity

Fyall and Garrod (1998) said 'the principal dilemma for heritage attractions is how to satisfy visitors' expectations, and manage their impact, without compromising the authenticity of the visitor experience itself' (see also Chapter 4).

Growing commercial pressure and increased visitor expectations have placed increasing pressure on heritage attractions to adapt their management and product presentation. Landorf (2009) discussed the idea of the 'commodification of heritage for tourist consumption and the impact of this process on authenticity', inferring a 'fine line' between authenticity and the translation of heritage and its components into a more marketable commodity. 'On the negative side, misappropriation of a cultural tradition can create conflict with local stakeholders and an unsatisfactory experience for tourists seeking authenticity' (Teo and Yeoh, 1997, cited in Landorf, 2009). The question is how far can heritage organizations go in order to maintain a balance between authenticity and marketable commodity? Furthermore, should they indeed be more concerned with sustainable preservation activities rather than turning heritage into yet another commodity? Yet it is this commoditization that forms an often useful strategy to attract visitors, offer education services and generate income.

'Improving the entertainment value of visitor experiences is generally viewed as incompatible with the conservation and educational goals implicit in the management of most heritage sites' (Garrod and Fyall, 2000; Malcolm-Davies, 2004, cited in Landorf, 2009). Studies have shown that heritage managers often have a limited understanding of tourists or tourism. There is a belief that the skills and understanding of heritage sites managers must be improved if sustainable heritage tourism is to be implemented. In addition, the fragmented nature of the tourism industry plays a role in hindering the facilitation of sustainable heritage tourism management. Markwell *et al.* (1997), in their case study of visits to historic houses in England, also outlined the skills shortage of heritage managers, indicating that 'house operators ... do not, generally, possess the skills, either in market research, or in the presentation of their attraction, to confront and manage change'.

> Since the 1960s there has been a dramatic growth in the number of museums and heritage attractions opening in this country ... They

constitute a culture industry which substitutes escapist commodified leisure for authentic experience and by doing so have fostered conformity, passivity and political indifference among participants turned spectators. This is seen largely as a consequence of the way in which history, as interpreted in commercially driven museums, has become sanitised, entertaining and inauthentic. (Goulding, 1998)

Lunn (2007) in his focus on war memorialization in Thailand, in particular the impact of the 1950s war film *The Bridge on the River Kwai*, said 'it is difficult to escape the essentially tourist-driven sense of enterprise associated with such memorialization and not to see the process as having little direct historical engagement for the majority of the Thai population'. 'The Death Railway experience', argued Lunn, 'has, for many visitors, become a packaged and rather sanitised experience'.

Events at historic sites

Events are becoming commonplace at most tourist attractions and heritage sites are no exception, although they tend to focus primarily upon a related period in history or generic cultural traditions. Often a historic house will host a range of activities and events related to its own history, plus a couple of music concerts that may or may not be related to the period of the property but will be in keeping with the historical context of the venue (e.g. classical rather than rock music), with some exceptions (see Chapter 10).

Volunteers and serious leisure

Many organizations in the tourism sector rely heavily on volunteers, none more so than heritage attractions. This is primarily because of the economies involved and the fact that many places would not be financially sustainable without volunteers. There is also a strong link between heritage and the enthusiasm it generates in communities, the members of which are keen to share their knowledge with visitors to an area. As an example, a National Trust stately home receiving 100,000 visitors a year will rely on up to 250 volunteers to keep it working, in addition to the staff employed in the management of the property and its ancillary services such as shops, restaurants, events and front of house.

This 'serious leisure' also extends beyond the interpretive role of tour guides to 'closed-season' activities, such as working in conservation, restoring contents, cleaning the property and helping with management tasks. It further manifests itself in outdoor conservation activities and working holidays for volunteers. Although very few organizations keep accurate records of volunteering, it has been estimated than in 2005–2006 at least 476,000 people volunteered in the heritage sector in England, representing 1.2% of all adults (English Heritage, 2007).

Media Representation

Heritage appears in a range of visual media, including news stories, documentaries and fictional film. While documentaries generally raise awareness of heritage sites in a positive way, offering a broadly educational overview of a site's historic legacy and development, the depiction of heritage sites in films arguably has a detrimental effect on the actual site (Winter, 2002; Lunn, 2007)

In recent years, many heritage sites have acted as the locations for films and documentaries. Such sites include Angkor Wat in Cambodia, used as the setting for the Hollywood Blockbuster *Tomb Raider*; Lacock Abbey and Alnwick Castle, UK, used as the settings for various interior and exterior scenes of Hogwarts in the *Harry Potter* films; and Carnforth Station near Lancaster, UK, which was used for the platform scenes in the 1945 film *Brief Encounter*.

Location filming is often more cost effective and realistic than constructing an artificial film set. In addition, it can provide significant economic benefits to an area because of cast and crew requirements for local facilities and amenities such as accommodation and catering. However, one of the problems arising from location filming is that the economic impact, in terms of cast and crew expenditure, is often

only short term, and the long-term economic benefits of increased visitors to a site (for both the site and the surrounding local area) may be outweighed by negative environmental and social impacts. These include damage to the site through increased visitor traffic (pedestrian or otherwise), lack of awareness of local culture and, perhaps most pertinently, a perception of the site based on an alternative, commodified culture, rather than an 'authentic' experience based on an understanding of the site's heritage. Such an experience may only be 'authentic' in so far as it will be based upon a representation of the site's history and development, which in turn is based upon historic records and translation of those records into a portrayal of the site that is as accurate as possible according to available information. Nonetheless, it may be argued that this is a situation to which heritage sites should aspire, in order to allow future generations to benefit from their inheritance (see Chapter 14).

Future Research

This chapter has explored many of the key issues facing heritage tourism, as well as the concepts and definitions of the subject. Key areas for future research include the following:

- Stakeholder participation in heritage planning and management (from the grass-roots level).
- Authenticity, in terms of the ways in which heritage and culture are presented and explained to others.
- The impacts of media representation on heritage sites.
- The idea of international funding, with a multitude of rights in terms of operational decisions and input, but limited recognition of the cultural constraints or idiosyncrasies of destinations and sites.
- Improving the skills of heritage managers in order to operate effectively.
- The motivations and behaviours of heritage tourists.

According to Landorf (2009), it is important to understand the motivations and behaviours of heritage tourists in order to be

---

Case Study 13.3. Angkor, Cambodia.

Angkor in the Siem Reap province of Cambodia became a UNESCO WHS in 1992 and is one of the most important archaeological sites in South-east Asia (UNESCO, 2010). The area can be seen as defined by four distinct regions: tropical forest, cultivated land, isolated villages and architectural remains of the Angkorian period. The Angkor complex consists of 200 monuments spread over an area of 400 square kilometres. Monuments include the Khmer temples, built between the 7th and 13th centuries by Khmer kings. Among the most famous and therefore most popular temples are Angkor Wat and the Bayon temple at Angkor Thom (UNESCO, 2010).

In the 1990s Angkor became a key focal point for Cambodia's agenda of modernization and growth, combined with a desire to reclaim what had been lost in two decades of conflict and social upheaval. According to Winter (2008), Angkor played a key 'role in the emergence of two key industries: heritage and tourism. The development of a "cultural heritage" industry promised the restoration of identity, history, cultural sovereignty and national pride. International tourism promised much needed socio-economic development.'

The filming of *Lara Croft: Tomb Raider*, a Hollywood blockbuster starring Angelina Jolie, created tourism management issues and highlighted the damage that can occur to historic monuments, natural resources and traditional culture. Wager (1995) identified that 'unsustainable types of speculative tourism would only serve only to enrich a small number of largely foreign investors who will take the profits out of the country, thus excluding the majority of the Cambodian people from receiving the full economic benefits from a tourist boom'.

Winter (2002) described the filming of *Tomb Raider* as a 'contradictory clash of … cultures', arguing that the film 'creates new narratives for tourists; ones that undermine the efforts of conservation agencies looking to formalise serious, cultural tourism across the site.'

The key focus of the problems experienced with Angkor was that the objectives of the Authority for the Protection and Safeguarding of the Angkor Region (APSARA) – the Cambodian-run management body set up as one of the key conditions of World Heritage Listing – were almost entirely focused around conservation. In addition, UNESCO had remained detached from APSARA in an endeavour to maintain an autonomous, self-funded and empowered Cambodian management authority and to detract from criticisms of 'cultural imperialism', something to which UNESCO remain extremely sensitive in an advanced post-colonial context' (Winter, 2002).

From a Cambodian government perspective, it was felt that the film would bring both international attention and economic benefit to the country (Winter, 2002). Naturally, there was an expectation that growth in tourism arrivals would result from the increase in global attention, thus bringing much-needed revenue to alleviate the country's financial deficit. This case study highlights, therefore, the need for careful and balanced management of preservation, access and interpretation given the myriad stakeholders and different agendas that may be involved.

---

able to sustainably manage heritage sites. In addition, the impact of stakeholder participation requires further understanding in order to evaluate the impact of tourism (Landorf, 2009). Arguably colonization is still prevalent at heritage sites worldwide, where local communities are marginalized in what may be seen as a misguided focus on unsustainable economic impact, rather than positive social impacts through local community involvement in planning and management. Evans (2004) supported this notion:

> These magnificent structures, silent tributes to the Maya's vast knowledge of astronomy and the ability of their engineers, force us to meditate on the destruction of the Amerindian civilisations, initiated on a large scale by the Spanish Conquistadors and clergy of the great 'civilising' empires of Europe. As Cambiassi (1997: 23) reminds us: 'This destruction continues even today in the form of exploitation and denial of the cultural identity of the descendants of the Maya and other Amerindian civilizations.'

The authenticity of heritage sites and their representation is a continuing debate in heritage tourism. Whether a site should be sanitized and presented as a commodity rather than an actual representation is a matter for further debate.

The 1972 International Treaty adopted by UNESCO called the Convention concerning the Protection of the World Cultural and Natural Heritage an agreement that 'aims to secure the necessary financial and intellectual resources to protect World Heritage sites'. The Convention requires countries:

> To recognise that the sites located on their national territory, and which have been inscribed on the World Heritage List, without prejudice to national sovereignty or ownership, constitute a world heritage 'for whose protection it is the duty of the international community as a whole to cooperate'. Without the support of other countries, some of the world's outstanding cultural and natural sites would deteriorate or, worse, disappear, often through lack of funding to preserve them. (UNESCO, 2008)

cultural) that influence heritage and tourism in these destinations.

Given the role of heritage in many tourist destinations, it is essential to understand and empathize with the nature, scope and context of heritage sites, and to understand their centrality within the historic development of the place where they are found and within the tourism industry that has grown around them. Even the most modern and contemporary cities of the world rely on their heritage to give them identity and to give those who live there a sense of locality and a shared personal and societal heritage.

Conclusion

This chapter has summarized the key issues around heritage as a tourism resource. As discussed in this chapter, it is essential to understand the link between culture and heritage and the valuable role that these phenomena play in the making of tourism spaces. The themes that exist around research in heritage tourism are multitudinous because of crossovers between the different research perspectives, which include tourism and heritage management but also involve the social sciences, conservation science, architecture and archaeology.

Using the case of Angkor, Winter (2008) demonstrated that the social consequences of heritage-related tourism can be extensive and suggested that it is essential for attention be paid to the processes (political, economic, social and

Review Questions

1. Consider and discuss the following statement made by Ashworth and Bruce (2009): 'The more distinctive and dramatic the [heritage] experience, the less likely is the tourist to return'. Are tourists more or less likely to return to a heritage site after a 'distinctive and dramatic' experience? Why?
2. What are the key debates with regard to defining heritage tourism?
3. Consider media representations of heritage attractions. What are the positive and negative impacts of such representation, both on the attractions themselves and the local area?
4. Evaluate the key argument for and against charging for entry to heritage attractions such as cathedrals and national museums.

References

Anholt-Gfk Roper (2009) *The Anholt-Gfk Roper NBI 2009 Report Highlights.* Anholt-Gfk Roper, New York.
Ashworth, G. and Bruce, D. (2009) Town walls, walled towns and tourism: paradoxes and paradigms. *Journal of Heritage Tourism* 4, 299–313.
Chartres, R. (2007) The real scandal over cathedral charging. *The Telegraph.* Available from: http://www.telegraph.co.uk/comment/personal-view/3640216/The-real-scandal-over-cathedral-charging.html. Accessed July 6, 2010.
Dallen, J.T. and Boyd, S.W. (2003) *Heritage Tourism.* Pearson Education, Harlow, UK.
English Heritage (2003) *Heritage Counts. The State of the Historic Environment.* English Heritage, London, UK.
English Heritage (2007) *Heritage Counts 2007.* English Heritage, London, UK.
ePolitix.com (2009) *Free entry to national museums highly valued.* Press release. Available from: http://www.epolitix.com/stakeholder-websites/press-releases/press-release-details/newsarticle/free-entry-to-national-museums-highly-valued///sites/visual-arts-and-galleries-association. Accessed July 6, 2010.

European Travel Council (2005) *City Tourism and Culture: The European Experience*. European Travel Council, Brussels, Belgium.

Evans, G. (2004) Mundo Maya: from Cancun to City of Culture. World Heritage in Postcolonial Mesoamerica. *Current Issues in Tourism* 7, 315–329.

Fyall, A. and Garrod, B. (1998) Heritage tourism: at what price? *Managing Leisure* 3, 213–228.

Goulding, C. (1998) The commodification of the past, postmodern pastiche, and the search for authentic experiences at contemporary heritage attractions. *European Journal of Marketing* 34, 835–853.

Hede, A.-M. (2007) World Heritage listing and the evolving issues related to tourism and heritage: cases from Australia and New Zealand. *Journal of Heritage Tourism* 2, 133–144.

Landorf, C. (2009) Managing for sustainable tourism: a review of six cultural World Heritage Sites. *Journal of Sustainable Tourism* 17, 53–70.

Lunn, K. (2007) War memorialisation and public heritage in South-East Asia: some case studies and comparative reflections. *International Journal of Heritage Studies* 13, 81–95.

Markwell, S., Bennett, M. and Ravenscroft, N. (1997) The changing market for heritage tourism: a case study of visits to historic houses in England. *International Journal of Heritage Studies* 3, 95–108.

McMorran, C. (2008) Understanding the 'heritage' in heritage tourism: ideological tool or economic tool for a Japanese hot springs resort? *Tourism Geographies* 10, 334–354.

Swarbrooke (2001) *The Development and Management of Visitor Attractions*, 2nd edn. Butterworth Heinemann, Oxford, UK.

UNESCO (2008) *World Heritage Information Kit*. The World Heritage Centre, Paris, France. Available from: http://whc.unesco.org/documents/publi_infokit_en.pdf. Accessed July 6, 2010.

UNESCO (2010) *World Heritage List*. The World Heritage Centre, Paris, France. Available from: http://whc.unesco.org/en/list. Accessed July 6, 2010.

VisitBritain (2010) *Culture and Heritage Topic Profile – February 2010*. Available from: http://www.visitbritain.org/Images/Culture%20%26%20Heritage%20Topic%20Profile%20Full_tcm139-184566.pdf. Accessed July 6, 2010.

Wager, J. (1995) Environmental planning for a World Heritage Site: case study of Angkor, Cambodia. *Journal for Environmental Planning and Management* 38, 419–434.

Wall, G. and Black, H. (2004) Global heritage and local problems: some examples from Indonesia. *Current Issues in Tourism* 7, 436–439.

Winter, T. (2002) Angkor meets *Tomb Raider*: setting the scene. *International Journal of Heritage Studies* 8, 323–336.

Winter, T. (2008) Post-conflict heritage and tourism in Cambodia: the burden of Angkor. *International Journal of Heritage Studies* 14, 524–539.

14 Tourism and Film

Dr Glen Croy and Sine Heitmann

Introduction

Film-induced tourism is a relatively recent area of tourism research (Croy and Walker, 2003; Beeton, 2005). Often, our initial consideration of film-induced tourism is of high-profile films and their impact on tourist numbers. For example, the films *Close Encounters of the Third Kind*, *Crocodile Dundee* and *The Lord of the Rings* are habitually noted for their reported effects on tourist numbers. The influence on tourist numbers is one aspect of the tourism and film relationship but there are none the less many more influences, and this chapter's aim is to highlight and introduce these other aspects. This chapter provides an introductory discussion to the relationship between tourism and film. First, film tourism definitions present a more inclusive context for considering the relationship. Second, a brief discussion of the film-induced tourism phenomena identifies the exceptional nature of this. Third, an overview of current film tourism studies highlights four emergent themes that form the basis for the discussion of this chapter. These four themes are film's role in tourists' pre-visit and on-site experiences; film's role in destination promotion; the impacts of film tourism; and, finally, the representations of people, cultures and places as related to tourism. The chapter concludes with an outline of future areas of research.

Definitions

Importantly, early academic mentions of the role of film in tourism were presented in the 1960s (e.g. Boorstin, 1961), while the first tourism and media-specific studies were presented in the 1990s (Butler, 1990; Riley and Van Doren, 1992; Tooke and Baker, 1996). Film now has a commonly reported tourism-inducing role, although often this is overstated, even concerning the above-noted films. Furthermore, the complexity and subtlety of film's roles are only beginning to be understood (Beeton, 2005). This growing understanding of the film and tourism relationship is reflected in film tourism definitions. Even with the relatively recent focus on film tourism, there is already a range of definitions and understandings of the concept.

Early studies presented the terms 'movie-induced tourism' and 'television-induced tourism' (Riley *et al.*, 1998). These terms present movies or television as 'pulling' forces for tourists to sets or actual locations. Thus, the primary role of movies and television is to generate awareness, desire and action to visit the screened locations. In each of these, the focus has been solely on fictional media, rather than documentaries or travel programmes. Most focus of research so far takes film tourism as the potential to generate tourism post-release of a film (hence the suffix 'induced' in many definitions). More recently, Beeton (2005) presented a more inclusive definition of 'film-induced tourism'. Film, in this case, includes movies, television and other screened media, such as videos and DVDs. Busby and Klug (2001) and Beeton (2005) noted that film-induced tourism comprises many aspects, including film as a tourist motivator, film as part of a holiday, celebrity film tourism (e.g. 'Hollywood homes' tours), film as nostalgia (visiting film locations that represent another era), constructed film attractions, film tours, film theme parks, film festivals and film as vicarious travel. Beeton (2005) concluded a definition of film-induced tourism as a broad-brush term related to 'visitation to sites where movies and television programmes have been filmed, as well as to tours to production studios, including film-related theme parks. What is of interest here is the tourist activity associated with the film industry, be it on-site in the field, or at (or near) the production studio'.

Further to these definitions, the identification and study of other media-inducing tourism has created an overarching term of 'fictional media tourism'. Fictional media is the presentation of fictions through different media. As well as movies, television, DVDs and the like, fictional media includes literary works, art and music as tourism-inducing agents (Tighe, 1986; Squire, 1993; Busby and Klug, 2001; Croy and Walker, 2003). However, this chapter will maintain a focus on film tourism. Of additional note are other disciplines' perspectives of this phenomenon. Karpovich (2010) has identified cultural and media discipline perspectives of film tourism, and their terminology of 'cinematic tourism', 'cult geography', 'media tourism' and 'symbolic pilgrimage'. While all studying the same thing, the different disciplines also take different perspectives (see later).

As is highlighted through Beeton's (2005) definition, film-induced tourism is much more than the role of films in attracting visitors; it especially also includes the activities at these sites. All the same, film has other roles in tourism, less evident than these influences on tourist behaviour. Some of these roles may not even be explicitly evident to the tourists themselves. The rest of this chapter will discuss the current understanding of the explicit and less evident roles of film in tourism.

Film-inducing Tourism: The Exception to the Rule

While many of the accounts of film and tourism relationships are about the direct inducing influence of film on tourist numbers, there are actually limited results in support of this. This role of film is largely a socially constructed 'truth' (Beeton, 2006), repeated enough times that people believe it. The limited studies that have assessed the role of film on visitor numbers have shown cases of dramatic changes in visitor numbers, including a 74% increase in tourist numbers to Devils Tower National Monument the year after the release of *Close Encounters of the Third Kind* and an additional 39% after the film's television release (Riley and Van Doren, 1992). All the same, these direct indicators did not specifically assess the role of the film in tourists' visits to the location. Past visitation trends indicate that these jumps in tourist numbers were exceptional, and as such there appears to be a strong relationship with the film. A later study for the local tourism association did identify that one-fifth of tourists had the film as an initial knowledge point about the area. The later result does not mean that tourists visited the area because of the film, although it does show a potential influence of the film. Other films reported upon include *Field of Dreams*, *Deliverance*, *Thelma & Louise* and *Steel Magnolias*, with each of their associated locations either not having any visitation prior to the films or experiencing a jump in tourist numbers (Riley and Van Doren, 1992). Tooke and Baker (1996) also completed a similar analysis on the influence of British television programmes on tourist numbers, with similar findings.

Riley *et al.* (1998) furthered the analysis of the influence of film on tourist numbers over 12 filmed sites. They found, as a median for all 12 sites, that visitation increased 10% 1 year after a film's release, and tourist numbers continued to grow 5 years after release, up 77% on the release-year numbers. These median values indicate the exceptional impact of *Close Encounters of the Third Kind*, having a 74% increase 1 year after release.

More than just being on film, key features of the filmed locations, and the films themselves, have been presented as inducing tourism. These key features include the picturesque physical environments; association and reinterpretation of stories; thematic contents creating pilgrimage attractions; celebrity; human relationships; to become a part of the lives of those depicted on screen; and novel activities presented in the films

(Riley and Van Doren, 1992; Riley et al., 1998; Croy and Walker, 2003; Beeton, 2005). This list of reasons highlights a layer of complexity; the previously implied nature of just being in film is not an inducing agent in itself.

The studies' films also highlight other considerations and characteristics. These filmed locations had relatively low pre-film tourist numbers and were relatively isolated from other tourism-inducing effects (although some locations were nationally important and known); the films were relatively successful in audience coverage and box-office success and the visitors were largely domestic, in many cases within day-visit distance. Importantly, what these films also implicitly highlight is while there are many films with similar characteristics, not many have this evident impact on tourist numbers; these films may well be the exception to the rule.

Given the potentially exceptional nature of the previously studied films, the role of film as tourism-inducing needs to be very carefully considered (as explicitly noted by Riley and Van Doren, 1992; Riley et al., 1998). Unfortunately, without consideration of the actual role of film in inducing tourism, and without supporting evidence, vast overstatements are made. For example, with regards to The Lord of the Rings, NFO New Zealand (2003), Croy (2004) and Jones and Smith (2005) have highlighted the limited impact of the film trilogy on tourist numbers. All the same, statements are still made presenting the proposed vast influence of the films on New Zealand's tourist numbers (e.g. Grihault, 2003; Houpt, 2003; Tzanelli, 2004). These statements, repeated in the general and academic media, have created misconstructions of the role of film in tourism.

None the less, what these studies have provided is a role for film in tourism and indications that this role can be very influential. These studies have also highlighted that there must be other subtle roles for film in tourism, roles that may not be so evident in every filmed location.

Film's Tourism Roles

Four themes have emerged in the film tourism literature as the roles of films in tourism have developed beyond a direct influence on tourist numbers. These four film tourism themes are: (i) the role of film in the tourist experience; (ii) the role of film in destination promotion; (iii) the impacts of film tourism; and (iv) the representations of people, cultures and places as related to tourism. Beeton (2010) discussed this film tourism emergence as 'knowledge development', from an early focus on speculation and justifying the field through to higher inquiry of methodological and theoretical informing discussions. As the study of film tourism relationship has developed Beeton (2010) highlighted the increase in multiple voices and growing multidisciplinary inquiries. She has portrayed the initial studies as 'speculating' on the relationship between tourism and the media (e.g. Butler, 1990), and these were followed by studies 'justifying' the relationship by showing the influence through numbers and demonstrating an industry relevance (e.g. Riley and Van Doren, 1992; Tooke and Baker, 1996). As indicated above, the study of tourism and film relationships has built on this important foundation. The next level Beeton (2010) presented was that of 'business research', presenting the how and why of the relationship between tourism and film, and the impacts of the relationship. This level has increased the theoretical, methodological and informing nature of the research. Three of the noted themes appear to be in this level of inquiry, specifically the role of film in the tourist experience, destination promotion and impacts of film tourism. The third level of Beeton's (2010) model is 'higher inquiry' emphasizing postmodern and multidisciplinary perspectives of the relationships, and particularly foci on identity, myth and fantasy. The fourth theme of representations is captured in this level. Each of these four roles is introduced and discussed here.

The role of film in the tourist experience

An increasing number of studies have investigated the roles of film in tourist experiences. Building upon earlier studies, a number have focused on the on-site experience, although importantly a number have also investigated the roles of film in the pre-visit stages of tourists' experiences. For the pre-visit stage of the tourist experience, film has roles in raising awareness, forming images, developing expectations and making decisions. Investigating these roles will serve to uncover the complexity of film's role in motivating on-site visits and the activities undertaken.

Pre-visit roles of film

Even in the early studies, Butler (1990) noted the role of the media as a primary source of information about places and the increasing influence of movies and television. Riley and Van Doren (1992) also noted the potential of the media as 'vehicles of recognition' 'to facilitate an increased awareness of the destination'. What these studies were identifying is that film media informs viewers about places and brings new potential destinations to mind. Croy and Wheeler (2007), in their introductory discussion of image formation, highlighted the role of film as often being a first opportunity to become aware of places, and as such even consider them as potential tourist destinations. For many reported film tourism destinations, it could be argued that the key role film played was showing that these places existed. An identified key goal of Tourism New Zealand's use of *The Lord of the Rings* was to do just this: to raise the awareness of a country far from most of its international tourist markets (Croy, 2010). More often, though, it is likely that film images add to pre-existing images of places, rather than being the first point of awareness (Iwashita, 2006).

All the same, just being aware of a place is not sufficient in making that place a tourism destination. The related discussion is of film's role in destination image formation. To be a potential tourist destination, there needs to be a positively appraised image in the minds of potential tourists. Here, film can play a significant role. As indicated by Riley and Van Doren (1992), destinations need potential tourists to hold comprehensive images, unlikely to be formed through advertising. Image-formation researchers have also noted that film is perceived more credible than advertising and is likely to have a lasting impact (Gartner,

1993). Film, in movies, television programmes, DVDs and the like has a number of distinct advantages over advertising. The audience has chosen to view the film, there is longer engagement than 30 seconds, there is a captivating story, there are purposefully picture-perfect representations of places to match the story and there are celebrities acting in these places. These features allow the audience to become aware of, familiar with and even develop complex images of these places (Croy and Wheeler, 2007; di Cesare *et al.*, 2009). Increased exposure, via viewing the film again or viewing other films produced (or set) in the area, allows even greater levels of image familiarity and complexity. The film itself may motivate viewers to seek further information about the place seen (di Cesare *et al.*, 2009). Again, as Riley and Van Doren (1992) noted, with the extended exposure to places through film, there is a higher level of image complexity and less perceived risk in decision making. Thus, increased exposure to places, through a chosen and believable medium, creates safer expectations of the likely experiences in the destination. These expectations may be of the places and people represented or of the story being told, as such including the noted reasons for attracting tourists. It must be noted that there is an expected intelligence on the part of the audience to distinguish between place, people and story, even if the expectation is to relive the story in the place (as compared to Torchin's (2002) mythical television tourist).

As such, film plays a role in the tourist pre-visit stage; it has a role in raising awareness of places, creating familiar and complex images of places and creating expectations of possible experiences. These roles make the decision-making process safer by reducing or dispelling barriers, or are at least perceived to do so (Croy, 2010). Importantly, if there is high perceived risk of the decision, film alone is not likely to be the sole information source and the image created is likely to be informed by a number of other sources to make the decision safer (Croy and Wheeler, 2007).

In this pre-visit stage, the destination choice and reason for visiting are not presupposed to be for the purpose of seeing film sites or reliving the film. The role of film has instead been one of awareness and image formation. These images have then informed rather than necessarily directed the decision-making process or destination choice. With this perspective, the subtle roles of film (and fictional media in general) are much more pronounced than what can necessarily be assessed at the on-site phase of the tourist experience.

On-site roles of film

Much of the film tourism studies of the tourist experience have been undertaken on-site, usually at filmed sites (places screened in movies or on television). These studies have primarily assessed what motivated tourists to be there and what makes up their experiences (also see Chapter 3). Heitmann (2010) suggested that film motivates travel, and especially that the film acts as a trigger for or a reinforcement of already existing motivations. Macionis (2004) proposed a model of film tourist motivations using push and pull factors for film tourists. She noted that films can highlight disequilibrium or push from home, and at the same time highlight pull attributes of potential tourist destinations. Furthermore, Macionis (2004) proposed that as tourists' interest in a film increases, they are more likely to be a purposeful film tourist. For the film tourist, visiting the film site would lead to higher levels of self-actualization, increasing role of push factors in the decision and the decreasing need for destination authenticity (with more emphasis on film authenticity). The opposite would be true for the incidental film tourist.

Macionis' (2004) proposed model has similarities to McKercher and du Cros' (2003) cultural tourist typology, and likewise, further studies have identified a range of film tourists. The more research that is completed, the more it appears that film is not a specific and primary motivator for travel or even to visit a specific place (Busby and Klug, 2001; NFO New Zealand, 2003; di Cesare et al., 2009; Macionis and Sparks, 2009). The niche of film-specific tourists is in fact very small. Busby and Klug (2001) found 5.3% of visitors to Notting Hill noted the film of the same name as a reason. Research into the influence of *The Lord of the Rings* found that 0.3% of visitors had the films

as a main although not the sole reason for visiting New Zealand, and an additional 9% noted the films as a reason, though not main reason (NFO New Zealand, 2003). In both the Notting Hill and New Zealand cases, a majority of visitors had actually seen the respective films and importantly associated them with the place being visited. As such, it is believable that film did play a role in the image of the place, even if not directing the decision.

Similar to the Notting Hill and New Zealand findings, di Cesare et al. (2009) identified that 4% noted a definite influence of film on destination choice (though not noting how significant that role was). Macionis and Sparks (2009) also identified that just over 4% of their sample had stated film as a prime reason for the visit to the site (but not necessarily for the holiday as a whole). Overall, the research indicates that while visiting filmed sites is popular, the film is often not the only or even the most important reason for visiting these destinations. The 'purposeful' film tourist, using McKercher and du Cros' (2003) term, is a small niche, and more often film tourism is an incidental tourist activity (Macionis and Sparks, 2009). Macionis and Sparks (2009) further identified that the small niche segment is similar for ethnically motivated markets and those motivated to visit dark tourism sites, and McKercher and du Cros' (2003) cultural tourists (13%). Figure 14.1 presents a film tourist adaptation of the cultural tourist typology model (McKercher and du Cros, 2003). Importantly, as noted, the existing research suggests that the vast majority of 'film tourists' are incidental, casual or serendipitous; there is a very small number of purposeful film tourists.

While not a primary reason for visiting a place, a number of factors motivate tourists at filmed sites (for further discussion on tourist motivation, see Chapter 3). Many studies have proposed film tourism motivations or reasons for visiting these sites (as highlighted above), although very few studies have actually assessed tourists' motivations. Macionis and Sparks (2009) is one of these studies. They identified three factor motivations: personal involvement with the film (2.69/5 dimension mean, 26% variance explained), a novel experience of

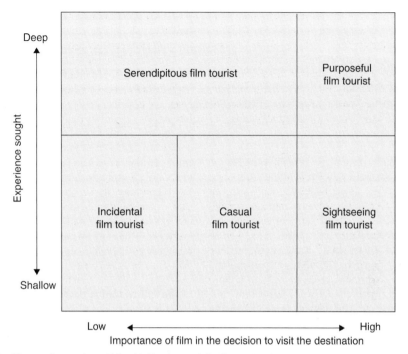

Fig. 14.1. Film tourist typology. (After McKercher and du Cros, 2003.)

visiting filmed sites (3.92, 18%) and the status of visiting filmed sites (3.12, 13%). The novelty of a film tourism experience was the greatest motivator; however, as indicated by the means and variance explanation, it was not overly powerful, further reflecting the incidental nature of visiting filmed sites. None the less, for some locations – such as Paris, Beijing, London, New York, Mumbai and Los Angeles (Beeton, 2005; Iwashita, 2006; Croy and Wheeler, 2007) – it is very difficult to disassociate a place from movies and television. As such, disassociating the tourist experience from image sources can also be very difficult. Consequently, film, while not an obvious motivator to the tourists themselves, might still have played a role in their travel experiences and decisions. The role of film in tourist motivations may therefore be difficult to determine (Busby and Klug, 2001; Roesch, 2009; Heitmann, 2010).

As an activity, film tourism is still big. A large number of visitors do travel to filmed sites and film-associated sites such as studios, theme parks, festivals and premieres (Beeton, 2005). Karpovich (2010) notes that more tourists visit Disneyland Paris than the Eiffel Tower and more visit Disney World than the Washington DC monuments. While the actual numbers may be taken with scepticism, these film destinations are very successful world tourism attractions. Of course, the Eiffel Tower and monuments of Washington are also filmed sites in themselves, and again for tourists to disassociate these icons from film is very difficult. Interestingly, Croy and Buchmann (2009) identified that a third of participants on a *The Lord of the Rings* tour had not read the books nor seen the films; they were on the tour because of friends' recommendations or just a means to access the New Zealand High Country. As such, even those on film tours may not be induced or motivated by film, further complicating the measurement difficultly.

Tooke and Baker (1996) and Frost (2009) noted the role of film in inducing tourism to the places where films were set, rather than where they were filmed. Often noted is the filming of *Braveheart* in Ireland and the film's influence on the image of and visitation to Scotland (Beeton, 2005; Frost, 2009; Karpovich, 2010). Other studies have highlighted the role of film, be it movies or television, in directing people to dislocated places, places not set nor used for filming (Torchin, 2002; Sydney-Smith, 2006). This dislocated motivation is exemplified by the opening of a replica *Field of Dreams* field in Japan (Springwood, 2002) and the popularity of film theme parks (Beeton, 2005). The dislocated experiences highlights issues of authentic experiences. Authenticity is discussed later.

For the film tourist, purposeful or incidental, film still appears to play a role in the experience. Roesch (2009), in his book, *The Experiences of Film Location Tourists*, reviews previous studies and highlights the diverse range of activities and desires undertaken at filmed sites. These experiences range from wanting to see the actors, to be where the important personalized events in the film took place, to create new film-associated experiences and to share the 'community' of the filmed theme. For the tourists Roesch (2009) interviewed on film tours, activities undertaken included taking photographs to show the general film area and to locate themselves there when showing friends and family back home. None the less, equally or even more important for film tourists was capturing the filmed sights to re-present the filmed images. Further than image capturing, film tourists simulated and re-enacted the films, mentally and physically, at times dressing as the filmed characters. Similarly, Beeton (2006) drew on an interview at an Australian television location, *Sea Change*, with the couple staying in the main character's television home. While the wife noted that the wonderful filmed scenery was the influence for their holiday, the husband responded that she had been acting as the lead character the whole time they were there. Film tourists also collect souvenirs of their visits. Important to Roesch's (2009) participants was the social interaction with the expert guide and the other film tourist participants, although there was a noted displeasure of sharing the time with passive or 'uninformed' fans and the at times overcrowding nature of a group. Other film tourists have been identified as conducting similar activities (Carl *et al.*, 2007; Croy and Buchmann, 2009; Kim, 2010).

Further to the pre- and on-site film tourist experience, Torchin (2002) briefly outlined her post-site film tourism experience and the implications for interpreting her television viewing and recollecting her actual visits.

Overall, film may play a very significant role for tourists, although one that is not fully appreciated even by the tourists themselves. Film, as a vehicle for awareness and image formation, creating expectations of places, people and experiences, and consequently as a decision-making reference, plays a number of roles. All the same, the role of film in directly motivating a visit and deciding on a destination has been shown to be very small. Visiting film sites is generally motivated by novelty, prestige and personalization, and the activities undertaken are, especially by purposeful film tourists, to engage with the film on-site (Fig. 14.2).

The role of film in destination promotion

Given the media's proposition that film generates tourism and the selective grazing of the research that highlights the potentially exceptional nature of these propositions, emphasis has been placed on film's role in destination promotion. In highlighting this, it is important to also note that most destinations actually attract film for the economic impact of film production and promote these productions to attract further production (Croy and Walker, 2003). However, there has been increased awareness of the potential for tourism impacts and, as such, film attraction has developed into a secondary outcome for some locations (Hudson and Ritchie, 2006; Beeton, 2008a; Croy, 2010).

The role for film in destination promotion is to reinforce the role of film in tourists' pre- and on-site experiences, create awareness, form an image, provide further information about the filmed locations, develop expectations, influence decisions and provide opportunities for the personalization of the film – to create an overarching positive tourist impression of the place. Studies on the use of film for tourism promotion have identified the perceived benefits of being filmed. Hudson and Ritchie (2006) noted that the main perceived benefits were stronger destination image or brand, positive economic impacts and higher tourist visitation.

Fig. 14.2. Tourists at Jungle Temple, Cambodia (*Lara Croft: Tomb Raider*). (Photographs © Glen Croy.)

Similarly, Croy and Walker (2003) found that the economic and employment impacts of film production and, on a secondary level, the potential impact on tourist visitation, were the perceived benefits. They also identified, at a third level, the benefits of image enhancement and cultural development.

A number of marketing strategies for the use of film to aid destination promotion have been proposed. Importantly, in the considerations of strategies, film should only be seen as one attribute of destination promotion and needs to be undertaken strategically (Croy, 2010). Beeton (2005) presented three destination-marketing recommendations. The first is for film-themed festivals, and especially community-focused festivals (see also Beeton, 2008a). Second is for tangible film representations, such as sets, statues, guidebooks and collections. Third is for the re-naming of sites or areas to more explicitly link them to a film. In presenting these recommendations, Beeton (2005) was very careful to note that all marketing should be within the consideration of the location and its interests, and that too successful promotion may lead to very unwanted impacts. Croy (2010) and Hudson and Ritchie (2006) also highlighted the need to be selective in marketing strategies, the importance of fitting within the destination and having a strategic plan for image management. They presented a range of potential film tourism strategies, such as promoting filmed locations to tourists, including a film-tourism website presence; generating media publicity of filming and the tourist experiences at the filmed sites; leveraging the films, such as using the filmed stars in tourism promotion and selling film memorabilia; and attracting further film productions (Hudson and Ritchie, 2006).

Overall, film has important roles in creating awareness for and promoting destinations. However, any promotion needs to be undertaken strategically, aligned with the destination's goals.

The impacts of film tourism

As implied in the above discussions, film tourism has the potential to create impacts, both positive and negative (Beeton, 2008b). The largely unconsidered influence of film on tourism has resulted in very reactionary impact planning, once the local community has felt the negative impacts or, to a lesser extent, impacts on the environment have become evident (Beeton, 2005). More so now, collaborative proactive planning for (the positive) potential film tourism impacts is more evident (Hudson and Ritchie, 2006; Beeton, 2008a; Heitmann, 2010). All the same, many of the negative impacts appear to be afterthoughts. Most impacts attributed to film tourism (both negative and positive) reflect the impacts generally attributed to tourism.

These impacts include an increase in tourist numbers and subsequent rise in revenues and employment; modification of tourism infrastructure; diversification of the tourism product; host–community interaction, cultural exchange and conflict; commodification and loss of authenticity; multiuse of the natural and cultural environment; and many more (Schofield, 1996; Tooke and Baker, 1996; Beeton, 2001, 2005, 2006, 2008a, 2008b; Croy and Buchmann, 2009; Heitmann, 2010). Importantly, as Heitmann (2010) noted, there is the potential for these impacts to be reinstated or reinforced with progressive releases of movies and television programmes to paid-for television, DVD and again on television, although she also highlighted that with the increasing turnaround and new media presented, this reinforcing influence may be reduced.

While locations primarily focus initially on the positive impacts of increases in revenue, more visitors, higher awareness, increased employment and new business opportunities, awareness of the negative impacts has increased. Two cases of film tourism impacts are very prominent in the tourism literature. First, the study of Australia's Barwon Heads represented in the television series *SeaChange* (Beeton, 2001, 2005, 2006, 2008b) and second, England's Goathland represented in the television series *Heartbeat* and more recently as Hogwarts' railway station in the *Harry Potter* series of movies (Mordue, 1999, 2001; Beeton, 2005, 2007, 2008a, 2008b; O'Connor *et al.*, 2009). In both cases, the tourist type and number changed. Especially in Goathland, the number of tourists swamped the village, displacing the residents (even if temporarily) from their town. For Barwon Heads, the traditional budget visitors were displaced, real estate prices increased and the amenities were changed to be tourism rather than local focused. Due to the changes, the villages the tourists saw on screen were unobtainable. Additionally, and importantly, the villages' residents saw dramatic impacts on their way of life, especially in the smaller village of Goathland.

As well as the contests and conflicts between local and tourist desires, film has also highlighted potential conflicts between different groups of tourists (Croy and Buchmann, 2009; Roesch, 2009). Traditional or pre-film tourists and film tourists can want different experiences, though competing for the same spaces for that experience, as also noted in the displacement of the Barwon Heads' budget visitors. Roesch (2009) also highlighted the potential for conflict between tour and independent film tourists, and even within tours.

The natural and cultural environment within a destination is subject to pressure from both the film industry and the resulting increase of tourism activity. Case studies have highlighted impacts during filming, such as modification of the environment by the film crew (Forsyth, 2002) and negative reactions from the local community because of disruptions in daily routines (Beeton, 2005). The relationship between film production and the local community has knock-on effects on how the community then deals with the increase of tourism after the release of the film (Beeton, 2008a, 2008b). As such, strategic relationships between the destination, tourism and film producers are recommended (Hudson and Ritchie, 2006; Beeton, 2008a, 2008b; Cynthia and Beeton, 2009).

As shown by this discussion, there is the potential for many positive as well as negative impacts from film tourism. As Beeton (2008b) and Heitmann (2010) have recommended, an inclusive and consultative planning framework is needed to adequately include and respond to the varying goals of the stakeholders. Importantly, film tourism planning should be part of the broader destination and community plan (Beeton, 2008b; Heitmann, 2010). The currently dominant planning approach within tourism development highlights sustainability and includes characteristics of long-term planning, partnerships and cooperation between all stakeholders and consideration of the economic, environmental and sociocultural well-being.

Applying stakeholder theory, Heitmann (2010) identified key stakeholders, including community representatives, the tourism association, the destination management organization (DMO), film office, local government and film producers – all of which are directly and indirectly involved in (film) tourism planning (see Fig. 14.3). The integration of all stakeholders in the development process safeguards the sustainable management of the tourism product, and if films trigger existing types of tourism (e.g. ecotourism, heritage tourism) then existing good practice from these arenas can be taken into account and applied to any new

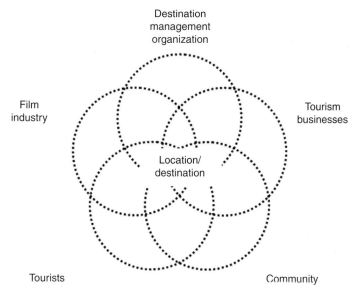

Fig. 14.3. Film tourism stakeholder. (Adapted from Heitmann, 2010.)

developments. However, while good in theory, there are practical challenges to minimizing negative impacts and allowing sustainable film tourism planning. One of the first challenges is that these different stakeholders are not homogenous entities, but overlap (i.e. local residents own tourism businesses or are part of DMOs). Second, as each stakeholder's role and interest in film tourism planning varies, so does their level of involvement and participation in the planning process.

Close cooperation between DMOs and the film industry is essential. To date, there is limited evidence that the film industry has been actively included or even interested in the tourism planning process. The film industry has a different agenda: creating the film it wants, not the tourism image that DMOs or the community wants (Beeton, 2005). Once the filming process has finished, there is limited or no involvement from the film industry as its priority lies in marketing and promoting the film, not the destination. Benefits of DMO and film partnerships have been recognized, albeit with a more instrumental approach (Croy and Walker, 2003; Hudson and Ritchie, 2006a; Cynthia and Beeton, 2009; Croy, 2010). The UK and USA have shown some initiatives in forms of government-funded schemes that are targeted at promoting the destination for future film locations (e.g. CanagRetna, 2007; Olsberg|SPI, 2007).

DMOs have a high interest in influencing film tourism destination development and can have a significant influence in the product development and marketing processes (see above). However, the power to influence in the early stages of the film-making process is limited, as DMOs have little or no control over how or for whom the destination is presented (Croy and Walker, 2003). Even if DMOs have the opportunity to work with the film industry at point of shooting, there is no influence on the filming, storyline, cinematography or other aspects of the film. This also means that there is no direct influence over the audience or target group of the film and any subsequent film tourists. None the less, as Croy (2010) identified, destination managers' emphasis should be on managing fluid image formation and destination image, not control.

Crucially, the local community is a primary stakeholder as, after all, it is their home and they will feel the immediate and cumulative impacts. With good management practices, communities can actively participate and be involved in the process and impacts on the physical environment can be kept to a minimum. Unfortunately, even if community participation is completed 'tourists will often come to see a famous site regardless of the immediate community's wishes' (Beeton, 2007). Furthermore, just as DMOs are limited in exercising control over the image portrayed, the community has to live with the consequences of the image projected on screen. For example, *Slumdog Millionaire* has meant that the slum community has become an object of the tourist gaze, subsequently reinforcing criticisms of tourism as a vehicle of commodification and objectification; the community is resisting this portrayal. This contest reflects differences in the interpretation of the film by local and international audiences (Blakely, 2009).

Finally, and following on from the last point, we encounter one variable that is beyond control and impacts significantly on the overall success of film tourism, which is the success of the film itself (Heitmann, 2010). Film tourism products and services are automatically and intrinsically linked to the fil+m and its success. Nevertheless, multiple releases and re-releases of the film cannot guarantee a continuous success of the tourism product. Films are for entertainment, which is becoming increasingly short-lived and more volatile to consumer behaviour than ever before, thereby challenging film tourism right from the beginning.

The preceding discussion highlights that the management of film tourism impacts depends on a range of variables. First, effective community participation depends on previous experiences and involvement in the planning process. Second, the appeal and location of destinations varies, and subsequently influences the success of a location in becoming a tourism destination. Third, the interest of the film industry in tourism is important, but lacking. Fourth, the success of the film may have an impact on the level of potential tourism interest. Finally, as already implied, tourists and the influence film has on their variety of motivations and desired experiences are crucial for managing film tourism impacts.

Representations of people, cultures and places as related to tourism

The critical interpretation of film presentation and representation is a much-increased feature of contemporary life and in tourism. Television series such as *House of Cards*, *Spin Doctors* and *Absolute Power* and films such as *Conspiracy Theory* and *Wag the Dog* have reflected, or arguably influenced, society's growing distrust of representation and presentations in the media. None the less, the power and influence of film has increased tremendously (Liebes and Curran, 1998). This power of representation has gained critical attention in the tourism literature (Andsager and Drzewiecka, 2002). The power of film for image presentation and interpretation creates or reinforces gaze and in this there is a critical cultural interpretation and definition of what an image is, means and does (Urry, 1990; Andsager and Drzewiecka, 2002; Ateljevic and Doorne, 2002; Dunn, 2006). To briefly expand and clarify, the critical cultural perspective 'is concerned with the process of representation; that is, how meaning is constructed through pictures, narratives, and other objects and language' (Andsager and Drzewiecka, 2002).

Film has been identified to reinforce, provide and maintain the norms of society, and as such is a significant influence in the creation of images and perceptions of people, place, race, country and culture (Aitken and Zonn, 1994; Benton, 1995; Terry-Chandler, 2000). Conversely, film is also a force that creates, modifies and challenges the norms of society. Critiques of film have consequently increased because of the representations of society and specific groups within society (Jackson, 1992). Aitken and Zonn (1994) exemplify this in 'the way spaces are used and places portrayed in film reflects prevailing cultural norms, ethical mores, societal

structures, and ideologies. Concomitantly, the impact of a film on an audience can mould social, cultural, and environmental experiences'. Much of the research on the representations of tourism in film has been fed into tourism from the perspectives of cultural and media studies.

Concerning tourism, it appears that travel shows have moved from depicting, educating and informing us of places to entertainment about people in places, with the focus definitely on the people (Dunn, 2006). This has also occurred through the fictional portrayal of tourism. These entertaining representations are still educating viewers on what it is to be a tourist, with the thoughts, motivations, behaviours and interactions not only reflecting but also moulding experiences. Film representations present not only a way of doing, but also a way of seeing and interpreting the tourist sights/sites and people of the destination (Gibson, 2006; Iwashita, 2006). Iwashita (2006) highlighted that these film-generated images are often 'reduced' to filmic stereotypes of places. None the less, these images motivate travel and suggest what tourists should see, and tourists consequently validate their travels by seeing what they saw at home, on television or in the cinema. Jenkins (2003, after Urry, 1990) described this as a 'hermeneutic circle' or 'circle of representation', where tourists travel to recapture the images that motivated them to travel. This is captured in Roesch's (2009) outline of film tourists' activities.

Other studies of film have focused on representations of history and their consequent influence on destination image and the destination itself (Frost, 2004, 2006; Mercille, 2005). Frost (2009) also assessed the role of runaway filming and the potential implications for authentic experiences, comparable to television tourists' experiences (Torchin, 2002). Similarly, Sydney-Smith (2006) commented on the creation of the postmodern or 'nowhere' place in film. In this, the location of the screened sites cannot be located for tourism and is not meant to be located. Related, Buchmann (2006) assessed the role of myth making, incorporating existing physical features and images from literary and film sources. She noted that these contested myths and realities create challenges for tourism and the provision of authentic experiences. Importantly, these fictional, more powerful, image builders can overwrite the real stories, histories and communities of the film-depicted places (Croy and Buchmann, 2009). This raises questions, debates and impacts related to authenticity, including for tourism.

Authenticity raises complex questions, especially in film tourism, as films create new images and stories for existing and potentially relatively unknown places (Fig. 14.4). As film may be the information source for tourists, what is perceived as authentic and what will be an authentic experience can create contests, both personally and with the location (Macionis, 2004; Croy and Buchmann, 2009). With these new images, film locations are examples of hyperreal places and simulacra in which reality and artifice are mixed and 'cognitive and imaginative dimensions overlap' (Couldry, 1998). Even with just film-specific tourists, different layers of authenticity and simulation take place before the decision to travel to a film location. A number of films are adaptations of literary works, and the first instance of authenticity is judged against how well the film portrays and presents the written story. Once the filmgoer becomes a tourist, they may judge authenticity against how well reality (i.e.

Fig. 14.4. Samurai village, New Zealand (*The Last Samurai*). (Photographs © Glen Croy.)

landscape and scenery, but also individuals and communities) resembles what has been seen on screen (Rojek, 1997).

Overall, film offers a representation. This representation can generate new tourism demand, with its associated impacts. These impacts can create very powerful changes to tourist perceptions of people and place, and their potential experiences. These new perceptions can be very different to the actual people and places, and the pre-existing histories and stories of these places. The ensuing contests spark debates on what is authentic as a destination, travel and images.

Further Research and Conclusions

This chapter has probably raised many more questions, and areas to investigate, than it has provided answers – as should be expected for a relatively new developing body of knowledge. Note should be made of the relationship and overlap with broader areas of tourism research, such as motivations, destination image and authenticity, and how these broader areas have informed the current film-focused research and the potential to add further detail to these discussions. It has also been highlighted that other fields of research, outside of tourism, can and will provide greater understanding of the tourism and film relationship, including marketing, media studies and cultural studies. Tourism, and film tourism in particular, is not isolated from its conceptual foundations, nor should it be. All the same, strengthening these conceptual foundation links and film tourism structures requires further research. The first related implication from this chapter is that research should inform our constructions, and we should be critical of generalized relational statements such as 'films induce tourists'.

Second, existing tourism and other research can provide great insights into the relationship between tourism and film, and we need to draw on this to inform our understandings. As such, it is important to base contextual film tourism research in conceptual frameworks, and provide contributions to the context and concepts. Within this second implication is the suggestion of using other bodies of knowledge to gain further insight into film–tourism relationships.

More practically, this chapter has implied that film tourism is far more inclusive than tourism at filmed sites and far more complex. Even tourists at filmed sites may not be there because of the film and their motivations and activities can be quite diverse, delivering very different experiences. A variety of film tourists exist, and the vast majority do not associate their travel experiences with film. This highlights another implication: that the relationship between tourism and film is often subtle and may not be apparent to the tourists themselves, let alone researchers investigating the relationship. Furthermore, with the subtle roles of film in tourism, the functional use of film in tourism promotion can be much more diverse than as an attraction. Film, as an added awareness and image formation agent and as an expectation builder, has had growing use.

Of greatest use for destination planners is that film has been identified as having a range of impacts on tourism and the destination, economy, community and environment. Awareness of this provides destination planners with the opportunity to be proactive and plan to maximize positive impacts, while eliminating the negative. Rather than having largely reactive responses to the negative impacts, destination planners can prepare prior to films even being shot and align with other destination and community plans.

Finally, the representation role of film and its creations of new authenticities has great potential implications for overwriting and creating new stories to be explored by tourists. Destinations will need to be especially vigilant to the impacts of these changes on tourists and, importantly, the community. The destination will need to deliver and educate tourists as to the destination's story, in most cases needing to connect tourists' filmed images to the authentic place.

In conclusion, film's role to induce tourism is only one aspect of the relationship between tourism and film. This chapter has noted that film tourism is much more than visiting movie sites. Film tourism also includes other media, including television, DVDs and other filmic representations (of fictions). All the same, tourist visitation of these sites appears to be an exceptional phenomenon and only one influence of film on tourism. Film tourism also includes travelling to film festivals, film studios, theme parks and other associated places. Furthermore, there are other roles for film in tourism, which may not be so evident at filmed locations. In the pre-visit stage, films raise awareness and form images of destinations. These images also create expectations of places, people and experiences, and then inform destination decision-making processes. In the growing research of film tourists, visiting film sites is to engage with the film on-site and is motivated by novelty, prestige and personalization.

Given these indirect and direct roles of film in the tourist experience, film has important roles in creating awareness of and promoting destinations. The use of film for promotion needs careful consideration for its match with the community and destination's goals. This careful consideration is especially important as there are many potential negative and positive impacts from film tourism. As such, film tourism will need to fit within an inclusive destination and community planning framework, including the variety of stakeholders and their goals. Film, and film tourism, does not only have physical impacts on a destination. Film representations can powerfully affect tourist perceptions of people and place, and their experiences with these people at these places. The influences of film on tourists, and their desired experiences, can create new versions of authenticity and identities for destinations.

Overall, this chapter has provided several insights into the new area of film tourism research. It has highlighted new levels of complexity in an often-reported simple relationship between seeing something on film and then visiting that place. Importantly, it is crucial to be curious and critical of generalizing relationship statements and further inquire as to the how, why and new perspectives, as film tourism research has begun to do (Beeton, 2010). Film tourism is a very interesting area of research, and an area that needs this research to add detail and expand the body of knowledge.

Review Questions

1. Identify your favourite film (movie or television programme) – name and describe where it was set. What else has helped form your image of the location?

2. Consider how tourism motivation (see Chapter 3) can be applied to film tourism. To what extent can these motivations contribute to the understanding of film tourist motivations?

3. What strategies can be deployed to engage stakeholders, and especially the film industry, more actively in the film tourism process?

4. Highlight examples where a film has resulted in conflicting representations of the destination. What can be done to avoid potential film representation conflicts?

References

Aitken, S.C. and Zonn, L.E. (1994) Re-presenting the place pastiche. In: Aitken, S.C. and Zonn, L.E. (eds) *Place, Power Situation and Spectacle: A Geography of Film*. Rowman and Littlefield, Lanham, Maryland, pp. 3–25.

Andsager, J.L. and Drzewiecka, J.A. (2002) Desirability of differences in destinations. *Annals of Tourism Research* 29, 401–421.

Ateljevic, I. and Doorne, S. (2002) Representing New Zealand: tourism imagery and ideology. *Annals of Tourism Research* 29, 648–667.

Beeton, S. (2001) Smiling for the camera: the influence of film audiences on a budget tourism destination. *Tourism Culture and Communication* 3, 15–25.

Beeton, S. (2005) *Film-Induced Tourism*. Channel View Publications, Clevedon, UK.

Beeton, S. (2006) Understanding film-induced tourism. *Tourism Analysis* 11, 181–188.

Beeton, S. (2007) The good, the bad, and the ugly: CSR, film, and tourism: two cases of filming in a small community. *Tourism Review International* 11, 145–154.

Beeton, S. (2008a) Understanding film-induced tourism. *Tourism Analysis* 11, 181–188.

Beeton, S. (2008b) *Community Development through Tourism*. Landlinks Press, Collongwood, Victoria, Australia.

Beeton, S. (2010) The advance of film tourism. *Tourism and Hospitality Planning and Development* 7, 1–6.

Benton, L.M. (1995) Will the real/reel Los Angeles please stand up? *Urban Geography* 16, 144–164.

Blakely, R. (2009) Slum tours get Slumdog Millionaire boost. *The Times Online*, January 21, 2009. Available from: http://www.timesonline.co.uk/tol/news/world/asia/article5555635.ece. Accessed February 18, 2009.

Boorstin, D. (1961) *The Image or What Happened to the American Dream*. Penguin Books, Victoria, Australia.

Buchmann, A. (2006) From Erewhon to Edoras: tourism and myths in New Zealand. *Tourism Culture and Communication* 6, 181–189.

Busby, G. and Klug, J. (2001) Movie-induced tourism: the challenge of measurement and other issues. *Journal of Vacation Marketing* 7, 316–332.

Butler, R.W. (1990) The influence of the media in shaping international tourist patterns. *Tourism Recreation Research* 15, 46–53.

CanagRetna, S. (2007) Lights! Camera! Action! Southern states efforts to attract filmmakers' business. Paper presented at the Southern Legislative conference of The Council of State Governments.

Carl, D., Kindon S. and Smith, K. (2007) Tourists' experiences of film locations: New Zealand as 'Middle-Earth'. *Tourism Geographies* 9, 49–63.

Couldry, N. (1998) The view from inside the 'simulacrum': visitors' tales from the set of Coronation Street. *Leisure Studies* 17, 94–107.

Croy, W.G. (2004) The Lord of the Rings, *New Zealand, and Tourism: Image Building with Film*. Working Paper (10/04). Monash University, Melbourne, Victoria, Australia.

Croy, W.G. (2010) Planning for film tourism: active destination image management. *Tourism and Hospitality Planning and Development* 7, 21–30.

Croy, W.G., and Buchmann, A. (2009) Film-induced tourism in the high country: recreation and tourism contest. *Tourism Review International* 13, 147–155.

Croy, W.G. and Walker, R. (2003) Rural tourism and film: issues for strategic regional development. In: Hall, D., Roberts, L. and Mitchell, M. (eds) *New Directions In Rural Tourism*. Ashgate, Aldershot, UK, pp. 115–133.

Croy, W.G. and Wheeler, F. (2007) Image formation: a research case. In: Hall, C.M. (ed.) *Introduction to Tourism in Australia: Development, Issues and Change*, 5th edn. Pearson Education, Australia, pp. 1–11.

Cynthia, D. and Beeton, S. (2009) Supporting independent film production through tourism collaboration. *Tourism Review International* 13, 113–120.

di Cesare, F., D'Angelo, L. and Rech, G. (2009) Films and tourism: understanding the nature and intensity of their cause-effect relationship. *Tourism Review International* 13, 103–112.

Dunn, D. (2006). Singular encounters: mediating the tourist destination in British television holiday programmes. *Tourist Studies* 6, 37–58.

Forsyth, T. (2002) What happened on 'The Beach'? Social movements and governance of tourism in Thailand. *International Journal of Sustainable Development* 5, 326–337.

Frost, W. (2004) Reshaping the destination to fit the film image: Western films and tourism at Lone Pine, California. In: Frost, W., Croy, G. and Beeton, S. (eds) *International Tourism and Media Conference Proceedings, November 24–26, 2004*. Tourism Research Unit, Monash University, Melbourne, Victoria, Australia, pp. 61–68.

Frost, W. (2006) Braveheart-ed Ned Kelly: historic films, heritage tourism and destination image. *Tourism Management* 27, 247–254.

Frost, W. (2009) From backlot to runaway production: exploring location and authenticity in film-induced tourism. *Tourism Review International* 13, 85–92.

Gartner, W.C. (1993) Image formation process. *Journal of Travel and Tourism Marketing* 2, 191–215.

Gibson, S. (2006). A seat with a view: tourism, (im)mobility and the cinematic-travel glance. *Tourist Studies* 6, 157–178.

Grihault, N. (2003) Film tourism: the global picture. *Travel and Tourism Analyst* 5, 1–22.

Heitmann, S. (2010) Film tourism planning and development: questioning the role of stakeholders and sustainability. *Tourism and Hospitality Planning and Development* 7, 31–46.

Houpt, S. (2003) Our next stop will be Frodo's hut. *The Globe and Mail*. Available from: http://www.globeandmail.com/servlet/ArticleNews/printarticle/gam/20030104/RVTRAV. Accessed 23 January, 2004.

Hudson, S. and Ritchie, B. (2006) Promoting destinations via film tourism: an empirical identification of supporting marketing initiatives. *Journal of Travel Research* 44, 387–396.

Iwashita, C. (2006) Media representation of the UK as a destination for Japanese tourists: popular culture and tourism. *Tourist Studies* 6, 59–77.

Jackson, P. (1992) Constructions of culture, representations of race: Edward Curtis's 'way of seeing'. In: Anderson, K. and Gale, F. (eds) *Inventing Places: Studies in Cultural Geography*. Longman Cheshire, Melbourne, Victoria, Australia, pp. 89–106.

Jones, D. and Smith, K. (2005) Middle-earth Meets New Zealand: authenticity and location in the making of *The Lord of the Rings*. *Journal of Management Studies* 42, 923–945.

Karpovich, A.I. (2010) Theoretical approaches to film-motivated tourism. *Tourism and Hospitality Planning and Development* 7, 7–20.

Kim, S (2010) Extraordinary experience: re-enacting and photographing at screen tourism locations. *Tourism and Hospitality Planning and Development* 7, 59–75.

Liebes, T. and Curran, J. (eds) (1998) *Media, Ritual, and Identity*. Routledge, London, UK.

Macionis, N. (2004) Understanding the film-induced tourist. In: Frost, W., Croy, G. and Beeton, S. (eds) *International Tourism and Media Conference Proceedings, November 24–26, 2004*. Tourism Research Unit, Monash University, Melbourne, Victoria, Australia, pp. 86–97.

Macionis, N. and Sparks, B. (2009) Film tourism: an incidental experience. *Tourism Review International* 13, 93–102.

McKercher, B. and du Cros, H. (2003) Testing a cultural tourist typology. *International Journal of Tourism Research* 5, 45–58.

Mercille, J. (2005) Media effects on image: the case of Tibet. *Annals of Tourism Research* 32, 1039–1055.

Mordue, T. (1999) *Heartbeat* country: conflicting values, coinciding visions. *Environment and Planning A* 31, 629–646.

Mordue, T. (2001) Performing and directing resident/tourist cultures in *Heartbeat* country. *Tourist Studies* 1, 233–252.

NFO New Zealand (2003) Lord of the Rings *Market Research Summary Report*. NFO, Wellington, New Zealand.

O'Connor, N., Flanagan, S. and Gilbert, D. (2009) Stakeholders' perspectives of the impacts of film- and television-induced tourism in Yorkshire. *Tourism Review International* 13, 121–127.

Olsberg/SPI (2007) Stately Attraction: *How Film and TV Programmes Promote Tourism in the UK*. Film Council, London, UK.

Riley, R. and Van Doren, C. (1992) Movies as tourism promotion: a push factor in a pull location. *Tourism Management* 13, 267–274.

Riley, R.W., Baker, D. and Van Doren, C.S. (1998) Movie induced tourism. *Annals of Tourism Research* 25, 919–935.

Roesch, S. (2009) *The Experiences of Film Location Tourists*. Channel View Publications, Clevedon, UK.

Rojek, C. (1997) Indexing, dragging and social construction of tourist sights. In: Rojek, C. and Urry, J. (eds) *Touring Cultures – Transformations of Travel and Theory*. Routledge, London, UK, pp. 52–74.

Schofield, P. (1996) Cinematographic images of a city – alternative heritage tourism in Manchester. *Tourism Management* 17, 333–340.

Springwood, C.F. (2002) Farming, dreaming, and playing in Iowa: Japanese mythopoetics and agrarian Utopia. In: Coleman, S. and Crang, M. (eds) *Tourism: Between Place and Performance*. Berghahn, New York, pp. 176–190.

Squire, S.J. (1993) Valuing countryside: reflections on Beatrix Potter tourism. *Area* 25, 5–10.

Sydney-Smith, S. (2006) Changing places: touring the British crime film. *Tourist Studies* 6, 79–94.

Terry-Chandler, F. (2000) Vanished circumstance: Titanic, heritage and film. *International Journal of Heritage Studies* 6, 67–77.

Tighe, A.J. (1986) The arts/tourism partnership. *Journal of Travel Research* 24, 2–5.

Tooke, N. and Baker, M. (1996) Seeing is believing: the effect of film on visitor numbers to screened locations. *Tourism Management* 17, 87–94.

Torchin, L. (2002) Location, location, location. The destination of the Manhattan TV tour. *Tourist Studies* 2, 247–266.

Tzanelli, R. (2004) Constructing the 'cinematic tourist' – the 'sign industry' of *The Lord of the Rings*. *Tourist Studies* 4, 21–42.

Urry, J. (1990) *The Tourist Gaze*. Sage, London, UK.

15 Dark Tourism

Dr Crispin Dale and Neil Robinson

Introduction

The term 'dark tourism' was first coined by Lennon and Foley (1996) to describe the relationship between tourism attractions and an interest in death and the macabre. Others have referred to this activity as 'thanatourism' (Seaton, 1998), 'morbid tourism' (Blom, 2000) and 'blackspots' (Rojek, 1993), with a fascination for visiting places where death has occurred. This chapter aims to explore the concept and practice of dark tourism. It will initially review what is understood by dark tourism before discussing its scope. The chapter is structured around a series of themes that have emerged from the literature. This includes an appraisal of the following aspects of dark tourism: exploring the dark and motivations for visiting sites associated with dark tourism; internationalizing the dark with the Disney-ization and McDonaldization of dark tourism attractions; politicizing the dark and issues concerning propaganda and the communication of political ideology through dark sites; investigating the dark through the concept of cold case reviews and dark tourism vacations; mobilizing the dark and its relationship to the emotional and physical movement of visitors and dark sites/exhibits; and managing the dark concerning environmental, educational and financial issues. The chapter concludes by discussing the future of dark tourism as a vocational and academic activity. Contemporary issues associated with the sociology of death and the manner by which modern society addresses death and dying are also appraised.

Defining the Dark

The origins of the academic debate associated with dark tourism are multilayered from a classical perspective. Dark tourism has a long history and has been described as a 'thanatoptic tradition dating back to the visitation of sites such as the battlefield of Waterloo and the natural disaster of Pompeii' (Seaton, 1998). While often appearing to grow out of the morbid curiosity for death and disasters of the 19th and 20th century, dark tourism has origins much further back in time.

Indeed, as early as the 11th century individuals were visiting locations associated with the darker side of travel, with places such as Jerusalem in the Middle East and more specifically the location of Christ's crucifixion proving popular venues for travellers visiting the Holy Land during the crusades. In more recent years, the Grand Tour (see Chapter 1) was an opportunity for the wealthy and curious to experience Europe. Sites such as the classical ruins of the Coliseum (a death chamber) proved to be a must-see location on the Grand Tour. The fascination with death and indeed mental instability is a curious subject matter and one that was studied at great length by the Victorians. Visits to St. Mary Bethlehem Hospital (aka Bethlem Hospital, Bethlehem Hospital and Bedlam) were common, as were visits to view the clinically insane. This form of dark voyeurism was popular with the wealthy middle class of the Victorian period, tapping into people's mental psyche and reinforcing antiquated beliefs associated with punishment, retribution and death.

© CAB International 2011. *Research Themes for Tourism*
(eds P. Robinson, S. Heitmann and P.U.C. Dieke)

From a typological perspective, dark attractions themselves can be classified into a number of different types, ranging from death sites (e.g. the site of JFK's assassination) to the re-enactment of staged events (e.g. English Civil War re-enactments by the Sealed Knot Society) (Seaton, 1998; Blom, 2000) and prisons (e.g. Alcatraz in San Francisco) (Wilson, 2008). Miles (2002) delineated between dark sites associated *with* and sites *of* death, disaster and depravity. He contrasts between the Auschwitz museum and the USA Holocaust Memorial Museum, Washington DC. The former is where the act of death actually occurred, while the latter is a commemorative museum located a significant distance away. In his analysis, Miles also differentiates between time and spatial factors. He acknowledges that the distance of the remembered event in terms of time and space influences the extent to which the attraction is darker or darkest tourism.

From a thanatological perspective, Stone and Sharpley (2008) chose to move away from the traditional narrative, based around supply, and concentrated more specifically on the consumption of dark tourism. Their research built upon an earlier conceptual paper by Stone (2006) that introduced a typological framework that attempted to theoretically illustrate the differing levels at which dark tourism can be viewed. Stone (2006) attempted to conceptualize the differing components of dark tourism in a light to dark framework. Dark sites were placed in an almost linear-style format, with the commercial-like dark dungeons of Merlin Entertainments at one end (lightest) and sites associated with genocide and mass extermination (darkest) at the other.

One note here is that a typological framework associated with the supply of dark tourism entities is possibly too subjective and tries to compartmentalize such sites into neatly defined segments. Not only do sites appear as fee-paying manifestations of private enterprise, but they also display theme-like commercial characteristics associated with commemoration, education and some questionable levels of authenticity. It is arguably too simplistic to put in order those dark attractions that represent the macabre. In addition, the methodological tools employed to rank those darkest are rarely discussed or explained (e.g. the criteria used, such as visitor numbers, tourist spend, death count at site, level of authenticity, gore value). Such common philosophical observations, as made by Stone (2006) and more importantly as displayed within the light to dark framework, share commonalities with the works of Lennon and Foley (2000). They suggested that many dark sites are 'established institutions like cemeteries and museums' and this is indeed a common trait shared with many of those dark attractions within Stone's (2006) typological framework.

Expanding the debate further, Stone's (2006) conceptual framework does offer the academic community a hook on which to hang its dark cloak. Indeed, while still academically fragile, the study of dark tourism has greatly benefitted from the creation of a light to dark framework as this creates a foothold which researchers can start from and, in some cases, be critical of. From a supplier perspective, Stone correctly set out in some detail the characteristics and traits associated with each of the product types. The framework also establishes a typological viewing frame through which a clearer understanding of supply can be obtained and ultimately the motivations that facilitate consumption.

Exploring the Dark

Although sun, sea and sangria holidays retain their popularity, it is acknowledged that there has been a trend towards alternative tourism experiences of cultures and histories (see Chapter 1) (Robb, 2009). This has precipitated a desire to experience more obscure tourism sites and attractions, with dark tourism being a feature of this. Motivations for visits to dark locations or shrines are themselves complex and disparate, resulting in a multitude of reasons for engagement with the macabre. It is further acknowledged that consumer experiences and motivations for visiting dark tourism sites is an under-researched field (Sharpley and Stone, 2009).

Chapter 3 has discussed the different theories associated with tourist motivation. While the motivations for consuming the dark are complex and multilayered, trying to deconstruct such a phenomenon is challenging. It is further acknowledged that the experience is subjective and will vary from one individual to another with their relationship to the dark tourism site (Robb, 2009). Dunkley (2005) provided a framework for understanding the different reasons and interests for visiting dark tourism sites. These include the following:

- Visiting sites such as cemeteries and grave-sites for contemplation for possibly spiritual and retrospective purposes.
- Thrill and risk seeking in the form of visiting attractions such as the running of the bulls in Pamplona.
- Validation and the confirmation of events that may have happened such as crime, murder or disaster.
- Authenticity and the need to acknowledge the reality of a place's or person's existence.
- Self-discovery and the intrinsic desire to learn.
- Visiting iconic sites that have immortalized key events, for example assassinations (e.g. the Dakota apartments where John Lennon lived) and significant landmarks (e.g. Checkpoint Charlie in Berlin).
- Convenience when an attraction is located in a famous city (e.g. the Coliseum, Rome).
- Morbid curiosity and visiting sites where death or disaster have only recently occurred.
- Pilgrimage for religious purposes (e.g. to Mecca) or to disaster sites (e.g. Ground Zero).
- Remembrance and empathy when visiting, for example, war cemeteries or the clock tower at Old Trafford to acknowledge the Munich plane crash of 1958.

In light of these differing motivations it is also important to note that the basis for grief-based tourists visits to dark sites can be driven by a 'pseudo-relationship' (Stone, 2009a) to the mediatization of the person or event. Yet Stone refuted the notion of moral panic that is often perpetuated by the media and contended that there is merely only 'talk' of panic.

At the heart of the dark tourism consumption debate is the notion that as moral human subjects, few if any who have died have come back to inform us of what death and dying is really like (Lazarus and Jesus not included). For one to pass over and experience the afterlife and return must itself be the ultimate in travel. But with the absence of the authentic or here and now, a visit to a dark site, with all its manifestations of previous dark activities, arguably comes a close second to experiencing the afterlife itself. What is arguably at the heart of the dark tourism debate is the fear of death and mankind's mortality, resulting in wanting to experience, albeit at arm's length, some tangible components of death. It was Woody Allen who famously said, 'I am not afraid of dying, I just don't want to be there when it happens.' This possibly typifies, and goes part way to explaining, the human psyche and its fascination with death. Contemporary history is littered with examples of sites that are associated with death and dying. The next section of this chapter appraises the growth in commercialized dark sites.

Internationalizing the Dark

A growing trend has seen commercial sectors move into the dark forum. The commodification of death (Wilson, 2008) has resulted in leading attraction operators capitalizing upon this form of tourism. While many of these enterprises offer a themed experience, their contribution should not be underestimated. Organizations such as Merlin Entertainments are at the forefront of developing dark tourism products with their portfolio of entertainment like products, which include the 'Dungeon' attractions located in York, London and Edinburgh. These attractions attempt to commodify dark experiences and the visitor is directed through a series of interconnecting rooms to experience and bear witness to hangings, floggings, public executions and the plague. An argument associated with these commercial attractions is that the magnitude of such atrocities or human disaster is often underemphasized or over-commercialized, resulting in the historical context of the loss of life being missed (Robinson and Dale, 2009a).

Many dark tourism attractions replicate aspects of Disneyization (Bryman, 1999) and McDonaldization (Ritzer, 1998) in their approach to presenting death. Disneyization acknowledges that wider society has become increasingly commercialized and orientated towards experiences that draw upon animation and recreation. It manifests itself in everyday life and commodities of consumption (Bryman, 1999). Bryman argued that many components of the tourism industry (e.g. restaurants such as the Hard Rock Café, Planet Hollywood and Rainforest Café) are based on cultural themes, including music, film and ecology. Theming is a marketing device to generate demand and is used as a method within dark tourism attractions. These 'dark fun factories' occupy the lighter edges of Stone's (2006) dark tourism spectrum and are predominately entertainment based. They are highly visual and arguably sensationalize death.

Las Vegas, USA, a city that actively advocates excess, is interlaced with intentionally designed lodgings based around dark themes. Accommodation providers such as the Caesars Palace, Treasure Island, Excalibur and Luxor hotels and casinos – the last with its King Tut Museum and Tomb – all play a fundamental role in the Disneyization of the dark. Caesars Palace delivers a product based upon the splendour of the Roman Empire. Yet its origins are based around the general and dictator of the Roman Republic, Julius Caesar, who created civil war and was later assassinated in a frenzied knife attack. The chronological distance from the past, to a large extent, legitimizes the production and consumption of the attraction. Ethical issues become paramount when mock-ups of real life murder locations are created and promoted as 'a dark-themed lodging experience'.

Ritzer (1998) contended that wider society has replicated the principles of McDonaldization. This includes the drive towards uniformity, commonalities, production and efficiency. Such principles have been replicated in theme parks in the tourism industry through their methods of operation, direction of visitors, queuing systems, merchandising and control systems. McDonaldization is reflected in dark tourism attractions such as the London Dungeon, where viewing is ticket timed, scripting of cast members is the norm and merchandising is available at every opportunity. The contention

is that such systems are fine when presenting fictional events, but become more of a problem when reality is morphed to mirror the construct of a theme. This is the case at Alcatraz, where many of the inmates have been portrayed in a particular manner as depicted by Hollywood. The Bird Man of Alcatraz was made famous by the 1962 Hollywood film of the same name. Actor Burt Lancaster portrays Robert Stroud (the real Bird Man of Alcatraz) as a kind and caring individual, imprisoned by a system that was out to get him. In reality, Stroud was disliked by his fellow prisoners and was an inherently violent person, notwithstanding the fact that he had also committed murder. A key driver is to order and make the attraction consumable for tourists. However, this has the potential to sanitize what is being portrayed (Robb, 2009) and subsequently raises arguments concerning authenticity. Issues of authenticity have been discussed at great length within dark tourism literature (see Lennon and Foley, 2000). Indeed, a key component of the tourism product is the consumption of the authentic, with visitors often remarking on how good or bad each experience is in light of the experience received at each venue. Mimesis, where actors or even tourists act out a part, is not uncommon in these types of attractions (Robb, 2009) – and yet 'live' interpretation is criticized for trivializing the subject matter (Wight, 2006). Citing Walsh, Wight observed that 'dark subject matter in exhibitions lies on the authenticity of form, rather than that of experience'. This can undermine the historical value of the attraction.

Politicizing the Dark

While dark tourism has often been associated with visiting sites akin with death and destruction, such sites should in no way be underestimated as an effective tool in the art of political manipulation, disinformation and propaganda. The word 'propaganda' is associated with the intentional manipulation of information for political purpose (Robinson and Dale, 2009a). Indeed, history is littered with examples where information has been used to actively sell, reinforce or aid a particular political mantra by one collective of individuals against others. This format can take many forms and nowhere is this more prevalent than at certain dark attractions or sites that attempt to rebrand or sell a particular version of events that ties in with the present status quo of a particular regime.

Beech (2000) introduced the notion of de-Nazification and this works well in underpinning the notion of propaganda by political parties. In the case of those concentration camps that were preserved by the Russians at the end of World War II (e.g. Auschwitz in Poland), the Russian leadership may be praised for preserving such sites so that future generations can view the evil that can be perpetrated by political regimes that go unchecked. However, this was not the intended purpose of the Russian authorities. The sole intention was to send a political message to the Russian people and further afield as to the evils of those political ideologies that adopt a non-communist manifesto or advocate a democratic basis of political leadership. It must be remembered that Hitler's political regime grew in strength in part aided by the democracy of the ballot box and the vitriolic political attacks that Hitler aimed at communism. In response, the Russians kept the camps as a reminder of the evils that can be fostered under political systems advocated by Western democracies. It can be argued, therefore, that the real reason for preservations was more politically led than from respect for the dead.

It is important to remember that the Communist political party, under the control of Stalin (a grand master of political skulduggery, subterfuge and propaganda), had for years been involved in propaganda. Stalin extensively used images of children to develop his image as Father of the Nation (many of which can still be seen today) and was not averse to removing the images of his political opponents (as in the case of Nikolai Yezhov, who Stalin had executed and was later airbrushed from a picture of them together). Looking into the historical past, a number of dark attractions employ differing levels of propaganda in an attempt to advance a political doctrine, message or viewpoint. In some cases these messages are justifiably correct, whereas others have skewed history around a particular ideology. It is only when history is looked into that we see the full extent to which propaganda is used. The use of propaganda at dark sites shows how visitor perception can be easily managed, with some components of history being displayed in a particular way so as to influence opinion. This is illustrated by Case Studies 15.1 and 15.2.

Investigating the Dark

The development of dark tourism has evolved much over recent years with the growth of niches, which are derivatives of the original dark tourism concept. One such niche area that has yet to be fully discussed in the literature is that associated with visiting murder sites. This genre of dark tourism exploits a popular fascination for people to explore the circumstances surrounding premeditated death,

---

Case Study 15.1. Cyprus (Nicosia).

Two dark attractions based in Nicosia, Republic of Cyprus, are themed around dark history, pre independence from Britain. The first site (the National Struggle Museum) contains information and artefacts relating to the National Liberation (The Cyprus Emergency) between 1955 and 1959 with the purpose of removing British rule. The second dark attraction is the Central Jail of Nicosia. The jail contains the graves of 13 members of the EOKA (National Organization of Cypriot Fighters), nine of who were hanged by the British. Today, the cemetery, cells and gallows are a museum. The jail is still used as a penal institution.

It can be argued that both sites follow a pronationalist political agenda. There might be sympathy with the executed fighters and the harsh measures implemented by the British in an attempt to minimize the impact of the conflict. However, little is made of those individuals, including approximately 371 British troops and innocent civilians (including Greek and Turkish Cypriots) (Carter, 2005), murdered by those sympathetic to the EOKA. Independence was granted in 1960.

Case Study 15.2. North Korea.

North Korea is an example of where political doctrines associated with communism are played out to the full. Many of the country's inhabitants live a meagre existence, in part due to political isolation, sanctions and mismanagement by the communist political dynasty. The political message, however, is one of harmony and happiness, where all children are cared for and the Communist system cares for all its inhabitants. Every part of a tourist visit is therefore tightly controlled (tourist numbers to North Korea are low and a visa is required). The reality is that North Korea has high child mortality rates, an ageing infrastructure and limited opportunities for its inhabitants.

The representation of aggression is played out on the border between North and South Korea, where representatives of the opposing sides (i.e. soldiers) display loyalty to their chosen political ideology. This manifests itself in the physical stance of the soldiers on duty, heavy surveillance akin to that of Orwell's Big Brother and the use of imagery in an attempt to justify a particular viewpoint.

namely the act of murder itself and the concept of the cold case review. Over recent years the media have been responsible for creating interest in areas related to detection and crime solving, which would normally have fallen under the media radar. The constant appeal of detective programmes on television demonstrates the interest of people in understanding the mystery of crime. Indeed, the success of shows such as *Crimewatch*, *Cold Case*, *Cracker*, *Sensing Murder*, *CSI (Crime Scene Investigation)*, *Criminal Minds* and so on has fuelled the appetite for this kind of subject matter – although it may be contended that the portrayal of crime in such programmes is increasingly sensationalized and has blurred fantasy with reality.

One philosophical viewpoint that has attempted to address those lesser-researched areas of dark tourism is that of Gibson (2008). Gibson's discussion of the relationship between serial murder and the American tourism industry is in itself seminal, in so much that it correctly identifies the juxtaposition that exists between the negative ramifications of serial murders in a geographical setting or population and the huge interest often expressed by visiting tourists, resulting in high demand for traditional hospitality services (e.g. board, lodging, souvenirs, photo opportunities).

Gibson (2008) starts his discussion by looking at the phenomena of serial killers in the context of the USA and comments that 'serial murder has become more frequent in recent years and offenders tend to kill larger number of victims'. He goes on to appraise the notion of dark tourism and thanatourism (terms that he uses interchangeably) with reference

to traditional manifestations of such sites as cemeteries, churchyards and war zones. Such a classification of sites is akin to that detailed by Stone (2006) in his conceptual light to dark framework. Gibson (2008) noted that in the same way that certain genres of dark tourism have resulted in increased academic interest, the same can also be said in relation to those individuals who choose to visit locations associated with serial murder. The main commonality here, and a general consensus held by a number of academics within the dark tourism field, is that death attracts spectators and locations associated with serial murder are in no way different.

Gibson (2008) described the implications that serial murder has on the USA tourism industry and how adverse actions such as the ongoing act of murder on a large scale within a geographical region can have disastrous consequences on the tourism sector. Such actions result in a general pattern of public awareness with reduced consumption of tourism activities, often out of perceived fear associated with the actions of one individual or a small collective of individuals. Such is the paranoia often displayed during such times that people become withdrawn, reluctant to travel or, in a worse-case scenario, call off any planned vacation activities. However, such negative events can themselves act as a catalyst for unplanned money-making ventures for the business savvy and unethical entrepreneur who offers services for those willing to engage in this form of dark voyeurism either during or after the terrible event (examples include Praia da Luz, Portugal, the site of the Madeleine McCann abduction;

Soham in the UK, the site of the abduction and eventual murder of Jessica Chapman and Holly Wells; and Hyde in UK where Dr Harold Shipman committed numerous murders of patients in his care). Such cases have themselves been documented in contemporary history and have been played out extensively within the world's media, all of which probably contributes towards creating demand. In the case of Madeleine McCann, tours of the surrounding locality where the abduction occurred, the apartment where the family were staying at the time of the abduction and the restaurants at which Kate and Gerry McCann (and friends) were dining at during the night of the abduction have all been incorporated in a tour (Watts, 2008).

Continuing on from the notion of contemporary murder sites as possible stablemates with the more traditional forms of dark tourism, Gibson (2008) attempted to re-engineer his observations by interlacing other lines of investigation in an attempt to better explain the fascination of society with death and destruction. One such theoretical construct used by Gibson is that of Seltzer (1998), namely wound culture theory. Wound culture theory works on the premise that violence within society has become a key component of modernity. This often manifests itself in scenes played out at a road accident (the rubber-necking actions of individuals passing the scene) and the public's insatiable appetite with viewing and 'collective gatherings around shock, trauma and the wound' (Seltzer, 1998). Such a notion might in part explain the motivations and actions displayed by consumers who visit the darker parameters of Stone's (2006) model. Continuing further into the world of Seltzer and wound culture theory, it can be noted that the human psyche often harbours a desire to be shocked and actively seeks out the physical manifestations of wounds, both physically and metaphorically. This might go in some way to explain society's growing interest in reality television, a format in which wound culture is developed for all to see. Sites associated with murder offer the visiting tourist opportunities to connect with possible wound appreciation, possibly sharing some commonalities with *Schadenfreude* (pleasure derived from the misfortunes of others).

Tapping into tourists' motivation for experiencing more authentic and real situations, coupled with the continued fascination for solving crime, the cold-case vacation offers an opportunity for the dark tourism industry. In this context, dark tourism has the potential to reinvigorate and create opportunities for solving cold-case crimes. The concept of the cold-case vacation raises a number of ethical issues, not least the sensationalism that such an experience may offer. Indeed, due to the sensitivity of various crimes, issues of interpretation should be uppermost in the minds of dark tourism providers when developing a product of this nature.

Mobilizing the Dark

The mobility paradigm has gained significance within tourism research in recent years (Hannam, 2008). Indeed, Burns and Novelli (2008) noted the argument 'that there is no such thing as tourism: only production, consumption and mobility'. Nevertheless, mobilities are deeply intertwined with the everyday activity of tourism and 'the perpetual movement throughout the world' (Hannam, 2009). Mobilities and their relationship to dark tourism come in different forms. There is the mobility of the tourism experience and the emotional connection that is made between the exhibit and death. Mobility can produce a lack of connection and emotional nearness (Larsen *et al.*, 2006) – although within the context of dark tourism it may be argued that visitors are seeking an emotional connection and to arguably confront the realization of death. There is a recognition that dark sites have the potential to 'mediate between life and death' (Sharpley and Stone, 2009) and in this respect, we are describing the mobility of the experience between life and death. There is an acknowledgment that death is inevitable and the dark exhibit or attraction acts as a point of reference for this experience. Stone (2009b) described this as 'mortality moments'. That is, moments when an individual questions his/her own existence and reconciles the relationship between life and death. According to Stone, the dark tourism site acts as a means for confronting these moments at a perceived 'safe distance'. From a mobility perspective, there is the collapsing of time and space (Harvey, 1990) so that life and death become synonymous in the location where they are being experienced. Metaphorically, and also physically, this involves the 'death of distance' (Cairncross, 1997, cited in Larsen *et al.*, 2006). This is in terms of both memorization of the experience and the physical locality where the experience takes place. The desire to be at the locality where the incident took place is symbolic of the often-mass visitations to disaster sites such as Ground Zero in New York.

Dark tourism is characteristic of a number of Urry's (2002) interdependent mobilities. First is 'physical travel' and the actual movement of people to the dark attraction or exhibit so as satisfy a particular need or desire, as discussed earlier in the chapter. Dark tourism is taken to a different stage when physical travel is driven by the act of observing or participating in death itself. This is probably the most extreme form of dark tourism and takes Stone's (2006) spectrum to a further level of darkness. The observation of public hangings in Iran and North Korea is evidence of the mobilization of people to events of this nature. Visitors go to war sites to experience places where death has taken place. Yet actually joining the forces to go to war can arguably be a dark tourism motive. This is further symbolized in suicide or euthanasia tourism, where people travel to clinics to end their life. This may be motivated by the presence of an incurable illness such as motor neurone disease or multiple sclerosis, which, paradoxically, can render those affected immobile. Dignitas in Switzerland, for example, offers services to those who wish to end their life (Pidd, 2009).

Second is the 'physical movement' of artefacts to and around dark exhibits or attractions. This can be a staged representation (MacCannell, 1973) of the site and its associated artefacts and objects. For example, at Auschwitz the 'Arbeit Macht Frei' ('work will set you free') signage has been relocated to a different position on the tour (Wight, 2006). Wight also noted the reorganization of exhibits to other parts of the site. The original sign has since been stolen and replaced with a replica (Connolly, 2009), further illustrating the mobility of exhibits to satisfy tourist demand.

Another example is the mobility of dark exhibits from other locations to convey a representation of the place. For example, the display of Egyptian mummies at the British Museum has been taken from its original setting in Cairo. Sites of death may also be relocated to a different place; examples include the Titanic exhibition at the Museum of Science and Industry in Manchester, UK, and the Washington Holocaust Museum in Washington DC, USA.

Third is 'imaginative travel' where there is the potential for hyperreal experiences through the representation of the dark exhibit. In this respect, there can be mobilities of memorization through the validation of an experience that has happened. In the concentration camps of World War II there was mass mobilization of people, often to their deaths. In stark contrast there is now the mobilization of tourists to experience what it must have been like in the camps. Tourists experience, through the re-creation and imagination, the actual mobility of the death camp. This is developed through walking tours and visualization techniques such as television displays and verbal presentations by guides. This generates representations of a place in the minds of visitor through mobile memories.

The fixed exhibit displays of many dark sites, when the flow of people and objects is likely to be moveable, rely on visitors to mobilize their memories and imagination in forming a representation of the place. Knox (2006) illustrated the example of Glencoe in Scotland, where war that is not connected with contemporary life can still have significance to the representation of a place in the visitor's mind. However, as discussed earlier, these can be misrepresentations that politicize places and fail to acknowledge the role of propaganda (Hughes, 2008). The imagination is further mobilized through the adoption of myths and mythical characters at dark tourism sites. Examples include re-creations of events such as the Jack the Ripper tours in London, which give visitors an experience that takes them back in time. Wilson (2008) also conveyed the notion of 'celebrity prisoners', such as Chopper Read, at prison sites in Australia. Such experiences require careful management and the following section discusses these issues in further detail.

Managing the Dark

Managing any dark experience is fundamental to creating a positive outcome for all stakeholders. The management of dark tourism sites and attractions is obviously important, but to what extent should they be managed differently? As the above discussion has noted, issues of commercialization and interpretation of dark tourism exhibits can impact upon visitor experiences. The management of dark tourism is therefore essential in delivering a balance between the ethical portrayal of the exhibit while enabling visitor satisfaction at an intrinsic level. In doing so, the following criteria should be taken into consideration: acceptability, suitability and ethics of display.

Acceptability relates to the nature of the subject matter being presented. The commodification of death, and its presentation as an attraction, maybe perceived by some as unacceptable. What is morally acceptable to some may be inapprehensible to others. In this respect, different consumers will have differing thresholds of acceptability and the attraction will need to manage this. In addition, there are cultural dimensions to what is deemed acceptable. Examples include the decision not to show pictures of the 'jumpers' (individuals who jumped from the Twin Towers) in some of the 9/11 exhibitions, and the Body Works exhibition that displays anatomical exhibits post death (albeit with the permission of the deceased, pre death).

Suitability refers to the nature of the dark site or activity that is being presented. Indeed, question marks pertain when the commercialization of dark sites is based upon the immediacy of a particular event. This was apparent with the media reaction towards the creation of tours documenting the fatal crash of Princess Diana in Paris (Schofield, 1998) and the disappearance of British child Madeleine McCann in Portugal (Watts, 2008). As mentioned previously, issues concerning elapsing of time and the scale and intensity of the event in the human consciousness are, to some extent, significant when understanding the suitability of a dark attraction or exhibit.

The ethics of display concerns the moral impact that an attraction or exhibit may impose upon an individual or group. The morality debate surrounding dark tourism has been discussed extensively by Stone (2009b). He has acknowledged the negation of religion and individualization and moral confusion in society as factors influencing the moral reasoning for visiting dark sites. He has further argued that a 'collective constitution' and individualized embodiment can arise from such visits, thus resulting in the questioning of morality and ethics in society. Nevertheless, the ethics of display are bought into question when dark attractions become packaged alongside stag excursions (e.g. http://www.lastnightoffreed om.co.uk/stag-packages/krakow/auschwitz-ex perience-weekend). From a management perspective, the ethics of an attraction require sensitivity and appropriate interpretation.

It is acknowledged that each of these criteria is based upon a value judgement and is also influenced by supply and demand factors. Indeed, further to these criteria are issues concerning the generic management of the attraction. This can be analysed from three different, yet interrelated perspectives: the financial model, the environmental model and the educational model.

The financial model is geared towards the overall success and profitability of the attraction. This involves the development of a 'darsumer' market, a term used to describe consumers of dark tourism products that commercialized operators attempt to retain through marketing processes (Robinson and Dale, 2009b). This includes promotional activities and relationship building with customers to encourage brand loyalty and repeat visits. This latter point is pertinent when a themed attraction provider offers dark attractions at multiple locations. Indeed, as mentioned earlier, Merlin Entertainments is at the forefront of developing dark tourism products with its portfolio of 'dartainment' products. Dartainment is a term describing dark attractions that attempt to entertain (Robinson and Dale, 2009b). For example, Merlin Entertainments provides its 'Dungeon' themed concept in London, York, Edinburgh, Hamburg and Amsterdam. The imagery that is often used in the promotions of commercialized dark attractions typically uses red and black as a means of representing blood and darkness, respectively.

The environmental model considers issues of preservation, conservation, information and sustainability. Dark sites can be located in properties and areas that require protection. Visitor management is therefore essential to ensure the conservation of the site and its associated exhibits. Dark sites that have increased susceptibility to tourism activity are those in natural settings such as battlefields (e.g. the Somme, France) and those of historical origin, such as monuments and buildings (e.g. the Coliseum, Rome). The management of visitors is essential so as to minimize the potential impact on the attraction and environment.

The inevitability of queuing where visitor numbers have exceeded capacity can impact upon the tolerance levels of visitors. This is an important factor as the emotions of visitors may be heightened due to feelings of anxiety, fear and excitement, depending upon the nature of the dark attraction being visited. Effective visitor management strategies are required to minimize dissatisfaction. This may come in the form of shortening the length of queues through the use of advanced or timed ticketing, or altering the perceived entry time by posting likely waiting times. Actors can also be used to entertain queuing visitors as a means of distraction, as played out extensively at the London Dungeons.

The educational model acknowledges the balance between informing the visitor about what is being portrayed while also engaging them with the attraction or exhibit. This encompasses the 'edutainment' debate and the extent to which dark attractions and exhibits should offer an element of entertainment. The basis for the attraction or exhibit is key to understanding the level of entertainment value that is required. The themed 'fun factories' that occupy the lighter edges of Stone's (2006) spectrum require a level of entertainment that stimulates the reason for attending. On the other hand, darker yet still commercialized attractions require a sufficient level of educational matter so as to inform, but not offend, the visitor. This can be a challenging balance to meet, in so far as the presentation of the dark requires consideration of many different stakeholders. For example, those who were involved or had family members involved in the 9/11 terrorist attack on the World Trade Centre are likely to have a different view on the portrayal of a memorial museum than someone who had no direct relationship to the event. Providers of dark attractions must acknowledge the level of influence (Mendelow, 1991) of each stakeholder and stakeholder group when determining the portrayal and interpretation of attractions and exhibits.

Interpretation techniques are important for facilitating the understanding of attractions and can be based upon personal and non-personal techniques. Personal techniques include interpretation through guided walks, talks and presentations (e.g. the Dearly Departed Tours of Hollywood) and reconstruction of the past and events through role-play (e.g. ghost tours). Non-personal techniques include no third-party involvement, but rather the use of audiovisual displays, signage and self-guided tours (e.g. International Slavery Museum, Liverpool, UK). As mentioned earlier in the chapter, interpretation techniques are challenged when attractions attempt to glamorize and sanitize past events (Robb, 2009). Furthermore, to what extent should visitors be given the scope to make their own interpretations about the attraction? This discussion has already referred to imaginative travel as a means of mobilizing the past. It may also be argued that dark attractions have a purpose to inform how a better future can be developed by paying attention to the lessons of the past. This is the case of the Anne Frank Museum in Amsterdam, which raises issues related to nationalism and racism.

Future Research

While much of the established dark tourism literature discusses issues associated with supply and demand, visitor motivations and classification of sites, many authors have chosen to shy away from areas on the periphery of the dark spectrum, namely those with voyeuristic tendencies. Indeed, what should we say of those 'voyeurs' who possibly fall outside the parameters of both the Lennon and Foley (2000) and Stone (2006) models. Accounting for these so-called 'deviant' types (Lisle, 2007) is one area where contemporary research is lacking. A future development for the dark tourism genre might be further fragmentation into a number of subcomponents. The term 'dark tourism' is possibly too general for a subject matter that is by definition multilayered and complex. The early pioneers who have attempted to shed light on this subject matter should themselves be applauded. The dark-to-light framework does offer some attempt to classify or scale the dark tourism phenomena. In the same way that Jafari and Ritchie (1981) subdivided the differing components of tourism on a wheel, it can be argued that dark tourism is too generic a term and does not sufficiently cover all of the differing areas. A future challenge for the academic community is to develop a more extensive table of dark tourism with its differing subcomponents. This will allow a better understanding and mapping of the multidimensional themes associated with dark tourism. One possible starting point is a 'periodic table of dark matter' (Robinson and Dale, 2010). Although very much at embryonic stage, this table offers greater latitude to better map the numerous manifestations of dark tourism subject matter.

Conclusion

This chapter has reviewed a number of thematic directions that have evolved from the field and on which further research could be conducted. Although the ethics of dark tourism will inevitably be questioned, it may evolve from a niche to mass form of tourism. This, to some extent, is already occurring through the Disneyization and McDonaldization of dark

attractions, as discussed in this chapter. The multitude of motivations for visiting dark attractions and exhibits has the potential to exploit the sector further. The challenge for operators of these attractions and exhibits is their ethical and sustainable portrayal. Future management initiatives such as an ethical checklist of things to do and not to do when portraying or visiting a dark attraction may be a way forward in this respect. What is assured is that fascination with dark tourism, as both an area of research, and as a visitor activity, will continue to grow.

Review Questions

1. To what extent do Dunkley's reasons and interests encapsulate the full range of motivations for visiting a dark attraction or exhibit? Consider other potential reasons for visiting a dark tourism attraction or exhibit and illustrate this with examples.
2. Give examples of dark tourism attractions that have embraced the principles of Disneyization and McDonaldization. How have these principles manifested themselves in the attractions?
3. Discuss to what extent dark tourism attractions should be managed differently from other visitor attractions. In the context of dark tourism, when interpreting the past, to what extent is it appropriate to manipulate images and information? Explore dark tourism exhibits and attractions where this has occurred and evaluate the appropriateness of this.
4. Discuss, from an ethical perspective, some of the issues associated with participating in a Jack the Ripper tour.

References

Beech, J. (2000) The enigma of Holocaust sites as tourist attractions – the case of Buchenwald. *Managing Leisure* 5, 29–41.

Blom, T. (2000) Morbid tourism – a postmodern market niche with an example from Althorp. *Norwegian Journal of Geography* 54, 29–36.

Bryman, A. (1999) The Disneyization of society. *The Sociological Review* 47, 25–47.

Burns, P. and Novelli, M. (eds) (2008) Introduction. In: Burns, P. and Novelli, M. (eds) *Tourism and Mobilities: Local-Global Connections*. CAB International, Wallingford, UK, p. xxvi.

Carter, A. (2005) Nicosia's Murder Mile. Available from: http://www.britains-smallwars.com/cyprus. Accessed February 1, 2010.

Connolly, K. (2009) Poland declares state of emergency after 'Arbeit Macht Frei' stolen from Auschwitz. *The Guardian*, 19 December.

Dunkley, R. (2005) Dark tourism – cashing in on tragedy? Tourism Society Seminar Event. Kensington Close Hotel, London, October 17, 2005.

Gibson, D. (2008) The relationship between serial murder and the American tourism industry. *Journal of Travel and Tourism Marketing* 20, 45–60.

Hannam, K. (2008) Tourism geographies, tourist studies and the turn towards mobilities. *Geography Compass* 2/1, 127–139.

Hannam, K. (2009) The end of tourism? Nomadology and the mobilities paradigm. In: Tribe, J. (ed.) *Philosophical Issues in Tourism*. Channel View Publications, Clevedon, UK, pp. 101–113.

Harvey, D. (1990) *The Condition of Postmodernity: An Enquiry into the Origins of Cultural Change*. Blackwell, Cambridge, Massachusetts, USA.

Hughes, R. (2008) Dutiful tourism: encountering the Cambodian genocide. *Asia Pacific Viewpoint* 49, 318–330.

Jafari, J. and Ritchie, J.R.B. (1981) Toward a framework for tourism education: problems and prospects. *Annals of Tourism Research* 8, 13–34.

Knox, D. (2006) The sacralised landscapes of Glencoe: from massacre to mass tourism, and back again, *International Journal of Tourism Research* 8, 185–197

Larsen, J., Urry, J. and Axhausen, K. (2006) *Mobilities, Networks, Geographies*. Ashgate Publishing, Farnham, UK.

Lennon, J. and Foley, M. (1996) JFK and dark tourism: a fascination with assassination. *International Journal of Heritage Studies* 2, 198–211.

Lennon, J. and Foley, M. (2000) *Dark Tourism – The Attraction of Death and Disaster*. Continuum, London, UK.

Lisle, D. (2007) Defending voyeurism: dark tourism and the problem of global security. In: Burns, P. and Novelli, M. (eds) *Tourism and Politics: Global Frameworks and Local Realities*. Elsevier, Oxford, UK, pp. 333–346.

MacCannell, D. (1973) Staged authenticity of social spaces in tourist settings. *The American Journal of Sociology* 79, 589–603.

Mendelow, A. (1991) *Stakeholder Mapping*. Proceedings of the Second International Conference on Information Systems, Cambridge, Massachusetts, USA.

Miles, W.F.S. (2002) Auschwitz: museum interpretation and darker tourism. *Annals of Tourism Research* 29, 1175–1178.

Pidd, H. (2009) Suicide tourism leads Swiss to consider ban on assisted dying. *The Guardian*, 29 October.

Ritzer, G. (1998) *The McDonaldization Thesis*. Sage Publications, Beverly Hills, California.

Robb, E.M. (2009) Violence and recreation: vacationing in the realm of dark tourism. *Anthropology and Humanism* 34, 51–60.

Robinson, N. and Dale, C. (2009a) Politicising the Dark. Dark tourism lecture, University of Salford, Salford, UK.

Robinson, N. and Dale, C. (2009b) Wanted man: A conceptual review of the role of dark tourism in facilitating the exploration of unsolved cold case murders, Paper presented at the Tourism Experiences: Meanings, Motivations, Behaviours conference. University of Central Lancashire, Preston, UK.

Robinson, N. and Dale, C. (2010) Introducing the Dark. Dark tourism lecture. University of Salford, Salford, UK.

Rojek, C. (1993) *Ways of Escape*. Macmillian, London, UK.

Schofield, H. (1998) Europe anger at Diana tour. BBC News Online. Available from: http://news.bbc.co.uk/1/hi/world/europe/150674.stm. Accessed March 1, 2010.

Seaton, A.V. (1998) Guided by the dark: from thanatopsis to thanatourism. *International Journal of Heritage Studies* 2, 234–244.

Seltzer, M. (1998) *Serial Killers: Death and Life in America's Wound Culture*. Routledge, New York, NY.

Sharpley, R. and Stone. P.R. (eds) (2009) *The Darker Side of Travel: The Theory and Practice of Dark Tourism*. Channel View Publications, Clevedon, UK, pp. 23–38.

Stone, P. (2006) A dark tourism spectrum: towards a typology of death and macabre related tourist sites, attractions and exhibitions. *Tourism: An International Interdisciplinary Journal* 54, 445–460.

Stone, P. (2009a) Making absent death present: consuming dark tourism in contemporary society. In: Sharpley, R. and Stone. P.R. (eds) *The Darker Side of Travel: The Theory and Practice of Dark Tourism.* Channel View Publications, Clevedon, UK, pp. 23–38.

Stone, P. (2009b) Dark tourism: morality and new moral spaces. In: Sharpley, R. and Stone. P.R. (eds) *The Darker Side of Travel: The Theory and Practice of Dark Tourism.* Channel View Publications, Clevedon, UK, 56–74.

Stone, P. and Sharpley, R. (2008) Consuming dark tourism: a thanatological perspective. *Annals of Tourism Research* 35, 574–595.

Urry, J. (2002) Mobility and proximity. *Sociology* 36, 255–274.

Watts (2008) Madeleine Tourists 'Should Be Ashamed'. Sky News Online. Available At http://news.sky.com/skynews/Home/Sky-News-Archive/Article/20080641314705. Accessed December 14, 2009.

Wight, C. (2006) Philosophical and methodological praxes in dark tourism: controversy, contention and the evolving paradigm. *Journal of Vacation Marketing* 12, 119–129

Wilson, J.Z. (2008) *Prison: Cultural Memory and Dark Tourism.* Peter Lang, New York, USA.

16 LGBT Tourism

Carol Southall and Dr Paul Fallon

Introduction

Like many forms of what are generally described contemporarily as niche tourism products (e.g. consider also dark tourism, film tourism and faith tourism) lesbian, gay, bisexual and trans-gendered (LGBT) tourism is essentially nothing new. Its origins are commonly dated back to the Grand Tour at least, but may even pre-date this form of tourism. Readers will probably be more familiar with the term 'gay tourism', which is commonplace in the existing academic litera-ture, although the term 'gay' technically refers to a narrower market of gay men and lesbians. 'Gay tourism' is in fact often used in a wider, more generic sense as a surrogate for LGBT tourism, which may reflect that 'gay tourism' is a more recognizable or user-friendly term. Admittedly, the use of the term 'gay tourism' in the academic tourism literature is appropriate since its focus to date has been on gay and lesbian travel (i.e. tourism related to homosexual men and women) (Hughes, 2006).

Consequently, it is necessary to explain the preference for the use of the term 'LGBT tourism' in this chapter, despite the fact that much of the content is limited to gay and lesbian travel because of the lack of literature relating to bisexual and transgendered travel (Hughes, 2006). First, a number of key organ-izations within the industry explicitly acknow-ledge this more inclusive concept in describing their activities. For example, the mission of InterPride – the international association of Pride festival organizers – is to 'promote Lesbian, Gay, Bisexual and Transgender Pride on an international level, to increase network-ing and communication among Pride organ-izations and to encourage diverse communities to hold and attend Pride events and to act as a source of education' (InterPride, 2010). Similarly, the International Gay and Lesbian Travel Association (IGLTA) identifies itself as 'the leading global organization dedicated to connecting businesses in the LGBT tourism industry' (IGLTA, 2010). Such wider inclusive acknowledgement of the LGBT community is not restricted to tourism. For example, in 2009 President Barack Obama proclaimed June to be LGBT month in the USA; this followed Bill Clinton's proclamation of June as Gay and Lesbian Pride Month in 2000. It should be noted that June represents a significant month in the LGBT calendar since the Stonewall riots took place in Greenwich Village in 1969, which resulted in the first Pride marches in the USA in 1970. The second main reason for the wider focus is directly related to the theme of this book. Given the lack of literature on bisexual and transgendered travel, it is expected that this approach will provide readers with a stronger platform from which to debate and research wider issues – including the use of the terms 'gay' and 'LGBT' tourism, if appropriate – than is currently the case.

The significance of LGBT tourism is in-creasing, with more and more destinations and businesses looking to target LGBT travellers. LGBT travel now represents a market that was estimated to be worth US$76.5 billion in 2006 (Out Now, 2010). The purpose of this chapter is therefore to summarize the 'story' of the LGBT tourism phenomenon to date and encourage readers to take the 'story' forward, for example by means of debate and further research. This picks up the baton already passed on by Hughes (2006), who explained in his book *Pink Tourism: Holidays of Gay Men and Lesbians*:

> gay and lesbian tourism should be of interest and concern to more than merely commercial suppliers or market researchers. Holidays are opportunities for many gays and lesbians to 'make sense' of their lives. Hopefully, this book will stimulate others to undertake further investigations of this important field.

Given the overarching tourism theme of this book, it is suggested that readers contextualize LGBT tourism within existing tourism frameworks with which they are familiar in order to stimulate initial debate and then use this to develop issues and ideas for further research. This should enable readers to consider more eclectic issues, perspectives and sources as relevant, since the majority of tourism frameworks are inherently multidisciplinary (Hughes, 2006).

A Growing 'Niche'

It is becoming increasingly apparent as we move into a new decade that LGBT tourism represents a significant, growing and increasingly diverse and global formal tourism phenomenon. This point is illustrated by a relatively few statistics and developments (the fact that these are mainly related to gay tourism may be indicative of the lack of information relating to bisexuals and transgendered people's travel or the ongoing use of the term 'gay tourism' to refer to LGBT tourism):

- The total buying power of the USA LGBT population in 2006 was estimated to be US$641 billion (an increase of 5% from 2005) – it was estimated to exceed US$800 billion by 2008. This buying power is similar to that of African-Americans in the USA (Pink Advertising, 2010).
- In 2003, it was estimated that the value of the LGBT tourism economy was worth approximately $140 billion (Tebje, 2004).
- In the USA, more gay and lesbian travellers hold valid passports than the overall American public – 88% of gay men and 57% of lesbians in comparison to 29% of the overall American public (The Travel Institute, 2010).

- Many National Tourist Boards now have a dedicated 'gay' section on their websites. For example, VisitBritain uses 'GayBritain' to offer current updates regarding events and festivals, gay cities and gay history and culture. It is estimated that gay and lesbian people living in the UK spent a total of £4.7 billion on leisure travel in 2007 (Out Now, 2010) – approximately twice the value of the UK cruise market (Powell, 2010).
- In 2005, Go Pink China became the first China-based travel company to offer gay-friendly tours. Primarily Western clients are offered city tours of Beijing, Shanghai and Xi'an and customized adventure trips to the Silk Road, Yunnan, Sichuan and elsewhere. Sightseeing is enlivened with 'insider stories about gay empires, gay affairs in the Forbidden City and the gay history of China.' Go Pink had 100 clients in 2006 and approximately 300 in 2007 (Moxley, 2008).
- The Gay Days 2009 travel expo attracted more than 13,000 attendees (Gay Days, 2010).
- The 2008 World Travel Market in London included an 'Out Now Gay Marketing Masterclass' given by Ian Johnson, CEO of Out Now. In his presentation, Johnson referred to the £47.2 million spent on gay honeymoons in 2007, with more than 8,700 couples entering into civil partnerships and each couple spending more than £5,000 on average on their honeymoon.
- The first book specifically covering the marketing of gay and lesbian tourism – *Gay and Lesbian Tourism Marketing: The Essential Guide for Marketing* by Jeff Guaracino – was published in 2007.
- Up to 350 Pride events take place across the globe annually – 2010 will see the first all-gay overnight cruise at the Amsterdam Gay Pride festival.
- The 1999 Sydney Gay and Lesbian Mardi Gras attracted almost 750,000 visitors, including more international tourists than other Australian annual events (Markwell, 2002).
- The inaugural International Gay Games held in San Francisco in 1982 attracted 1350

athletes of 12 different nationalities, while the 2002 Games held in Sydney attracted 11,000 athletes (Waitt and Markwell, 2006).

- Notions of gay couples as 'DINKs' ('double income, no kids') are inaccurate – surveys show that significant numbers of gay and lesbian households include children (Hughes, 2006), for example from previous relationships and/or conceived or adopted in existing ones. This represents a significant opportunity for the development of more family-oriented products and services.

In addition to emphasizing the size and value of the LGBT travel market, these data also emphasize the development of a LGBT tourism industry along similar lines to that of the wider tourism industry, for example in terms of the contribution and development of distribution, destinations, attractions, events and new products. Significantly, and although admittedly selective, the facts and figures also indicate that the development of LGBT tourism has been mainly Western-centric to date, notwithstanding the growth of active LGBT communities around the world.

Understanding LGBT Tourism

One of the most common frameworks for understanding tourism generally is the systems approach (e.g. Leiper, 1979; Mill and Morrison, 2001). Within this approach, the complex, dynamic and multidimensional nature of tourism and its inter-related parts – including consumers, service providers and environments (e.g. PESTEL: political, economic, sociocultural, technological, environmental and legal) – can be more fully considered. Weaver and Opperman (2000) acknowledged this systemic nature in their formal definition of tourism as 'the sum of the phenomena and relationships arising from the interaction among tourists, business suppliers, host governments, communities, origin governmental organizations, in the process of attracting, transporting, hosting and managing these tourists and other visitors'. This summary is beneficial to both practitioners and academics alike, especially in terms of encouraging more holistic thinking related to both inputs and outputs of tourism development, as well as multiple stakeholder perspectives.

Consequently, this chapter advocates, albeit mainly on an implicit rather than an explicit basis, the adoption of a systemic approach to the study of LGBT tourism, emphasizing that consideration needs to be given not only to the LGBT market and the LGBT tourism industry, but also to the broader tourism industry and wider PESTEL environments, especially those of a political, sociocultural, legal and economic nature. Furthermore, this framework enables not only drivers for but also barriers to the development of LGBT travel in different parts of the system to be identified and understood. As an example of this, it should be remembered that the 'celebration' of LGBT tourism that exists in some parts of the world is not necessarily one that is yet shared globally. A 2010 report on state-sponsored homophobia cited 76 countries in which homosexual acts are illegal and a further three countries where the legal status of homosexual acts is unclear (Ottosson, 2010). Homosexuality is punishable by the death penalty in a further five countries and in parts of a further two countries. Responses to this approach have subsequently been made in more liberated tourist-generating regions, with the UK's Foreign and Commonwealth Office offering guidance and travel tips for travellers to such destinations in order avoid problems.

A fundamental question relating to the study of LGBT tourism is 'what is LGBT tourism?' The answer to this question enables relevant research issues such as the size, value, impacts and future of the phenomenon, as well as operational research issues relating to populations and sampling, to be considered accurately. In an attempt to offer the reader a definition that acknowledges the complex and multifaceted nature of LGBT tourism, reflecting its systemic nature, but that also provides a relatively simple mechanism to understand the phenomenon and inform further study, we propose the following definition:

> LGBT tourism may be broadly defined as any tourism activity, either specifically designed to attract the LGBT (lesbian, gay, bisexual and transgendered) market, or one that, by nature and/or design, appeals to and is ultimately

pursued by the LGBT market. The interaction between the suppliers, managers, facilitators and consumers of the LGBT tourism product and service, and their subsequent relationship, is an integral part of the concept.

The term 'gay tourism' is sometimes used in a more generic way to refer to LGBT tourism. Readers should also note the use of other terms to refer to the phenomenon. For example, Hughes (2006) noted the use of 'pink tourism', reflecting the initial use of pink triangles to denote gay men in concentration camps in Nazi Germany and its more recent employment as a symbol of community. Tebje (2004) identified that in South Africa the term 'queer tourism' is used to describe LGBT tourism, emphasizing that regional differences may also need to be taken into consideration. Graham's (2002) delineation into subcategories emphasizes not only the multidimensional nature of gay and lesbian travel, but also acknowledges its evolution over time:

- Homosexual tourism – this represents a relatively narrow focus on travel for the purposes of enjoying more sensual and sexual freedom than one would be able to at home. This is exemplified by travel by homosexual males from Northern Europe to the Mediterranean in the 18th century.
- Gay tourism – this is a more recent and broader phenomenon which acknowledges gays and lesbians as well as their interactions with wider 'social, cultural, economic, political and health dimensions of life'. It centres on gay and lesbian enclaves – mainly but not exclusively urban areas in Euro-American countries – and events, including Pride festivals.
- Queer tourism – this more specifically encompasses the gay and lesbian histories that are co-present, but often hidden, at places and in events. Such histories are ubiquitous – for example, and as already acknowledged, Go Pink China tour guides enliven their tours with 'insider stories about gay empires, gay affairs in the Forbidden City and the gay history of China.'

To date, the academic tourism literature has focused almost exclusively on the gay and lesbian traveller aspects of LGBT tourism, and

has also emphasized gay males more than lesbians. Consequently, the bisexual and trans-gendered aspects of LGBT tourism have largely been ignored. Some tourism issues related to bisexual and transgendered people have been considered in non-tourism journals – for example, Padilla (2008) considered the relationship between tourism and the bisexual behaviour of male sex workers in the Dominican Republic outside of the tourism-specific literature. Therefore, readers interested in these aspects are encouraged to carry out a broader investigation of literature to inform their studies.

The History of LGBT Tourism

The significant development within LGBT tourism relates to the commercial recognition of the 'gay travel market' and the subsequent development of the formal gay tourism industry from the 1970s onwards. Understandably, one of the main drivers for this recognition is economic, essentially based on market characterizations – initially among gay men – of high income, high travel propensity and high travel spend (Hughes, 2002, 2004). However, commerce is not the only driver for the development of LGBT tourism, and other forces – especially those related to political, legal and social change – have also played key roles, emphasizing that the market needs to be considered within broader non-commercial societal developments, including changes in attitudes, behaviour and regulation by various communities.

It was not until the 1990s that the concept of gay tourism became incorporated into mainstream tourism provision. This hesitancy was not because there was no market; indeed, on the contrary many tour operators and destinations were fully aware of the market potential. Their fear, however, was that catering for the gay community would lead to a boycott of their products by their existing clientele. For example, in the USA, general targeting of the gay market started in the late 1970s, but slowed down with the emergence of AIDS (Becker, 2006). In 1992, however, presidential candidate Bill Clinton hired an advertising and PR firm specializing in reaching the gay and lesbian community to help him get the gay vote. This represented a turning point from which there has been no looking back.

While commercial acknowledgement is more recent, gay tourism itself dates back much further than may be expected. The Grand Tour, for example, taken by men of nobility in the Victorian era, involved not only cultural education but also, for some men, afforded the opportunity to more freely express their sexuality in societies where homosexuality was more accepted than in the UK (Clift *el al.*, 2002). As already noted, Graham (2002) referred to this form of tourism, therefore, as 'homosexual tourism'. This exploration of sexuality as an unwritten yet prevalent aspect of the Grand Tour was also explored by Littlewood (2001), who said that 'the erotic opportunities of the Grand Tour were homosexual as well as heterosexual.' The idea of freedom of expression of sexuality has been a recurrent theme throughout history and arguably it is no less prevalent or pertinent in an exploration of today's tourism industry in an 'enlightened world', than it was over 100 years ago. Undoubtedly, gay tourism represented an elite activity until the latter part of the 20th century (Clift *el al.*, 2002) when the gay neighbourhoods, or 'gaybourhoods', which were formed as a result of de-industrialization, became attractions and consequently tourist destinations in their own right. Examples of such destinations include the Castro area of San Francisco, Canal Street in Manchester, Greenwich Village in New York, 'Le Village' in Montreal and Le Marais in Paris.

Greenwich Village in New York not only represents a key site in the history of LGBT tourism, but also emphasizes the need to understand the wider environmental context in which the phenomenon has developed. The Stonewall Riots of 28 June 1969, which took place in the Village, were a definitive series of events that marked the start of the gay rights movement in the USA and around the world. At the time, it was common for police to raid bars that were known to be frequented by the LGBT community under the pretext of checking alcohol or liquor licences (Carter, 2004). The reality was that many people were arrested without good reason and their names published in newspapers, causing them to lose their jobs. A police raid on the gay bar the Stonewall Inn in Greenwich Village caused a violent reaction in which the LGBT community, long persecuted and marginalized for their lifestyle, fought against persecution (New York Area Bisexual Network, 2010). A year later on 28 June 1970, the first Gay Pride marches took place in New York, Chicago and Los Angeles to commemorate the anniversary of the riots. These initial marches have now blossomed into more than 350 Pride events that will be held worldwide in 2010, including the first ever march in Jamaica in April 2010 (D. Mills, Vice President for Member Services, InterPride; personal communication, 9 April 2010). Furthermore, the increased visibility of LGBT communities has resulted in part from the staging of Pride events worldwide, while these lucrative events attract tourists and have reinforced recognition of the increasing economic value of the LGBT community.

A more recent development for LGBT tourism has been the shift towards the more inclusive term of 'LGBT' and away from the term 'gay' as a generic for these communities. This reflects a wider shift in usage. For example, in 2009 President Barack Obama – following a precedent set by Bill Clinton in 2000 – proclaimed June to be LGBT month in the USA. This shift has undoubtedly been influenced by the work of groups such as the New York-based Bisexual Political Action Committee, which succeeded in renaming Pride events being held in New York City in 2010 to LGBT Pride events for more inclusivity (and also to acknowledge the fact that it was the LGBT community that was involved in the original Stonewall incident in 1969) (New York Area Bisexual Network, 2010).

Until the mid-1990s, gay travel essentially remained separate from mainstream travel in terms of targeted products and services and target marketing. As would be expected, exclusively gay destinations and facilities clearly benefitted from this trend. Around this time, perhaps in part due to the increasing recognition of the value of the market, its increasing visibility and acceptance, and the confidence such acceptance inspired, gay and lesbian travellers appeared to break away from the confines of strictly all-gay environments. This is not to say that gay and lesbian people did not travel before this time; however, those to whom all-gay environments did not appeal may well have travelled somewhat more subtly, integrating with friends and family, both heterosexual and homosexual, and pursuing a less 'homosexualized' experience. 'With the increasing, and for the most part, positive recognition of gay and lesbian rights on the world stage came recognition by mainstream operators of the value of what came to be known as "the pink pound"' (Southall, 2009). The search for a '"recession-proof" market niche' (Holcomb and Luongo, 1996 in Clift *et al.*, 2002) identified the gay market as a distinct possibility.

How many LGBT people prefer to visit destinations and travel with operators that are specifically tailored towards their needs is debatable, and there are limited statistics available to confirm this. Gay-specific travel organizations appear to attract only a small minority of LGBT travellers. This may be for a number of reasons:

- There are few LGBT-specific travel organizations in the UK and worldwide, compared to mainstream operators, thus those operators that do exist are able to charge a premium for their services that may be unaffordable to the majority of the market.
- There is a lack of awareness of LGBT-specific travel organizations within the LGBT community.
- LGBT travellers prefer to carry out their own research and make their own independent arrangements, as is a current trend within the tourism industry generally.

Certainly the trend towards independent travel is one that is supported by Kaur Puar (2002) who indicated that 'far and away the greatest source of revenue from gay travel is independent travel [and] the internet is projected as the element that will continue to alter how gays and lesbians travel ... Due to the relative anonymity of internet use, travellers may access information without outing themselves.'

Indeed this apparently under-researched correlation between LGBT internet use and the notion of 'outing' oneself may be considered a potential future area of research.

The Value of LGBT Tourism: The 'Pink Pound', 'Pink Dollar' or 'Dorothy Dollar' – Just How Valuable are They?

The section entitled 'A Growing Niche' at the beginning of this chapter outlines some key statistics pertaining to the perceived value of LGBT tourism. One of the difficulties, however, in establishing the true value of the LGBT tourism market has historically been the lack of available, current and ongoing research into the LGBT community on a global scale. Additionally, until recently and arguably despite recent attempts, the bisexual and transgender aspect of LGBT tourism has not been fully researched. Thus there are clear inconsistencies in terms of both definitions used and research emanating from selected definitions. Consequently, statistics pertaining to the value of the market may be somewhat dated and there are often differences in statistics quoted, dependent on the source and scale of the research. What is clear is that the LGBT market is often depicted as one with high levels of disposable income. Whether this is indeed the case is debatable as it may be argued that the 'pink pound' is not as powerful as was first thought. Indeed, there may be some misguided assumptions about the demographic. For example, it is indeed the case that not all gay and lesbian people are high-earning professionals with a high level of disposable income. The notion of the 'pink pound' is also compromised by the high proportion of expensive one- or two-person and urban household lifestyles. The DINK is often associated with the gay market and yet the number of gay families *with* kids is increasing. Not only this, but arguably much of the research carried out to date has relied on those factions of the gay community who are able and willing to inform. Those who are 'out' tend to be in a position where they are secure enough in their lives and professional stature to participate in research. It appears to be these people who become representative of the whole community. What is important is how LGBT people spend their money. It is argued that LGBT people are more likely to 'live for the moment' and thus have a higher-than-average propensity to travel. Additionally, it is generally established that favoured expenditure is leisure and travel products and services. The power of the 'pink pound' or 'pink dollar' is often purported to be high, 'but its power lies not just in its direct purchasing ability but also in the market which it encapsulates' (Southall, 2009).

It has been estimated that in 2007, gay and lesbian people living in the UK spent a total of £4.7 billion on leisure travel. They also spent £47.2 million on gay honeymoons. What is clear is that the value of the LGBT market sector is hugely important to the industry, both from a domestic and an international perspective. What is also clear is that it remains difficult to ascertain the true value of the market due to discrepancies in all aspects of research, from definitions to methodology.

Gay population estimates for the UK vary between 1% and 20% of the adult population. The huge differential is accounted for by the existence of numerous definitions and variations in research methodology. However, in 2005, the UK government announced gay demographics for the first time, estimating the figure at around 6% of the population or 3.6 million adults (Govan, 2005).

Further recognition of the importance of the market will be evidenced in what is billed to be the largest ever gay market tourism research study of the LGBT community: the 2010 Out Now Global LGBT Market Study. Research will focus on the tourism and leisure patterns of the estimated 35 million gay and lesbian people living in 14 countries across Latin America and Europe. Among those countries being surveyed are the UK, France, Germany, Spain, Italy, Argentina, Mexico and Brazil (Out Now, 2010). At the time of writing, no survey results are available. However, it is clear that this survey will fill a gap in available statistical research and enable further and more comprehensive and correspondingly more insightful assessment of the value and importance of gay tourism.

LGBT Events

Events represent one of the most visible and dynamic components of the LGBT tourism system. Waitt and Markwell (2006) noted that organized LGBT events are nothing new, but 'the number, diversity, and size of events are new characteristics'. From an economic perspective, events show the 'pink pound' at its strongest – attracting large numbers of visitors within short time frames, making significant injections of revenue into local economies and potentially stimulating further visits at other times of the year by linking LGBT communities together, both internal and external to the destination (Waitt and Markwell, 2006). Crucially, these impacts are achieved by the various components of both general tourism as well as specifically gay tourism supply (i.e. transport, accommodation, marketing and hospitality working together to attract and satisfy visitors). On a wider scale, LGBT events also enable destinations to promote their gay-friendliness, notwithstanding that this approach may not always be supported by all sides of the local community (Visser, 2003). Case Study 16.1 emphasizes the role of events as part of a 'bigger picture' – including a tolerant political and social setting, a proactive gay community, a broader quality tourism product, targeted marketing and recognition of the significance of collaboration – in the development of Cape Town as South Africa's 'gay capital' (Tebje, 2004).

Pride events are arguably the most visible and ubiquitous LGBT events. Contemporary Pride events include not only marches, but also parades, rallies, festivals, arts festivals and other cultural activities, as well as acknowledging intersex and other emerging sexual identities in addition to LGBT communities (InterPride, 2010). However, a wide variety of other events and series of events – including sporting mega events such as the Gay Games (visit http://www.gaygames.com for an interesting timeline of the Games) and gay tourism expos (Stuber, 2002) – have emerged more recently, catering for both the growing demand and supply sides of the LGBT tourism phenomenon.

The global development of Pride events, and of organizations involved in such development, emphasizes the dynamic, systemic nature of the LGBT tourism phenomenon. Pride events are now organized in a highly sophisticated manner at both international (e.g., InterPride)

Case Study 16.1. Cape Town.

LGBT, or queer, events have played a major role in establishing Cape Town, South Africa, on the global LGBT tourism map. The new liberal constitution following the demise of apartheid in the early 1990s gave equality before the law in South Africa, which resulted in the growth of both gay organizations and spaces (Visser, 2002). Cape Town represented one of the main beneficiaries of the post-apartheid tourism boom, but visitor growth started to wane in the mid 1990s. To counteract this decline and further stimulate international tourism, niche markets such as adventure, sport, convention, cruise and gay tourism were identified (Visser, 2002). By 2001, it was estimated that 10% (i.e., approximately 80,000) of its international visitors were gay. Although there was no specific overriding 'master plan' designed to attract the market, Visser (2002) and Tebje (2004) have identified a number of effective strategies that were adopted.

Partnership development:

- The Gay and Lesbian Association of Cape Town Tourism Industry and Commerce (GALACTTIC) was created in 1999 to represent the specific interests of this sector of the tourism industry. The GALACTTIC website provides links for *inter alia* accommodation, tours and transport, restaurants, bars and theatres. A representative of Cape Town Tourism sits on the board of this organization.
- The gay community represents a key member of Cape Town Tourism, playing a significant role in the development of the city's tourism strategy.
- Cape Town Tourism collaborates with the 'Gaynet' website, providing information for gay and lesbian travellers to Cape Town.
- The gay community and Cape Town Tourism produce a 'Pink Map' that lists the city's gay-friendly facilities, including accommodation, restaurants, pubs and massage parlours. The official visitor's guides to the city (http://www.cape-town.org) also include a 'gay and lesbian' tourism section.
- Cape Town Tourism contributes to the development and promotion of the city's 'pink' events in the city.
- Cape Town Tourism works closely with gay distribution channels – such as tour operators, travel agents and media – to provide promotional and other information and material on this market.
- Representatives of Cape Town's 'pink' tourism industry sit on international bodies such as InterPride.

Market communication:

- General characteristics such as Cape Town's natural beauty and cultural diversity, its value for money and its developed tourist infrastructure are used to present Cape Town as a multifaceted and world-class tourism product.
- In 2001, Cape Town hosted the International Gay and Lesbian Travel Association's biannual symposium, attended by more than 1000 travel retailers from 35 countries. The symposium was partly sponsored by South African Tourism and provided a perfect PR opportunity for the destination, especially for the lucrative American and European markets.
- Targeted communication through the international LGBT media, in particular publications such as *Spartacus*, has promoted Cape Town as a gay-friendly city.

Product development:

- Events: the Mother City Queer Project (MCQP) represents the most important gay event taking place in Cape Town. It is now in its 14th year and has an international following (for more details on this event, visit http://www.mcqp.co.za/). Originally a one-night party, MCQP has developed into a week-long event. A huge costume party, based around a new theme each year to keep its appeal fresh, is its main feature. In 2000, the 'Toy Box'-themed event generated more than R50 million. MCQP appeals not only to the 'circuit queens' who attend all the big queer parties around the world, but also to a wide variety of other segments of the pink market. Cape Town also hosts a Gay and Lesbian Film Festival, which has received sponsorship from South African Tourism, emphasizing the significance of the gay market for the national tourism office. An unsuccessful bid was made to host the 2010 Gay Games, partly on the basis that Cape Town's gay-friendly image would boost its chances of winning the bid (the eventual winning host destination was Cologne).
- Accommodation: a diverse range of accommodation exists specifically for the pink market, catering for all budgets and interests. In 2004 there were approximately 35 accommodation establishments catering for this niche market.
- Tour operators: a number of inbound tour operators catering specifically to the gay and lesbian travel industry have emerged. Cape Town Tourism works with these to promote the city as a gay-friendly destination.

and national (e.g., Gay Pride UK) levels. As already noted, the original Pride events solely comprised marches that took place in New York, Chicago and Los Angeles on 28 June 1970 to commemorate the anniversary of the Stonewall riots. However, not all events directly commemorate the Stonewall riots (Waitt and Gorman-Murray, 2008). For example, the Chill-Out festival, which takes place annually in Victoria, Australia, originated as a type of recovery party from the Sydney Gay and Lesbian Mardi Gras in 1997.

Changing Legislation: Civil Partnerships and Discrimination

Travel for LGBT people

At the UN General Assembly in 2008, the UN declaration supporting the rights of LGBTI (lesbian, gay, bisexual, transgender and intersex) people was presented. The declaration on human rights, sexual orientation and gender identity has the support of 66 countries worldwide and condemns human rights violations of LGBTI people.

In a 2010 report on state-sponsored homophobia (Ottosson, 2010), 76 countries were identified in which homosexual acts are illegal. Many of these countries are located in Africa and Asia. South Africa is one of few African countries to acknowledge gay rights. More frighteningly, in five countries and in parts of a further two countries, homosexuality is punishable by the death penalty.

In 2006 the UK's Foreign and Commonwealth Office began to offer travel advice to LGBT people in order to raise awareness of legal issues and cultural differences worldwide with regard to acceptance of homosexuality. Recognizing that there are many countries worldwide in which homosexual activity is illegal, the Foreign Office sought to offer guidance and travel tips for LGBT travellers, some of which include avoiding excessive physical shows of affection and researching the situation in a destination before departure (Foreign and Commonwealth Office, 2010).

Marriage and civil partnerships

According to the International Gay and Lesbian Association, 27 countries offer same-sex couples most or all rights of marriage. Most of these countries are in Europe and include the Netherlands, Denmark, Germany and the UK. Those outside Europe include South Africa, Canada, New Zealand and Australia. In the USA, President Barack Obama has publicly stated that he supports civil partnerships and federal rights for LGBT couples, as well as opposing a constitutional ban on same-sex marriage (The White House, 2009). Despite this, same-sex marriages are only legal in a small number of US states.

The Civil Partnership Act (2004) came into force in the UK in December 2005. The Act enables same-sex couples aged 16 years and over to obtain legal recognition of their relationship. The first day that couples could form a civil partnership was 19 December 2005 in Northern Ireland, 20 December 2005 in Scotland and 21 December 2005 in England and Wales. The number of civil partnerships formed was at its highest level in the UK between January and March 2006. According to the Office of National Statistics (ONS, 2009), this 'reflected the fact that many same-sex couples in long-standing relationships took advantage of the opportunity to formalize their relationship as soon as the legislation was implemented'. The total number of civil partnerships formed since the Civil Partnership Act came into force in December 2005 up to the end of 2008 was 33,956 (ONS, 2009). The number of civil partnerships formed in the UK fell by 18% between 2007 and 2008.

In 2008, 53% of people forming civil partnerships in the UK were male. The average age at the formation of a partnership was 41.8 years for men and 40 years for women. Interestingly, almost a quarter of all partnerships formed in the UK in 2008 were formed in London and 'it was also the region of the highest proportion of male civil partnerships compared with female' (ONS, 2009). One of the main benefits of civil partnerships for the tourism industry has been the growth in gay honeymoons.

Equalities law

The Employment Equality (Sexual Orientation) Regulations (2003) offer legal protection against discrimination and harassment in the workplace. The regulations make it unlawful 'to discriminate against a person on the grounds of their sexual orientation in employment and vocational training (including further and higher education)' (Department for Communities and Local Government, 2007).

The Equality Act (Sexual Orientation) Regulations (2007) makes it unlawful to refuse people goods, services (such as hotel rooms), facilities and education on the grounds of their sexual orientation. The additional purpose of the Regulation is to widen markets for both suppliers and consumers (Department for Communities and Local Government, 2007). Of interest here is the fact that it is unlawful for a same-sex couple to be refused a double-room in a hotel, for example, because this might cause offence to other customers – or for an individual to be refused entrance to a gay-friendly bar because he/she is not gay. Organizations that design their products and services for gay and lesbian customers (e.g., gay clubs and bars, gay hotels and gay tour operators) are within their rights to do so, according to the legislation, as long as they make their goods and services available to people of any sexual orientation. Such organizations would not be required, by law, to redesign their products and services to suit the needs of heterosexual customers.

According to the Department for Communities and Local Government (2007):

> There is some evidence that discrimination currently leads some gay men and lesbians to reduce their use of some types of service or else to direct their business to towards known 'gay-friendly' service providers, leading to a lack of choice, diminished competition and higher prices. Even service operators that do not discriminate themselves can lose custom if the perceived risk of discrimination leads potential clients to restrict themselves to designated gay-friendly establishments. With regards to participation, an associated increase in service uptake has clear benefits to the industries involved and to the utility of lesbians, gay men and bisexual consumers.

In March 2010, a new law that criminalizes incitement to homophobic hatred came into effect as part of the Criminal Justice and Immigration Act (2008). According to the Ministry of Justice (2010) the legislation makes it unlawful to incite hatred on the grounds of sexual orientation, similar to pre-existing laws for race and religion. The legislation does not make it illegal to tell jokes about or criticize homosexuality, nor does it affect discussion or criticism of sexual practices, which is still be allowed.

Such changes in legislation have been welcomed by the gay community. However, in a 2007 Stonewall publication focusing on the attitudes of British people towards gay and lesbian people (Cowan, 2007), Ben Summerskill, Stonewall's chief executive said that 'changing the law, however tough that may seem at the time, is often the easy part – changing hearts and minds is much harder.'

The findings of the Stonewall report (Cowan, 2007) indicated that more than nine in ten people supported legislation protecting lesbian and gay employees from discrimination. Additionally the report found that almost a fifth of people consider television to be responsible for 'anti-gay prejudice'. More worryingly, over half blame tabloid newspapers. Furthermore, more than four in five British people think that the media relies too much on clichéd stereotypes of gay people.

Popular LGBT Destinations

As Clift *et al.* (2002) indicated, the number of holiday destinations now welcoming gay and lesbian visitors is considerably greater than that 20 years ago, when openly gay travellers were generally only to be found in recognized 'gay-friendly' destinations. This trend, it is argued, has come about through more effective marketing, advances in equality and human rights, and progression in technology. According to Southall (2009):

> The question remains; are the increases in gay and lesbian travel a result of general travel trends,

e.g. globalization, where the cheaper cost of international travel, increased accessibility of far-flung destinations and the proliferation of tourism organizations make travel more accessible to all, or is this niche-market still as lucrative for those investors willing to take the time and effort to recognize and satisfy their needs?

For LGBT travellers, the ability to relax on holiday means that the choice of destination and accommodation is often made on the basis of perceptions of tolerance and gay-friendliness. Actual holiday activities of sightseeing, eating out, drinking and sunbathing are unlikely to vary greatly from those pursued by heterosexual travellers. This is supported by Pritchard *et al.* (2000), who concurred that 'gay and lesbian consumers share much in common with tourists in the straight community'.

Interestingly, in a study of the correlation between sexuality and holiday choice, the holiday preferences of gay men and lesbians were found to differ. Pritchard *et al.* (2000) found that the factors influencing gay men's choices of destination were aspects of culture and architecture, whereas lesbians were more concerned with the gay-friendliness of a destination. The need for acceptance is strong for gay people but more so, argued Pritchard *et al.*, for lesbians than for gay men.

As previously stated, it was only in the mid-1990s that 'gay and lesbian travellers appeared to break away from the confines of strictly all-gay environments. Until this time gay travel had essentially remained separate from mainstream travel and exclusively gay destinations and facilities benefited from this trend' (Southall, 2009). The ability to escape the prejudices encapsulated in the home environment was, for many, the main attraction of an all-gay enclave. As Pritchard *et al.* (2000) said, 'In straight tourism spaces, the same prejudices which exist in their home environment would be in evidence and hence the holiday would not offer escape'.

As noted earlier in this chapter, there are numerous destinations in which homosexuality is illegal and even some where the death penalty still applies to those 'caught' engaging in homosexual behaviour. What is clear, however, is that as society changes, so too does legislation, and previously inaccessible destinations (inaccessible due to prohibitive legislation,

rather than physical access issues) will become increasingly accessible to the gay market. Nonetheless, issues of safety and acceptance appear to be key in the decision-making process of gay travellers.

In 2008, Outtraveler.com published a list of top up-and-coming destinations: 'We chose some of these cities for their burgeoning gay goings-on or progressive LGBT [lesbian, gay, bisexual and transgender] rights policies; some for their spectacular artistic and architectural wonders; some for their thrilling joie de vivre that's getting people in travel circles talking'. The list included Santiago, Chile; Valencia, Spain; Marseille, France; Dublin, Ireland; and Cardiff, Wales. Many other destinations are as popular now as they were two decades ago, including London, New York, Sydney and Amsterdam.

Mainstreaming LGBT Travel – 'Mainstream' versus 'Gay' Travel Organizations

One of the main problems of gay destinations and hotels is that 'while [they] may be oases of safety, they can also serve to ghettoize homosexuals and paradoxically heighten their vulnerability' (Pritchard *et al.*, 2000). This can deter gay travellers who may feel that 'being conspicuously gay in a gay resort [is] possibly less safe than when holidaying in a straight destination' and additionally 'gay spaces [are] in danger of heterosexual encroachment and absorption due to the attractions of gay nightlife' (Pritchard *at al.*, 2000). Being singled out, and ostracized, as obviously gay outside of the confines of a gay destination or hotel is not what gay travellers wish to experience and this may, ironically, be the reason for reticence, on the part of the gay traveller, to frequent such places. Many gay and lesbian travellers may also be unaware of specialist gay travel companies, particularly in the UK. It is argued that even those who are aware may not necessarily book with a gay travel organization or select a gay destination or hotel, preferring instead to book a holiday with a mainstream operator or book independently. For the mainstream operators who provide for gay and lesbian travellers, there remains considerable scope for market differentiation.

In the 1990s American Airlines undertook significant promotional work with the LGBT community, including sponsoring Pride events. Today, 'the airline [is] regarded as the most popular airline among American gays and lesbians' (Clift *et al.*, 2002). In an industry such as tourism, where products and services are increasingly similar and interchangeable, companies are seeking new ways to differentiate themselves and create distinct market profiles. American Airlines recognized that gay marketing would be a strategic differentiator for them and they are a clear example of an organization that has remained the market leader in the gay travel niche. Offering a dedicated LGBT sales team and an opportunity to 'Fly with your friends at American Airlines', the airline clearly anticipates and identifies the travel needs of their gay market and even produces a gay newsletter, 'Rainbow News', which gives information and overviews of LGBT events (Southall, 2009).

In 1998, 'London became the world's first major city actively to campaign internationally for the gay and lesbian market' (Clift *et al.*, 2002). As with American Airlines, London recognized the need to find new ways to differentiate itself and create a distinct market profile. More recently, in October 2009, London opened its first centre dedicated to LGBT visitors. The Gay Tourist Office opened in London's Soho district to provide visitors with LGBT-specific information about the capital.

Case Study 16.2. Philadelphia and South Carolina.

In November 2003, the Greater Philadelphia Tourism Marketing Corporation (GPTMC) officially 'came out' as a gay-friendly destination by introducing a successful campaign entitled 'Philadelphia. Get Your History Straight and Your Nightlife Gay'. The decision to target the LGBT market was based on statistical information indicating the potential economic return to be accrued from targeting this market. According to GPTMC (2004), 'Through secondary and customized marketing research, GPTMC identifies the high yield markets that can generate high tourism returns, such as the gay and lesbian travel market'. Hoping to cash in on what was then estimated to be a $54.1 billion gay travel market, the GPTMC developed its new campaign in partnership with 'the Philadelphia Gay Tourism Caucus – 55 regional organizations, including area Convention and Visitor Bureaus, represented by 85 members.' (GPTMC, 2004). According to GPTMC (2004), 'By mid-December [its] $200,000 media buy in gay-only media had generated $3 million in publicity in mainstream media such as … CNN, BBC Radio, … *USA Today* and the *Washington Post*'. The marketing campaign that followed targeted the US and Canadian markets through 'print, television, online and cooperative advertising'.

Economically the campaign was identified as a clear success, with average daily spending by the overnight gay traveller increasing from $179 in 2003 to $257 in 2004 (GPTMC, 2005). 'Over an 8-month period, we went from low on the "gaydar" to high on the list of popular destinations for gay travellers. Now, as an industry leader, we find other destinations looking to us for advice on how to develop a gay tourism marketing campaign of their own' (GPTMC, 2005).

According to GPTMC (2009) 'The gay-friendly section of the [web]site received over 100,000 page views in 2009', offering a clear indication of the importance of this method of communication for the LGBT tourism market.

In contrast to Philadelphia's destination marketing success story is that of the USA state of South Carolina. According to *The Guardian* (Baker, 2008) 'An advertising campaign launched on the London Underground during gay pride week [in July 2008] caused a political storm in South Carolina'. The posters were part of an advertising campaign designed to attract visitors to gay-friendly US states, with each destination (including Las Vegas, Washington, Boston and Atlanta) being described as 'so gay'. The advertisement was condemned by a South Carolina senator and the state's tourism department refused to pay the $5000 fee for the campaign appearance.

What is clear from these case studies is that targeting the LGBT market is still liable to cause controversy in some destinations, even those in countries perceived to be more accepting of LGBT people. Undoubtedly, however, the economic gain accrued from targeting the LGBT market is significant.

Future Research

LGBT tourism represents a relatively new area of study and is therefore ripe for research. Despite the appearance of the first published study on gay tourism in 1996 and a subsequent growth in interest since, Hughes (2006) noted that 'to date, relatively little is known about holidays of gays and lesbians and related issues'. Interestingly, the same author also suggested the existence of potential barriers to research in this area, including a tendency for tourism research to ignore marginalized groups, a reluctance by researchers to become personally associated with (and subsequently stigmatized by) the topic and the dominance of data from self-selecting 'out' respondents that may not be representative. Consequently, readers may wish to debate these research-related issues further, for example in terms of considering ways of moving the literature forward.

Given this paucity in the literature, research considering mainstream issues – including, for example, consumer behaviour, market size, value and demographics, marketing and distribution, impacts, and destination development – relating to LGBT travellers would be very welcome. Given the significance of festivals and events for the LGBT community and the development of LGBT tourism, and the recent emergence of events literature, specific research in this area would also be highly valuable.

Since the main focus of the literature has been on gay and lesbian travel (especially gay male travel) and has essentially ignored the bisexual and transgendered dimensions (Hughes, 2006), research relating to bisexual and transgendered people – notwithstanding potential issues relating to senses of identity – and also of lesbian dimensions of LGBT tourism would clearly be welcome. For example, Hughes (2006) reflected that the 'limited information about lesbians and their holiday experiences is a reflection of a more widespread lack of interest by market researchers in general and their perception of lesbians as being a market that is less worth pursuing than that of gay men'. Due to the commercial interest in LGBT tourism, perceptions and realities relating to value of segments within the market may warrant specific interest. Another dimension worthy of further research is the family unit, recognizing increasing conception and adoption among gay couples (Mulryan, 1995). Studies that compare the behaviours and impacts of various LGBT communities would also help identify individual segments to inform marketing responses. For example, Pritchard *et al.* (2000) found that the travel preferences of gay men and lesbians differ from each other, specifically with regards to factors affecting destination choice.

Given the shift in terminology from 'gay' to 'LGBT' tourism and Waitt and Markwell's (2006) comment that the 'gay tourism industry' is how the industry sees itself, a potentially interesting piece of research would consider how different members of the industry regard themselves, not just in relation to LGBT tourism but also to the wider tourism industry.

Conclusion

LGBT tourism represents a significant growing sector of the tourism industry. While the use of 'gay tourism' has predominated in the past, 'LGBT tourism' represents a more contemporary and inclusive term that is increasingly being used in general and by associated tourism organizations. The phenomenon of LGBT tourism is well established and generally well accepted in Western countries and LGBT tourism has an increasing global presence. One of the main reasons for the growth of the LGBT industry relates to the recognition of its economic value. However, it is clear that its development is linked to a wide array of environmental factors, especially economic, sociocultural, political and legal. The academic literature has followed the growth of the LGBT tourism industry, but by its own admission this still represents an under-researched area. It is clear that numerous opportunities exist for its further development.

Review Questions

1. What macro- and micro-environmental factors have led to the emergence of LGBT tourism?

2. What are the drivers for, and barriers against, the development of LGBT tourism? (You may wish to consider general or specific perspectives.)

3. Develop a marketing plan for a tourism organization of your choice for its development of the LGBT market.

4. What are the potential difficulties in researching LGBT tourism?

References

Baker, V. (2008) South Carolina – not 'so gay' after all. Wednesday. *The Guardian*, July 16. Available from: http://www.guardian.co.uk/travel/2008/jul/16/gay.travel. Accessed April 20, 2010.

Becker, R. (2006) *Gay TV and Straight America*. Rutgers University Press, Chapel Hill, North Carolina, USA.

Carter, D. (2004) *Stonewall: The Riots that Sparked the Gay Revolution*. St Martin's Press, New York.

Clift, S. Luongo, M. and Callister, C. (eds) (2002) *Gay Tourism: Culture, Identity and Sex*. Continuum, London, UK.

Cowan, K. (2007) *Living Together. British Attitudes to Lesbian and Gay People*. Stonewall, London, UK. Available from: http://www.stonewall.org.uk/documents/living_together_final_web.pdf. Accessed March 20, 2010.

Department for Communities and Local Government (2007) *The Equality Act (Sexual Orientation) Regulations (2007). Final Regulatory Impact Assessment*. Department for Communities and Local Government, London, UK. Available from: http://www.equalities.gov.uk/PDF/SexORegimpass2007.pdf. Accessed July 7, 2010.

Foreign and Commonwealth Office (2010) LGBT travellers. Available from: http://www.fco.gov.uk/en/travel-and-living-abroad/your-trip/LGBT-travellers. Accessed July 7, 2010.

Gay Days (2010) Expo Information. Available from http://www.gaydaysexpo.com. Accessed July 16, 2010.

Govan, F. (2005) Six per cent of population are gay or lesbian, according to Whitehall figures. *The Telegraph*, 12 December. Available from: http://www.telegraph.co.uk/news/uknews/1505277/Six-per-cent-of-population-are-gay-or-lesbian-according-to-Whitehall-figures.html. Accessed July 9, 2010.

Graham, M. (2002) Challenges from the margins: gay tourism as cultural critique. In: Clift, S., Luongo, M. and Callister, C. (eds) *Gay Tourism: Culture, Identity and Sex*. Continuum, London, UK, pp. 17–41.

GPTMC (2004) *Tourism 2004: Report to the Industry*. Greater Philadelphia Tourism Marketing Corporation, Philadelphia, USA.

GPTMC (2005) *Tourism 2005: Report to the Industry*. Greater Philadelphia Tourism Marketing Corporation, Philadelphia, USA.

GPTMC (2009) *Tourism 2009: Report to the Region*. Greater Philadelphia Tourism Marketing Corporation, Philadelphia, USA.

Holcomb, B. and Luongo, M. (1996) Gay tourism in the United States. *The Annals of Tourism Research* 23, 711–713.

Hughes, H.L. (2002) Marketing gay tourism in Manchester: new market for urban tourism or destruction of 'gay space'? *Journal of Vacation Marketing* 9, 152–163.

Hughes, H.L. (2004) A gay tourism market: reality or illusion, benefit or burden? *Journal of Quality Assurance in Hospitality and Tourism* 5, 57–74.

Hughes, H. (2006) *Pink Tourism: Holidays of Gay Men and Lesbians*. CAB International, Wallingford, UK.

IGLTA (2010) Our Mission Statement. Available from: http://www.iglta.org/facts.cfm. Accessed July 16, 2010.

InterPride (2010) Mission & History. Available from: http://www.interpride.org. Accessed April 20, 2010.

Kaur Puar, J. (2002) Circuits of queer mobility: tourism, travel and globalization. *Journal of Lesbian and Gay Studies* 8, 101–137.

Leiper, N. (1979) The framework of tourism. *Annals of Tourism Research* 6, 390–407.

Littlewood, I. (2001) *Sultry Climates: Travel and Sex*. John Murray Publishers, London, UK.

Markwell, K. (2002) Mardi Gras tourism and the construction of Sydney as an international gay and lesbian city. *GLQ: A Journal of Gay and Lesbian Studies* 8, 81–99.

Mill, R.C. and Morrison, A.M. (2001) *The Tourism System*, 4th edn. Kendall Hunt Publishing, Dubuque, Iowa.

Ministry of Justice (2010) *Offences of Stirring Up Hatred on the Grounds of Sexual Orientation*. Criminal Law Policy Unit Ministry of Justice, London, UK. Available from: http://www.justice.gov.uk/publications/stirring-up-hatred.htm. Accessed April 20, 2010.

Moxley, M. (2008) Little pink book. *The Guardian*, 28 June. Available from: http://www.guardian.co.uk/travel/2008/jun/28/gayandlesbiantravel.china. Accessed July 9, 2010.

Mulryan, D. (1995) Reaching the gay market. *American Demographics* 17, 46.

New York Area Bisexual Network (2010) A brief trip thru bisexual NYC's history. Available from: http://www.nyabn.org/Pages/WhoWeR/OurHistory.html. Accessed May 7, 2010.

ONS (2009) *Statistical Bulletin: Civil Partnerships in the UK*. Office for National Statistics, Newport, UK.

Ottosson, D. (2010) State-Sponsored Homophobia: A World Survey of Laws Prohibiting Same Sex Activity Between Consenting Adults. The International Lesbian, Gay, Bisexual, Trans and Intersex Association, Brussels, Belgium. Available from: http://old.ilga.org/Statehomophobia/ILGA_State_Sponsored_Homophobia_2010.pdf. Accessed July 7, 2010.

Out Now (2010) 2010 Out Now global LGBT market study. Available from: http://www.outnowconsulting.com/latest-updates/2010-out-now-global-lgbt-market-study.aspx. Accessed May 1, 2010.

Padilla, M. (2008) The embodiment of tourism among bisexually-behaving Dominican male sex workers. *Archives of Sexual Behaviour* 37, 783–793.

Pink Advertising (2010) Pink Rand to be researched in SA. Available from http://pinkads.blogspot.com. Accessed July 16, 2010.

Powell, F. (2010) Keynote speech. Presentation given by the director of the Association of Cruise Experts at the Tourism Society's 'Tourism and Transport' event. University of Wolverhampton, Wolverhampton, UK.

Pritchard, A., Morgan, N., Sedgley, D., Khan, E. and Jenkins, A. (2000) Sexuality and holiday choices: conversations with gay and lesbian tourists. *Leisure Studies* 19, 267–282.

Southall, C. (2009) *Gay and Lesbian Tourism*. Tourism Insights, VisitBritain, London, UK.

Stuber, M. (2002) Tourism marketing aimed at gay men and lesbians: a business perspective. In Clift, S., Luongo, M. and Callister, C. (eds) *Gay Tourism: Culture, Identity and Sex*. Continuum, London, UK, pp. 88–124.

Tebje, M. (2004) South Africa's promotion to the gay market. Available from: http://www.tourismknowledge.com/South_Africas_promotions_to_the_Gay_market.pdf. Accessed March 16, 2010.

The Travel Institute (2010) Niche market statistics from the Travel Institute's line of lifestyle specialist course. Available from: http://www.thetravelinstitute.com. Accessed April 8, 2010.

Visser, G. (2002) Gay tourism in South Africa: issues from the Cape Town experience. *Urban Forum* 13, 85–94.

Visser, G. (2003) Gay men, tourism and urban space: reflections on Africa's 'gay capital'. *Tourism Geographies* 5, 168–189.

Waitt, G. and Gorman-Murray, A. (2008) Camp in the country: Renegotiating gender and sexuality through a rural lesbian and gay festival. *Journal of Tourism and Cultural Change* 6, 185–207.

Waitt, G. and Markwell, K. (2006) *Gay Tourism: Culture and Context*. Haworth Hospitality Press, Binghamton, New York.

Weaver, D. and Opperman, M. (2000) *Tourism Management*. John Wiley & Sons, Queensland, Australia.

The White House (2009) Lesbian, Gay, Bisexual, and Transgender Pride Month, 2009. Press release. Available from: http://www.whitehouse.gov/the_press_office/Presidential-Proclamation-LGBT-Pride-Month. Accessed July 9, 2010.

17 Gastronomy and Tourism

Ghislaine Povey

Introduction

Gastronomy as a discipline has advanced significantly since the early 1990s, with theory in the spheres of culinary arts, culinary science and technology developing pace. There is now, debatably, an embryonic underpinning philosophy (Hegarty, 2009). Gastronomy in the eyes of many academics includes a plethora of complementary areas of study including humanities, geography, history, anthropology, ethnography and sociology. Hegarty (2009) defined gastronomy as the following:

> The essence of gastronomy is found in the knowledge, aesthetic, and experimental sensory expressions, as well as in the emotion, excitement, love, fun, and theatre experienced, which gastronomes, gourmets, connoisseurs, practitioners, and food scholars develop while engaging with gastronomy. Gastronomy is essentially a manifestation of social behavior. It is open to questions such as why people choose the food/dishes they do when they eat and why they choose to enter a particular restaurant in a street full of restaurants.

Gillespie (2001) identified 38 'differing subjects, callings, professions and trades' that contribute to gastronomy. Gastronomy also includes the practical and technical aspects of food production, from the anthropological study of what is cooked and how it is cooked in differing cultures to the cutting-edge 'molecular gastronomy' of Heston Blumenthal, TV chef and proprietor of the The Fat Duck, one of the world's leading restaurants. This chapter considers gastronomy within the tourism perspective and therefore does not cover technical and practical aspects.

Humans are the only beings on earth that ritually prepare and eat food together, a habit that is true of all human cultures. Many authors opine that the practice of cooking and eating together is very important to the continuance of our species (Hegarty, 2009). Eating is an everyday activity for all humans; it is not an option (Ignatov and Smith, 2006). If we do not eat then we do not survive. Consequently, whatever else is happening in society – a birth, death, war or natural disaster such as the earthquake in Haiti in January 2010 – a priority activity is to prepare food and eat. In many more developed societies the act of food preparation has been dissociated from the act of eating, as can be seen by the huge rise in the numbers of 'ready meals' being consumed (Gillespie, 2001; Mintel, 2010). In today's postmodern society, gastronomy is increasingly crucial to our identity formation (Ignatov and Smith, 2006). At a very profound level food and culture are intrinsically interlinked, and there is a strong academic vein that has explored this. The roots of food and drink are literally deep in 'the terroir', the soil and climate of an area. When visitors eat a locally grown and produced meal they are actually consuming the destination itself (Povey, 2006). Partaking of food and wine tours is seen to be a cultural activity (Howe, 1996; van Westering, 1999; Ignatov and Smith, 2006).

Gastro-tourism activities include a broad spectrum of food and culinary activities, generally created to enhance visitors' experiences while at a destination (Smith and Costello, 2009). These can include factory visits; eating in restaurants, café bars and tea shops; farmers' markets; taste workshops and lectures; wine- and other drink-tasting experiences; and vineyard and orchard tours. In fact the phenomenon of gastro-tourism is now widely recognized as a defined segment of the tourism industry (Cohen and Avieli, 2004; Ignatov and Smith, 2006; Kivela and Crotts, 2006; Okumus et al., 2007; Smith and Costello, 2009; Devesa et al., 2010).

The Importance of Gastronomy in Tourism

Gastronomic tourism has been shown to be a valid segment to which destinations can market, and it can conceivable offer a valid tourism approach for areas not blessed with natural attractions such as sea or snow (Kivela and Crotts, 2006). Quan and Wang (2004) identified three benefits that gastronomic tourism can give to destinations. First, gastronomic tourism can be used by destinations to develop rural tourism and boost the agricultural economy. Second, when destinations do have gastronomic resources these can be easily used to develop trails, food festivals and a gastronomic tourism destination image. Third, foods can be included as part of another attraction such as a mega event and become a part of the tourism offer in this manner. In addition, food festivals and celebrations add greatly to a community's pride and self-value and can enhance local life, as has been the case with the annual Ludlow Food Festival (Quan and Wang, 2004).

The study of food and tourism is complicated. As well as there being a defined group of visitors who are there purely because of the destination's food, there are also visitors who do not have gastronomy as their main reason for travel but who are keen gastronomes, and who will seek out authentic food and often base their judgement of the destination upon that food. Gastronomy can thus be either a primary or secondary motivator for tourists (Quan and Wang, 2004; Okumus et al., 2007).

Gastronomy has been identified as a travel motivator (van Westering, 1999). It is particularly common among tourists who are comparatively close to home. Key factors for satisfaction among gastronomic visitors are related to their motivation, including the range of gastronomic options and the 'conditions of stay', including ease of car parking and suitable accommodation being offered (Devesa et al., 2010).

The Meal Experience

Central to the study of gastronomy is the concept of the meal experience, the plethora of aspects that are included, from the consumers' perspective, in the consumption of a meal either in or supplied by a restaurant. When studying gastronomy it is insufficient just to study the meal. The place it is eaten, the surroundings, the food service, the music being played while eating and a superfluity of other factors all influence the meal experience (Hegarty, 2009). A restaurant meal is similar to a theatrical performance, with service staff (and, in the case of display kitchens, chefs) playing significant roles in the production, alongside the decoration of the site, which in turn creates the ambiance. When dining on holiday, memories can be made (Kivela and Crotts, 2006).

The terms 'gastronomy' and 'culinary tourism' are often used, and in the eyes of the majority of tourists and tourism professionals they are mostly interchangeable. For some, however, the use of the word 'gastronomy' implies the inclusion of 'fine dining' with a high level of culinary skill used to create masterpiece dishes from exquisite ingredients of the highest possible quality. Generally, food tourism is defined as tourists visiting a destination specifically to sample the food products offered there. Some authors would add that the food should be unique to the destination (Smith and Costello, 2009).

According to Smith and Costello (2009) gastro-tourists are likely to have at least a bachelors' degree and to participate in this type of tourism without their children, usually in parties of two adults. They are also likely to eat more in local restaurants and participate in cultural attractions than other types of tourist (Smith and Costello, 2009).

Case Study 17.1. Motivations for gastro-tourism in Bordeaux, France (by Dania Pisarz).

This research was part of a wider study into tourism and gastronomy in France, with particular focus on local food's role. Bordeaux was chosen for the study as it is synonymous with food, wine and gastronomy tourism. It hosts a biennial wine event. Weekly wine and cheese tasting tours are organized, where the neophyte can savour three different Bordeaux wines accompanied by a large selection of French cheeses. Tourists are also invited to follow a gourmet trail grouping together some of the best addresses to find fine food and drink (Bordeaux Tourism, 2007).

For this study, 210 questionnaires were distributed at French tourist offices and via email to members of Ludlow Slow Food. Fifty per cent of the sample questionnaires were completed in English and the rest in French.

The results of this research clearly showed that food and drink tourism is seen as having an important place in the travel experience. An average of 63% of respondents judged gastronomy as very important or important in their choice of a destination, and the idea that discovering the gastronomy of a country can be the primary motivator to travel to that destination was supported. Indeed, 16% of participants agreed that a country's gastronomy is a very important component when choosing their holiday destination and 47% described it as important.

Conversely, just less than one quarter of respondents saw gastronomy as a basic component in their choice of destination. It can thus be concluded, from the statistics, that gastronomy can be considered as central to travelling.

However, with nearly 60% of respondents not seeing the importance of gastronomy in their choice of destination or when on holiday, the argument for seeing gastronomy as a niche tourism sector was also supported.

Atmosphere and authenticity

The importance attached to experiencing the atmosphere and authenticity of a venue when having a meal also emerged in the results, as did the benefits of using local restaurants. Over 80% of respondents appreciating a meal outside their accommodation clearly showed the importance of the physical motivator. Categories explaining why a meal outside of their accommodation was appreciated by tourists were identified. These included 'atmosphere and authenticity', 'better food, better prices', 'choice and variety', 'novelty and discovery' and 'relaxation'.

Developing a market for local foods outside the area

In addition to consumption of traditional foods while on holiday, two thirds of the sample stated that they took some traditional food home. While approximately one third of those questioned said they never took food home, most of those were Australian and American citizens, who are subject to strict laws regarding repatriation of foods. There is clearly a potential pool of consumers willing to buy an area's foods, which if sufficiently concentrated could form a useful market for local food producers and processors.

The value of social interaction

Many tourism contexts involve a social interaction with other people. The satisfaction linked to an experience may be derived not only from the individual act of consumption but also from the fact that all sorts of other people are also consumers. Eighty-eight per cent of respondents in this survey stated that having a meal on holiday was a way to increase social interactions and eight out of ten tourists considered eating in a restaurant frequented by locals as important. In addition, 94% of people agreed that they enjoy sharing a meal with someone on holiday. There was an agreement that such meals can reinforce the emotional bonds shared by a family.

When asked about the sociability aspects of a meal with strangers, this was still significant, if slightly less than that with family and friends. Interestingly, 69% of respondents stated that they would not hesitate to go to a restaurant alone. When verbally asked about their reasons, the majority of participants stated that they would not have an opportunity to experience a local restaurant when they were back at home.

Sociological Aspects of Gastronomy

Lifestyle analysis is an area which is considered by some researchers to hold the key to understanding why tourists eat what they eat. Hjalager (2004) has analysed concepts developed by Bourdieu (1984 in Hjalager, 2004) in the context of gastronomy and tourism. Bourdieu (1984) developed different lifestyle groups (Table 17.1), the daily habits and customs of which and the values with which they are imbued affect all their decisions and choices. These lifestyles are not just defined by class. They are governed by a range of aspects such as educational level and family backgrounds. Individuals can, if they acquire the means, change from one group to another (Hjalager, 2004). These lifestyle groups have both advantages and disadvantages for destination managers; while they can give an excellent insight into consumer behaviour, they can also be misleading as, for example, different nationalities have different lifestyle groups. Hjalager (2004) asserted that this lifestyle theory can be useful when we try to explain why fast-food chains such as McDonald's continue to be financially successful in the face of widespread criticism of their industrial food product in

tourist destinations. The driveways of hotels offering 'all-inclusive' packages are often seen strewn with families trooping back to their hotel carrying bags of McDonalds, for which they have paid a premium price, rather than consuming the local food products readily available within their hotel. Bordieu's lifestyle groups provide a framework to explain why tourists' food supply and choices cannot be consistently addressed, by reflecting the complexities of the tourist's lifestyles (Hjalager, 2004). These sociological aspects of gastronomy tourism need much research to investigate how effectively Bordieu's framework can be applied to tourists across different cultures and nationalities.

Place

Some see the increased interest in food heritage and traditions as a modern construct invented to enable modern tourists to look back into the past. The reality is that tradition is constantly evolving and changing (Mykletun and Gyimothy, 2010). Probably due to the centrality of the tourist gaze in tourism research since the

Table 17.1. Lifestyle groups and their tastes.

Lifestyle group	Attributes	Likes	Dislikes
Employers	Rich but lacking in culture Complicated meal preparation Lack of economic restraint	Bakery products, wine, game and luxuries such as foie gras	Fresh fruit and vegetables, fresh meat and restaurant and canteen meals
Teachers	Poor but very cultured Simple meal preparation with pre-prepared elements Low cost sought Disapprove of heavy and rich foods eaten by other classes	Bread and dairy products, fruit preserves, ethnic restaurants and canteen meals	Wine and spirits, expensive meats and fresh fruit and vegetables
Professionals	Quite well off and quite cultured Light healthy foods prepared, rejection of fatness, and emphasis on slimness which becomes social convention	Meat (often good cuts), fresh vegetables, seafood and restaurant meals	Preserved meat, bakery products, sugar and canteen meals
Workers	Poor both economically and culturally Food tends to take long, slow cooking Prefer to eat and drink well and be generous with hospitality	Like economical, heavy, stodgy, nourishing food, bread, dairy products and cheap cuts of meat	Fresh fruit and vegetables, restaurant and canteen meals and seafood

Adapted from Seymour (2004).

beginning of the 21st century, taste (and thus traditional foods) has been clearly linked to place (Hjalager and Corigliano, 2000). Cohen and Avieli (2004) used this in their analogy of food with handicrafts. Alongside the linking of taste to place in tourism theory, there has been a growing link with locality developed by the Slow Food movement (as discussed in Chapter 9) and the rapid development of EU regulations regarding local foods and their labelling as regards quality, provenance and typicality.

Food in Destination Marketing

Good destination marketing is important because it is a mechanism by which the tourists' expectations can be managed (Quan and Wang, 2004). If expectations are unrealistically high then the tourist will inevitably be disappointed with the reality. Food is seen as one of the key tangible and intangible goods and services within a destination's portfolio (Okumus *et al.*, 2007) and can be a primary motivation to travel (Quan and Wang, 2004). Given that eating is thought to be one of the most pleasurable activities during a holiday, good food adds value to a destination's image (Okumus *et al.*, 2007). The high value placed upon food's role in the attractiveness of any destination can be linked to the fondness of source market populations for out-of-the-ordinary food experiences, often sought at ethnic restaurants. This familiarity with the food is thought by some to develop consumers' tastes and endear destination cuisines to them (Okumus *et al.*, 2007). This is not universally accepted for reasons that are discussed in the next section, where we investigate the challenges of consuming an unfamiliar cuisine.

Destination marketing presents the marketer with the challenge of increasing visitor numbers, while ensuring sustainability. To attract tourists the destination has to be exotic, yet not offer any threat; it needs an image of 'safe exoticism' (Okumus *et al.*, 2007). Research has indicated that with good marketing and wise use of images, tourists can be persuaded to spend higher amounts on local and authentic foods (Telfer, 2000). Both food and tourism imagery in the form of photographs

in promotional materials are fundamental to 'selling the dream' and attracting tourists to a destination. Well-produced marketing materials can positively influence tourists' decision making; ill-produced materials, however, can have a derogatory effect and cause them not to choose a destination (Okumus *et al.*, 2007). It is better to do nothing than to do something in an amateurish way. Okumus *et al.* (2007) asserted that an understanding of tourists' own culture is important to well-produced materials so that images congruent to their culture and its prejudices and taboos can present the destination's food appropriately.

Du Rand and Heath (2006) explored the role of gastronomy in destination marketing and derived a framework for best practice. They noted that the use of food as part of the marketing mix of destinations was underdeveloped, while highlighting the central role that food plays in the formation of national identity in tourists' eyes. Their recommendations to destination development and marketing teams included the following:

- Develop partnerships to enhance gastronomic tourism as a niche or part of the general destination product offer, such as linking food and wine tourism in an area. This agrees with work done in the Niagara region of Canada (Telfer, 2000).
- Use unusual foods to develop a brand (e.g. the sheep's heads in the Case Study 17.2, later).
- Develop themes that link food to other activities such as heritage (explored later in this chapter).

The Challenge of the Unfamiliar

While many tourists purport to want to eat local food, the reality is that the vast majority consume their meals within the perceived safety of an international hotel. Initial research suggested that the only concerns held by tourists reflected practical issues such as health and hygiene in certain destinations (Cohen and Avieli, 2004).

Food is a key attraction to any destination and is widely featured prominently in promotional literature by many destinations. In 2002, the Culinary Institute of America was set up to assist the promotion of culinary tourism at destinations. There is, however, a scarcity of research into the engagement of tourists with local gastronomy. Much of what is written refers to Eurocentric destinations with cuisines very similar to those of the tourists' own. Cohen and Avieli (2004) noted that much tourism research has been made into visual aspects of tourism from Urry's 'tourist gaze' to the general prioritization of the sightseer as the prototypical tourist. They went on to assert that the other bodily senses are largely neglected. This may seem irrelevant, but upon further consideration there are significant differences between looking and tasting. It is easy and safe to look at a sight. Eating or drinking, however, has an immediate potential risk (Cohen and Avieli, 2004). It involves ingesting the actual environment into the body. If it is poison or dangerous in some other way, it can lead to death. By travelling out of their home environment, tourists put themselves into a situation where they may be confronted by food and drink that are very different from the familiar and which may constitute a physical risk. Food when travelling can be simultaneously frightening, fabulous and fun (Rozin, 1999).

The allure of local food is heavily featured in literature, which is full of professional pictures of succulent, colourful, appetizing food. It is playing the same role as 'food porn', which is consumed by the masses in developed countries, featuring an ever-growing cast of celebrity chefs and food writers. The reality for the tourist, however, is far more threatening. While for some the novelty of an unusual food is an attraction as a small part of a wider holiday experience, the reality is that we all have to eat daily to survive. A trip to a museum with a disturbing subject can be avoided, but if there are no palatable, familiar foods available then a tourist's daily existence can become traumatic, with the tourist having to consume unpalatable, disgusting or even frightening foods.

Fischler (1988) identified that individuals have either a 'neophobic' or 'neophilic' tendency to taste. This means that tourists are likely to either suspect or welcome new taste experiences. This is likely to have been formed by both biological and cultural stimuli (Fischler, 1988). Even within cultures there are likely to be differences between different social groups and classes (Cohen and Avieli, 2004). Gastronomic tourism is likely to exacerbate this tendency. Some tourists, particularly in destinations perceived to be particularly exotic, will not taste new foods until they are assured that they are based upon familiar and acceptable ingredients and prepared in a way that is tolerable. Sometimes conditions in food preparation areas are perceived to be insanitary and tourists are dissuaded from consuming (Cohen and Avieli, 2004). Increasingly, however, tourists are actively seeking new food experiences, wishing to expand their taste vocabularies.

Tourists to South America have been observed to have suitcases full of tinned meat and fish, 'in case there's nothing available'. Ironically some of this included corned beef from Argentina. Cohen and Avieli (2004) cited the case of Israeli tourists taking crackers and instant meals in case they find that the food offered at the destination does not meet their religious rules. Many Westerners, however, have an increasingly wide daily cuisine that often incorporates foods from their tourist destinations. Nevertheless, when in a resort they are faced with a plethora of unfamiliar choices from food outlets that operate in unfamiliar ways, the rules of which they do not know. While to some this is exciting, for the majority this is a source of apprehension, diffidence and irritation (Cohen and Avieli, 2004).

Barriers to Tourists' Enjoyment of the Gastronomic Experience

Cohen and Avieli (2004) identified a number of impediments to tourists' appetite for new taste.

Hygiene and health

Illness can spoil a holiday, and this is a key reason for the prevalence of suspicion regarding local food. A day lost to illness-induced inactivity on holiday represents a much greater loss than a day spent in the tourist's normal daily life. There is also the tendency for health professionals to intensify tourists' health concerns before they go on holiday, often warning patients about numerous food dangers. Many guide books and other media advise of the dangers of various ailments, stressing their links to food and causing avoidance of local products. Water in particular is often the focus of many dire warnings. On their return home tourists often over-exaggerate any illness they have suffered, gaining greater sympathy from friends and relatives.

Local eating habits and table manners

How we eat is culturally based. In Western culture the use of utensils and apportioning food to individuals is seen as civilized, differentiated from animalistic devouring of foods. While Western cultures perceive that contact between food and fingers is unhygienic, other cultures, such as some found in Asia, prefer to scoop balls of rice with their fingers and dip them in a shared pot of sauce or curry. In other situations tourists are intimidated by the eating utensils offered to them, such as the fear with which many Westerners view chopsticks. While it is considered acceptable for Asian hosts to show Western visitors how to use chopsticks, it could be considered insulting if the Westerners were to reciprocate and show them how to use Western utensils, as to do so would infer that they lacked civilization. Attitudes to raw ingredients also differ greatly between cultures. While in the West it is still acceptable (although widely criticized) to keep live lobsters in cases in restaurants and cook them at the table, the vast majority of Western tourists would find the cages of live chickens, rabbits, rats, cats and dogs in Asia or guinea pigs in south America unacceptable. Sometimes tourists will order these animals, observe (even taking photographs) their killing and preparation for the table, and then be unable to face eating the dish.

Communication gap

Many tourists cite their inability to understand menus and communicate with restaurateurs as a key factor in their avoidance of local establishments. Tourists will rarely visit establishments that are used extensively by local people, gaining reassurance from the presence of other visitors. Particular concerns arise around embarrassment due to their ignorance of local gastronomy and worries about being overcharged or scammed in some other manner.

Representation of Destination Food

It is commonly thought that ethnic restaurants in the tourist's home country give a clear insight into the destination's culinary lexicon, but this is not necessarily the case. First, ethnic restaurants tend to offer a limited range of iconic dishes rather than representing local cuisine. Tourists familiar with destination cuisines from ethnic restaurants from home tend to stick to the dishes with which they are familiar and the names of which they know. This in itself can lead to problems as dishes tend to be made palatable to the restaurant's local population. In the UK, for example, chicken tikka masala, one of the most popular 'Indian' dishes eaten, was actually developed in the UK in response to customers wanting the authentic Indian chicken tikka to be served with a sauce or gravy. Ethnic chefs also have to use ingredients available in their new area, which affects the taste. Despite the proliferation of ethnic restaurants, they are largely visited by a small percentage of better-off, culturally sophisticated consumers. It should be remembered that popular ethnic dishes become naturalized, becoming so much part of the culinary landscape that people forget they used to be exotic. In the UK, many dishes that were considered exotic and ethnic are now so established that they are thought to be British by much of the population. A good example of this is the adoption of the spaghetti bolognaise. When served in the UK it now has very little similarity to the original dish and would not necessarily be recognized by someone from Italy.

Tourism destinations develop culinary establishments that cater specifically for the tastes of tourists. Here they can adapt local foods to meet the preferences of the visitors and provide a taste of home for neophilic tourists. These dishes can become part of the destination culinary lexicon often creatively adapted, becoming genuine original *sui generis* cultural products. Restaurants and bars are typically a spontaneous development of an existing facility where tourists and locals eat side by side before the site becomes a fully tourist-oriented facility. Alternatively, they can be 'implanted' by outsiders (often the big fast-food companies). These tend to attract local youngsters as well as providing a 'bubble' for tourists. Some of these establishments have to adjust to local customs, for example by not selling products incongruous to local culture (e.g. pork products in Muslim countries). High-class restaurants in international hotels attract local elites.

Gastronomic Authenticity

Gastronomy has also been linked to wide-ranging discussions and developments in theories of authenticity and the consumption of authenticity. This is of clear importance for tourist destinations that are increasingly concerned with providing authenticity. Gastronomic images are used on postcards as a representation of authenticity (Markwick, 2001). Beer (2008) discussed meal authenticity. He viewed authenticity in the context of meals as being a triumvirate relationship between three key factors:

- The self – the individuals themselves and the sum of their experiences.
- The thing – what is actually being experienced.
- The other – the ways in which society defines what is authentic.

In this context, the challenge for producers of gastronomy tourism is that of understanding 'the other' in their visitors' culture as much as in their own. They are thus in a position where they can provide what is an authentic experience for the visitor. They need to ensure that through clever marketing visitors perceive actual authenticity as being authentic or through staging events for tourists, the actual authenticity for the host population is not lost. It is also important to consider that each

individual from within every culture has actually been exposed to a myriad of different experiences, and so each person may perceive the authenticity of an experience differently (Reisinger and Steiner, 2006). While aspects of gastronomic authenticity can be legislated, with standards being set, for the individual it will always come back to this subjective, personal construct (Reisinger and Steiner, 2006; Morgan *et al.*, 2008). For tourists who are aspiring to experience authenticity, the whole question of food and meal authenticity becomes a priority (Buckland, 2007).

Buckland (2007) linked tourists' perceptions of food authenticity to two important types of media: the travel guidebook and the food writer. He looked particularly at the case of Mary Frances Kennedy Fisher, who wrote about French food for Americans based on her extensive travel experiences. She is considered responsible for linking France to food and its history in the American psyche (Buckland, 2007).

Stages in the Development of 'Authentic' Local Food Experiences

The aim of most tourist-oriented establishments is to provide palatable but 'authentic' local foods. However, there is much discussion regarding how that authenticity is judged by the tourist. Many foods undergo adaptations that do not deem them inauthentic to tourists and in fact enhance their appreciation. According to Cohen and Avieli (2004), this is a staged process.

Preparatory stage

Two issues are of interest here: raw materials and food preparation. For many tourists, an authentic dish has to be made from authentic ingredients. However, many individuals are repulsed by certain traditional ingredients such as dog, snake or duck's feet found in some South-East Asian gastronomies. Tourists find that exclusion or replacement of this type of ingredient makes dishes more acceptable, without denigrating its authenticity.

Modern technologies are often employed in the food preparation of 'authentic' dishes for tourists, which does not affect authenticity when the preparation takes place out of the tourist's gaze. If the food preparation is seen, however, it becomes performance art and an intrinsic element of the authenticity. Operatives develop exaggerated styles, examples of which can be seen in many cocktail bars or in the flamboyant cooking of teppanyaki chefs.

The challenge for chefs is to keep the distinct elements that define the local gastronomy while mitigating them to enable tourists to access such foods within their palate range. If too much is taken out then the food becomes inauthentic, but if it is too changed then it fails to metonymically impress. Restaurants often offer a range of intensities to suit different palates.

Presentation stage

By definition this is firmly part of the front region, observed by tourists and comprising displays, adverts and interpretation of the dishes being offered. It is the means by which consumers judge the authenticity. In most tourist restaurants the menu is the key document. Cohen and Avieli (2004) made an analogy between the menu and a map, in that it guides newcomers through the gastronomic terrain, being diacritical to visitors and less important to those who know the area. In the same way as the tourist map, the tourist menu is adapted and simplified for visitors. The actual structure of a menu may also need to be adapted as cultures eat in different ways. Some cultures serve all the meal elements at the same time, while in Western culture it is traditional to eat several courses served separately. Putting meal components together can be challenging and tourist menus offer set meals to interpret the local gastronomy and all its elements into a format that tourists can understand. This process includes linguistic translation of the dishes alongside a cultural translation to enhance understanding. This means that the translation may not be literal. For example, 'the Thai tom yam may be reclassified as a (hot) soup, som Tam as (spicy) salad' (Cohen and Avieli 2004).

Augmentations to the menu, or at times replacements for it, are various 'culinary brokers' who interpret the local food for tourists, acting as intermediaries. These can include waiters, travel representatives, tour guides and local friends. They can recommend and explain dishes within the context of the visitor's culture. This can be helpful in that they can help visitors choose dishes they will prefer, but they may act to limit the range of dishes tourists try, based on their own prejudices.

Structure and style

Meal structure and service style are less important and, when not taking the set meal and allowing the restaurant to define the sequence. Customers ordering independently will tend to order according to their own preferences. Local customs of serving and eating, if significantly different from the tourists' own, tend to be seen as a nuisance rather than an indication of authenticity. The exception to this is a small number of tourists who see their ability to conform to local customs as a status marker, such as in asking for chopsticks if they are offered a fork and spoon.

The ambiance and floor plan of a restaurant contributes significantly to the perception of authenticity. Successful operators stage this authenticity, while ensuring the tourist's comfort. An example of this is Thai restaurants that dig out spaces in the restaurant floor so that tourists can experience sitting at the traditional low *kantok* table without being uncomfortable (Cohen and Avieli, 2004). Relationships between host populations and visitors can present a challenge and are often fraught with difficulty. Some restaurants in France have had to change their layouts, diplomatically separating tourist and local expatriate customers from local French customers. This is because visitors are often overheard moaning about the rudeness of the local population, who naturally resent this.

Different types of tourists are attracted to different types of food and demand different levels of authenticity. Recreational tourists tend to be less experimental and somewhat neophobic, while experiential tourists seek to vicariously experience the authentic life of others. The latter are far more likely to be neophilic. As destinations mature they tend to attract more recreational tourists while the more experiential tourists move on to less developed areas. Local restaurants carry more internationalized foods and local dishes become homogenized (Cohen and Avieli, 2004).

Salamone (1997) outlined an interesting example of the food differences between genuinely authentic restaurants and those developed for tourists – the original San Angel Inn, Mexico City, and the San Angel Inn run by the proprietor's son in Disney World as part of the Epcot World Showcase area. There are some differences in all areas between the two. In the original restaurant, the cuisine significantly reflects authentic Mexican haute-cuisine, rather than the 'Tex-Mex' food experienced by most Americans as Mexican prior to the San Angel Inn dining experience. The Disney World San Angel Inn endeavours to continue in the tradition of the original, but differences have been instituted to better meet the expectations of visitors. An example of this can be seen in the way the restaurants contextualize their cultural roots. In Mexico City, where the majority of customers are locals, the restaurant stresses its links to Europe; in Disney World, where the restaurant is mainly used by tourists, the emphasis is on both European links and the Native American aspects of Mexican culture. This is expressed in many ways, such as in background music and decor.

Links to Entrepreneurship

The linking of gastronomy to entrepreneurship is little researched, but an interesting study has been carried out by Mykletun and Gyimothy (2010) regarding the Voss sheep's head meal and its use as an 'adventurous tourism' product, as would be sought by one of Fischler's (1988) neophilic tourists.

Eating a sheep's head meal in this day and age would be challenging for many tourists of Western European origin. Historically, however, every part of a slaughtered animal was eaten and sheep's head was a traditional part of the St Andrew's Day meal in Scotland. Sheep's head meals would be more accessible to visitors from Asia and the Middle East. As discussed elsewhere in this chapter, Asian cultures eat a wide range of domestic animals as a normal part of their diet, although in China there is now a movement to stop the eating of cats and

---

Case Study 17.2. The sheep's head meal.

Mykletun and Gyimothy (2010) used the example of a traditional Norwegian meal, which has been successfully developed as a key element of tourist attraction in the town of Voss. The sheep's head meal, which is based on the traditional local foods of the area, is sold in a restaurant based in a 400-year-old farm storehouse located at Løne in Voss. Visitors can also participate in a guided tour of the production site where the sheep's heads are produced for commercial and participate in a *Smalahovelag*, a party where sheep's heads are consumed by friends and family.

The sheep's head production is no longer entirely traditional. Machinery has been introduced to speed up the process and the sheep's head consumption, which was habitually with 'sheath knives', is now associated with more commonly used cutlery. It is even consumed with beer and aquavit, a Norwegian liquor (Mykletun and Gyimothy, 2010). The Voss sheep's head meal plays a valuable part in the marketing of the area as a tourist destination (Hall *et al.*, 2003):

> As for the sheep's-head meal, its bouquet reminds the guest of smoked lamb's meat, but is 'sharper' and stronger in intensity. The mere sight of it may be alarming for the first-time consumer while eliciting positive expectations on the culinary side among the experienced meal participant. The meal is served with a half of a sheep's-head on the plate along with potatoes and 'mashed swedes' as in olden days, and decorated with parsley. The brown skin is in place and the head still has an open eye with eyelids 'glaring at the guest,' as well as an ear, the nose, lips, half a tongue and its teeth. It is obviously the head of a living creature that used to graze and eat hay. Anticipating consuming this part of the animal is an unfamiliar experience to most people, and may also elicit associations with food taboos.

(Mykletun and Gyimothy, 2010).

dogs by the better-off middle classes, many of whom are pet owners (Watts, 2010).

The consumption of a sheep's head does actually carry a higher health risk than eating other parts of the animal's body. Sheep's brains have been associated with the prion disease 'scrapie'. This is a close relative of bovine spongiform encephalopathy, which in turn has been associated with the human version, Creutzfeldt-Jakob disease.

In addition to this, the act of eating an animal's head is a recognition that the animal has been killed for consumption, which is offensive to many meat eaters. There is a huge psychological difference between eating a piece of food and seeing evidence of the live animal that gave it for consumption. Eating such a dish may imbue the consumer with status and be seen among the peer group as a badge of bravery. It engenders a wide range of emotional responses in those who attempt it.

Case Study 17.2, the sheep's head, is a successful use of gastronomy to attract tourists. An unsuccessful example is given in Case Study 17.3, which is based upon research by Plummer *et al.* (2006) looking into why the apparently popular Waterloo–Wellington Ale Trail failed.

Case Study 17.3. The Waterloo–Wellington Ale Trail.

The Waterloo-Wellington Ale Trail was a collaboration of six artisan breweries based in Ontario, Canada. The trail – a self-guided tour of the breweries – was launched in 1998 following successful negotiations between the participants the preceding year. The brewers shared a commitment to craft brewing with an emphasis on traditional techniques to produce full-bodied, distinctly flavoured, original beers. The group realized that there was a synergy in working together and there was a perceived need to cooperate and create a tourist product that would attract beer tourists and enable the breweries involved to sell their products directly to the consumers.

Despite much acclaim in the second year of operation and 10,000 participants, the trail met its demise in the 2000 (Plummer *et al.*, 2006). Individual breweries still offer tours independently, but fail to gain the added value derived from the synergistic activity.

Gastronomy and Heritage

One of the strongest links for all involved in gastronomy is that with heritage. The history of an area, both environmentally and culturally, will shape that area's cuisine. Both Povey (2006) and Harrington (2005) developed models identifying factors that influence the identity of traditional food. According to Harrington (2005):

> Regional flavor profiles, etiquette and regional recipes are predominantly derived through a continuous interaction and evolution of fashion, traditions, culture and climate. All cuisines and gastronomic traditions are created through a fusion of ingredients and techniques as a result of the marrying of diverse cultures, ethnic influences and history with the restriction of product availability and know-how.

For visitors there is an intrinsic link between an area's history and the consumption of heritage food. Food is a part of the cultural heritage that can literally be internalized and absorbed (van Westering, 1999). In heritage attractions the kitchen is often now featured and visitors are keen to try a taste of history. This is linked to the consumption of 'place' offered by gastronomic experiences. The development of food outlets at museums illustrates this point well. The Black Country Living Museum at Dudley in England is a good example of this. A confectionary shop, based in a period building, sell bags of sweets made to traditional recipes, while a bakery similarly sells cakes to visitors. A chip shop sells fish and chips traditionally fried in beef fat to give authentic flavour, while a vegetarian option is provided in the café. In addition, an on-site public house sells 'traditional cheese cobs'. Profits from these foods boost revenues and certainly please visitors. There have, however, been some instances in which the food has been less than completely authentic – for example, when a 'rocky road cup cake' was observed to be on sale in the baker's shop.

The use of food and drink establishments as heritage attractions is an important area of research. Howe (1996) identified the potential value of UK public houses as heritage attractions. She also suggested that the food served in these establishments should reflect local food heritage and culture (Howe, 1996). Josiam *et al.* (2004) defined the term 'historaunt' to define an historical restaurant. They researched the differences in behaviour and motivation between customers at a themed restaurant and a similar but authentically historical restaurant. Clear differences were identified, although the limitation of the study to one 'historaunt' and one other restaurant does limit its value. Visitors to the 'historaunt' were far more likely to be on their first visit and to be day trippers or tourists who were attracted to the restaurant because of its heritage and its official listing as an historical site. Josiam *et al.* (2004) went on to discuss the disadvantages of restaurants of being heritage sites as well as gastronomic attractions, particularly in the area of planning and development, where constant changes in health and safety legislation can be difficult to implement as it is often impossible to alter the heritage site to accommodate them.

Satisfaction with Gastronomic Experiences

While customer satisfaction in the food service setting has been extensively researched, as has tourist satisfaction in the general context (with gastronomy being viewed as an element of the wider tourism product), comparatively few researchers have addressed satisfaction in relation to gastro-tourists. Nield *et al.* (2000) revealed clues as to the determinants of satisfaction. This was one of the first studies to explore tourists' food service experiences (Nield *et al.*, 2000). It was, however, somewhat restricted in its construction.

Correia *et al.* (2008) found that the most important factors in achieving gastronomic satisfaction were related to availability of local courses, exoticism, presentation of food and the food service staff. They also found that price and atmosphere have clear parts to play in satisfying tourists. They went on to assert that restaurateurs need to add elements of originality to their menus, presenting their heritage foods in a modern way or adding a twist (Correia *et al.*, 2008). In studying gastronomic satisfaction, it is important to remember that this is very culturally specific and will greatly vary between

groups of tourists with different nationalities and backgrounds (Nield *et al.*, 2000).

Kivela and Crotts (2006) analysed gastro-tourist behaviour in the context of a phenomenological model of culinary tourist experiences developed by Hjalager (2003; in Kivela and Crotts, 2006). This is based on four gastro-tourist categories: (i) recreational; (ii) existential; (iii) diversionary; and (iv) experimental.

Kivela and Crotts viewed tourist food behaviour as being on a spectrum from existential to experimental (Fig. 17.1). Quan and Wang (2004) developed and applied a tourist experience model to food. They differentiated 'peak touristic experiences' (PTEs), which are the key destination attractions, from 'supporting touristic experiences', which are supporting factors such as comfort and convenience (Fig. 17.2). Without either the tourist's experience is less enjoyable. If the main attraction at the destination does not deliver satisfaction then no matter how good the hotels, food and other support services are, the visitor will not be satisfied. Conversely, the experience of the main attraction can be negatively affected by poor support services, which detract from overall satisfaction. Crucial to both factors are the day-to-day activities that the tourist experiences, the 'daily routine experiences'. In seeking novelty in food, tourists can be offered a familiar food prepared in an unusual way. An example of this is found in Jiangxi in China. In most of China rice is cooked in a pan or electric rice cooker, but in the tourist area of Jiangxi rice is cooked in bamboo. This adds a flavour dimension to the rice and makes its consumption part of the PTE (Quan and Wang, 2004). A meal that is in other ways ordinary can become a PTE when it is particularly memorable either because of the place it is eaten in or the enjoyment experienced during the meal. Crucial to the experience of becoming a PTE is that the food is memorable (Quan and Wang, 2004).

Within the context of this conceptual model, food can be viewed as an extension of daily routine experiences: if we wish to live, we have to eat. Alternatively it can be viewed as a destination attraction in its own right and represent a PTE. Where tourists are overtly

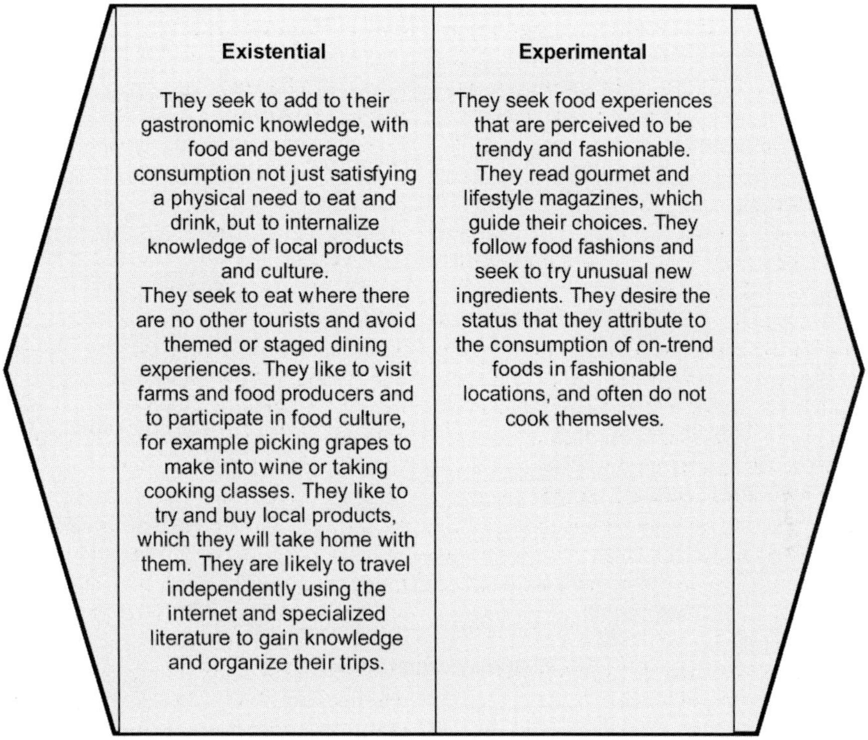

Existential	**Experimental**
They seek to add to their gastronomic knowledge, with food and beverage consumption not just satisfying a physical need to eat and drink, but to internalize knowledge of local products and culture. They seek to eat where there are no other tourists and avoid themed or staged dining experiences. They like to visit farms and food producers and to participate in food culture, for example picking grapes to make into wine or taking cooking classes. They like to try and buy local products, which they will take home with them. They are likely to travel independently using the internet and specialized literature to gain knowledge and organize their trips.	They seek food experiences that are perceived to be trendy and fashionable. They read gourmet and lifestyle magazines, which guide their choices. They follow food fashions and seek to try unusual new ingredients. They desire the status that they attribute to the consumption of on-trend foods in fashionable locations, and often do not cook themselves.

Fig. 17.1. Food behaviour spectrum. (Adapted from Kivela and Crotts, 2006.)

gastro-tourists then they will visit the destination for its food attractions, such as a food festival or wine region, and these will be PTEs. However, they or any other tourist may have a memorable meal that becomes for them a PTE. It should be remembered, however, that seeking variety in food is a perfectly normal activity and one in which most people engage regularly, as meals would be very dull if the same recipe was eaten daily (Quan and Wang, 2004).

Getz and Brown (2006) studied wine consumers in a region of Canada isolated from wine production. Wine consumers were chosen as they are more likely to want to participate in wine activities than those who do not drink wine. The researchers identified three categories of critical attributes of a successful wine tourism experience (Table 17.2).

Ignatov and Smith (2006) identified three types of consumer:

- Type 1: these individuals are more interested in wine tourism than anything else.

- Type 2: interested in food rather than wine. They like dining out as well as visiting farmers markets and similar attractions and events.
- Type 3: interested in both food and wine. They want to participate in the whole food and wine experience. They want to experience a range of activities tied to gastronomy.

All of these tourists influence the destination as they are all viable segments (Ignatov and Smith, 2006).

Future Research

There is a need for future research in this area. Several writers have identified areas for future research in gastronomic tourism marketing, including: market profiles of gastro-tourists and wine tourists; the ethnic groups of visitors, particularly from the perspective of finding out if gastro-tourism is typically an ethnically

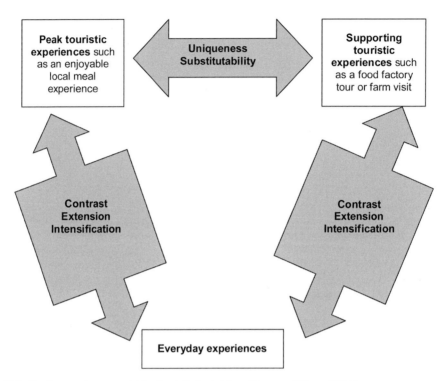

Fig. 17.2. Tourist experience model for food. (Adapted from Quan and Wang, 2004.)

European pursuit; and the propensity for tourists to participate in learning activities around this area (Hjalager and Corigliano, 2000; Heaney *et al.*, 2004; Josiam *et al.*, 2004).

There is also a need to further explore the relationships between culture, heritage, food and restaurants, both from a heritage and restaurant perspective (Howe, 1996; Salamone, 1997; van Westering, 1999; Josiam *et al.*, 2004; Mykletun and Gyimothy, 2010). Likewise, there is need for research in areas relating to gastronomic authenticity, including

Table 17.2. Critical features of the wine tourism experience: a consumer perspective.

Key product feature	Attributes	Related features
Core wine product	Visitor-friendly wineries Knowledgeable winery staff Wine festivals Familiar wineries	Large number of wineries to visit Famous wines Winery group tours
Core destination appeal	Attractive scenery Pleasant climate Moderately priced accommodation Easy to obtain information Well-signposted wine trails	Lots to see and do Opportunities for outdoor recreation
Cultural product	Unique accommodation with regional characteristics Fine dining and gourmet restaurants Traditional wine village	Speciality shops or markets selling local farm produce

Adapted from Getz and Brown (2006).

the staging of meal experiences and the balance between authenticity and modern production techniques (Mykletun and Gyimothy, 2010).

Conclusion

This chapter discussed current research in the area of gastronomy within the context of tourism. It particularly looked at the importance of gastronomic tourism as a niche market and the role of food within the overall tourism experience. A case study of the motivations of tourists in Bordeaux, France, was included, which identified motivations in relation to gastronomy. The chapter then explored the role of gastronomy in destination marketing and the representation of food to tourists.

Gastronomic authenticity has been investigated, and elements in the development of authentic gastronomic tourism experiences outlined (Cohen and Avieli, 2004). The negative aspects of food for tourists and the challenges they presents were also identified and analysed. The gastro-tourism link with entrepreneurship was outlined and case studies from Norway and Canada were included. The fundamental relationship between gastronomy and heritage was discussed. Lastly, the chapter explored key research in satisfaction with the meal experience in the gastro-tourism context, and key concepts were identified and discussed.

It is clear that gastronomy plays a crucial role in travel motivation, being either a primary or secondary motivator for most tourists. Its use and representation in destination marketing materials is very important and an image of 'safe exoticism' is valuable. Tourists want gastronomic adventures but within a safe environment, and tourism industry professionals need to recognize that for many consumers unfamiliar food and dining experiences can be threatening. Given the intrinsic relationship between food and culture, and the links between heritage and food for all stakeholders, it is important that interactions between hosts and visitors are monitored and managed to ensure that all participants benefit from these exchanges. Destination entrepreneurs are a vital part of this process as they develop authentic gastronomic experiences that are perceived to be 'safe' by tourists.

Review Questions

1. Consider a tourism destination you know well. What capacity exists to develop gastronomic tourism?

2. Critically evaluate the management and marketing of food and wine tourism in a destination of your choice.

3. Considering the nature of the tourism and hospitality industries, evaluate the way in which gastronomic tourism strengthens the relationship between these two sectors.

References

Beer, S. (2008) Authenticity and food experience – commercial and academic perspectives. *Journal of Foodservice* 19, 153–163.

Buckland, B.S. (2007) Eating authenticity; M.F.K. Fisher and American visions of France. *Petits Propos Culinaire* 83, 81–91.

Bordeaux Tourism (2007) *Bordeaux Tourisme.* Number 85. Bordeaux Tourist Office, Bordeaux, France.

Bourdieu, P. (1984) *Distinction.* Harvard University Press, Cambridge, Massachusetts, USA.

Cohen, E. and Avieli, N. (2004) Food in tourism: attraction and impediment. *Annals of Tourism Research* 31, 755–778.

Correia, A., Moital, M., Ferreira Da Costa, C. and Peres, R. (2008) The determinants of gastronomic tourists' satisfaction: a second-order factor analysis. *Journal of Foodservice* 19, 164–176.

Devesa, M., Laguna, M. and Palacios, A. (2010) The role of motivation in visitor satisfaction: empirical evidence in rural tourism. *Tourism Management* 31, 547–552.

Du Rand, G.E. and Heath, E. (2006) Towards a framework for food tourism as an element of destination marketing. *Current Issues in Tourism* 9, 206–233.

Fischler, C. (1988) Food, self and identity. *Social Science Information* 27, 275–292.

Getz, D. and Brown, G. (2006) Critical success factors for wine tourism regions: a demand analysis. *Tourism Management* 27, 146–158.

Gillespie, C. (2001) *European Gastronomy into the 21st Century.* Butterworth-Heinemann, Oxford, UK.

Hall, M., Mitchell, R. and Sharples, L. (2003) Consuming places: the role of food, wine and tourism in regional development. In: Hall, M., Sharples, L., Mitchell, R., Macionis, N. and Cambourne, B. (eds) *Food Tourism Around the World. Development, Management and Markets.* Butterworth Heinemann, Amsterdam, Holland, pp. 24–59.

Harrington, R.J. (2005) Defining gastronomic identity: the impact of environment and culture on prevailing components, texture and flavors in wine and food. *Journal of Culinary Science and Technology* 4, 129–152.

Heaney, R.G. and Robertson, G. (2004) The great Australian bite: travel patterns of culinary visitors. *Tourism Research Report* 5, 37–50.

Hegarty, J. (2009) How might gastronomy be a suitable discipline for testing the validity of different modern and postmodern claims about what may be called avant-garde? *Journal of Culinary Science and Technology* 7, 1–18.

Hjalager, A.M. (2004) What do tourists eat and why? Towards a sociology of gastronomy and tourism. *Tourism* 52, 195–201.

Hjalager, A.M. and Corigliano, M.A. (2000) Food for tourists – determinants of an image. *International Journal of Tourism Research* 2, 281–293.

Howe, G. (1996) An untapped heritage resource – the British Public House. *International Journal of Wine Marketing* 8, 41–52.

Ignatov, E. and Smith, S. (2006) Segmenting Canadian culinary tourists. *Current Issues in Tourism* 9, 235–255.

Josiam, B.M., Mattson, M. and Sullivan, P. (2004) The Historaunt: heritage tourism at Mickey's Dining Car. *Tourism Management* 25, 453–461.

Kivela, J. and Crotts, J.C. (2006) Gastronomy tourism: a meaningful travel market segment. *Journal of Culinary Science and Technology* 4, 39–55.

Markwick, M. (2001) Postcards from Malta: image, consumption, context. *Annals of Tourism Research* 28, 417–438.

Mintel (2010) *European Food Retailing Briefing.* Mintel, London, UK.

Morgan, M., Hemmington, N. and Edwards, J.S.A. (2008) From foodservice to food experience? Introduction to the topical focus papers: extraordinary experiences in foodservice. *Journal of Foodservice* 19, 151–152.

Mykletun, R.J. and Gyimothy, S. (2010) Beyond the renaissance of the traditional Voss sheep's-head meal: tradition, culinary art, scariness and entrepreneurship. *Tourism Management* 31, 434–446.

Nield, K., Kozak, M. and Legrys, G. (2000) The role of food service in tourist satisfaction. *Hospitality Management* 19, 375–384.

Okumus, B., Okumus, F. and Mckercher, B. (2007) Incorporating local and international cuisines in the marketing of tourism destinations: the cases of Hong Kong and Turkey. *Tourism Management* 28, 253–261.

Plummer, R., Telfer, D. and Hashimoto, A. (2006) The rise and fall of the Waterloo–Wellington Ale Trail: a study of collaboration within the tourism industry. *Current Issues in Tourism* 9, 191–205.

Povey, G. (2006) Factors influencing the identity of regional food products; a grounded theory approach. *Cyprus Journal of Sciences* 4, 145–157.

Quan, S. and Wang, N. (2004) Towards a structural model of the tourist experience: an illustration from food experiences in tourism. *Tourism Management* 25, 297–305.

Reisinger, Y. and Steiner, C.J. (2006) Reconceptualising object authenticity. *Annals of Tourism Research* 33, 65–86.

Rozin, P. (1999) Food is fundamental, fun, frightening, and far-reaching. *Social Research* 66, 9–30.

Salamone, F.A. (1997) Authenticity in tourism: the San Angel Inns. *Annals of Tourism Research* 24, 305–321.

Seymour, D. (2004) The social construction of taste. In: Sloan, D. (ed.) *Culinary Taste: Consumer Behaviour in the International Restaurant Sector.* Elsevier, Butterworth-Heinemann, Oxford, UK, pp. 2–22.

Smith, S. and Costello, C. (2009) Segmenting visitors to a culinary event: motivations, travel behavior, and expenditures. *Journal of Hospitality Marketing and Management* 18, 44–67.

Telfer, D. (2000) Tastes of Niagara: building strategic alliances between tourism and agriculture *International Journal of Hospitality and Tourism Administration* 1, 71–88.

Van Westering, J. (1999) Heritage and gastronomy: the pursuits of the 'new tourist'. *International Journal of Heritage Studies* 5, 75–81.

Watts, J. (2010) Chinese legal experts call for ban on eating cats and dogs. *The Guardian,* 26 January.

18 Religious Tourism

Peter Wiltshier

Introduction

This chapter considers the importance placed by the guardians or stakeholders of religious tourism to the provision of services for visitors, with special reference and examples taken from the Anglican Church in England. The outcomes and output of religious tourism research are assessed for the twin purposes of meeting the expectations of the both the institutions as religious spaces and the extent to which tourism can support these places. Tourism that includes visits to a church, shrine or place of pilgrimage offers all visitors a clear and unambiguous attraction, yet spiritual and religious tourism remains a most understudied area (Ron, 2007). People now travel for a variety of complex personal needs as they aim for some spiritual nirvana or self-actualization (Hall, cited in Timothy and Olsen, 2006).

Religious Tourism Today

There is now a proliferation of information for visitors concerning churches, religious sites and monuments with a focus on beliefs, mythology and legends, many of which constitute the basis for a rich heritage and cultural tourism. Britain, much like well-established cultural and heritage destinations in Europe and Asia, offers the visitor a wealth of man-made sites of pilgrimage and spiritual significance for a truly global audience. Within the confines of these islands we find evidence that domestic visitors are becoming more involved with this variety of

heritage tourism. In 2003, Opinion Research Business conducted research that found that 90% of people in England go into a church building at least once in any year (Sheppard, 2006). Researchers are in no doubt as to the growing importance of religious sites for tourism, and their importance in economic as well as sociocultural terms as sites of current and former worship (e.g. Shackley, 2001; Timothy and Olsen, 2006). Authors debate whether religious and heritage sites actually improve our knowledge in a politically neutral manner. That is, sites of religious tourism may lead to an understanding and knowledge that reinforces spiritual prejudices and emphasizes differences in belief systems, and therefore their physical manifestation in the tourism products (Andriotis, 2009; Poria and Ashworth, 2009). Religious tourism can effectively help identify and promote the unique aspects of destinations in increasingly homogeneous global tourism.

Tourism management can be used by religious sites to benefit the site and the community as well as the visitor. Partnerships between hosts and guests that link the sacred and the secular can be explored for the mutual benefit of all stakeholders. Some sites take advantage of localized resources that deliver a successful tourism product to the visitor and to their own community and the financial rewards are then clearly identifiable to all of these stakeholders. This chapter acknowledges the partnership approach to this type of tourism development and notes that it is very much a customized and location-specific model of accessible tourism development that is proposed for the future (see also Chapter 7). Models of management of religious sites that focus on the essential requirements for the benefit of the site, for the interpretation of beliefs and values that reinforce identity, and perhaps unique aspects of that site, are important for consumers, hosts and guardians of sites and for the future health of the tourism industry.

In the 21st century our attention, when considering the demand side, is focused on the human need for personal development and continuous personal development based upon self-actualization or the realization of personal goals and achievements. These can be linked with a spiritual or belief-based component of development. Effectively, this places tourist facilities adjacent to and within cities such as Mecca, Rome, Istanbul, Athens, Benares, Jerusalem and Santiago de Compostela. In addition, perhaps more local destinations, such as one's familial church or temple, are now at centre stage for worship and for tourism. A dual purpose is common for many religious sites. This dual purpose – sacred worship and secular (non-religious) tourism – creates special demands on the religious infrastructure, including the staff responsible for sacred worship and individuals and teams with responsibility for destination management. This duality brings special problems for site managers as well as for theologians and the clergy. The skill sets needed by the clergy for effective worship and sacred purposes are not questioned here. However, the management of religious sites creates an agenda that has, as yet, been largely unexplored. The skills that are now required for effective tourism management both emphasize the sacred purpose and mission and identify ways to maximize the revenue that is needed for ongoing site maintenance (McKercher *et al.*, 2008; Levi and Kocher, 2009; Collins-Kreiner, 2010).

Historical Perspectives

In order to successfully integrate religious sites within tourism it is essential to map the history and contemporary objectives of the local community against the hardware that religious buildings, regalia and mementoes contain. The brand identity and key selling message are usually reinforced by these components. The evidence is used to reflect contemporary practices and consider ways in which tourism can benefit from the presence of heritage and cultural sites identified through religious tourism and ways in which tourism can support the mission and strategies of the religious site.

This chapter extends the management of religious and sacred site paradigms discussed by both academics and practitioners (Shackley, 2001, 2005, 2006; Lane, 2005; Busby, 2006; Olsen and Timothy, 2006; Timothy and Conover, 2006; Rivera *et al.*, 2009). It is important now to identify ways in which stakeholders can measure the value and positive outcomes and output of non-worship visits to religious sites and to then identify whether these sites should be open for visitors or kept closed to conserve heritage and enable worship. The big question may be whether it is cost-effective to manage these places as cultural heritage sites. A further question is the extent to which religious sites, and those that manage them, value or consider the place as a cultural heritage site for the benefit of a wide range of stakeholders. A destination has a dual responsibility for maintaining the religious infrastructure for worship and visitation, and therefore ambiguities arise in identifying how best the destination and site can be funded and managed.

In the UK, Salisbury Cathedral, a famous Norman church, attracts 300,000 visitors each year (as tourists and as worshippers). The ambiguity arises from a donation being sought for admission from all visitors. The admission charge is neither compulsory nor welcomed by visitors. The cathedral needs the funds to cover the costs of managing a world-class visitor attraction as well as maintaining a significant site of worship. In addition, the admission fee covers the costs of staffing and interpretation for visitors, but not quite so transparently also covers some of the costs incurred in maintaining the cathedral for worship or sacred use. At York Minster, visitors pay an initial admission fee, a further fee to visit the Treasury and an additional charge to climb the tower to see views of York.

Case Study 18.1. How benefits can outweigh costs.

York Minster (which alone attracts 800,000 visitors each year), Lincoln Cathedral and Lichfield Cathedral are important sacred spaces in the UK that attract both domestic and overseas visitors. The major issues for these sacred sites concern effective and efficient management that maximizes the experience for visitors and minimizes the costs incurred in managing that experience, together with the provision of additional services that also need to represent value for money, such as tour guides or an audio tour.

The concern for site managers revolves around minimizing the cost in exchange for service provision, while ensuring the experience has satisfied the visitor and created an opportunity for the visitor to sense history, temporarily join a community of cultural importance and experience a mystic thrill. To successfully manage the site, the provider should add value in terms of food and drink, music and performance.

The experience should be linked to a partnership with visitor attractions in relatively close proximity. These partnerships create another option for additionality and include retail shops, museums, heritage buildings such as monuments or castles and stately homes. In York, for example, the City Walls and National Railway Museum are within walking distance of the cathedral. Visitors, except those treating the visit as pilgrimage or travelling for spiritual reasons, often need a compelling reason to participate in religious tourism as there is usually physical effort required in exchange for the benefits of the visit.

Visitors currently record in visitor books how awestruck they have felt and how inspired they have been by both the stories of the sites and the magnitude and magnificence of the sites themselves. They have further commented on positive interpretative experiences, where some of the value of admission may be transcribed into a more tangible benefit.

In considering public policy and strategy for regional community-based tourism development we may identify how religious tourism can meet the challenges of sustaining communities, more so in rural locations; how religious tourism can foster stronger and more effective relationships with communities; and how religious tourism can help non-traditional users, including young people, to engage with destinations.

Without doubt, the prime reason that anyone with responsibility for the conservation of historic buildings will continue to encourage visitors is the need to raise revenue to cover restoration and meet maintenance costs of church estates and church yards (see Chapter 13). Not only do visitors provide an income stream, they also open up opportunities for practical career developments in management and health and safety, all the while maximizing returns on the investment in infrastructure while providing employment and possible new and diversified skills in rural locations, as well as opportunities for volunteering (see Chapter 13). It is recognized that there are inherent difficulties and unexpected additional costs in site management created by inappropriate visitation and even vandalism and theft (McKercher *et al.*, 2008). However, it is acknowledged that developing partnerships, new businesses and new careers aligned with restoration and rejuvenation is a long-term and complex strategy; it requires detailed and painstaking work and reflection and years of human effort (Lane, 2005). A management focus in examining tourism as a business opportunity for any religious site does not preclude the need to consider spiritual activity, an experience that provides meaning for consumption by a wide audience and, above all, an inspirational experience (Rivera *et al.*, 2009). Many religious buildings dedicate a quiet area for visitors who wish to engage in contemplation and reflection.

Defining Religious Tourism

Religious tourism may be conceived as the ways in which religious sites relate to visitors' needs. One definition is provided by the Churches Tourism Association (2007) as 'promoting best practice in welcoming visitors to places of worship and developing the tourism potential and visitor experience of a unique part of our historical and contemporary sacred heritage'.

Woodward (2004) defined religious tourism as consumer-led and explained that 'Tourist

---

Case Study 18.2. Simplicity and maintenance: the example of Hrastovlje, Slovenia.

This special place of devotion and pilgrimage is located within 30 minutes' drive of both Trieste in Italy and the delightful ancient Venetian port city of Piran in Slovenia. The church at Hrastovlje (Fig. 18.1) is an example of a religious site that has yet to become commodified. In the 1950s a church caretaker removed the whitewash inside and found breathtaking Biblical frescoes dating back to 1490. The village's name translates into English as 'the place of oaks'. There is a well-known fresco of the 'death dance', pictorially describing the human journey from birth to death, which is typical of religious iconography from the period.

This ancient, yet noble and simple structure comprises a Romanesque church; an impressive bell tower or campanile; and an incredible eight-metre high surrounding defensive stone wall to protect Christian worshippers from the raiding Turks.

It is a beautiful and simple setting in which to commune with your spiritual side, wonder at the 12th century building with its highly descriptive and glorious painted frescoes and acknowledge an epoch in which humans held their faith and beliefs in awe, asked few questions about life's direction and abided by the sacraments.

---

activity at religious sites represents an important source of income for many faith institutions and organizations, generating funds for repairs and maintenance'. Busby (2006) suggested that such tourism is in effect driven by sacred consumption and 'contemporary tourism has its roots in religious pilgrimage'. In fact, many of the major cities in the world have grown through their associations with historic pilgrimage and the wealth generated through this early form of tourism.

Religious tourism can be based upon three paradigms. The first is in the promotion of service within tourism. The second concerns the sufficiency of partnership and networks to support development; and the third is a focus on the quality of the product and sustainability (Zairi and Whymark, 2000; Shackley, 2001; Saravanan and Rao, 2006). From the consumers' perspective, consideration needs to be given to demand from individuals with complex, diverse and even chaotic needs, who are internally focused and rational. Increasingly, relational church administrators are aspiring to become more inclusive, aware of diverse needs, proactive, nurturing and

Fig. 18.1. Trinity Church, Hrastovlje, Slovenia.

Case Study 18.3. Contemporary travellers visit spectacular sites of former pilgrimage: Monolithos, Rhodes, Greece.

If you hire a car in Rhodes and travel leisurely south on the western coastline of this Dodecanese island, past olive and citrus groves dotted on hillsides and along an almost deserted coastline south of the busy Diagoras Airport, you will eventually come to a cliff-top site called Monolithos. The village is nondescript. Visitors seem to come for delicious honey from the surrounding pine forests. But as you drive down the tortuous road towards the beach, Monolithos, a dramatic Venetian castle, rises above. Monolithos is perched just beyond the village on a 300-foot-high rock. Just like a pilgrim, you must walk from the car park and café up the narrow pathway and steps to the almost deserted castle. On the top of the rock there is a small church dedicated to Saint Panteleimon. Adjacent to the pretty whitewashed church, complete with an icon and candles yet to be lit, is another ruined chapel, a relic of earlier times. No one approaches you for a donation. Even the honey seller has disappeared as you return to the foot of the castle to travel onwards, refreshed by the fantastic Aegean views west as the sun sets (Fig. 18.2). This is indeed a spiritual journey for all of humanity.

Rhodes is home to many religions, including sun worshippers. A common spatial theme, repeated all over this lovely and sparsely settled island, is the location of sites of worship and celebration on mountain tops. These sites range from Monolithos and Kameiros in the west to Lindos in the east and Ialysos at the northern tip – this last special site with spectacular views over the sea to Turkey and Marmaris. Religion was well defended from these splendid vantage points. Today's sun worshippers cluster around, and never venture very far from, the somewhat congested resort of Faliraki and its beach, which is approached from Diagoras Airport by a multi-lane highway.

Fig. 18.2. View west from ruined chapel, Monolithos, Rhodes.

externally focused (Cohen, 1996; Powell and Geoghegan, 2005).

Commentators within religious organizations are aware of the need to become more responsive to individuals, to recognize diversity in needs and a new response of recognizing mobility (Jackson, 2002). Fundamentally, Jackson, speaking about Christian churches identified the Church's requirement to review strategies to become proactive and engage the 'relational' approach, perhaps to attract young people while focusing on resolving financial difficulties. The Church's needs are identified through a mission, which includes becoming 'energised by faith', outwardly looking at local and global issues, taking risks in facing the costs of change, nurturing communities in lay matters and leadership, being aware of diverse needs and significantly focusing on doing the 'basics well', while being relaxed about what is not being done (Warren, 2004). Shackley identified the need to position religious sites as service providers between visitors and specific sites of tourism or visitation. The following factors were perceived by Shackley as facilitators of service delivery: (i) sales promotional intermediaries; (ii) collateral; (iii) technology; (iv) access to facilities; (v) feedback and reviews; (vi) interpretation; (vii) monitoring and review action; (viii) volunteers from within communities; (ix) sacred activity – worship.

Shackley (2001) considered these as enablers of a postmodern eschatology and of relational religious tourism, to relate consumption and sacred needs to the specific sites of worship as sacred places rather than as secular heritage sites, and as drivers of new (religious) tourism management.

Supply Issues: Diversity and Identity

The paradigm of association and partnership, of working with an integrated vertical and horizontal supply chain, has been well documented through the multidisciplinary construct of tourism (Mowforth and Munt, 1998; Crouch, 1999; Shaw and Williams, 2004; Hall, 2005; Beech and Chadwick, 2006). The duality of place is a theme identified

through the need to manage the 'convergence of sacred and secular space' (Olsen, 2006).

Moreover, it is necessary to identify and capture the central role of volunteers and amateurs in services for visitation and tourism (Olsen, 2006). This theme of managing people and visitors through volunteers should be explored, identifying skills needed within the management structures to meet complex and contradictory demands from sacred and secular visitors, managing traffic and visitor flow, providing effective interpretation services, understanding strategic intent and a central theme to manage the important 'sense of place' (Olsen, 2006).

Management approaches may be predicated upon diversity and identity created and embedded within communities (see the model of cultural, territorial identity; Ray, 1998). Visitors arriving at a church for non-worship purposes may well be seeking information regarding ancestors and significant milestones in their families' lives such as births, marriages or burials (genealogy). They might also be interested in the history of the area, the local vernacular style and architecture and wildlife within religious open spaces (graveyards and unusual sites such as Whipsnade Tree Cathedral), in different religions and philosophies or just in 'having a look round'. This suggests that religious sites must meet the needs of diverse groups of people and diverse visitor needs.

Tacit knowledge – 'know how' as well as 'know what' – requires skills of an interdisciplinary nature, drawn from multiple projects and processes, to devise tourism management strategies for religious sites. Volunteers and lay workers will therefore require a wide set of skills and skills development to create 'communities of practice'. Appropriate skills development for volunteers is broadly similar across a range of consumer-facing roles (be it volunteering in a stately home, at a country park, within a zoo or in a church), yet specific provision for volunteer training and skills development in churches is almost non-existent and funding uncertain.

Religious tourism sites can draw on diverse mentors and exemplars of best practice to help adjustments in current practices as well as structures. Lessons can be acquired from supportive projects that focus on new ways of information gathering, analysing, communicating, negotiating, networking and resourcing that can be drawn from local, regional and global spatial studies. Church tourism depends on resources to maintain the fabric of heritage sites, manage the damage caused by visitor numbers and weather, and address the need for archaeological conservation, crowd control and managing access and visitor capacity. To some extent, managing peoples' expectations of sites requires psychological skills that are not in the standard repertoire of church wardens and volunteers (Shackley, 2001). Few religious sites can afford to be open to visitors seven days a week even during daylight hours without fear of vandalism and theft, although some buildings have installed alarms and CCTV (often funded through donations), which reduces insurance premiums to facilitate more flexible and more regular opening. Regrettably, it is common to find many churches closed to avoid petty vandalism, often emanating from local communities.

Olsen (2006) identified a dual-management model to incorporate internal as well as external management issues. In terms of internal management, key themes to be explored and developed include managing worshippers as well as secular visitors and the context of worship conflicting with the context of visiting. Internal issues also include managing finances, contradictions in selling goods and services, accessibility of sites, preservation and conservation of sites, interpretation, managing toilets, and food and beverage consumption. External issues relate to government intervention, musealization, hardening of sites, contestation of usage, cooperative planning and managing elites. Shaw and Williams (2004) identified the following as key indicators for sustainable church tourism development: access, support, market research, community involvement, plurality, training and partnerships.

Many factors emerging as priorities for sustainable successful tourism partnerships with churches derive from consumers' increasing individualism as embracers of niche activities, coupled to government deregulation and devolution of responsibilities in skills acquisition to the local level (Leitch, 2006). Rotherham (2007) identified that challenges are present in the deregulation and devolved responsibilities for managing infrastructure and sites and therefore the necessity to endeavour, through management practices, to broaden any benefits to communities as well as to churches and to develop communities in the future. He also identified that motivations from current and predicted demand come jointly from spiritual motivation and impulse visiting, as well as pull factors such as family connections, links to famous people, literary connections and a growing fondness for the architecture of churches. He finally concluded that risk increases with greater demand for a wider range of purposes and that costs associated with these (e.g. insurance, repairing vandalism and other damage) are not matched by incomes.

Accessibility

Shackley (2001) identified key resources and skills required to actively manage religious sites where visitors are welcome. These include skills to control visitors through managing car parking, bus parking and access, directing visitors and managing flow, moderating accessibility, managing queues, dealing with vandalism and graffiti, managing damage to site infrastructure, conservation, noise from crowds and the physical presence of worshippers and visitors for other purposes. In addition, a range of other skills is also valuable for the strategic management of religious sites, including events management, the ability to manage funding applications (e.g. for restoration, interpretation) and fundraising, and the appointment of conservators who can identify and maintain the fabric of buildings, tombs and monuments.

This theme is reinforced by promoting tourism in sacred space (Shackley, 2001). To link consumption to church facilities and 'services' it is possible to locate visitors and sites through a variety of enablers. These enablers are intermediaries, technology, access, interpretation and feedback, monitoring activity reports, feedback from volunteers, and community trust and levels of use for worship and sacred activities (Shackley, 2001). For a further discussion around accessibility, see Chapter 12.

Partnership

The concept of partnership or involvement in a network or trail is important in successful site management. The costs incurred in interpretation, promotion and management can be ameliorated through partnership. Partnership in the sense of horizontal integration within the destination's attractions and features can lead to greater visibility for the site and for the destination and an intelligent, well-mapped trail can support understanding and create a low-cost promotional opportunity through clever cooperative marketing.

This demands connectivity, partnership and vertical and horizontal integration using business supply chains (Hall, 2005). Matching the sacred needs of the Church with the key themes being sought through ministry include energizing the congregation and the clergy through faith, creating an outward-looking focus through engaging communities both locally and for a global 'audience', seeking spiritual guidance, not seeking to satisfy all, taking risks (related to change and growth), creating high levels of community involvement and engagement and leading on lay work as well as spiritual tasks, increasing awareness of diverse needs and becoming inclusive, focused on basics and relaxed about 'what is not being done' (Warren, 2004).

Quality issues

Performance measurement and the quality of the visitor experience determine a possible series of interventions (Zairi and Whymark, 2000; Beech and Chadwick, 2006; Saravanan and Rao, 2006). Key indicators for benchmarking the performance of services should be constructed in addition to specific market

segments to be reviewed for expectations and satisfaction. Religious organizations managing sites often have a minimal budget for promotion and therefore need to consider ways in which they can achieve quality systems through economies of scale wherever feasible. Such a list of services is based upon research conducted by the author and could potentially include the following provision for visitors: bookstalls; burial, church records and historical documents; interpretation (e.g. brochures, flyers, leaflets, booklets), which can be both free and cost-recovered; commentary; audio tours; free gifts; informal chat opportunities; information boards and displays; internet access; libraries; musical space; playing of musical instruments (and a dedicated area for this); quiet space for thinking and reflection; refreshment space; shelter; and a visitor book.

Community Involvement

The measure of community involvement outside worship is considered relevant to the provision of services to visitors or tourists. Both are dependent on the careful coordination of resources such as volunteers and a managed promotional campaign. There is ample evidence of campaigns for the preservation of church monuments and fabric (e.g. Jackson, 2002; Warren, 2004). Community involvement can be defined as the active provision of services and activities at church venues for persons resident in the local area.

There are several aspects to community involvement, reinforcing the concept of partnership and collaboration between suppliers in tourism: (i) the urban involvement of churches; (ii) the degree of conviction about the involvement that will be considered; (iii) the levels of innovation and proactivity; and (iv) the perspective of the local action groups, such as the local Women's Institute and Scout and Guides movements. Many of these groups use spaces such as churches or meeting halls for flower festival events, mother and toddler groups, parish meetings, youth groups and other activities.

Fig. 18.3. Interpretation at All Saints' Church, Bakewell.

Managing the Visitor Experience

Management of visitors and their expectations is essential to ensure the successful delivery of religious tourism. To link this consumption to facilities and services it is necessary to include a variety of enablers. These enablers are the intermediaries, technology, access and interpretation that facilitate the visitor experience (Fig. 18.3) (Shackley, 2001).

Many religious sites produce a brochure, which may range from a small folded leaflet to a full-colour guidebook, although in some instances many small tourism attractions, religious sites included, have identified the value of a website in lieu of a document. Others maintain a supply of leaflets for casual visitors and aim to recover costs through donations made by visitors within the church. Major churches often have a shop on site for sales of relevant books, gift items and cards.

Case Study 18.4. Derbyshire Churches

Churches in Derbyshire (Fig. 18.4) have been important draw cards for visitors since the Norman Conquest. Early records confirm visitors' interest in the Saxon churches around Castleton in the north of the county and Repton in the south. The historical relationship between the sacred and secular became important in the minds of many visitors. The incentive to visit in the third millennium is not much different to that incentive of the first and second. The history of Christianity in Derby goes back well over a thousand years (Page, 1970). Pevsner mentions the relationship between the countryside and the built environment in his seminal work of 1953: 'the centre, especially north of a line from Ashbourne to Belper, is all country rightly popular with tourists'. He continues 'Derbyshire [did] not possess a cathedral nor many parish churches as spectacular as those of East Anglia…instead of grand churches there are grand houses'. A later publication celebrates many of the churches that informed this research, including the parish churches of Breadsall, Ashbourne, Wirksworth, Bakewell, Eyam, Hope, Tideswell, Youlgreave and Derby. St Michael's and St Mary's in Melbourne is significant and attractive to both worshippers and visitors as Derbyshire's most complete Norman church (Anderson, 1984).

Many a fine country house was and still is associated with a church. Some of these early churches are now considered at least as historically important as the country house. Many of the churches in the grounds of historic properties also still function as places of worship within their communities. A further theme reflects the industrial past of the diocese, which is mainly primary industries; mining, manufacturing and quarrying. The production of lead for church and domestic roofing and spouting has been central to the evolution of several communities within the diocese.

Current research identifies a lack of apparent awareness of the existing promotional and development agendas and agencies available throughout the diocese. The 2006 study of community use of churches showed evidence of expertise available throughout the diocese and a multifaith approach towards supporting tourism as a regeneration tool was supported (Sheppard, 2006). Another key issue, which may be worrying for some, is the ageing population in the rural areas of the diocese: 46% of the

Fig. 18.4. An architectural gem, All Saints' Chapel, Steetley.

population is aged over 45 years (Sheppard, 2006). Educating and disseminating good practices will be somewhat hampered by lack of ready access to information technology services and providers in many churches throughout this sample. Table 18.1 identifies potential churches and visitor segments within the diocese.

One such supportive and informative project was the Cascade project. The Cascade project, pioneered in the diocese by the district and county council's local tourism officers together with the diocesan tourism advisers, was launched in 2003 at ten sites within the diocese and was useful in connecting key churches through one brochure. However, this project needs essential ongoing research to support its continuation. Since 2003, the district and county tourism structures have changed and it is felt that this change has not aided the collaborative project that Cascade was intended to become. When questioned, several churches knew nothing of Cascade and its intent.

Unfortunately many of the smaller churches with special features, notably church architecture such as Chellaston alabaster monuments (Fig. 18.5), reredos (screens), piscinas (basins) and sedilias (seating), which were in regular use by the clergy, do not have sufficient information provision for visitors. This may be deliberate to avoid paying hefty insurance premiums (under valuation) and to minimize bringing the value of such items to the attention of those who may wish to steal or damage them. Church wardens allude to the difficulty of protecting valuable features from damage and theft. This is an interesting area worthy of further investigation.

St Lawrence Church at Eyam, which is celebrated as a historical outpost of the plague in the 17th century, has a school-visit programme that is cost-effective and incorporates a multifaith approach to visitors. Interestingly, the church does not insist on a specific fee for any group wishing to visit, but most schools automatically make a donation. Donations made by organized groups cover the costs of administration, cleaning and organizing the visits. Over the past 20 years sufficient brochures, displays and packs for teachers have been made available and costs have been recovered using this voluntary donation regime.

Many of the churches in Derbyshire contain Chellaston alabaster effigies and carved monuments that are rare and delicate. They cannot be maintained and kept presentable without significant professional restoration and appropriate funds for such maintenance. Numerous other tombs, woodworks and other features are present throughout the county's churches, which are all splendid examples that draw in visitors to the churches. Where such invitations to visitors exist there must be a greater effort made to encourage visitors to give donations in exchange for relevant and accessible interpretation, which should connect churches with the setting and landscape, with other churches and with other buildings to help create a better understanding of the church's environment and its place in history. These features not only attract visitors in their own right, but they also enhance the possibility of connectivity between a church and its parish and raise important funds for ongoing preservation and conservation.

A sense of invitation

St Peter's Church in Derby offers a city welcome to visitors, as does the Church of St Mary's and All Saints, Chesterfield. The focus of the clergy on extending a warm invitation year round to both current and new visitors is notable. No distinction is made between worshippers in the traditional sense and casual passers-by who have a need for engagement with the building for quiet prayer, meditation or 'neutral' space where the visitors' needs are paramount.

Food, drink and entertainment

Several churches celebrate visitors and reward guests and key stakeholders with the opportunity to eat and drink within the church building. All Saints' Church in Breadsall is a good example of a place where sponsors are recognized and the contribution that they have made over the year is celebrated in feasting. Recognition of benefactors to St Lawrence's Church in Ticknall is shown in Fig. 18.6.

Open for the business of genealogy

The issue that emerges as fundamental to all churches is the accessibility of the church to all visitors. Visitors, in addition to worshippers, can and do anticipate help in tracking ancestors and visiting graves

Continued

Case Study 18.4. Continued.

Table 18.1. Defining visitors (market segments) – an examination of motivation and satisfaction.

Visitors	Example churches	Concept and good practice
University graduates and their families	Cathedral of All Saints, Derby	Plurality Interfaith and non-traditional users
Theatre, performance artists and audience	Church of St Mary's and All Saints, Chesterfield	Visitor experience Churchyard performances – Roman re-enactments
Benefactors	Clergy in Chesterfield	Features and benefits Peter Ball sculpture 'Madonna and Child'
Seekers of advice at times of crisis	St Peter's Church, Derby	Partnership From debt counselling to helping the homeless
Seekers of counsel	St Peter's Church, Derby	Plurality and partnership Open-door policy
Gourmets	St Edmund's Church, Castleton All Saints' Church, Breadsall	Food and beverage Café, soup kitchen
Wedding guests	All Saints' Church, Breadsall	Opportunities An average wedding ceremony contributes £400 to the church concerned
Special interest organizations, historical societies	All Saints' Church, Breadsall	Genealogy and Partnership Erasmus Darwin Foundation celebrations
Summer-time passers-by	Ashbourne Deanery	Innovation Displays at Alsop, Tissington, Fenny Bentley, Parwich and Thorpe
Schools and students	St Lawrence Church, Eyam	Innovation Organized school-tour parties
Hoodlums and vandals	St Lawrence Church, Eyam	Innovation Donor-funded alarm system
Volunteers	Any of the churches	Community involvement Rotas and staff in attendance for interpretation
Shoppers	Any of the larger town churches	Visitor experience Books, toys, gifts, cards, souvenirs
Craftspeople	Church of St Mary's and All Saints, Chesterfield	Innovation 'Madonna and Child'
Villagers, townspeople, residents	Any of the churches	Training and skills Pantomimes, flower festivals, mother and toddler groups
Day-trippers	Any of the churches	Information provision Cascade project (see text)
Walkers, hikers	Church of St Giles at Hartington for proximity to shopping and refreshments/ toilets	Information provision
Museum curators, technicians and archivists	Any of the churches	Community involved Partnership
Genealogists	Church of St Mary's and All Saints, Chesterfield	Genealogy Partnership
Gardeners, horticulturalists	St Bartholomew's Church, Hognaston	Partnership, features and benefits Flower festival each May
Pensioners, veterans	All Saints' Church, Breadsall	Community involved, invitation by church to take tea, coffee, cakes
Young local residents	New Mills United Reform Church, New Mills	Training and skills, invitation Youth 'hang out'

Fig. 18.5. Scarce relic in All Saints' Church, Breadsall.

and tombs as part of the service provided by the Church. A secondary issue is the idiosyncratic way in which churches are open or closed other than at times of worship. The Church of St Lawrence at Whitwell is an example of such confusion. The church is open while local schools are open and locked when schools are closed. Apparently this resulted from concerns by the parish over the inappropriate behaviour of young people in the church. While this situation is regrettable, it has the effect of denying worship and visits during holidays and at weekends. It has the potential to alienate the church from the very people that it may well seek to serve.

Continued

Case Study 18.4. Continued.

Fig. 18.6. Benefactors of St Lawrence's Church, Ticknall.

Networks and Partnership

The concept of partnership is central to developing a relationship between the multiple sectors and organizations involved in tourism. Not only do churches form the central monumental, historic and inspiring feature of the man-made environment in several towns and villages, but they also form the core of the visitor offer made by each destination. Most churches are located close to a museum, shopping centre or famous stately home and, in most cases, a transport hub (e.g. a railway station or bus depot).

Churches acknowledge this centrality and focus on the infrastructure and retail experience. Some churches are anxious that worshippers and visitors can manage to attend street fairs and stalls in the market places and pedestrian precincts, but find it difficult to worship in a church. The link must be made between the church and its neighbouring retail, transport and service businesses. This link would serve to integrate the offering of events and special activities and would enable the partners to share not only the costs of hosting events, but also the benefits of organizing and developing various sacred and secular activities as equal partners.

Future Research

Commodification or commoditization (the possible loss of unique cultural meaning and identity) of religious sites can cause obvious distress to worshippers and pilgrims. We see this as often at Uluru, Australia, as we do at Westminster Abbey or Canterbury Cathedral. The sale of goods and services at such sites is widespread and anticipated with some trepidation by visitors as they enter and leave the site. These souvenirs, often mass produced away from the site itself, are often collected by visitors to commemorate a sacred visit, as occurs at Fatima in Portugal or Lourdes in France. Relics are copied; religious scripts are reproduced; and vernacular and sacred architectural mementoes created in resins are freely distributed as faithful copies. We can question the need of non-worshippers to possess copies of special, even unique keepsakes. We cannot question the need for the site to sell mass-produced items to generate surplus for reinvestment in site protection and interpretation. Here lies the paradox. Is it fair, or equitable, to continue to support the production of these gimcracks in far-away places? Does the purchaser have any notion of whether an income is generated for the sacred site? We do have a duty of care to the special site and to its guardians. To that end, it is fundamental to assure visitors and worshippers of the importance of making a contribution to their visit. It is imperative that sacred visits to sites of worship and pilgrimage are not sullied by outright greed. What sympathetic businesses and tour operators must consider is ways in which we can all support the ongoing management of religious sites with ethical and responsible practices.

Conclusion: Themes in Religious Tourism

There is a repeated theme that religious sites seldom generate community-led social capital when considered as tourism venues or attractions. Of course, the notion of network and partnership is well understood, but what is not apparent is the opportunity to equally share costs and profits associated with the formalized networks and partnerships that are indeed possible. As Taylor (2003) described, the process of community development through acquired social capital is observed through building confidence in accomplishments and viewing these positively as success stories, and by creating links with services, suppliers and users through the media. These will lead to empowered communities where citizens can develop jobs and assets supported by new forms of governance to facilitate these outputs.

This chapter has identified and promoted ways in which the accessible religious history of communities can be managed. It encourages stakeholders to consider placing the concept of old doors opening to new visitors. With the benefit of technology, strategic approaches to management and some measure of coordination and centralized support for parish initiatives, we can anticipate a more fruitful relationship between religion and tourists in the third millennium.

The views of parishioners and local residents are required in any strategic plan to adopt tourism as a strategy for development and coherence. An inventory of festivals, attractions, events, archives and records should be prepared to inform potential funders and collaborating organizations and individuals (both for profit and not for profit). Tourism organizations are potentially unaware of the extensive inventory available and could benefit from this information being made accessible.

Success stories could be promoted and distributed through existing channels, but also through destination management organizations. Specific exemplar sites may be used in a religious education programme to encourage good practice for visitors (and for residents). Supply chain initiatives could also be further explored. Provision of food, drink and appropriate entertainment through music, dance, theatre and art and craft displays can enhance existing attractions and events.

Partnerships with volunteer and profit organizations linking consumables, human resources, trades-people, genealogists, historians and trainers could enhance the services provided for hosts and visitors. Networks and collaboration between existing partners could be broadened to anticipate alternative users and uses of existing sites.

However, religion and tourism are not easy or necessarily natural partners in development. There are some straightforward resourcing issues to address in managing people, promotion and distribution of the product. Tourism places religious sites, especially places of worship such as churches, as sites of heritage interest. At present, sacred issues, spiritual development and self-actualization are seemingly secondary issues and ill-defined by the key partners.

Review Questions

1. Church tourism requires a substantial contribution from volunteers. Identify opportunities through skills that volunteers offer to the construction of religious tourism.

2. Partnerships, networks or clusters are critical to success in developing religious tourism. Can you determine partners and networks that churches need to make, or belong to, to facilitate religious tourism?

3. Discuss effective ways of branding and developing religious tourism with limited funds for marketing.

References

Anderson, J.J. (1984) *Churches of Derbyshire*. Wye Valley Press, Wye Valley, UK.

Andriotis, K. (2009) Sacred site experience: a phenomenological study. *Annals of Tourism Research* 36, 64–84.

Beech, J. and Chadwick, S. (2006) *The Business of Tourism Management*. FT Prentice Hall, London, UK.

Busby, G. (2006) The Cornish church heritage as a tourist attraction: the visitor experience. Doctoral thesis, University of Exeter, Exeter, UK.

Churches Tourism Association (2007) Churches Tourism Association (Online). Available at: http://www.churchestourismassociation.info. Accessed September, 2007.

Cohen, E. (1996) The sociology of tourism: approaches, issues and findings. In: Apostolopoulos, Y., Leivadi, S. and Yiannakis, A. (eds) *The Sociology of Tourism: Theoretical and Empirical Investigations*. Routledge, London, UK, pp. 51–74.

Collins-Kreiner, N. (2010) The geography of pilgrimage and tourism: transformations and implications for applied geography. *Applied Geography* 30, 153–164.

Crouch, D. (1999) *Leisure Tourism Geographies*. Routledge, London, UK.

Hall, C.M. (2005) *Tourism: Rethinking the Social Science of Mobility*. Pearson Prentice Hall, London, UK.

Jackson, B. (2002) *Hope for the Church: Contemporary Strategies for Growth*. Explorations, London, UK.

Lane, B. (2005) Sustainable rural tourism strategies: a tool for development and conservation. *Intra American Journal of Environment and Tourism* 1, 12–20.

Leitch, S. (2006) *Lord Leitch's Review of Skills; Prosperity for all in a Global Economy – World Class Skills*. Final Report, HM Treasury, London, UK.

Levi, D. and Kocher, S. (2009) Understanding tourism at heritage religious sites. *Focus* VI, 17–21.

McKercher, B, Weber, K. and du Cros, H. (2008) Rationalising inappropriate behaviour at contested sites. *Journal of Sustainable Tourism* 16, 369–385.

Mowforth, M. and Munt, I. (1998) *Tourism and Sustainability: New Tourism in the Third World*. Routledge, London, UK.

Olsen, D.H. (2006) Management issues for religious heritage attractions. In: Timothy, D.J. and Olsen, D.H. (eds) *Tourism, Religion and Spiritual Journeys*. Routledge, London, UK, pp. 104–119.

Olsen, D.H. and Timothy, D.J. (2006) Tourism and religious journeys. In: Timothy, D.J. and Olsen, D.H. (eds) *Tourism, Religion and Spiritual Journeys*. Routledge, London, UK, pp. 1–23.

Page, W. (ed.) (1970) *The Victoria History of the County of Derby*. Dawsons, Folkestone, UK.

Pevsner, N. (1953) *The Buildings of England: Derbyshire*. Penguin, London, UK.

Poria, Y., and Ashworth, G. (2009). Heritage tourism – current resource for conflict. *Annals of Tourism Research* 36, 522–525.

Powell, F. and Geoghegan, M. (2005) Beyond political zoology: community development, civil society, and strong democracy. *Community Development Journal* 41, 128–142.

Ray, C. (1998) Culture, intellectual property, territorial rural development. *Sociologia Ruralis* 38, 3–20.

Rivera, M.A., Shani, A. and Severt, D. (2009) Perceptions of service attributes in a religious theme site: an importance satisfaction analysis. *Journal of Heritage Tourism* 4, 227–243.

Ron, A. (2007) Book review: tourism, religion and spiritual journeys. *Annals of Tourism Research* 34, 547–548.

Rotherham, I. (2007) Sustaining tourism infrastructures for religious tourists and pilgrims within the UK. In: Raj, R. and Morpeth, N.D. (eds) *Religious Tourism and Pilgrimage Management*. CAB International, Wallingford, UK, pp. 64–78.

Saravanan, R and Rao, K.S.P (2006) Development and validation of an instrument for measuring total quality service. *Total Quality Management* 17, 733–749.

Shackley, M. (2001) *Managing Sacred Sites: Service Provision and Visitor Experience*. Continuum, London, UK.

Shackley, M. (2005) Service delivery at sacred sites: potential contribution of management science. *European Journal of Science and Theology* 1, 33–40.

Shackley, M. (2006) Visitor management at world heritage sites. In: Leask, A. and Fyall, A (eds) *Managing World Heritage Sites*. Butterworth Heinemann, Oxford, UK, pp. 84–95.

Shaw, G. and Williams, A. (2004) *Tourism and Tourism Spaces*. Sage, London, UK.

Sheppard, D. (2006) *More than Bricks and Mortar: A Study of the Community Use of Church Buildings*. Church of England, Industrial Mission Derbyshire, Derby, UK.

Taylor, M. (2003) *Public Policy in the Community*. Palgrave MacMillan, Basingstoke, UK.

Timothy, D.J. and Conover, P.J. (2006) Nature religion, self-spirituality and New Age tourism. In: Timothy, D.J. and Olsen, D.H. (eds) *Tourism, Religion and Spiritual Journeys*. Routledge, London, UK, pp. 139–156.

Timothy, D.J. and Olsen, D.H. (2006) *Tourism, Religion and Spiritual Journeys*. Routledge, London, UK.

Warren, R. (2004) *The Healthy Churches' Handbook: A Process for Revitalizing Your Church*. Church House Publishing, London, UK.

Woodward, S. (2004) Faith and tourism: planning tourism in relation to places of worship. *Tourism and Hospitality Planning and Development* 1, 173–186.

Zairi, M. and Whymark, J. (2000) The transfer of best practices: how to build a culture of benchmarking and continuous learning – part 2. *Benchmarking: An International Journal* 7, 146–167.

19 Health and Medical Tourism

Dr Richard Tresidder

Introduction

The tourism industry is continually developing and expanding to meet the needs of changing consumer expectations. The significance of undertaking or consuming tourism has always had a link with the associated benefits of health, well-being and rejuvenation. However, there is a new niche within the market that takes this further and may be defined as medical tourism. Medical tourism differs from other forms of health-based tourism by the fact that the trip or vacation involves some form of medical intervention, which may vary from simple plastic surgery to liver or kidney transplants. Medical tourism can be defined as a niche in the sector by the fact that tourists travel from their home for the purposes of gaining medical attention (Connell, 2006), and as part of this experience they travel using the existing tourism infrastructure. Often, as part of the medical intervention, they will stay in a hotel and undertake activities just like any other tourist. What differentiates medical tourists from others is that the trip is not motivated by the need to escape from everyday life or search for new experiences through travel. Rather, the major motivation for travel is to confront health or lifestyle problems in a focused manner.

This chapter analyses the nature of health and medical tourism, the impacts they have on host communities and the ethical issues that accompany some of the treatments purchased by tourists. Over the past two decades there has been a sharp growth in both health tourism and medical tourism, and although both are concerned with notions of health and well-being, the implications for tourists and host communities are very different. The growth in these areas has seen the development of specialist facilities and destinations, including those provided on cruise ships, such as spas and therapy centres (see chapter 20). This niche has extended into new and deterministic areas that expand health and well-being tourism into new and often controversial areas of medical procedures and invasive surgery.

Historical Background

In order to assess the significance of medical tourism it is important to understand how the sector has developed. It may be argued that medical tourism is just an evolution of health tourism, and that with current developments in spa treatments and resources there has been a blurring of the boundaries between the two. One of the major motivations for undertaking the activity of tourism, apart from visiting new places or meeting new people, is the rejuvenation element of the tourist experience. The idea is that by pampering him/herself, or undertaking a holiday to escape the pressures of everyday life, the traveller is able to experience feelings of rejuvenation, relaxation and well-being. The significance of an individual undertaking tourism and the benefits it brings can be traced as far back as Classical Greece and Rome, where treatments and even the ownership of seaside second homes were common for the wealthy (Jackson, 1990). The purpose of such activities was explicitly aimed at promoting health and vitality for the individual. As such, health tourism has existed for many centuries. This is exemplified by the Roman Empire, where a tourism infrastructure existed to facilitate access to thermal health spas (Bender *et al.*, 2002). These were constructed throughout Europe and still provide the foundations of many of the world's most identifiable resorts and destinations, such as Aix, Aachen, Bath and Baden. Spas have played an important part throughout the centuries, not only in recreation but also in restoring physical and mental health. They also cross the divide to medical tourism in countries such as Hungary by offering a form of rehabilitation that continues today (Bender *et al.*, 2002).

During the medieval period, bathing was seen as a dangerous activity as it was thought to spread disease and licentious behaviour and many destinations closed as a result of the public's moral outrage. From the 15th century there was a renaissance as mineral waters were identified as possessing certain health-giving medicinal qualities and used as a remedy for many ailments. By the beginning of the 16th century visitors were encouraged to take the waters internally and externally. Resorts such as Buxton (UK) still market the health-giving qualities of their mineral water, packaging and selling it through a global distribution network. The fashion for taking the waters in the 16th century was a direct result of the increased urbanization within Europe, where the growth of cities was unfortunately not accompanied by proper or efficient sanitation systems. As a result, sewage and industrial waste led to the pollution of water supplies, in turn causing a massive rise in diseases such as cholera. For many people during this time, mineral water provided one of the only natural and clean forms of drinking water. This led directly to an increased interest in and a rejuvenation of Europe's spa resorts. The popularity of the spa resorts continued to gain momentum in the 18th and 19th centuries, leading to an increased significance of spa towns and reinforcing their role in the contemporary travel and tourism industry.

By the 18th century the relationship between tourism, health and water was well established. Its popularity led to the development of seaside towns as destinations (Hassan,

2003), and it was noted that taking the waters, or bathing in spa baths or the sea, led to health benefits. This created wealthy tourist destinations, today characterized by the evidence of neo-classical architecture in historic 'spa towns'. By the 19th century this niche tourism had become established and the trend for spa resorts had extended to the colonial and ex-colonial territories (Connell, 2006) such as Virginia and Pennsylvania in the USA. Significantly, the spa towns' importance as a tourism resource became cemented in cultural activities, and the taking of the waters was accompanied by a significant entertainment network that became the social centre for Georgian polite society. The spa resorts thus became not only places for health and well-being, but also offered escape, opportunities for social networking and a means in which to indulge in social and hedonistic activities. This led to the development of large hotels, fashionable housing, opera houses, theatres, public houses, tea rooms and meeting places. It may be argued that the European spas of the Georgian era laid the foundations for the contemporary health and well-being industries.

This trend was further accelerated with the advent of trains and the democratization of travel. The ability to travel longer distances cheaply and safely, in conjunction with a rise in people's disposable income and the establishment of the new middle classes, enabled the great seaside resorts of Europe to develop (Hassan, 2003). For the first time taking the waters, and in particular the trend for taking sea water, was now available to a large number of people. With the increasing number of destinations, the trend to visit the seaside in order to take the waters, sea air or to sunbathe led to the seaside becoming established as a centre for health and well-being (Swarbrooke and Horner, 2007). It offered an 'escape to sun and light' in order to avoid 'the deep depressions on ill-health suffered by inhabitants of damp and foggy cities' (Hassan, 2003). Visiting the seaside allowed urban tourists to escape polluted industrial areas where light and sunshine were often shrouded by smog, and as such the search for sunshine became a central element of the tourist experience. As a result, sunshine became seen as a significant element of healthy living.

By 1931, sunbathing as an activity was being championed by the British Health Resorts Association, which promoted health tourism and led to the commercialization of seaside resorts as playgrounds and health resorts (Hassan, 2003). The relationship between tourism and this notion of escape continues today, but in the form of more esoteric activities such as yoga, meditation and alternative experiences or therapies in which tourists find themselves seeking some form of inner peace or self-actualization. Rather than escaping the smog of cities, today's traveller now searches to escape from the fast pace of life and technology, which are broadly the same motivations that supported the development of spa and seaside resorts in the past.

The development of spa resorts during the 20th century as centres for health and well-being has seen them adapt to the needs and desires of contemporary tourists by diversifying from just offering mineral water or non-invasive beauty therapies or treatments to a range of alternative therapies, electrical treatments and clinical treatments for medical conditions such as psoriasis and rheumatoid arthritis (Tsankov and Kamarashev, 1996), as well as physiotherapy and minor cosmetic operations, dentistry and other treatments. These treatments and developments have blurred the boundaries between medical tourism and traditional health and well-being tourism and have motivated the development of medical tourism as a specific and growing niche.

Defining Medical Tourism

It is important to make a distinction between health tourism and medical tourism. The two products are very different, with different market segments and different sets of impacts and ethical issues. Henderson (2004) stated that tourism and health share a close relationship that can be both positive and negative in nature. It is recognized that tourists face many health problems while travelling (e.g. deep vein thrombosis, malaria) as well as the risk of sustaining injuries during the trip. However, tourism is more often associated with good health and the search for this has shaped contemporary tourism practices. There is a belief that taking a holiday contributes to physical and emotional well-being, underpinning the perceived benefits of participating in tourism. Henderson (2004) identified health tourism as being reliant upon 'mineral water and climate', but also includes 'sun and fun' activities where health is either a principal or secondary purpose. For Laws (1996) health tourism was 'leisure taken away from home where one of the objectives is to improve one's state of health'. The interest in this aspect of tourism has led to the widespread development of resorts and destinations that specialize in the provision of health and well-being tourism. Health-related tourism is booming (Henderson, 2004) and spas are no longer simply places to take the waters or undergo treatments, but have instead become places that mix pampering and wellness by offering relaxation, fitness and stress relief. The health and well-being benefits of undertaking such forms of tourism can be seen as a by-product of the tourism experience and are usually supplemented by the usual activities of sightseeing, experiencing local culture and enjoying the environment.

Medical tourism is different because the medical treatment becomes the primary motivation for the visit and the usual tourism activities become secondary to the medical element. Medical tourism can be defined as undertaking a medical intervention away from the home country, where the medical element is the central theme of the activity. It has emerged because affordable, accessible transport (e.g. low-cost airlines) has made it easier for people to travel long distances to overseas countries to obtain medical, dental and surgical care while simultaneously being holidaymakers in the conventional sense. This definition may be seen in opposition to Garcia-Altes (2005) definition of health tourism as 'people travelling from their place or residence for health reasons'. As a result, medical tourists' motivations are different to those other types of tourists. Their needs are very specific and related to the medical condition, and rely on available expertise and facilities rather than hotel or destination experiences or facilities, thereby allowing the medical need to dictate the travel decisions.

Figure 19.1 shows how the sector may be classified and segmented. Health tourism offers a more traditional tourism experience, whereby the customer is pampered with the major motivation of relaxation and rejuvenation, and fits within more established notions of tourism. Cosmetic tourism, although involving a medical element and often an operation, commonly mixes the procedure with usual tourist behaviour. For example there has been an unprecedented rise in the number of New Zealanders (Yang *et al.*, 2009) searching for low-cost cosmetic surgery in Asia (Henderson, 2004) in order to undergo surgery while enjoying exotic environments and cultures (Yang *et al.*, 2009). This category falls very much into what de Arellano (2007) defined as 'scalpel safaris' or 'rainforest and rhinoplasty'

packages. The final category of medical tourism is defined by the fact that the explicit purpose of the trip is to purchase and have a medical treatment or to purchase health services abroad (this increasingly includes travelling for the purposes of euthanasia, now termed 'suicide tourism'). Although this definition may also be used for cosmetic procedures, the motivations and experiences are very different for the traveller as the trip is undertaken on medical grounds rather than for aesthetic purposes, and is generally used to improve the quality of the individual's life through a medical intervention. Although both may come under the same definition, the motivations, facilities required and ethics differ and it can be argued that these niches or sectors are clearly interrelated and reliant upon each other.

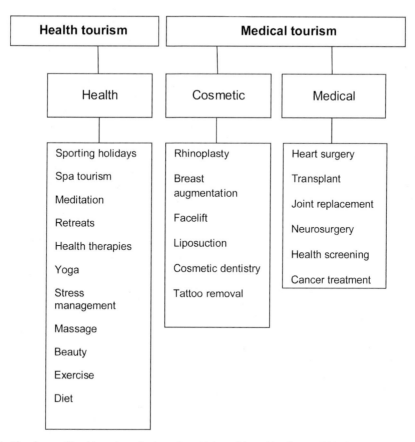

Fig. 19.1. The shape of health and medical tourism. (Adapted from Henderson, 2004.)

Reasons for Growth

The development of the medical tourism market is being driven by a number of social, demographic, cultural and economic factors (Garcia-Altes, 2005).

Ageing populations

Improvements in medical care, diet and lifestyle have led to people in developed countries living longer. This has placed pressure on home medical services as each year an increasing number of older people seek medical interventions to treat diseases and afflictions that accompany old age (e.g. hip or knee replacements) (Lagace, 2007). This has led to long waiting lists for operations and as older people are also often wealthier than they have been before, they have the ability to buy medical services cheaply and to jump queues, which is increasingly attractive for this demographic.

Lifestyle changes

We currently live in world that is influenced by celebrity and media images of the perfect body. Cosmetic surgery was previously the preserve of the rich. However, the opportunity to have cosmetic surgery in more affordable destinations, while simultaneously enjoying a holiday, has democratized the ability to have the perfect body or smile. Travelling to another country also provides the tourist with a degree of anonymity, whereby it is possible to have a treatment and recover without family, colleagues or friends knowing that they have had cosmetic surgery. As a result, cosmetic tourism now plays a significant role in the medical tourism niche.

Tourism alternatives

Cosmetic surgery is a natural extension of the experiences offered by spas and health clubs. The barriers to such forms of tourism have thus been broken down and medical tourism has just become another accepted niche in the contemporary tourism industry.

Nature of generating health systems

Home health systems may be too expensive or the medical treatment identified not covered under health insurance policies in tourists' own countries. The home health service may not offer the treatment for economic, political, religious, ethical or medical grounds; the waiting list for treatment may be prohibitively long; or the individual may not be eligible to join the list. By travelling to certain countries where the regulatory and ethical guidelines differ, the individual may be able to undergo operations or medical procedures outside of local ethical or legal constraints. For example, in many countries abortion is still illegal or there are strict limits on the stage of pregnancy at which abortions may be undertaken. These can be extended or removed by having the procedure carried out elsewhere in the world. Thailand established itself as a major centre for medical tourism in the 1970s by offering sex change operations, and at the extreme end of the sector there are clinics in Switzerland that allow patients to undergo euthanasia. The different cultural and social values of host countries allow tourists to find treatments and services that are be sanctioned in their own countries.

Shortage of organs

Transplant tourism can be seen as one of the most controversial elements of medical tourism. It is a small element of the sector, but it raises more moral and ethical questions than many others types of treatments. With advancements in medical practice and technology, transplant surgery is continually developing new approaches for transplanting body parts from one individual to another. However, the major barrier for people needing transplants is not technology, but rather the availability of organs. For example, in the USA in 2007 there were 101,943 waiting-list candidates, with another person being added to the list every 14 minutes. This is in contrast to the availability of organs, with fewer than 8,000 organ donors in 2008 and fewer than 22,000 transplanted organs. The result of this disparity between the availability of and need for organs is that 15% of patients on the waiting list die each year while waiting for a liver transplant (Rhodes and Schiano, 2010). Therefore, one of the major motivations for undertaking medical tourism is the fact that by going to China or India it may be possible to purchase an organ and undergo transplant surgery, thus bypassing waiting lists and organ availability. This raises a number of ethical issues that are examined later in this chapter.

Medical Tourism and Globalization

Tourism has always been at the forefront of the globalization process as people have travelled across borders and boundaries, interacting and engaging in cultural exchanges and business with host communities. As such, the infrastructure to support international travel is already well established. As a consequence, international tourism in the form of medical tourism has led to 'globalization of health care' (Lagace, 2007) or, it can be argued, to the democratization of health care. This section examines some of the major reasons that medical tourism has become a clear and identifiable niche in the contemporary tourism industry. For de Arellano (2007), 'Medical tourism, or travel with the express purpose of obtaining health services abroad' has enabled people to jump hospital or transplant waiting lists by seeking medical care abroad. In some instances, however, the only difference from gaining treatment is the location rather than the service. De Arellano (2007) provided the following example:

> For a patient in, say, New York or Washington, DC, who may be under the care of an Indian physician and a Jamaican or Filipino nurse, going abroad for medical services may not seem dissimilar to care at home. And the promise of comparable services at lower cost, with some exotic travel thrown in, is often tempting. As a result, patients are increasingly looking for new horizons in medical care, including elective surgery and long-term care. Some countries, such as India, Brazil, the Philippines, and Thailand, are actively capitalizing on the trend, offering health

care/resort packages that promise the best of medicine with the attractions of tourism at a fraction of what equivalent health services would cost in the United States.

The significance of this for patients (or tourists) is that they receive 'first-class services at third-world prices'. Economics – in the form of the cost of the service – is key to the emergence of the niche and although other factors have been identified, the considerably lower costs in the world's medical destinations are a major incentive for medical travellers. These 'cheaper' destinations include many less developed or developing countries (Bookman and Bookman, 2007) and major centres include India, Thailand, South Africa and former European Communist states such as Lithuania (Budiani-Saberi and Delmonico, 2008). This economic consideration, in conjunction with access to facilities and organs that are not available in (more expensive) Western countries, means that these countries are increasingly attractive to medical tourists.

Medical Tourism and Economic Development

Tourism has always been seen as one of the major strategic tools in the economic armoury of developing and less developed countries with all the benefits it brings in terms of infrastructural development, international investment and foreign exchange. Medical tourism still brings these traditional benefits, but also enables countries to develop their own niche in the international tourism marketplace, while having the additional benefits of improving the destination's health services and encouraging medically trained locals to either stay in the country or to return from practicing overseas. Countries that actively promote medical tourism do so for self-serving reasons, as investing in the medical industry is a means to increase the gross domestic product, upgrade facilities, generate foreign exchange and boost tourism, which of course bring benefits to local communities and regional and local economies. It is argued that the development of a medical tourism industry has a trickle-down approach, whereby local communities and populations also benefit in terms of facilities and employment opportunities (de Arellano, 2007).

Destinations such as India, Thailand and Singapore have explicitly used medical care as an element of their tourism strategy (Connell, 2006) to boost international tourism numbers. In addition, countries with less strong international tourism profiles such as Belarus, Latvia, Lithuania and Hungary have significantly developed medical tourism alongside their more traditional offerings of health, well-being and spa tourism. Saudi Arabia has started to develop a medical tourism strategy by linking medical tourism with pilgrimage (Hajj) to create packages that target medical tourists from throughout the Gulf States. The significance of medical tourism for national economies is illustrated by Bies and Zacharia's (2007) analysis of medical tourism in India. They state that medical tourism in India has increased at the rate of 30% per year and that the Apollo Hospital in Delhi had more than 60,000 medical tourists in a 3-year period between 2001 and 2004. The Apollo Hospital Group has over 8500 beds across 50 hospitals; it also offers health insurance services and runs clinical research divisions. It has treated over 16 million patients from 55 countries and the services are offered with direct links to the Incredible India tourism marketing campaign and web resources.

Medical tourists are attracted to countries such as India by the fact that operations are 80% cheaper than in the USA. By 2012 it is estimated that tourism will have generated US$20 billion for the Indian economy (Bies and Zacharia, 2007) and medical tourism has become one of the most important components of the country's tourism industry. The Apollo Hospital Group has become a significant provider of medical tourism in Asia and can be seen as just one example of the scope of the services and size of the investment being made. Similar organizations can be seen throughout Asia (Henderson, 2004); for example, the Bumrungrad International Hospital in Bangkok treated 55,000 US patients in 2005, of whom three-quarters flew directly from the US. It is possible to purchase medical treatment packages (including medical care and accommodation) pre-travel from the hospital's website.

Medical tourism is a central strategy for economic growth (Bookman and Bookman, 2007) for many countries, but needs regulation to oversee the quality and ethics of provision. It also needs legal, political and economic stability, but often governments who are entering the medical tourism niche fail to address the issue of saturating the market with provision, thus destroying the impact of medical tourism for the country as they will be competing with other providers. The significance of the sector has not been lost on Western medical groups in Europe and the USA, who are starting to compete by offering reduced prices, discounts and interest-free credit for treatments. One of the major barriers for medical tourism providers is the perception by tourists that the facilities and services may not be up to 'Western standards', although this is often not the case. Western providers are using this uncertainty as an element in their marketing campaigns. In addition, a number of concerns have been raised relating to the ethical nature of some governments and service providers within the sector, focusing mainly around the supply of body parts and organs and the care given after the operation.

Ethical Issues

The first ethical issue revolves around the very nature of medical tourism and the idea that a tourist will travel from a rich country to a poor country to exploit the resources of a destination. In the case of medical tourism this often means using body parts from local people, which have either been purchased from them or have been taken after their death through an accident or execution (Rothman et al., 1997). This type of exploitation follows some of the early debates in tourism surrounding the host–guest relationship and the impacts tourism can have on the local culture or society (see Chapter 6). Medical tourism may be seen as a clear example of the inequality of international relations between the rich and poor, north and south or first and third worlds, and raises the major concern that the sustainable and ethical tourism lobby has expressed for the past 20 years: that tourism often exploits the resources of a destination. In addition to the ethics of such a form of tourism, more significantly there are also medical ethics to consider, especially for transplant tourism. Although transplantation raises a number of ethical issues, the main two revolve around the origins of the organ and how that organ is allocated. These issues become especially complicated when applied to visitors who are purchasing organs (Rhodes and Schiano, 2010) as this can sometimes lead to kidnap and murder (Rothman *et al.*, 1997). Organs are traditionally sourced from a number of places and each has a differing ethical impact.

First, organs are harvested from recently deceased donors who have been killed in an accident or other mishap. Although this is the most traditional means of sourcing organs and body parts, the ethical issue is how the organ is allocated and how the recipient is chosen. The economic superiority of the medical tourist often results in the organ being allocated to the highest bidder, potentially denying a local person the chance of a transplant.

Second, people in the host countries sell their organs for financial gain. Although it may be argued that people have the freedom to do what they like with their own bodies, the economic reality of living in a less developed country is one of poverty and the only thing someone may have to sell is their body. Again this raises many issues in relation to the inequality of the world's economic system and the power of developed countries over poorer ones. In addition, transplant tourism has been associated with significant problems for those who sell their organs: the money they receive is limited and they are frequently swindled out of the fee. The surgery used is often substandard and the after-care that should be made available is not (Budiani-Saberi and Delmonico, 2008). Furthermore, this has led to an illegal and ethically questionable trade in human body parts and organs.

In December 2003, an international organ trafficking ring was broken. It was revealed that transplant recipients had paid $100,000 to the ring for a kidney transplant, while living donors had been paid $800. At the Second Global Consultation on Critical Issues in Human Transplantation in 2007 the World Health Organization (WHO) estimated that organ trafficking accounts for 5–10% of kidney transplants throughout the world. Many of these organs will have been purchased for medical tourists (WHO, 2007).

Third, and most controversially, governments may sell the organs of executed prisoners to transplant tourists. In China, 90% of transplanted organs come from executed prisoners (Huang *et al.*, 2008). The ethical and moral implications of this activity are significant. For example, it provides incentives to increase the death penalty rather than to give long custodial sentences because the financial rewards in providing organs for transplant tourism are so great. However, it must be noted that China has stated that Chinese citizens will now be given priority for organs in line with the Istanbul Declaration that condemned transplant tourism (Huang *et al.*, 2008).

Future Research

There is clearly scope for considerable research into medical tourism in all its forms, although there are considerable challenges relating to the ethics of this form of research, which may provide some contentious results. As the extreme ends of the niche continue to develop, such as travel for euthanasia, so the complexities and sensitivities of research deepen.

There is also scope to further investigate the renewal of seaside resorts and the development of major spa resorts. These are predicated upon the recognition of new forms of health and well-being tourism and an increased recognition of the need to live more healthy lifestyles. There are also links to other forms of tourism and to the idea of travel to take part in activities that are predominantly health based, such as yoga and meditation.

Conclusion

Medical tourism is a significant niche in the contemporary tourism industry. It is not a new phenomenon and has its origins in the traditions of tourism as offering escape, rejuvenation, health and well-being. The development of medical tourism is the logical progression from the health and well-being and spa industry and the niche reflects the changing social and cultural environment as well as demographic changes. When analysing the significance of the sector it is important to identify that there are three strands – health, cosmetic and medical tourism – each of which has differing ethical, moral and technical requirements. Although medical tourism has become a significant element in the tourism offering and a focus of many developing countries (because it offers a distinct niche in which to cement their role within the international tourism industry) (Bookman and Bookman, 2007), it does have benefits in terms of encouraging investment in medical resources and encourages qualified staff to stay in or to return to their home countries. However, medical tourism raises certain ethical and moral questions that need to be answered by governments, medical providers, the tourism industry and ultimately the tourist, as to the morality and acceptability of such tourism in relation to the sourcing of organs and body parts, and the economic superiority of transplant

tourists within the host–guest relationship. Nevertheless, medical tourism is a significant niche that will continue to grow. In order for the niche to develop sustainably it needs international regulation to protect the host or donor and the guest or recipient. Such regulation needs to be implemented without driving the sector underground and into the arms of the illegal groups that operate on its margins.

Review Questions

1. Critically evaluate the challenges of managing medical tourism in a way that is safe and ethical.

2. Assess the changes in lifestyle that have led to an increase in health and medical tourism.

3. Critically evaluate the relationship between medical tourism and the general principles of sustainability and social responsibility.

References

Bender, T., Balint, P. and Balint, G. (2002) A brief history of spa therapy. *Annals of the Rheumatic Diseases* 61, 949.

Bies, W. and Zacharia, L. (2007) Medical tourism: outsourcing surgery. *Mathematical and Computer Modelling* 46, 1144–1159.

Bookman, M. and Bookman, K. (2007) *Medical Tourism in Developing Countries*. Palgrave MacMillan, New York.

Budiani-Saberi, D. and Delmonico, F. (2008) Organ trafficking and transplant tourism: a commentary on the global realities. *American Journal of Transplantation* 8, 925–929.

Connell, J. (2006) Medical tourism: sea, sun, sand and surgery. *Tourism Management* 27, 1093–1100.

de Arellano, A. (2007) Patients without borders: the emergence of medical tourism. *International Journal of Health Services* 37, 193–198.

Garcia-Altes, A. (2005) The development of health tourism services. *Annals of Tourism Research* 32, 262–266.

Hassan, J. (2003) *The Seaside, Health and the Environment in England and Wales Since 1800*. Ashgate, Aldershot, UK.

Henderson, J. (2004) Healthcare tourism in Southeast Asia. *Tourism Review International* 7, 11–121.

Huang, J., Mao, Y. and Millis, J.M. (2008) Government policy and organs transplantation in China. *Lancet* 372, 1937–1938.

Jackson, R. (1990) Waters and spas in the classical world. *Medical History* 10, 1–3.

Lagace, M. (2007) *The Rise of Medical Tourism*. Harvard Business School, Working Knowledge, Boston, MA.

Laws, E. (1996) *Health Tourism, A Business Opportunity Approach*. Routledge, London, UK.

Rhodes, R. and Schiano, T. (2010) Transplant tourism in China: a tale of two transplants. *The American Journal of Bioethics* 10, 2–11.

Rothman, D.J., Rose, E., Awaya, T., Cohen, B., Daar, A., Dzemeshkevich, S.L., Lee, C.J., Munro, R., Reyes, H., Rothman, S.M., Schoen, K.F., Scheper-Hughes, N., Shapira, Z. and Smit, H. (1997) The Bellagio Task Force Report on transplantation, bodily integrity, and the international traffic in organs. *Transplantation Proceedings* 29, 2739–2745.

Swarbrook, J. and Horner, S (2007) *Consumer Behaviour in Tourism,* 2nd edn. Butterworth Heinemann/ Elsevier, Oxford, UK.

Tsankov, N. and Kamarashev, J. (1996) Spa therapy in Bulgaria. *Clinics in Dermatology* 14, 675–678.

Yang, Y,. Al-Ani, S., Bartlett, G. and Moazzam, A. (2009) Cosmetic tourism – its true cost. *ANZ Journal of Surgery* 79, A60.

WHO (2007) *Second Global Consultation on Critical Issues in Human Transplantation: Towards a Common Attitude to Transplantation. Report.* World Health Organization, Geneva, Switzerland.

20 Cruise Tourism and the Cruise Industry

Patsy Morgan and Lisa Power

Introduction

The aim of this chapter is to introduce readers to the cruise industry. This is an increasingly important tourism sector and an area of academic research that is underrepresented in the tourism field of studies. The study of the cruise industry is complex because it changes rapidly and information quickly becomes outdated as cruise ships change hands and new products and services are created to cater for this dynamic market. Itineraries find cruise ships along coastlines, on all the oceans of the world and on inland waterways. Shore-side excursions are offered not only to ports but also to a variety of inland destinations, such as to Hluhluwe Game Reserve in South Africa or an evening at the Hermitage in St Petersburg. Onboard activities and facilities have diversified to such an extent that they now include not only ballroom dancing, musical productions and gambling in casinos but also rock-climbing, edutainment and celebrity-endorsed restaurants. Today, the marketing and promotion of the cruise sector is still, despite the internet, predominantly through travel agents as the variety of cruise products on offer presents the prospective cruise tourist with a complex range of choices and options. Cruise ships are diversifying to meet the needs of an increasing market and varied customer base and are no longer the preserve of the rich and elite. The cruise sector now provides a product for everyone. Ships offering traditional elegance and decor that evoke classic cruising traditions are offered alongside new entrants onto the market, namely the world's first mega ships – floating holiday resorts.

Definitions

It is important to explain exactly what is meant by the different terms used in cruising. To cruise means to sail from place to place for pleasure, calling at a succession of destinations, or to sail, journey or move about by means of a cruise ship. Cartwright and Baird (1999) defined cruising as 'a multi-centre holiday where you take your hotel with you from centre to centre'. This emphasizes the essence of the cruise, which incorporates transport (the ship), accommodation in the form of cabins or berths, food and drink in on-board restaurants and eateries, entertainment, retail and other leisure facilities such as swimming pools and spas. Cruise ships have developed into floating resorts on the sea where passengers can enjoy all of the facilities and amenities of a holiday resort without having to leave the ship (Wood, 2000).

A cruise ship or cruise liner is a floating passenger vessel used commercially for pleasure voyages. Cruise ships come in all shapes and sizes, some with as few as 100 passengers and others with over 5,000 passengers. Ships' designs vary to operate in different waters such as crossing the Atlantic, ambling in the Caribbean, coping with ice in the Arctic or gentle river cruising. Ocean liners value speed and traditional luxury, while cruise ships value amenities rather than speed.

A cruise trip is a passage of time spent on board a cruise ship and at cruise destinations. A trip can last for two nights (a short cruise), 2 weeks (an average cruise) or up to several months (a world cruise). A cruise voyage can be a round trip with several en-route stops (e.g. a Mediterranean cruise starting and finishing in Southampton); a fly cruise (e.g. flying from London to Barbados, then sailing around the Caribbean and returning to London by air from Barbados); or a fly cruise that involves flying to one destination and sailing to another or vice versa (e.g. flying out to New York and sailing back to Southampton).

A cruise destination is a port where shore excursions take place. These can be organised by the ship or independently by passengers. It can also refer to a specified area such as the Baltic, Alaska, the Mediterranean or the Caribbean.

Cruise tourism is tourism based around cruise ships where different suppliers and organizations within the cruise industry, such as airlines and tour operators, work together to provide cruise holidays. The diversity of cruise tourism is not just about holidays. Cruise ships are becoming increasing attractive for other sectors such as business cruise tourism, where business meetings, incentive conferences and exhibitions (MICE) are held on cruise ships.

A cruise tourist is a person who spends at least one, but usually two nights or more on a cruise ship, usually for leisure purposes.

The History of Cruise Tourism

It was cargo rather than passengers that was transported on the initial ocean-going vessels. In the early days passengers used a ship as a means of transport to get from A to B (hence the word 'liner'), usually as quickly and efficiently as possible. During the 1890s to 1920s, transatlantic voyages took new emigrants from Europe to the USA. They travelled on ocean liners and passengers were segregated depending on class. The poorer passengers were housed in third class. This was also known as 'steerage' because those travelling in this category were accommodated on the same level as the control linkages for the

rudder. On some ships, third-class passengers were expected to provide their own food and drink and sleep anywhere in the hold where suitable spaces were available (Tibballs, 1998; Cartwright and Baird, 1999). Each category of passenger, first, second and third class, had their own designated area, separated into different dining rooms with their own menus, cabins and facilities. The film *Titanic* illustrates some of these differences; here, the facilities on board included 840 state rooms, libraries, a swimming pool, a Turkish bath and even elevators.

In 1922, the first official cruise on a ship built specifically for the purpose of travelling from port to port with on-board luxury and leisure took place. Cruise companies realized that carrying passengers was a lucrative business and it was with this commercial venture in mind that the early development of passenger cruising rather than passenger transport took place. Despite the loss of the *Titanic*, some of the most ostentatious and decadent ship-based travel took place between the 1920s and 1940s, when the rich and famous, film stars and politicians dominated the passenger lists. For wealthy travellers who were able to afford high levels of comfort and service at home, these were reproduced on board. The exceptionally high standards demanded by first-class passengers were reflected in the prices paid (Mancini, 2004).

Cruising came to a standstill during World War II when many ships were commandeered for active duty, carrying soldiers, cargo and ammunition or being used as floating hospitals (Cartwright and Baird, 1999). The introduction of transatlantic commercial airlines from the late 1950s to the mid 1960s saw journey times across the oceans cut dramatically and for a time cruises declined in popularity. The cruise companies responded by diversifying their products and the introduction of the fly cruise saw a resurgence in the cruise sector. The popular *Love Boat* television series in 1975, filmed on board a Princess cruise ship, was a strong influence as it presented to a wide audience a romantic and intriguing image of life on-board ship (Douglas and Douglas, 2004).

As the millennium approached, modern purpose-built cruise ships were developed to accommodate cruise tourists seeking unique experiences, a wide range of different itineraries

Table 20.1. An abbreviated chronology of cruise ships since 1840.

Year	A summary of some of the major cruise lines and ships
1840	The first transatlantic crossing. The 700-tons wooden paddle-wheeler *Britannia* departs from Liverpool, UK, for Halifax, Nova Scotia, Canada
1857	The Peninsular and Oriental Steam Navigation Company (P&O) makes the first sightseeing cruise to the Mediterranean on *SS Ceylon*
1869	The White Star Line is formed with the *Oceanic*
1873	*Baltic Liner* (White Star Line) crosses the Atlantic (eastward) in 7 days, 20 hours and 9 minutes
1875	Thomas Cook takes 21 passengers on the *President Christie* to the North Cape
1876	White Star Line's *Britannic* crosses the Atlantic (westward) in 7 days, 16 hours and 35 minutes
1881	P&O's *SS Ceylon* is bought by Oceanic Yachting Company and refitted. This is considered the first Ocean Pleasure Cruise Ship for the European Market
1897	The world's largest ship, the German *Kaiser Wilhelm der Grosse* (14,300 t), is launched with capacity for 558 first-class, 338 second-class and 1074 steerage passengers
1900	Hamburg America Line builds the world's first cruise ship – *Prinzessin Victoria Luise* (24,400 t), with 119 staterooms accommodating approximately 400 passengers
1907	The White Star *Adriatic* is the first cruise ship to have a swimming pool
1910	The White Star Line launches the *Olympic* ocean liner with 1054 first-class, 5010 second-class and 1,020 third-class passengers
1912	*RMS Titanic* departs Southampton 10th April 1912 on its maiden voyage to New York. It strikes an iceberg and sinks on 15th April 1912, resulting in the deaths of 1517 of the 2223 passengers and crew
1920	Prohibition sees the growth of 'booze cruises' around the coast of America
1922	The first official around-the-world cruise is undertaken by the Cunard ship *Laconia* (18,000 tons) with all first-class accommodation
1931	Work stops on the *Queen Mary* because of the economic depression
1932	Launch of the French liner *Normandie*, famous for its grand interior designs
1936	The *Queen Mary's* maiden voyage from Southampton to New York with 1805 passengers and 1101 crew. In 1938 it crosses the Atlantic westbound in 3 days, 21 hours and 48 minutes
1938	*Queen Elizabeth* launched
1940	*Queen Mary 2* and *Queen Elizabeth* begin war duty and engage as troop carriers
1948	Cunard's *Caronia* (34,000 t) is first cruise liner built after World War II
1952	The American ocean liner *United States* (53,000 t) captures the Blue Ribbon award for the fastest crossing of the Atlantic
1958	Transatlantic commercial jet passenger service begins (BOAC). Transatlantic travel is reduced from 6 days to 6 hours
1959	Holland America's *Rotterdam* passenger liner is built
1960	The French passenger liner *France* is launched and enters service in 1963 Maiden voyage of Italian Line's *Leonardo da Vinci* ocean liner crosses the Atlantic to New York
1969	*Queen Elizabeth 2* maiden voyage to New York
1970	Royal Caribbean (founded in 1968) introduces *Songs of Norway* cruise ship in Miami, Florida
1972	Carnival Cruise Lines is founded
1977	Norwegian Cruise Line develops the first private-island concept with Great Stirrup Cay in the Bahamas
1982	*Queen Elizabeth 2* and *Canberra* are used as troop transport by the British navy in the Falklands war
1985	Carnival launches *Holiday*, the first of the mega cruise ships
1988	Royal Caribbean introduces the *Sovereign of the Seas* cruise ship, the first large, modern cruise ship (73,000 t, 2690 passengers)
1990	Carnival Cruise Line introduces the family-friendly *Fantasy* cruise ship
1994	Walt Disney Company starts the Disney cruise venture
1998	Princess Cruise Line introduces the *Grand Princess* cruise ship (109,000 t) Carnival Corporation acquires Cunard Line

Table 20.1. Continued.

Year	A summary of some of the major cruise lines and ships
1999	*Voyager of the Seas* sets a record for the number of passengers on a single cruise ship (3497)
2000	Costa Cruises builds *Atlantica*
2002	Royal Caribbean International expands its fleet with *Brilliance of the Seas* and *Navigator of the Seas*
2006	Costa Cruises is the first international cruise company to schedule regular cruises in China and Asia
2007	RCI takes delivery of *Liberty of the Seas* (160,000 t, 3634 passengers)
	A new company, Azumara cruises, is created by Royal Caribbean Cruise Line
	Final sales for the *Queen Elizabeth II* world voyage, and the liner is sold to Dubai
2008	Cunard Line's *Queen Victoria* makes its maiden voyage (90,000 t, 2000 passengers)
	P&O's *Ventura* (3100 passengers) is the largest ever cruise ship for the UK cruise market
	The maiden voyage of Royal Caribbean International's *Independence of the Seas*
	Smoking is banned on many cruise ships
2009	Royal Caribbean International's *Oasis of the Seas* is the largest cruise ship in the world, with 5400 passengers on its maiden voyage
2010	Celebrity Cruises cancels the first leg of launch celebrations for *Celebrity Eclipse* to divert the ship to repatriate more than 2000 British tourists stranded by the eruption caused by the Eyjafjallajökull volcano in Iceland

Adapted from Polsson, 2009.

and destinations and on-board leisure and entertainment. Recent trends have seen more affordable cruises being offered to a wider market on mega ships on the one hand, and on the other a more exclusive, intimate ultra-luxury on smaller ships (Wood, 2000).

Leading Cruise Brands

The cruise industry is constantly changing through mergers and acquisitions (Kwortnik, 2006). There are many cruise ships owned by a range of global companies, but the dominating top three are Carnival Corporation, Royal Caribbean Cruise Line (RCCL) and Star Cruises. Between them, these three hold the biggest share of the cruise market (Dowling, 2006; Peisley, 2006). While these major cruise brands are discussed below, it is highly recommended that the reader takes time to explore the vast range of different brands and cruise ships that make up this global phenomenon. This would help to further clarify the major cruise brands within the global industry.

Carnival Corporation

The Carnival Corporation owns Carnival Cruise Lines and many other cruise brands. It is the biggest British–US company in the cruise industry. Its ships sail to all over the world, including the Mediterranean, the Caribbean, Northern Europe, Alaska, America, the Middle East and the Far East. There are currently 22 Carnival Fun Ships operating from the USA. The Costa Cruises brand, which caters for the Italian market, operates a further 13 ships. Aida cruise ships are for the German-speaking market. Carnival UK, based in Southampton, is the umbrella organization for major brands such as Cunard, P&O Cruises, The Yachts of Seabourn and Ocean Village (where the ships are currently being phased out of Carnival UK and transferred to Carnival Australia). The Yachts of Seabourn offers small cruise ships (with an average of 200–450 berths) and is the most upmarket of the Carnival UK brands, offering all-inclusive premier cruising.

The Royal Caribbean Cruise Line

RCCL was formed in 1968 when three Norwegian shipping companies pooled their resources. In 1970, the first RCCL cruise ship entered service, the *Song of Norway*. This ship is interesting in that it was one of the first ships to be 'stretched', which means that the ship was cut in two and an 85-foot mid section was added to increase the passenger capacity from 700 to just over 1000 passengers. From the 1970s the company developed rapidly, acquiring not only more ships but also its own exclusive destination on the northern coast of Haiti. The brands that form RCCL are Celebrity Cruises, Royal Caribbean International and Azamara Club Cruises.

Continued growth and mergers have created a strong brand. The largest cruise ship in the world, *Oasis of the Seas*, was formally named in November 2009. Its sister ship, *Allure of the Seas*, is due to make its debut in December 2010 (Cruise Critic, 2010). Both these ships can carry an average of 5400 passengers. RCCL provides sea–land holidays in Alaska, Canada and Europe, as well as all sea cruises.

Star Cruises

The third largest cruise brand is Star Cruises, which started with six ships but now owns a total of 11 ships and is the leading brand in the Asia-Pacific region. Star Cruises was formed in 1993 and is responsible for developing the cruise industry in the Asia-Pacific region. It caters to Asian passengers and Western passengers who are interested in Asian destinations. It has also penetrated the mature markets in North America and Europe by acquiring the Norwegian Cruise Line in 2000, adding another 11 cruise ships to the corporate brand. Norwegian Cruise Line was one of the original cruise lines. It introduced freestyle dining and the concepts of facilities and activities for children and family groups, which are apparent on most international cruise ships today. The diversification into land-based integrated resorts and entertainment businesses has led Star Cruises to change its name from 'Star Cruises Limited' to 'Genting Hong Kong Limited'.

Cruise Ships – The Core of the Cruise Industry

Cruise ships are at the heart of the industry and are its core product. The key development in cruise ships has been growth in terms of size (Fig. 20.1).

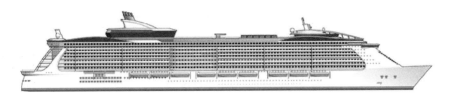

Royal Caribbean International: *Oasis of the Seas* (2009)

Cunard: *Queen Mary 2* (2004)

White Star Line: *Titanic* (1912)

Fig 20.1. Comparison of some of the well-known ships built in the 20th century. (Adapted from Wise, 2007; Global Security, 2008.)

Although different in size, in reality cruise ships can really only offer four different categories of cabins – although if you examine cruise brochures, up to 20 different categories may be on offer. The cabin choices are as follows:

- Inside: no window, inside corridor or porthole.
- Outside: with porthole or sea-view.
- Balcony: allows the passenger outside access without going on deck.
- Suites: mini, junior, deluxe, grand, superior, owners, penthouses and staterooms.

The location of the cabin is reflected in the price, with the best cabins deemed to be those higher up in the ship. However, the lower and more central the cabin's position, the less roll and sway is felt as the ship sails. The size, location, amenities and price of the four different cabin types form passengers' choices.

Royal Caribbean International refers to its cabins as staterooms. *Independence of the Seas* and *Oasis of the Seas* have the unique feature of internal cabins with a view of the atrium or the boardwalks and parks (Royal Caribbean International, 2010).

The size of the ship is measured by gross tonnage, which can be confusing. Gross tonnage refers to the calculation of the volume of a ship – in other words, the measurement of space – not the weight. Gross tonnage is promoted as the space-to-passenger ratio (Table 20.2). As the volume of the ship increases it enables not only more passengers to be carried, but also additional facilities and amenities to be incorporated into the design. As ships' sizes have increased, so have their costs (Table 20.3).

Ships today are often older ships that have belonged to different cruise companies over the years and changed not only ownership, but also name. For example, *Ocean Village 2* (part of Carnival UK) started out in 1990 as *Crown Princess*, but during the last 20 years has changed brand, name and registry. It became *Ocean Village 2* in 2007 to meet the demands of a new viable, younger target market. On the 16th November 2009, *Ocean Village 2* was deployed to the Carnival Australia fleet for economic reasons. Following extensive refurbishment and a repaint, it is now currently sailing under the name *Pacific Jewel*.

Table 20.2. Classification, size and examples of cruise ship.

Classification of ships	Example	Number of passengers (approx.)	Tonnage (approx.)
Resort ships	RCI *Oasis of the Seas*	5400	220,000
Mega ships	P&O *Ventura*	3100	115,000
Large ships	P&O *Oceana*	2016	77,000
Medium-size ships	Cunard *Queen Elizabeth*	2200	92,000
Small ships	Global Maritime *Marco Polo*	826	22,080
Boutique/ultra-luxury ships	Seabourn *Odyssey*	450	32,000

Table 20.3. Comparing the growth of three cruise liners.

	Name of ship		
	Titanic	*Queen Mary 2*	*Oasis of the Seas*
Date in service	1912	2004	2009
Company	White Star Line	Cunard	Royal Caribbean International
Price ($, est.)	7.5 million	800 million	1.2 billion
Gross tonnage (t, approx.)	46,328	152,000	220,000
Length (m)	269	345	360
Passengers	2,434	2,620	5,400
Crew	885	1,253	2,100

Adapted from Wise, 2007.

Products and services of cruise ships

Cruise companies strive to offer the ultimate cruise experience and hope to achieve this through the products and services they offer. These can include restaurants, bars, state-of-the-art spas and health and fitness facilities, retail shops, libraries, theatres, casinos, food outlets and other amenities to meet the needs of the different target markets. RCCL has introduced wave surfers, climbing walls and indoor ice-rinks to attract the family and the younger, active markets. P&O's cruise ship *Aurora* has golf simulators, while *Ventura* has a rock-music school and offers circus skills classes. Most cruise ships provide a variety of entertainment including West-End shows, quizzes, dance classes, art auctions, talks from experts and cookery demonstrations, to name but a few. Most ships now ask for passengers' credit card details prior to boarding as ships tend not to deal with cash on board (Dickenson and Vladmir, 2008). All passengers are given an identity card that serves two purposes: (i) it is used to record all purchases that take place on the ship and at the end of the voyage bills are settled prior to final disembarkation; and (ii) the identity card acts as a security mechanism to allow passengers on and off the ship at ports of call.

The products and services available on cruise ships depend on the size and age of the ship, with resort ships so-called because they resemble resort hotel complexes. As a rule of thumb, smaller ships offer a more personalized service as the ratio of passenger to crew is greater than on resort ships. Smaller ships tend to offer more exotic itineraries at a more relaxed pace, with an emphasis on luxury and elegance. The decor can be contemporary or classic and the facilities reflect the target markets that the company wishes to attract.

The ideal ambiance for an ultimate cruise experience is down to passenger choice and cost. Modern design is about efficiency, spaciousness, high standards of elegance and luxury, with ships striving to create their own character and identity. In a very competitive marketplace, cruise companies seek to gain competitive advantage by introducing new facilities and activities. The business market is attracted by onboard conference facilities com-bined with a cruise experience, while romantics are enticed by the opportunity to renew their vows or even be married by the captain while at sea.

Food and drink on cruise ships

One of the most important features of cruise ships is the choice of restaurants. Generally cruise ships carry an average of 3500 passengers, who all need to be 'fed and watered' up to 24 hours a day (Douglas and Douglas, 2004). Restaurants are in many ways retailers of time, service and customer experiences and it is the differentiation of cruise restaurants that helps to form the unique part of the cruise brand (Muller, 1999). According to Hall and Sharples (2003), food and its consumption is considered one of the major factors in determining the choice of cruise holiday. Leading cruise ships boast of five- and six-star food standards where choice and service of food is given high priority. The image and taste of food can vary and it is the variety of food – which includes midnight buffets, chocolate fountains and exotic cocktails – that is part of the gastronomic appeal to passengers. Dining varies from formal dining where passengers enjoy full restaurant service to 'freedom dining', a term used for buffet-style, self-service or freestyle dining where diners, depending on their level of accommodation, have greater freedom to choose from a range of restaurants. Regardless of accommodation status, dining for all passengers is part of the cruise package with meals included in the price of the voyage.

Some cruise companies have recently introduced celebrity-endorsed restaurants, which is another product/service to enhance extra spending on-board ships. For example, at the time of writing, Marco Pierre White is the celebrity chef for the P&O *Ventura*; James Martin is the celebrity chef for Ocean Village ships; Gary Rhodes is associated with the P&O ships *Oriana* and *Arcadia*, both of which have a Rhodes Restaurant; and Todd English lends his name and expertise to the Cunard *Queen Mary 2*. This trend is likely to continue for the foreseeable future, as cruise ships use food as a badge of recognition and part of their brand identity.

Table 20.4. Short-haul cruises (UK) distribution.

	2004 (%)	2006 (%)	2008 (%)	% point change 2004–2008
Travel agent	43.3	51.5	55.9	12.6
Tour operator	37.8	31.0	37.2	–0.6
Made own travel/accommodation arrangements	8.6	12.3	15.9	7.3

From Mintel, 2009.
Base: adults aged ≥15 years who took a cruise for their last holiday. Taken from a TGI survey of around 25,000 adults.
Source: GB TGI , BMRB Winter Q1 2004/5-09 (Oct-Sept)/Mintel

Selling the Cruise Product

Because of the expansion of the cruise industry and subsequent growth in the capacity of cruise ships, aggressive marketing is required and for the time being at least travel agents' role in this process seems secure. In 2007, Carnival Corporation was the dominant player in main media advertising of cruising in the UK, with P&O as the top advertised brand. This was followed by Royal Caribbean International. Familiar high-street names such as the three largest travel agencies (The Thomas Cook Group PLC-owned Thomas Cook and the TUI Travel PLC-owned Thomson and First Choice) account for 25.6% of the estimated 6800 travel agencies in the UK (Keynote, 2009). One of these groups, TUI Travel PLC, has a direct link to the cruise sector, recently becoming the new owner of Island Cruises (TUI Travel, 2010). Other independent travel agents such as The Cruise Specialists and Bolsover Cruise Club specialize in cruise holidays and as such have become experts in this field.

Despite the rapid growth of direct sales in tourism, in 2008 travel agents in the UK were responsible for selling approximately 82% of all cruise holidays and 90% of all fly–cruise sells, including online, telephone and in-branch sales (Keynote, 2008). This is a particularly important market segment for travel agents as the percentage of consumers arranging their holidays independently rose to 40% in 2008 (Keynote, 2009). One of the reasons that consumers use travel agents rather than the internet to book their cruise holiday is the wide range of products on offer and the choices that need to be made. For example, prospective cruise holiday makers need to decide whether to cruise from home or foreign ports; whether their preference is for a large ship such as Royal Caribbean's 225,282-t, 5400-passenger *Oasis of the Seas* or a smaller, more intimate ship such as Seabourn's 10,000-t, 208-passenger *Seabourn Pride*; which cabin grade they would like; whether their preference is for a casual or a more formal atmosphere; whether they want a family-friendly or child-free ship; and, of course, which destinations they would like to visit.

A survey by Mintel (2009) highlighted that travel agents and tour operators are the main way in which a cruise holiday is booked in the UK (Table 20.4).

This is also the case for the American market, where 74% of cruisers booked at least some of their cruise with travel agents in 2009, although this was often age related (Table 20.5).

Over two thirds of the American 25–44 year age group, despite their familiarity with online processes, still used a travel agent when booking a cruise. When asked why, the following reasons for using a travel agent were provided (CLIA, 2008):

- 42% said agents provide the best service.
- 59% were extremely or very satisfied with agents, with an overall satisfaction of 93%.
- 78% of cruisers use travel agents for all types of travel planning, as compared to 44% of non-cruisers.

Many travel agents, in particular cruise specialists, take part in familiarization trips and

Table 20.5. Age-related bookings.

Segment	Age (years)	Bookings (%)
Seniors	≥ 55	77
Boomers	45–65	73
Generation Xers	25–44	69

From CLIA, 2008.

cruise seminars designed especially for them by the cruise companies. Travel agents make on-board visits to different ships to increase their product knowledge and can provide first-hand advice to potential customers about different cruise companies and the services they provide. They work on commission from the cruise operators and can expect to earn commission rates of between 12% and 18%. A number of travel agents operate websites dedicated to cruise sales and invest heavily in advertising cruise holidays. Some cruise companies such as Norwegian Cruise Line can only take cruise bookings online so the flights and transfers need to be booked separately and the travel agent can also provide assistance and expertise with this. For those who are not internet users, the high street travel agent plays a vital role.

Cruise Ports and Cruise Destinations

Cruise ports

A port is a complicated transport junction, a stopover or harbour on a marine gateway that enables maritime transport, cargo and cruise ships to enter and depart a destination. Cruise ships visiting different ports require an efficient infrastructure to process the large number of cruise tourists who embark and disembark (Gabe *et al.*, 2006). At the port, cruise ships must be docked and secured, passengers embarked and disembarked, provisions loaded and unloaded, and security procedures adhered to. Ports offer different services that may include pilotage (small pilot boats that guide the large cruise ships into and out of the port), towing, mooring, bunkering (storage) and waste disposal. They also offer passenger services such as customer clearance, passport checking and other duties that are part of the process for cruise voyages (Miotke-Dziegiel, 2007). Some cruise ports are designed for 'turnaround', a term used to describe a short period of time in which a cruise ship remains in a port for the sole purpose of processing passengers and loading fuel and supplies ready for the imminent voyage. This also provides opportunities for maintenance work such as painting, repairs, special cleaning and even renovations while the ship is in port. During turnaround, the cruise companies promote their ships by inviting travel agents and potential passengers to view the ships. In some cases, with prior invitation, these guests can enjoy a lunch on board.

In the UK, Southampton is the principle port and one of the largest in Europe. It has had up to eight major cruise ships in dock at any one time. If each cruise ship holds an average of 3000 passengers then, in this instance, approximately 24,000 passengers needed to be processed on and off the ships. Port authorities facilitate this process. Southampton Port is privately owned by Associated British Ports, which currently has 23 ports in its portfolio and is the largest operator of seaports in the UK. Ports in the UK fall into one of three categories of governance: they may be under municipal control, run by a trust or under private ownership (Associated British Ports, 2009). Southampton Port is of significant value because it is situated on the south coast of the UK and is the main gateway to the USA and many destinations in Europe. Because of the growth of the cruise market, a fourth passenger terminal costing approximately £19 million was built in 2008, designed to process passengers as quickly and efficiently as possible. The new Ocean Terminal was designed so that friends and relatives may stay with the passengers right up until departure.

According to Chesworth (2006) 'the main enticement to encourage ports to accommodate ships, passengers and crew is the amount of money passengers spend ashore'. Visitors from ships can indeed have a considerable economic impact on a port's city and surrounding communities. Some of the new resort ships cannot be accommodated by all ports. For example, Jamaica's Port Authority is investing around US$152 million to enable resort ships such as the Genesis Class to enter Falmouth harbour. Ships with more than 5000 passenger can be overwhelming during shore visits, where other issues relate to embarkation and disembarkation times for such large numbers of people. Ships that are unable to dock at smaller ports often anchor off-shore and use tender boats. Tenders are motorized boats (which in some cases are also used as lifeboats, holding approximately 120–140 passengers) that ferry passengers to and from the shore, where they visit places of interest and visitor attractions in the local surroundings. Passengers are also free to arrange their own on-shore activities and many explore the local sites the destination has to offer. A cruise ship can be worth approximately £1 million to a port city.

Cruise destinations

Most cruise voyages incorporate stops at different destinations. Apart from the transatlantic cruises, when ships can take up to 5 days to sail from Southampton to New York, cruise ships normally sail during the night and moor at different destinations during the day, giving passengers the opportunity to spend time on shore. Cruise destinations are divided into two categories: (i) traditional destinations such as the Caribbean, Western Mediterranean, eastern and North America, western USA, Mexico and areas such as Alaska, Norway and the Baltic region; and (ii) developing areas such as South America, the Amazon, Hawaii, Australia, New Zealand, the Antarctic, the Falkland Islands and the Far East, incorporating Japan, China and the Philippines. For the 2011, season P&O has 156 cruises calling at 270 ports in 90 countries, all with diverse social, cultural, historical and geographical attributes.

An interesting development with regard to destinations is the purchasing of private islands by cruise companies. Royal Caribbean International is the only cruise company to own two private islands, the CocoCay, a 140-acre private island situated in the Bahamas' Berry Island chain, and Labadee, a private beach peninsula located on the northern coast of Haiti. Both are for the exclusive use of the Royal Caribbean cruise passengers. Disney Cruise Line owns Castaway Cay, a 1000-acre island that is part of the Abacos chain of islands in the Bahamas. Holland America owns Half Moon Cay, which it occasionally rents out to other cruise companies (e.g. Costa Cruises). These privately owned islands are staffed by local people who boat to the island when they know a ship is visiting. The advantage of owning or renting a private island is that additional activities can take place that are different to those offered on-board ship (e.g. powerboat adventures, jet skiing, scuba diving, parasailing, water skiing, snorkelling, beach barbeques and beach games). Cruise passengers who use the island's facilities pay for the benefit of doing so. Teye and Leclerc (2003) referred to the ownership of private islands in foreign countries as a feature that contributes to the 'environmental bubble' all of who contribute to the 'pleasure periphery' of the cruise holiday. When passengers decide on what type of holiday to go on, the destinations can be a key deciding factor. For some, however, the cruise ship itself is the destination as it contains all the amenities and facilities that the passenger desires.

Working for the Cruise Industry

The increase in the size of cruise ships has created a demand for people to work in the cruise industry. Ships are sometimes referred to as floating hotels and, in a similar way to large land-based hotels, they have organizational structures that require a range of personnel with appropriate skills to ensure the ship operates with precision and efficiency while meeting the needs of the cruise passengers.

The captain is the highest ranking officer on board and is responsible for the operation of the ship. The second in command is the staff captain, who heads the deck department. Next in line is the first officer, who is responsible for navigation and overseeing bridge operations. On the technical side, the chief engineer is responsible for the management of the engines and electrical and refridgeration systems. Ships require a team of highly qualified mechanical and electrical maritime engineers as well as navigation officers to ensure the ship is kept in good working order and gets to the chosen destinations on time. In the hotel department, ranks and titles for officers vary from cruise line to cruise line. Sometimes called the hotel director or executive purser, this officer takes responsibility for the hotel operations of the ship, which include cabins, restaurants, bars and food supplies for passengers and crew (Gibson, 2006).

Most cruise ships will have a cruise director, who is a senior officer with responsibility for entertainment. Entertainment on board is carried out by performing artists, including dancers, acrobatics, singers, jugglers, comedians and musicians who are recruited by entertainment agencies. Ships also have a senior medical officer or doctor on board, who is the officer in charge of providing medical care for passengers and crew. Other senior roles may include passenger services managers, food and beverage managers and restaurant managers. Organizational structures may vary depending on the cruise company and the size of the cruise ship (Gibson, 2006). In addition to senior officers, a ship also employs crew members who work in diverse roles such as cabin stewards, housekeepers, waiters, bar tenders, laundry attendants, general galley assistants and cleaners. The crew will consist of a range of different nationalities where the common language is English. Cruise ships are multinational and staff originate from places such as Mumbai, the Philippines, Indonesia and Eastern Europe. Staff contracts may last between 6 and 9 months and long hours while on-board are the norm. Senior officers are usually employed directly by the cruise companies. In an international environment such as this, cross-cultural management, understanding and cooperation are essential. High levels of customer service are paramount, not only for the reputation of the cruise brand but also to create repeat business and memorable experiences for cruise passengers.

While cruise ships offer a range of employment, the industry has been criticized for ethnic recruitment, institutional racism and a stratified labour force – the different groups of employees (officers, staff and crew) have separate living and dining areas, a different intensity in interacting with passengers and considerably different pay. The ethnic cast is often reflected in the hierarchy, with European and North American staff occupying the higher ranks and Eastern European, Asian and Caribbean employees found on the lower levels of employment. These practices are facilitated by the strategic basis of recruitment agencies as well as the use of flags of convenience, which aid cruise companies in circumventing home country laws, taxes and maritime regulations. These employment patterns are mirroring common globalization processes, which are driven by economic savings and catering for the cruise ship passenger's needs (Wood, 2000).

Future Research

Tourism research really began in the early 1960s, but is generally an under-researched area. The cruise industry only started to gather momentum from the early 1970s when cruises became a alternative to land-based holidays as competitive pricing made cruising available to a wider range of tourists. The growth of cruise tourism has risen at a disproportionate rate to other tourism sectors. Cruise ships impact upon the destinations visited, although the impact of resort ships has yet to be tested as cruise ships carrying more than 5400 passengers, such as *Oasis of the Seas*, have only recently come into service. Research into the economic impacts of the cruise industry has highlighted the argument for more cruise ships in developing regions such as the Red Sea, the Indian Ocean and now the Far East, where ships are drivers for economic growth. However, cruise ships can pose a danger to the sociocultural environment when up to 5000 passengers arrive at once, especially at smaller ports. They also present an environmental danger to fragile marine ecosystems. For example, the increase in cruises in Alaska and the Polar regions is under scrutiny and research is ongoing to assess the impact of cruise ships on the environment. The typology of cruise passengers is changing, with passengers getting younger and more families cruising. In addition, the singles cruise market is increasing and the elderly are becoming more adventurous and active. Ongoing research is therefore essential to assess how supply can meet the demand of different market segments.

Conclusion

Study of the cruise industry is now recognized as a discipline in its own right and not just as an annotation of the tourism industry. The first

International Cruise Conference was held in 2008, enabling academic and industry practitioners to exchange knowledge. It is now recognized that academic research is crucial to the cruise industry. Because of this the Cruise Research Society was formed in 2010 and will function as a platform for future cruise research. One of the difficulties with cruise research is that cruise studies are on a 'shifting tide of knowledge' where information can change rapidly. What happens today is yesterday's knowledge and tomorrow's research enquiry.

Review Questions

1. Look at the chronology of cruise ships (Table 20.1). Carry out further research to assess how you think historical events have influenced the development of the cruise industry.
2. Assess how a cruise holiday differs from a traditional land-based holiday.
3. Why do you think the travel agent plays an important role in booking cruise holidays? Evaluate how this is likely to change in the future.

References

Associated British Ports (2009) Association of British Ports Interim Report 2009. Available from: http://www.abports.co.uk/files/abp%20subholdings%20uk%20ltd%20interim%20report%202009.pdf. Accessed May 1, 2010.

Cartwright, R. and Baird, C. (1999) *The Development and Growth of the Cruise Industry*. Butterworth-Heinemann, Oxford, UK.

CLIA, Cruise Lines International Association (2008) The Cruise Market Overview Statistical Data 2007. Available from: http://www.cruising.org. Accessed April 22, 2010.

Chesworth, N. (2006) The cruise industry and Atlantic Canada. In: Dowling, D. (ed.) *Cruise Ship Tourism*. CAB International, Wallingford, UK.

Cruise Critic (2010) *Allure of the Seas* Review. Available from: http://www.cruisecritic.com. Accessed May 2, 1010.

Dickenson, R. and Vladimir, A.N. (2008) *Selling the Sea. An Inside Look at the Cruise Industry*. Wiley, New York.

Douglas, N. and Douglas, N. (2004) *The Cruise Experience*. Pearson Hospitality Press, Australia.

Dowling, R. (2006) *Cruise Ship Tourism*. CAB International, Wallingford, UK.

Gabe, T.M., Lynch, C.P. and McConnon, J.C. (2006) Likelihood of cruise ship passenger return to a visited port: the case of Bar Harbor, Main. *Journal of Travel Research* 44, 281–287.

Gibson, P. (2006) *Cruise Operations Management*. Butterworth Heinemann, Oxford, UK.

Global Security (2008) Cruise Ships. Available from: http://www.globalsecurity.org/military/systems/ship/passenger-cruise.htm. Accessed April 3, 2010.

Hall, C.M. and Sharples, L. (2003) The consumption of experience or the experience of consumption? An introduction to the tourism of taste. In: Halls, C.M., Sharples, L., Mitchell, R., Macionis, N. and Cambourne, B. (eds) *Food Tourism Around The World: Development, Management and Markets*. Butterworth-Heinemann, Oxford, UK, pp. 1–24.

Keynote (2008) Travel and Tourism Market. Available from: http://www.keynote.co.uk/market-intelligence/reports/category/travel-and-tourism. Accessed April 29, 2010.

Keynote (2009) Travel and Tourism Market. Available from: http://www.keynote.co.uk/market-intelligence/reports/category/travel-and-tourism. Accessed April 20, 2010.

Kwortnik, R.J. (2006) Carnival Cruise Lines – burnishing the brand. *Cornell Hotel and Restaurant Administration Quarterly* 47, 286–300.

Mancini, M. (2004) *Cruising: A Guide to the Cruise Line Industry*. Thomson Delmar Learning, Canada.

Mintel (2009). *Short-haul Cruises – UK – April 2009*. Available from: http://academic.mintel.com/sinatra/oxygen_academic/search_results/show&/display/id=280431/list/id=280431&type=RCItem&list=list/display/id=394688. Accessed August 1, 2010.

Miotke-Dziegiel, J. (2007) Ports in development of maritime tourism – problems and challenges in the Pomeranian region. *Tourism and Hospitality Management* 13, 483–592.

Muller, C.C. (1999) The business of restaurants: 2001 and beyond. *International Journal of Hospitality Management* 18, 401–413.

Peisley, T. (2006) *The Future of Cruising – Boom or Bust 2015?* Seatrade Communications, Essex, UK.

Polsson, K. (2009) Chronology of Cruise Lines. Available from: http://kpolsson.com/cruiship/ship2009.htm. Accessed May 1, 2010.

Royal Caribbean International (2010) Balcony Staterooms. Available from: http://www.royalcaribbean.com/findacruise/cabinclass/cabinTypes/home.do?cabincls=Bandbr=R. Accessed May 1, 2010.

Teye, V.B. and Leclerc, D. (2003) The white Caucasian and ethnic minority cruise markets: some motivational perspectives. *Journal of Vacation Marketing* 9, 227–242.

Tibballs, G. (1998) *The Titanic. The Extraordinary Story of the "Unsinkable" Ship.* Readers Digest, New York.

TUI Travel (2010) Annual Report and Account 2008. Available from: http://www.ara2008.tuitravelplc.com/tui/pageshome. Accessed April 15, 2010.

Wise, J. (2007) World's Largest Ship Pulls 360s with Joystick. Available from: http://www.popularmechanics.com/science/extreme_machines/4217987.html. Accessed April 23, 2010.

Wood, R.E. (2000) Caribbean cruise tourism. Globalization at sea. *Annals of Tourism Research* 27, 345–370.

Conclusion

Peter Robinson, Sine Heitmann and Dr Peter Dieke

In the creation of this book, many academics have contributed their knowledge, ideas and research to explain, discuss and question contemporary themes in tourism. Within each chapter a broad range of ideas and concepts is presented, representing an even wider sphere of academic interest and research into each typology. These final pages consider and reflect upon the chapters that have been brought together in this publication. They explain the context within which they relate to each other, placing a focus on the way in which research themes will continue to develop and paying particular attention to the increasingly sub-divided notion of tourism to explain the importance of research in the context of tourism development.

We can divide and subdivide any industry until we are left with nothing more than parts; the components that when added together create a whole, but when apart are nothing more than individual phenomena. This can be easily exemplified with tourism because it is essentially intangible and relies upon aspects of sociology, semiotics and geography being brought together to create places where all stakeholders become actors and participants in tourism. Our motivation to travel (Chapter 3) is heavily influenced by the semiotics that construct and signpost places of interest and significance (e.g. historic houses, national parks, theme parks) or places that meet our needs at a given time (e.g. relaxation, excitement, adventure).

Historically, these motivations were relatively simple. Tourism emerged first as pilgrimage (travelling to sites of religious significance), then as education (the Grand Tour) and during the 1950s affordable, accessible transport opened up long-distance travel to the masses, creating what we commonly refer to as 'mass tourism' (Chapter 1). This is defined by large numbers of travellers moving en masse to destinations and resorts where, in many cases, a foreign country may be enjoyed in a 'safe' environment. The relationship between hosts and guests is performed through excursions and tours that offer glimpses of the physical and the re-created past, suggesting that much of what tourists experience is a representation of heritage presented as authentic for tourist consumption (Chapter 4).

As we have become more confident travellers – better educated, increasingly aware of the world around us and living within an increasingly globalized and smaller world – we have become increasingly curious about our surroundings. In Chapter 1, the author explored the idea of discovery as a traveller and this is a theme that was common among early tourists. In Chapter 5 we considered the role of images in the creation of tourism spaces, which influence expectations and the decision to travel. Just as painters produced images of far-away lands 200 years ago, so today marketers sell new and existing destinations as opportunities to 'discover' and 'explore' new places, even when they have already been explored, interpreted, presented and re-presented to the tourism consumer.

Very often there follows a common idea that a few adventurous tourists reach a destination first, the destination realizes the positive benefits of tourism and before long there is a booming tourism industry that brings with it numerous positive benefits, but also many disadvantages (Chapter 6). Tourism development (Chapter 2) has to be managed effectively to maximize the potential positive impacts of tourism and minimize the negatives, while offering access to sites and places that may have very important cultural values (Chapter 12). Sustainable tourism has been a central focus of tourism management since the Rio de Janeiro summit in 1992 and has evolved as a tool for tourism development, often being the catalyst for other types of tourism activity. Some of these were discussed in Chapter 6 as they are closely aligned to the principles of sustainability, and include pro-poor tourism, eco-tourism, green tourism and nature tourism. Contrary to their titles, these are often not particularly sustainable, but carry a positive marketing connotation. Other forms of tourism, such as community-based tourism (Chapter 7) and slow tourism (Chapter 9) provide new ways of addressing the old problems of sustainable tourism development through bottom-up approaches to destination development. These often include a focus on local traditions, local foods and local products and are defined by their generally more rural characteristics (Chapters 8 and 17).

In the introduction, we discussed the fact that many types of tourism are not discussed in this book. As we continue to research tourism, and as travellers continue to seek new experiences and new knowledge, so too new types of tourism will emerge. Some of these may be considered worthy of research. Events, for example, encompass a broad range of activities that are related to tourism. Some of these have historically been recognized as a tourism product (e.g. business travel), but the popularity of events and a growing interest in contemporary culture – often defined through arts and festivals – are creating not just new tourism products, but new ways of engaging with tourism and new tourist behaviours (Chapter 10). Similarly, sports tourism and adventure tourism (Chapter 11) has been recognized for some considerable time, while cultural (Chapter 12) and heritage (Chapters 13 and 18) tourism

have been the long-term mainstays of the core components of tourism destinations. Cultural and heritage, however, encompass many debates about ownership and access to a shared cultural heritage that requires sensitive management so that future generations are able to benefit from the continued existence of important sites.

Many new types of tourism have emerged in recent years. These include film tourism (Chapter 14), which has seen a huge growth in interest as destinations have realized the benefits of media coverage in its many forms, and dark tourism (Chapter 15), which has existed for some time, but has attracted a strong niche following through democratization and the increased accessibility of places associated with death and disaster. Likewise, research has for many years now discussed the lesbian, gay, bisexual and transgendered tourism market (Chapter 16), but has focused less on the full range of related tourist activities that comprise this important and valuable market sector.

This book has also discussed themes that are growing in importance. Chapter 9 introduced the idea of slow tourism and slow food. Indeed, 'food' as a product and activity of tourism has become increasingly important and central to many peoples' travel experiences (Chapter 17), offering opportunities to find new ways to integrate with tourism destinations. Likewise, religious tourism (Chapter 18) also offers new ways of exploring and relating to destinations, while using spaces designed for one purpose – worship – for something very different. It is important to recognize the synergies between the physical worship space and the opportunities such sites offer to travellers seeking local history, architecture and genealogical research, combined with opportunities to touch upon other niches such as wildlife tourism in historic and unmanaged graveyards.

Chapter 19 explored the origins of health tourism and the emergence of medical tourism as a potentially valuable tool for tourism development, but within the context of some difficult and controversial issues. The book concluded with a discussion around cruise tourism (Chapter 20), which offers an interesting and exciting glimpse of a fast-growing market that perfectly exemplifies the point made in Chapter 1: that these 'niche' products can easily become 'mass tourism'. Cruise growth outstripped all other tourism sectors in 2009 and is widely touted as the saviour of the high-street travel retailer because of the complexity of cruise bookings.

We recognized in the introduction that not every 'theme' in tourism would be discussed in this text. It is important to reiterate again that many of these are simply products; researchers should be cautious when researching these 'themes', recognizing that some niche markets are little more than specific products. Of course, these products may be valuable and may benefit a tourism destination in economic terms. Wedding tourism is one such example, but it rarely brings with it a level of debate and discourse that challenges and questions its impacts, morals and ethics in the same way that transplant tourism (Chapter 19) or paying for access to religious sites (Chapter 18) do. It would be easy to pigeonhole all types of tourism as 'themes' – woodland tourism, walking tourism, cycling tourism, teddy-bear tourism, castle tourism – but we argue here that these are products that fit into and across specific themes.

The key message that comes out of this text, then, is that there are indeed clear themes that provide interesting research topics. Why, for example, would a traveller choose to visit places associated with death and destruction and at what point does a desire for knowledge become voyeuristic behaviour? The fact that the majority of chapters include examples and case studies proves the value of these themes as real, practical and applicable ideas and discussions that are as important as research themes as they are in managing tourism. Each chapter provides ideas for future research and illustrates the debates that exist within each type of tourism.

Finally, *Research Themes in Tourism* was developed to provide an overview of a range of interesting, contemporary and emerging concepts in tourism. It has been written in a way that attempts to integrate theory and practice and to provide an overview of the underpinning areas of tourism that are essential to contextualize research. We hope that it provides both guidance and inspiration for researchers and practitioners alike and that, as a result, it furthers the opportunity for tourism development through a greater understanding of the shared responsibilities of all stakeholders.

Index